ACKNOWLEDGME

D0373429

This is to acknowledge those who contributed trail descriptions, photos, or other expertise to this book. The inclusion of their names does not necessarily mean they concur with its editorial content: John Allen, Bill Arthur, Ric Bailey, Dennis Baird, Phillip Blomquist, Julia Corbett, Don Crawford, Ernie Day, Jerry Dixon, Erik Fisher, Bill Francis, Paul Fritz, Dan and MaryAnn Green, Craig Groves, Elizabeth "Betsy" Hammet, Jerry Johnson, Robert N. Jones, Keith Kempski, Ann and George Matejko, Mike Panting, Donna and John Pinsof, C.P. Stokes, Karen Swafford, Nelle Tobias, Will Vernard, Jennifer Vervoort, Ron Watters, Charmaine Wellington, George Wentzel, and Craven Young.

John Allen is a Boise State University astronomer and conservation stalwart on behalf of the Payette National Forest country. His wife, Edwina Allen, is chair of the Northern Rockies Chapter of the Sierra Club. Bill Arthur is the regional representative for the Sierra Club in the Northwest—directs everything from Washington strategy for saving the Northwest's old growth forests, lobbying, to the annual Wenaha-Tucannon "decadence outing". Ric Bailey is a truck driver and president of the newly-revived Hells Canyon Preservation Council. Dennis Baird is the social sciences librarian of the University of Idaho and terror of the "cut-and-run" timber boys. Phil Blomquist ties flies, has two great hunting dogs, and is an outdoor writer. Julia Corbett, a former BLM employee, is also a former staffer for Idaho Governor John Evans.

Don Crawford is a professor of microbiology at the University of Idaho, creator of new life forms, photographer, and long-time Sierra Club leader. Ernie Day is a warhorse in the preservation of Idaho Wilderness and famous outdoor photographer. Jerry Dixon, friend of the South Fork of the Salmon River, is now teaching school near the Brooks Range in Alaska. Erik Fisher is a psychiatrist for the Veteran's Administration and Chairman of the Boise/Payette Backcountry Coalition. Bill Francis, a dear friend killed in an automobile accident, was a reporter for the Idaho State Journal. Paul Fritz is retired superintendent of Craters of the Moon National Monument and friend of new national parks. He knows absolutely everyone and is a prominent figure in National Parks and related preservation. Dan Green is working on his doctorate in forest economics at the University of Idaho. MaryAnn Green is a counselor for the Moscow, Idaho, school district. Elizabeth "Betsy" Hammet, call home. Jerry Johnson is an assistant professor of political science at Montana State University and former expert river runner. Rob Jones recently completed his doctorate in educational psychology at the University of Utah. Keith Kempski, our long-time hiking companion, is an energy specialist at the University of Wisconsin in Madison.

Ann Matejko, a former wilderness ranger, is a public affairs officer for the U.S. Forest Service and Jackie's co-author on a women's outdoor book. Her uncle, a member of the Seattle Mountaineers, invented the Therm-a-Rest mattress. George Matejko is a lands specialist for the U.S. Forest Service. Mike Panting is friend of the Caribou Range and won't let you go until you've had a tour of Forest Service perfidy in the area. Donna Pinsof is a supervisor for Gould/AMI (computer chips) in Pocatello and Sierra Club chair for Eastern Idaho. John Pinsof, mastodon bone-hunter, is working on his doctorate in paleontology at Idaho State University. Boy are those two tall!

C.P. Stokes is a legendary outfitter, raconteur, and mountainman of the central Idaho wilderness. Karen Swafford (last we heard) was somewhere in Antarctica. Nelle Tobias has fought unwise development proposals near McCall for a lifetime. Will Vernard has made protection of Long Canyon a realistic possibility. Jennifer Vervoort is former Forest Service seasonal employee—we have no idea where she is, if you see her, please let us know. Ron Watters is the director of the Idaho State University Outdoor Program, an outdoor writer, and instrumental in the establishment of the River of No Return Wilderness. Charmaine Wellington, feminist extraordinare, is an assistant professor of English at the University of West Florida and our springtime hiking companion. Pocatellan George Wentzel is a legendary flyfisher, outdoor writer, and former Green Beret. Craven Young astonished Sun Valley, got his law degree, and moved on.

The Hiker's Guide
to IDAHO

by

Ralph Maughan and
Jackie Johnson Maughan

FALCON™

Falcon Press® Publishers, Inc.
Helena, Montana

This book is in memory of grandmother Cleta Hancy Hansen,
b. December 15, 1901,   d. February 17, 1984.

—Ralph Maughan and Jackie Johnson Maughan, January 1990.

CAUTION

Outdoor recreation activities are by their very nature potentially hazardous. All participants in such activities must assume the responsibility for their own actions and safety. The information contained in this guidebook cannot replace sound judgment and good decision-making skills, which help reduce risk exposure, nor does the scope of this book allow for disclosure of all the potential hazards and risks involved in such activities.

Learn as much as possible about the outdoor recreation activities you participate in, prepare for the unexpected, and be safe and cautious. The reward will be a safer and more enjoyable experience.

PREFACE

This book is designed with something for everyone—from easy day hikes suitable for a picnic with children, to a strenuous climb of Mount Borah, Idaho's highest mountain.

It has been claimed that only the young and wealthy can use the backcountry. This may have been true a century ago when it was mostly the gentry who had the means, leisure, or desire to enter the wilds for pleasure. Today, however, that argument overlooks a few important events, such as the industrial revolution, mass transportation, the forty-hour work week, and the existence of millions of acres of public land in the western United States. Wilderness and backcountry use can be truly for everyone. The only real barriers are lack of information, lack of desire, and lack of Wilderness. This book can help remedy the first problem. The second is up to you. The third is up to all of us.

Backpacking and hiking are not inherently expensive. Grandma Gatewood (Emma Caldwell Gatewood, 1887-1973), who hiked the entire 2,000-mile Appalachian National Scenic Trail alone three times, did so with high-topped sneakers and a duffel bag. She was seventy-four years old when she completed her last traverse. Of course, you can spend a good deal of cash over the years acquiring the best and latest equipment. But whether your gear is vintage or vanguard, there is no return on recreational investment that parallels the millions of acres of wild country to which you have now gained access. Not only is the hiking itself literally free, it also represents freedom—freedom to come and go as you wish, make your own decisions, and find personal pleasures and satisfactions. It is a productive escape. It is a chance to smell the fir and columbine; to hear the breeze rustle through the quaking aspen, an intimate mountain stream, or the shuddering bugle of an elk. It's a challenge to see if you can hook a native trout, catch a watercolor sunset on film, or climb a stern king of a mountain. It's a chance to drink from an untainted spring—a form of sacrament, incorporating nature into yourself.

All this is there for the asking. Fortunately, Idaho has plenty of it.

Hiking need not exclude children or those not in the best of physical condition. Accordingly, hikes in this book range from easy to difficult. But it is beyond the scope of this book to tell you how to hike, backpack, or mountaineer. There are a good many books in print about the "how to" of using the backcountry. The intent of this one is to tell about the "where".

Included in this book are hikes from almost every undeveloped portion of Idaho. And, although there are some descriptions of trails in the more famous areas, such as the Sawtooth Wilderness and the White Cloud Mountains, we've deliberately emphasized the many splendid places that haven't gained a national reputation—yet.

The book contains 100 hikes, described by 30 (including ourselves) outdoor veterans. There are 22 new hikes, revisions to 43 former hikes, and new overviews, such as to the Hells Canyon National Recreation Area and the proposed Great Divide Wilderness. Two hikes in the first edition have been eliminated to be replaced by others which are more accessible, scenic, or interesting.

Our contributors were solicited because of their professional and/or avocational expertise. They have all given their personal impressions of the difficulty level or their respective hikes; consequently, the ratings may not be absolutely uniform. For the most part, contributors are sharing information about their favorite hiking areas. As Rob Jones said, "To be honest, a good deal of my motivation for writing a description of this hike in such a pristine and untrammeled area is to enlist support for the area from friends of the land...I had difficulty deciding to 'let the word out" about this precious area; however, if you come to quietly see and loudly support [its] continued wilderness character, your welcomed by me."

Idaho's wild places don't exist by accident. Most have been preserved only by years of effort on the part of many dedicated individuals and organizations. The environmental theme of our book should help you understand what the threats to Idaho's wild country are and what you can do to help.

Trail guides need to be updated periodically as trails are relocated, land management changes, and nature takes it course (as in the massive 1988 and 89 forest fires, the 1984 "monsoon" in the Pioneer Mountains, and the 1983 earthquake in the Lost Rivers). This is why sources for up-to-date information are listed with each hike. We strongly recommend that you check with these sources particularly for road conditions and trailhead information. If you have information to add, wish to contribute a description of your own, or have (yes, we mean it) criticisms, please get in touch via the publisher—Falcon Press, Box 731, Helena, Montana 59624.

CONTENTS

LOCATION OF HIKES

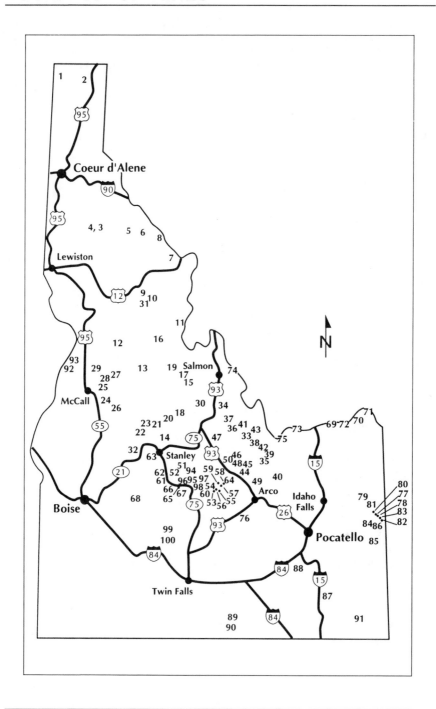

INTRODUCTION

STEWARDSHIP AND WILDERNESS

Idaho is blessed with more undeveloped country than any other state save Alaska. Overall, however, the amount of wild country is shrinking while recreational use has increased. Starting in the 1970s, usage in some western wilderness areas doubled or even quadrupled. While recreational use such as hiking poses less of a threat than development, there are still measures all visitors should take. It is becoming ever more crucial that users touch the land only lightly. As the famous poem of Henry Wadsworth Longfellow's closes, so should your journey:

> And the night shall be filled with music,
> And the cares that infest the day
> Shall fold their tents like the Arabs,
> And as silently slip away.

Most wilderness abuse comes from ignorance, not premeditation. Leave no litter; this includes bits of aluminum foil in the campfire ring. (Don't even leave a campfire ring—scatter the rocks). Perishables, such as toilet paper and sanitary napkins, should be either burned or carried out. Offal should be buried in the humus layer of the soil and latrines located at least 200 feet away from watercourses.

If at all possible, camp below timberline as alpine areas are very fragile and don't make good campsites anyway. They offer little wood and are subject to violent winds, storms, lightning, and cold.

Don't camp right next to a lake or stream. Camping here leads to water pollution and banks worn down to mud wallows. Don't use soap (including "biodegradable" soap) in a water source. Dip the water into your cook kit and dispose of the gray water well away from the water source.

Don't camp right next to the trail either—both for your privacy and that of everyone else. In addition to the matter of privacy, wild animals use the trails at night, including bears, skunks, and porcupines. So it's in your interest to camp away from the right-of-way.

Once all the earth was wild, but now only fragments of its four billion years of history before humankind are left, much preserved in the National Wilderness Preservation System.

In 1964, after years of political struggle, the United States Congress recognized the value of wilderness preserved with the passage of the Wilderness Act. The act empowered Congress to protect select parts of roadless public lands. It allows only for setting aside truly exceptional lands.

The designation of undeveloped public land as wilderness prohibits the use of motorized vehicles, construction of roads, buildings, logging, and most mining activity within its boundaries. It does not exclude limited livestock grazing, pack animals, hunting, fishing, or camping. Since it only applies to lands already without roads, and, by act of Congress, keeps it that way, wilderness designation is a very powerful method of keeping that status quo for select beautiful and/or ecologically valuable lands.

As of this writing, about 3.9 million acres (about 6,100 square miles) of wild country in Idaho have been preserved officially as part of the National Wilderness Preservation System. Presently, they are the Selway/Bitterroot, the Frank Church/River of No Return, the Sawtooth, the Hells Canyon, the Gospel Hump, and the Craters of the Moon National Monument Wilderness.

Most of Idaho's roadless country, however, has no protection: each year hundreds of square miles fall to the axe and bulldozer. This is usually accomplished through a system of political favors. The wildlands that have survived are usually either very popular (such as the Sawtooths) or high, cold, rocky, and dry. Lumber can't be profitably harvested in such locations unless made artificially attractive through subsidies from the public purse—"below cost" timber sales in which the public pays, often, not only for the road to the timber sale, but also for a portion of the timber itself because the timber is sold to the logging companies for less than its value. In other words, taxpayers are required to finance the destruction of their own forests!

In all, about 11 million acres of unprotected wild country (de facto wilderness) still survives on the public lands in Idaho. This is probably more than any other of the 48 states. Since the River of No Return Wilderness was created in 1980, the attention of Idaho environmentalists and conservationists has turned to these de facto wilderness lands. A coalition of Idaho environmental and outdoor groups, the Idaho Wildlands Defense Coalition, has been proposing that about four million of these acres be added to the 3.9 million acres of designated Wilderness in the Gem state. We refer to this proposal repeatedly throughout the book for it represents the dominant view of the environmental community in Idaho as to those lands so meritorious as to deserve this strong protection.

Others disagree. Some such as Earth First! propose more protection. Others, often bankrolled by resource extraction industries, still oppose all wilderness protection despite the rising concern about the health of the earth and its community of life. Since the defeat of Senator Frank Church in 1980, no wilderness has been designated in Idaho, and most Idaho politicians have been on the anti-environmental side.

Whether the wild country is protected will depend much on you. We feel those who enjoy and gain inspiration from the outdoors have a moral obligation to help pass it on to others.

All of the following organizations are actively involved in promoting the preservation and wise use of Idaho's public lands.

Committee for Idaho's High Desert Box 2863 Boise, Idaho 83701
Greater Yellowstone Coalition Box 1874 13 S. Wilson Bozeman, Montana 59515
Hells Canyon Preservation Council Box 903 Joseph, Oregon 97846
Idaho Conservation League (ICL has 12 chapters and five paid staff members.)
   State Headquarters Box 844 Boise, Idaho 83701
   Field Office Box 2671 Ketchum, Idaho 83340
Idaho Environmental Council Box 1708 Idaho Falls, Idaho 83401
Idaho Wildlife Federation Route 3, Cento Drive 6951 Twin Falls, Idaho 83301 (The
   IWF has five district organizations in Idaho.)
Sierra Club
   Eastern Idaho Group Box 1173 Pocatello, Idaho 83204

Middle Snake Group Box 552 Boise, Idaho 83701
Paloose Group Box 8787 Moscow, Idaho 83843
Sawtooth Group Box 2235 Hailey, Idaho 83333
Wilderness Society Idaho Field Office 413 West Idaho St., Suite 102 Boise, Idaho 83702.

Make It a Safe Trip

The best safety advice is the adage of the Scouts (although they don't always follow it themselves)—be prepared. For starters this means, most of all, carrying the necessary USGS topographic maps and a compass and knowing how to use them. For seconds, carry first aid and survival equipment. (If you have the maps and compass, you probably won't end up needing the survival equipment.)

Perhaps the third best advice is to tell someone where you're going and when you plan to return, specifically. File a flight plan. That way, if it comes down to it, a search and rescue team will know where to begin looking. (Remember that search and rescue teams generally must be put together by your loved ones and the local sheriff at your expense—unless you're lucky. Count on spending a lot of money being found.)

After these three caveats, safety advice can go on and on. There are probably other tips besides those listed here, but, after years of experience, we recommend the following:

—Watch the weather: be especially careful not to get caught on a ridge or exposed place during a lightning storm or at high altitude in a snow storm. If caught in a lightning storm, lie flat and abandon all conductive material—aluminum fishing rod containers, backpacks.

—Be super careful with fires. Don't put them where they could ignite tree roots, trees, dry grass, or blow out of control. Put them out completely before you go to bed or leave.

—Check the long-term weather forecast to avoid extended periods of cold, often snowy weather (even in early and midsummer).

—Don't hike at night.

—Don't split up your party unless everyone is very experienced.

—Avoid temptations to swim across lakes or streams.

—Stay on the trail unless you are an experienced hiker.

—Whether or not to hike alone is a judgment call based on your abilities and willingness to take what can undoubtedly be a risk.

—Don't slide down snowbanks or scree slopes unless you know for certain there are no cliffs or rocks at the bottom. (This requires either scouting the area or superior map reading abilities.)

—Know the symptoms and treatment of both hypothermia and altitude sickness. Hypothermia is the silent killer. Altitude sickness can affect even the strongest hiker and can make you feel like you've been on a week-long drinking binge.

—Study basic survival and first aid before leaving civilization.

—Don't eat mushrooms or other wild plants unless positive of identification.

—Find out as much as you can about the hike, especially any potential hazards, before you leave. This includes the condition of the road to the trailhead.

—Don't wait until you're confused to consult your topographic map. Look at it frequently to identify and keep track of the changing appearance of all major landmarks.

—Don't exhaust yourself or weaker members of your party by trying to travel too far, too fast. Be especially careful on rough terrain at the end of the day when everyone is tired.

—If you get lost, don't panic. Sit down and relax while you carefully go over the topographic map, study the terrain, and take readings from the compass. Plan your next move carefully, making sure you can get back to where you are now. Everyone gets lost at some point in difficult backcountry. Thousands have spent unplanned nights in the wilderness and survived. A few, a very few—usually those who panicked and ran wildly around—didn't make it. Remember that you have food and shelter all on your back. Consider your situation logically. If you're too tired or scared to do so at the moment or it's getting too dark to navigate, sleep on it.

—If your hike calls for wading a large stream, bring wading shoes or remove your socks and put your boots back on. This makes for more secure footing. Avoid the current's full force by keeping sideways to the flow. Slide, don't lift, your feet one at a time, making sure one foot is secure before seeking a new hold with the other one. Go slowly and deliberately. A hiking stick or branch works well for additional support. Place it upstream of where you are wading.

—Last, by definitely not least, stay clear of wild animals, especially those larger than you. In some places in Idaho, bears (including grizzlies) pose a hazard not present in most other states. While worry about bears is commonplace, the vast majority of injuries from animals doesn't come from bears. Almost all wild animals will "attack" if they sense that they are cornered.

Should I Drink the Water?

There are few backpacking pleasures that can top a cool drink from a high country lake or stream. Unfortunately, that cool sip from a cold mountain stream may be hazardous to your health.

The most common problem is wild strains of the normal intestial bacteria E. coli which is teeming in areas heavily used by humans or grazing animals. The most serious problem is the protozoan Giardia lamblia. The best measure to avoid both is the purchase of a water filter. These are available from mountaineering supply companies such as REI (Recreational Equipment, Inc., Box 88125, Seattle, WA 98138). They do cost a bit (about $225 for the Katadyn or $40 for The First Need), but are worth the investment if you hike a lot. If not, the second best option is to purchase water purification tablets such as Portable Aqua (the active ingredient is iodine) from a pharmacy or outdoor equipment store. Make sure to check the expiration date on the bottle.

E. coli will manifest in a few hours and is characterized by stomach pain and diarrhea. Giardiasis is caused by ingestion of the dormant cyst form of a protozoan. These cysts can survive, even in cold streams (40 degrees Fahrenheit), for up to three months and can be spread by domestic livestock, wild animals, and humans. Onset can occur from within several days to six weeks. Professional medical treatment is required. Since it is beyond the scope of this book to advise on how to treat these and various other medical problems, we strongly suggest you purchase a copy of Medicine for Mountaineering, published by the Seattle Mountaineers.

A final note—some backcountry water is drinkable without treatment. Use caution. Is the area very remote? Freely flowing springs which lack seepage areas above or around their margins are the best bet for a safe backcountry drink. If you do decide to try it, remember you do so at your own risk.

Hiking in Bear Country

Some believe that the threat posed by bears is overrated. We would concur when it comes to black bears. Grizzly country is something else again. We've seen numerous black bears and never had a problem. Ralph, however, was treed by a grizzly and there have been incidents of unprovoked attacks in which the camper did all the right things. What to do?

First, of all of the hikes in this book, only Targhee Creek in the Henry's Lake Mountains in Idaho presents more than a remote probability of grizzlies being present. Grizzlies also are occasionally sighted along the Continental Divide, particularly in the Centennial Mountains, in the Frank Church/River of No Return Wilderness, the Snake River, and Big Hole Mountains of the Idaho/Wyoming border, and the Selkirks of Northern Idaho, but the possibility of an encounter is exceedingly remote.

In general be cautious and alert. Don't hike alone, especially at night. Personally, we like groups of at least six. Watch for bear sign such as claw marks on trees, over-turned logs, and bear scat (especially fresh). Bears often defecate right on the trail. Be cognizant of the places bears prefer (those with lots of forbs, downed timber, the treeline between meadow and forest, and water sources). Leave your dog at home. It may run down the trail ahead of you, encounter a bear, and run to you for safety with an angry bear behind it.

*Monarch of the mountains—**Ursus arctos horribilus**, the grizzly bear. Give it a wide berth.*
Michael Sample photo.

It is still common practice to warn women during menses to avoid grizzly country. As of 1989, scientists at the Eighth International Conference on Bear Research and Management reiterated that there is no evidence that a menstruating woman prompts grizzlies to attack. Still, it seems prudent to be especially careful—use tampons rather than pads, change often, and, if possible, burn them before going to sleep. If you are still concerned, birth control pills will (as you know) stop the flow.

When hiking, a group of six or more, again, is a kind of insurance policy against encounters. But, should you see a bear at a distance, make a wide detour on the upwind side so the bear can get your scent. If a detour isn't possible, slowly back down the trail until safely out of sight. Then, make lots of noise (the more, the better) and slowly and noisily make your way up the trail again. The bear should be gone when you get back to your earlier observation point. If the bear is still there and you can't get safely around it, abandon your route. (Be sure not to force a bear into a position, such as cliffs, in which it cannot escape.) Although it isn't a foolproof method, making noise while hiking helps avoid bears. Many hikers hang bells from their packs. As a general rule, the noisier, the safer. Metallic sound seems more effective than human voices which can be muffled by natural conditions. Also, it's difficult to keep up a steady conversation during long hikes.

While in camp be extremely careful with food and garbage. Keep a clean camp. Don't camp in sites obviously frequented by bears. If you see a bear or fresh signs (those already mentioned plus bedding areas such as those dug into the root systems of fallen trees), pick another campsite. If possible, camp near tall trees that can be easily climbed. Sleep 175 feet from your camp-fire/cooking area and where you hang your food. Keep food and garbage out of reach at night. A good method is to suspend, from a tree, a ditty bag containing your food—at least ten to 15 feet high and five to ten feet away from the trunk. Do not sleep in the clothes you cooked in and don't keep them (or food!) in your tent. Avoid smelly foods (bears have an acute sense of smell) such as bacon, lunch meat, and sardines.

Burn combustible trash if regulations and natural conditions allow open fires. Burn cans and other incombustibles to remove odors. Then, dig them out of the ashes and pack them out. Don't bury trash in the backcountry (it's not only unaesthetic, but tacky).

Don't clean fish near camp. Burn the entrails, if possible. Never leave them around camp. The smell of fish, as mentioned, attracts bears. Camping at popular fishing sites requires extra caution.

In the event of a confrontation, try to remain calm. Don't panic and run (this, in the bear's mind, means you're acting like food). You can't outrun a bear anyway. If the bear stands its ground and doesn't seem aggressive, stand still. If it continues the unaggressive behavior, back very slowly and quietly away until out of sight. If the bear looks aggressive (stands up on its hind legs), start looking for a tree to climb. If it moves toward you, get up the tree fast if you're sure you have enough time. Make sure it's tall enough to get you out of reach. Most such confrontations are with grizzly bears; only the grizzly cubs can climb trees. Before starting for the tree, drop something like a pack or a camera to distract the bear. Stay up the tree until you're positive the bear has left the area. If you can't find or climb a tree, play dead. Curl up and clasp your hands over the back of your neck in a fetal position to protect the soft-tissue organs and your spinal column. This takes courage, to say the least, but it affords you the possibility of avoiding serious injury. Physical resistance, of course, is useless.

Publisher's note: Keep in mind these are merely general rules. they're probably the best, but, as always, it's dangerous to generalize. Certainly, there is no concrete formula for avoiding confrontations or for what to do when confronted. Dr. Charles Jonkel, one of the nation's leading experts on grizzlies, suggested trying to evaluate each individual situation based on these general rules. And by all means, Jonkel emphasizes, "Try to avoid an encounter."

Hiking With Children

Unless you are already an experienced outdoorsperson who is quite comfortable in the wilderness, it is not advisable to bring along babies or very young children.

Children between the ages of two and six are heavy to carry and don't have the stamina to walk. Let them hike for awhile, then carry them again. (This should definitely be a shared responsibility. It's sexist to assume that the woman is the only one who needs to worry about this.) At age six, children will start hiking longer distances, and they will be ready to carry a pack. Daypacks, fanny packs, and even children's backpacks can be purchased at most sporting goods stores. Start out easily with lightweight personal items like a treasured, but not delicate toy, clothing, toothbrush, cup, and snacks. Eventually, add a sleeping bag and some food. Children won't be able to carry their own complete gear until they have become good hikers—can hike the entire distance, no longer complain, and look forward to trips.

If the child has not been introduced to the wilderness in early years, motivation may be your most difficult task. A child often does not understand the purpose of leaving the security of home, television, video games, and friends for a tiring walk with "nothing to do". You can prevent or modify negative attitudes by introducing education about nature and outdoor activities at an early age (in advance of planning any particular trip).

Negative attitudes, we're sorry to say, may be less common among boys than girls. (However, our own daughters, by the time they'd reached the age of eight, did come to like the experience. They're grown now, and seem to remember their experiences fondly.)

Still, boys usually associate outdoors trips with masculinity. Our big, nine-year-old nephew, for example, not only carried all his own gear into a very remote area of the Frank Church/River of No Return Wilderness, but pesters us for more outings.

Hiking trips with younger children should be short—one-half day at the maximum—so the children can explore and enjoy themselves the rest of the day.

Teach children as early as possible what to do if lost. Giving children a whistle and attiring them in bright clothing will also aid in finding them. Other survival skills, such as navigating and fire building, should be taught as early as possible. Get them accustomed to paying attention to where they are and where they're going—note such things as streams, clearings, and the number of side canyons on the route.

Take care of your children's feet—just like you would your own. Boots are expensive and borrowed ones might work. Good athletic shoes are preferable to boots that don't fit. Be certain to check their feet for blisters (they won't know enough to do so themselves). Be sure to moleskin potential trouble spots.

(In general, you'll have to check their clothing, gear, and packs repeatedly.)

If you don't buy or adjust for your children the right-sized packs and footwear and all the necessary equipment to keep them warm or cool, don't expect them to enjoy the outing. Children feel aches and pains, freeze at night, and have a pack rub them wrong just like you do.

Finally, don't expect them to sleep alone. If you sometimes worry about bears or beasties, consider how a child feels. Also, spend time with them: build little rafts they can navigate down a mountain stream, encourage them to sing songs they've learned in school or at the campfire. Take time to give them snacks and rest along the trail. It's worth it.

Crossing Renshaw Creek. Don L. Crawford photo.

MAP LEGEND

Interstate	🛡00	Trailhead Parking & Described Trail	P⊢ - - -→			
U.S. Highway	🛡00	Route	....	Alternate Route	....	
State or Other Principal Road	(000)	Camp site	▲	Cross-Country Route	....	
Forest Road	[0000]	Ranger Station	♣			
Paved Roads	▬▬▬▬	Building	■	Cross Country Route	....	
Dirt Road	= = = = = =	Intermitent Creeks	⟋ ⟍ ⟋	Cross-country Route	....	
Bridge	⟩─⟨	River, Creek, Drainage	⟋⟍⟍↗			
Peak & Elevation	▲ MOUNTAIN 0000 ft.	Falls or Rapids	─//─			
Point Elevation	+	Meadow or Swamp	⁎ ⁎ ⁎			
Pass or Saddle	⟍⟋⟋	Springs	♂			
Mine or Tunnel	─◁	Lakes	⬤			
Continental Divide	●●●●●●●●●	Glacier	⬭			
State Boundary	▬▬▬	National Forest Boundary	▬▬▬			
State Boundary & Continental Divide	●●●●●●●●●	Wilderness Boundary	⊢⊢⊢⊢⊢			

Map Scale 0 0.5 1
Miles

Directional Orientation ⬆N

THE HIKES

Selkirk Mountains and Salmo-Priest Proposed Wilderness

Overview

In the far northwest corner of Idaho are found two of the state's more unusual hiking areas the headwater s of the Salmo and Priest rivers and the U-shaped valley of Long Canyon. Both areas are basically part of the Selkirk Mountains, a rugged, glaciated, 250-mile-long range stretching northward deep into British Columbia. The unique qualities of these two areas eastern stem from their remnant patches of virgin temperate rain forest, which grow clustered along the densely vegetated stream bottoms.

This "big tree" country is nurtured by heavy annual rain and snow falls, resulting in huge western cedars, Douglas-fir, and spruce all covered by a healthy growth of moss and lichen.

The lichen provides the major source of food for the only band of mountain caribou remaining in the nation. This endanger species requires old-growth forest for its habitat.

Another occasional visitor to the mountains and valleys of the Selkirks is the grizzly bear, which wanders down from Canada trying to re-establish itself in some of its former range.

Overall, the dense forests and rare wildlife of the Selkirks present an uncommon backcountry experience for the determined hiker.

HIKE 1 SALMO-PRIEST DIVIDE TRAIL

General description: An 18-mile loop offering a beautiful 3-day introduction into the proposed Salmo-Priest Wilderness, located in both Idaho and Washington and bordering Canada.

General location: Along and above the waters of the Salmo River. The trailhead is 105 miles north of Coeur d'Alene by road.

Maps: Continental Mountain and Salmo Mountain (7.5') USGS quads.

Special attractions: Mountain caribou (the most endangered large mammal in the U.S.), a remnant population of grizzly bears, plus bighorn sheep, deer, elk, cougars, lynx, bobcats, martens, fishers, wolverines—a rare concatenation of deep wilderness animals in a mountain forestland of ultimate splendor.

Season: Mid-July to late September.

Difficulty: Easy to moderately difficult (with the hard portions mostly in the Idaho part of the loop).

Information: Colville National Forest, 765 S. Main, Colville, WA 99114; (509) 684-3711; or Panhandle National Forest, 3815 Schreiber Way, Coeur d'Alene, Idaho 83814; (208) 765-7356.

The hike: The Salmo-Priest Divide trail offers an excellent introduction to the beauty and diversity of the proposed Salmo-Priest Wilderness, an area for which Idaho and Washington conservationists have struggled many years for wilderness designation. In the Idaho portion, a 14,700-acre wilderness is proposed.

The terrain is mountainous; elevations range from 2,720 feet on the Upper Priest River to 7,572 feet on Snowy Top Mountain. Snowy Top divides two principal watersheds, the South Fork of the Salmo River and the Upper Priest River. The Upper Priest is acclaimed as one of America's 37 most scenic wild rivers in the National Wild and Scenic Rivers Act. Gypsy Peak, at 7,309 feet, is the highest point in Washington east of the Cascades.

The trailhead starts at 6,000 feet on a saddle between Salmo Mountain Lookout and Shedroof Mountain. The road to the saddle is well-maintained and easily traveled by car once the snow melts near the first of July. To reach the trailhead from Spokane, take Highway 2 to Newport. Then take Highway 20 northward toward Canada. At Ione, Washington, cross the bridge over the Pend Oreille River and turn up the road to the Sullivan Lake ranger station. Just past the ranger station, take a right onto a well-maintained Forest Service road. Follow the signs toward Salmo Mountain Lookout. At the turn-off to the lookout go straight ahead; the trailhead is but one mile further.

From the trailhead (Trail #506), you'll wind for about 3.5 miles through large stands of cedar, hemlock, spruce, and white pine as you descend to the Salmo River at 4,000 feet. This part of the trail and the stretch along the Salmo River will remind you of the west slope of the Cascades, for they lie within an interior "coastal" storm track. The flora here is much like an inland rain-forest. Here giant red cedars, some nearly 3,000 years old and nearly 12 feet in diameter, stand guard over the Salmo River. Delicate carpet mosses, Canadian dogwood, maidenhair fern, and calypso orchids live on the forest floor.

Salmo River in the proposed Salmo-Priest Wilderness. Bill Arthur photo.

The well-maintained trail crosses over a good log bridge when you reach the Salmo River, and here you turn east to head upriver on Trail #530. You'll find several good campsites close to the river crossing. The next good campsite is about three miles. The Salmo's wild trout offer a challenge to the angler who wants to explore along the river.

After two miles along the river, Trail #530 turns to the north, away from the main river, and begins the ascent to the divide separating the Salmo and the Priest River drainages.

At this point the trail is not as well-maintained; it is usually overhung with heavy foliage, and there is some deadfall until you begin to gain elevation. One mile up the trail, where it crosses one of the feeder streams, you'll find the last good campsite before you reach the ridge. Be sure to fill your water bottles here.

From here, you leave the river to the 6,400-foot ridge, you gain about 2,000 feet in four miles. Just below the ridge is a small spring where you can resupply your water. Along the ridge, you'll walk six miles without finding water except during early snowmelt. However, you can camp near the ridge and melt snow as late as July.

Part of the ridge is rugged, offering fine views of Salmo Basin as you wind through large stands of hemlock and across small meadows. Wildlife abounds here, so be sure to keep a watchful eye. Bears, deer, and smaller game are frequently seen. Good campsites are plentiful for the first half-mile after reaching the ridge.

I recommend setting up camp and taking a side trip to Snowy Top Mountain. This 7,572-foot peak, the highest in the Salmo-Priest, is an easy walk from the trail. Snowy Top offers majestic views of both major river drainages; the rugged, wild mountain terrain to the south; and the peaks immediately north, which lead into Canada. Boundary Lake, on the international border, lies just below Snowy Top to the northwest. Snowy Top is bounded by numerous mountain meadows. Here I watched an eight-point (Royal) bull elk spend most of the day grazing in a meadow just below the summit.

From Snowy Top you can also see the major threat to this unique and beautiful *de facto* wilderness. The U.S. Forest Service is busily trying to "chainsaw" the area's boundaries with an ever-expanding number of clearcuts. Canada has already done so to the north. This wild country that remains is desperately in need of the protection given only by full wilderness classification by the U.S. Congress. If you're concerned about protecting this gorgeous area, get in touch with local conservation groups and find out how you can help.

Most of the smaller drainages you see are outside of the wilderness boundary as recommended by the Forest Service. Conservation groups are trying to get protection for a substantially larger area. This would protect these watersheds along with critical habitat for the caribou and extremely high-quality hiking area. The mountain caribou, now down to only about 16 animals, absolutely require the moss and lichens that grow only on such over-mature climax evergreen forests.

The last portion of the trail follows the Snowy Top divide for about 3.5 miles, drops down to a saddle (you lose about a thousand feet), then regains the elevation at Shedroof Mountain. If you spend your second night out on the Snowy Top divide, then your last day will entail an eight-mile walk out.

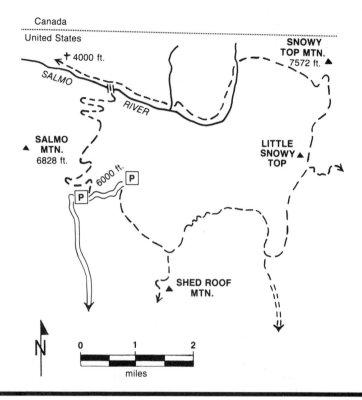

Canada

United States

SNOWY TOP MTN.
7572 ft. ▲

+ 4000 ft.

SALMO

RIVER

SALMO MTN.
▲ 6828 ft.

6000 ft.

P

P

LITTLE SNOWY ▲ TOP

SHED ROOF MTN.
▲

N

0   1   2

miles

The last day offers spectacular views of the surrounding mountains amid which the Priest River courses 3,000 feet below. Grouse, deer, bears, and other wildlife are often seen on the ridge.

As you drop into the saddle just before Shedroof Mountain, you'll find a small perennial stream. This is your last water. It's three more miles to the road. Once you reach the road, you'll find the loop is about .7 mile from being complete. You must follow the road for this distance back to your car.

In 1983, the mountain caribou was granted status as an "endangered species" on an emergency basis by the U.S. government. After visiting this area, please be sure to write to your congressional delegates supporting wilderness designation for the area. Otherwise, the Forest Service plans to relegate one of the most unique and threatened wildlife areas to second place behind logging.—*Bill Arthur* □

HIKE 2   *LONG CANYON*

General description: A good, reconstructed trail, running most of the 18-mile length of the narrow Long Canyon of Canyon Creek. It entails a 3, 000- to 4,800-foot elevation gain, depending on which route you take.

General location: Approximately 26 miles northwest of Bonners Ferry, Idaho, and three miles south of the Canadian border.

Maps: Pyramid Peak, Shorty Peak, Smith Falls, and Smith Peak (7.5') USGS quads; Kaniksu Forest Service map.

Special attractions: A splendid example of a northern climax rain forest. Abundant wildlife, including occasional grizzly bear and woodland caribou; mushroom hunting, and fishing.

Difficulty: Moderately difficult due to several steep pitches.

Season: June to October (depending on snow).

Information: Bonners Ferry Ranger District, Kaniksu National Forest, Rt. 4 Box 4860, Bonners Ferry, Idaho 83805; (208) 267-5561.

The hike: This area is one of the last two unlogged drainages of the American Selkirk Mountains. Parker Canyon, which lies next to it, is the other. Since this area is so exceptional and fragile, we ask that backbackers keep their parties small, select entry dates of light use (in the mid-week, for example), and use backpacking stoves instead of making fires.

This prime area consists mainly of hemlock, western red cedar, white pine, and larch in the middle one-third of the forest. The upper one-third and ridges are covered with Englemann spruce and sub alpine fir. Wildlife, including black and grizzly bears, woodland caribou, moose, deer, martens, abounds. Mushroom hunting in this rain forest, particularly in September, is fabulous. Two of the three highest mountains in northern Idaho flank Long Canyon: Smith Peak at 7,653, and Parker Peak at 7,670 feet. The drainage holds four large lakes.

The Long Canyon Trail in recent years has been improved vastly with both volunteer labor and Forest Service oversight and dollars. Use has become so heavy since the first edition of this book (when few even knew about Long Canyon), that a permit system may soon be required.

There are two possible entry points. The lower (northeastern) is recommended for those without high clearance vehicles. You will have to double-back on your route unless you're able to arrange a 22-mile shuttle.

To get to both trailheads, first head north from Bonners Ferry on U.S. Highway 95 for about 17 miles to the junction with Idaho Highway 1. Take Highway 1 toward Porthill, Idaho. About one mile past the junction, turn left onto the Copeland road. This road crosses the Kootenai River to end at the intersection with the paved West Side road.

To reach the lower trailhead, turn right at the intersection and drive past Parker and Canyon creeks. You'll end up about seven miles north of the intersection and one-half mile past Canyon Creek. Park on the right side of the road. The Forest Service hopes to have a developed trailhead at this site soon. The trail begins on the left side, one-half mile after an old logging road.

To reach the upper (southeastern) trailhead, turn left at the West Side and Copeland road intersection. Drive four miles south to the Side and Copeland road intersection. Drive four miles south to the unpaved Trout Creek Road.—

the first public road on your right. Take this road. The Trout Creek Road is very difficult and dangerous for the entire nine miles to the trailhead. The obvious trailhead leads to many different locations.

The lower trailhead provides a good, clear trail. Since it begins on private property (with access purchased by the Forest Service), hikers should note that no camping is allowed. Within a half-mile, you cross onto National Forest land, where logging ceases. The first two miles are through forest, then through slate, with a 1,200-foot elevation gain. This will quickly warm you to your task. The steepness of this entry is the very reason this canyon hasn't been logged. Canyon Creek itself is difficult to see or reach until you come to the first of four campsites five miles in. During late summer and fall, this campsite may be your first chance to get water.

The lower section's slate eventually yields to granite, signaling a gentler grade, although this trail is generally uphill all the way. From here on, the rock you encounter is granite, as is the entire 200-mile Selkirk Range. Two fires in this century have reduced the sidehill forest, but an adventurous trip down into the canyon bottom will reveal huge cedars and large windfall pools in the creek with 10-inch rainbow and brook trout to be caught. I stumbled into this bottom after getting slightly lost. After a night's rest, I tried fishing and discovered that the fish were unafraid and eager to try my flies. Restraint in fishing may be called for here, but difficult access and navigation to the canyon bottom before the three-mile point may impose restraint. Fishing is generally good throughout the length of the creek.

The ponderosa pine, aspen, and cottonwoods will have disappeared when you reach the first crossing of Canyon Creek just past the 7.5-mile mark. You'll find good camping at this point, with sites on both sides of the creek. This is where you enter the rain forest. This magnificent forest, about one-half mile wide, continues for seven miles. Apparently forest fires stop here due to the wetness. Experience has shown that clothing can't be dried, even during September, without a campfire, no matter how warm the weather. But then, that's why the mushrooms are so abundant.

In a major rehabilitation effort initially led by the Boundary Backpackers and subsequently joined by the Sierra Club, The American Hikers Society, the Panhanhandle Backcountry Horsemen's Association, and individuals and groups national and international, much maintenance has been done to improve this trail.

Still, this lowest creek crossing can be tricky even in September—and it's always very cold. The trail crosses back to the northwest side of Canyon Creek again, about two more miles up, at the 9.5-mile campsite. This, again, is a difficult crossing, but cross-country travel to look for a better crossing is strongly discouraged in order to maintain the earea for its unique wildlife. The woodland caribou is an endangered species and the Selkirk grizzlies are near extinction. Furthermore, the going is tough with huge windfalls and marshes full of devil's club.

The next campsite, the smallest, is located at the 9.5-mile crossing on the northwest side of the creek. The trail continues for about four miles on this side of the canyon through various forest arrangements until you reach the very large 13.5-mile camp. Here a large creek drains Smith Lake. It tumbles down in an apparently endless series of small waterfalls and flows into Canyon Creek at the only real flat in the valley bottom. You can actually sunbathe here! (This

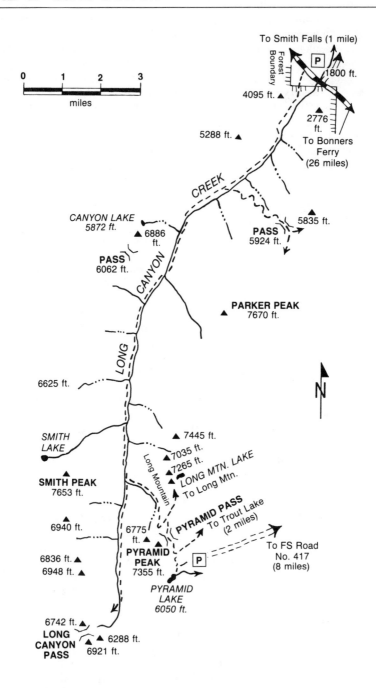

To Smith Falls (1 mile)

Forest Boundary

P

1800 ft.

4095 ft. ▲

2776 ft.

To Bonners Ferry (26 miles)

5288 ft. ▲

0   1   2   3
miles

CREEK

CANYON LAKE
5872 ft.

▲ 6886 ft.

5835 ft. ▲

PASS
5924 ft.

PASS
6062 ft.

CANYON

PARKER PEAK
7670 ft. ▲

LONG

6625 ft.

N

SMITH LAKE

▲ 7445 ft.

7035 ft.

7265 ft.

Long Mountain

LONG MTN. LAKE
To Long Mtn.

SMITH PEAK
7653 ft. ▲

6940 ft. ▲

6775 ft. ▲

PYRAMID PASS
To Trout Lake
(2 miles)

P

To FS Road No. 417
(8 miles)

6836 ft. ▲

6948 ft. ▲

PYRAMID PEAK
7355 ft. ▲

PYRAMID LAKE
6050 ft.

6742 ft. ▲

LONG CANYON PASS

▲ 6288 ft.

6921 ft. ▲

Hiking Parker Ridge with Pyramid Peak (left) and Lion's Head (right) in the background.
Will Venard photo.

is a rain forest, however, and sunny days are not the rule.)

Slightly more than one mile upstream, you'll find the final campsite just beyond the crossing of the main creek. This is a cozy spot straddling the trail. A small feeder stream supplies water. In another half-mile the hemlock-cedar forest begins to play out in the higher altitude (over 4,000 feet) and gives way to spruce and fir. In September huckleberries, present on most of the trail, flourish in abundance for picking.

The upper one-third of the canyon, past the 14.5-mile camp and the trail intersection to Pyramid Pass, has no campsites. This section also has the least-developed trail. In addition, most maps do not accurately locate the trail. It disappears on its way to Long Canyon Pass after it recrosses the creek about 3.5 miles upstream from the 14.5-mile camp, so the hike from here to Long Canyon Pass is cross-country. The head of Long Canyon is at the junction of the Lion's head, Smith Peak, and Pyramid Peak ridges, and is an excellent central location for cross-country hiking in the Selkirk portion of the proposed Long Canyon-Selkirk Crest Wilderness. Plans have been discussed for a higher camp and a connecting trail over the pass to form a loop down the neighboring Smith Creek drainage. The existing Smith Creek Trail is in total disrepair.

Entry from the upper trailhead will require your attention and maximum oxygen intake. It is 2.5 miles and 1,300 feet from the trailhead to Pyramid Pass, from which you drop into Long Canyon. One-half mile in, a trail to the left goes to Pyramid and Ball lakes. Proceed to the right. One mile further, a trail to the right leads to Trout and Big Fisher lakes. Proceed to the left. In dry seasons, the spring here is the last water for two miles. In about one more mile, you'll reach Pyramid Pass. One-half mile further you'll come to another trail intersection. The fork to the right continues on Parker Ridge north. These last miles of trail circle around Long Mountain to Long Mountain Lake. Take the fork to the left for the four and a half miles downhill. At the bottom you'll find the 14.5-mile campsite. From here you can follow the directions given for the lower trailhead.

Long Canyon proper covers about 20,000 acres. It represents about three percent of the timberland in Boundary County. The prime forest covers about 7,000 acres, and whether or not to log this virgin old-growth timber has been debated for years. Don Cambou's film, "Long Canyon: the Wilderness Issue," has helped publicize the area.

The Boundary Backpackers was formed in 1980 to maintain the canyon trail and to do what we could to protect the canyon's pristine state. Since then, the group has led the charge of those desiring to preserve Long Canyon and have it designated as wilderness. (The Selkirk Crest, south of Long Canyon, is a rocky, rugged area of glacial peaks, lakes, and ridges.) This proposal is supported by Idaho conservationists. The Forest Service has recommended only 22,875 acres of the area for wilderness.

Primary opposition to wilderness has come from the timber industry. Long Canyon supplies irreplaceable old-growth timber for wildlife, the only prime forest in north Idaho for primitive recreation, and a natural forest by which to gauge success in managing other forests. Those wishing to help protect and maintain the area may contact the Boundary Backpackers. (See the Information section at the beginning of the trail description for address.)—*Will Vernard* □

Grandmother Mountain Area

Overview

The Grandmother Mountain roadless area is a moniker given to a section of the Clearwater Mountains. Please refer to the overview for the Salmon River Mountains for general information about this area.

HIKE 3 *CRATER LAKE*

General description: A difficult half-mile hike with a drop of 480 feet on an extremely steep (no switchbacks) trail to a high mountain lake.
General location: One-half mile from Freezeout Saddle in the Grandmother Mountain Roadless Area about 20 miles east of Clarkia, Idaho.
Maps: Widow Mountain (7.5') USGS quad.
Special attractions: This is generally a secluded area because of its inaccessibility. The lake is stocked with grayling trout.
Difficulty: Difficult.
Season: Mid-July to mid-October.
Information: Coeur d'Alene District, Bureau of Land Management, 1808 North 3rd St., Coeur d' Alene, Idaho 83814; (208) 765-7356.

The hike: This is a good angler's overnight or dayhike. The trail is not only extremely steep, but is quite wet and slippery even into mid-July some years. Once down, however, you'll find a beautiful little lake with good fishing set in a deep cirque.

Access to Crater Lake is via the Freezeout Saddle Road from Clarkia, Idaho. A detailed description of how to locate the trailhead is given in the Marble Creek trail hike, which follows this hike. The turnout and parking area are approximately 5.4 miles by road east of Freezeout Saddle.

After parking in one of the spaces available at the turnout (6,150 feet in elevation), place all the gear you hold dear into your pack and walk in a generally westward direction up the obvious jeep trail for a few dozen feet. You will see a sign marking a foot trail to the lake. However, no trail will be evident. Continue up the jeep trail a few hundred feet while keeping an eye out for the trail on your right. The trail descends steeply and immediately. If you reach the end of the jeep trail and find yourself climbing upward across the top of the cirque wall, then you have gone too far. If that does happen, however, you can use the mistake to spend a little extra time climbing to take in a spectacular view of Crater Lake below to the northeast.

The unmarked foot trail is similar to other trails in the Grandmother Mountain roadless area—it isn't easy to find. Follow it as it descends *steeply* towards the lake. In some places the descent is from rock to rock while you grasp onto brush or other handholds. Don't get discouraged though, for it's only a half-mile down, and the climb back out is easier than the descent. When it is wet, however, the trip down is so slippery as to be dangerous to rear ends, cameras,

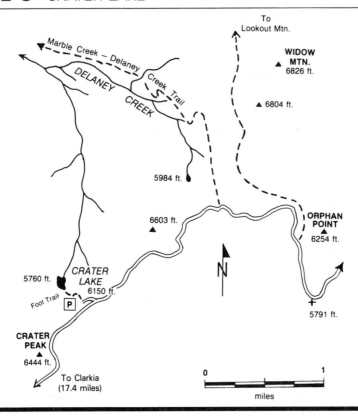

and fishing gear. Consequently, your hands should be free and gear tucked away safely in your pack.

The foot trail eventually follows a small creek bed down to the southern face of the cirque wall and ends in a small meadow right beside the lake (5,760 feet in elevation). From here you look across the alpine fir-rimmed lake to a massive cirque wall rising about 700 feet straight up. There are unmelted snowbanks on the north-facing side of the cirque through July, and a small stream enters the lake on the left side of the clearing. Due to the damp and delicate nature of this little meadow, it is not well suited for camping. Instead, explore the outlet end of the lake for a less fragile (and more secluded) campsite.

This lake is frequented by anglers despite the difficulty in reaching its shore. Because of its compact size, it only takes a few campers to crowd it. Therefore, the conservation-minded may prefer to make this a day hike or to take it in combination with a longer trip on some other trail in the Grandmother Mountain area.—*Don L. Crawford* □

A young hiker surveys sparkling Crater Lake from above. Don L. Crawford photo.

HIKE 4 *MARBLE CREEK VICINITY*

General description: A 15-mile hike on a good, little-used trail winding through subalpine meadows, high mountain lakes, rocky crags, and a forested canyon rich in wildlife.

General location: 40 miles northeast of Moscow, Idaho, and 20 miles east of Clarkia, Idaho, as the crow flies. It lies partly in the Panhandle National Forest and partly in the Coeur d'Alene District of the BLM.

Maps: Grandmother Mountain and Widow Mountain (7.5') USGS quads.

Special attractions: Good stream and some lake fishing, huckleberry picking, big game habitat, ample campsites, and terrain varying from mountain to lowland river.

Difficulty: Moderately difficult.

Season: Mid-July to mid-October. (The low elevation trailhead can be reached by April or May, but that in the high country is not accessible by sedan until early July.)

Information: Coeur d'Alene District, Bureau of Land Management, 1808 N. 3rd St., Coeur d'Alene, Idaho 83814; 208/765-7356: or Avery Ranger District, Panhandle National Forest, Star Route Box 1, Avery, Idaho 83802; 208/245-4517: or St. Maries Ranger District, Panhandle National Forest, Box 407, St. Maries, Idaho 83861; 208/245-2531.

The Hike: This is a 30,000-plus acre oasis of roadless area in a region otherwise characterized by extensive development. Marble Creek and several of the alpine lakes have good fishing, and this is huckleberry heaven in late summer and early fall. A marsh system in the area (Pinchot Marsh) is being considered by the BLM for classification as a Research Natural Area.

The Grandmother Mountain Roadless Area is well-known locally for elk and deer hunting and high elevation lakes that are heavily used in the summer. In the fall, hikers compete with bears for huckleberries. However, the Marble Creek trail is not heavily used once you get a few miles from its lower end.

The BLM administers most of the high elevation portion and is currently considering this for possible wilderness classification. The Forest Service administers the timbered lower elevation canyon and has long-term plans to log the area and build a road all the way up Marble Creek. Conservationists feel the two areas should be combined and 20,000 acres designated the Grandmother Mountain Wilderness.

Marble Creek can be entered from the Marble Creek trailhead (3,300 feet) or the Widow Mountain-Lookout Mountain trailhead (5,922 feet). The easiest route is to leave a shuttle vehicle at the Marble Creek trailhead (see map). This way you have a 15-mile, mostly downhill, hike. If you choose the shuttle option, allow at least two hours' recovery time.

To get to the lower (northern) Marble Creek trailhead, take Idaho Highway 3 to Clarkia. Turn east into town. The road soon curves sharply right and passes a gas station on the left. Turn left at the corner, follow the road through a residential area and around a curve left to cross the Middle fork of the St. Maries River. Immediately after the river crossing, you'll find a "T" in the road. Turn right and drive .6 mile to an intersection with a cabin on the right. Turn left toward Hobo Pass on the graveled Merry Creek Road (#1491). After 1.2 miles, turn right onto the Clarkia-Marble Creek road (# 321). Ignore the intersections and continue on the main road until you have driven about 5.4 miles. Here you come to another "T". Turn right, staying on road #321, and drive eight fairly steep miles over Hobo Pass. The trailhead is just east of the bridge over Marble Creek. There is a small campground. The trail is marked by a sign that reads Homestead Hump Trail #261.

If you start the hike at the high elevation (south) end of the Marble Creek Trail, the Freezeout Saddle road provides access to the Widow Mountain-Lookout Mountain trailhead as well as to a number of others. To locate the Freezeout Saddle road, instead of turning left towards Hobo Pass at the intersection marked by the cabin already mentioned, proceed straight and cross Merry Creek. You'll soon see a sign on the right identifying the Hatley Cow Camp. After about 3.5 miles, you will cross a creek and come to an intersection with

Bountiful beargrass blooms near Freezeout Saddle in the Marble Creek area. Don L. Crawford photo.

a BLM campground on the right. Turn left onto the Gold Center Creek road and begin your climb. This is a well-maintained dirt road. After about 4.2 miles, you'll come to a major intersection. Continue straight ahead on the marked Forest Service Road #301 toward Roundtop and Avery. This is the narrower of the two intersecting roads. The sign warns that only four-wheel drive vehicles are recommended beyond this point. It is, however, passable by sedans unless quite wet. There will be occasional rocks to avoid and a steep grade to maneuver.

Approximately 7.3 miles up Road #301, you come to a small rock outcropping on the left. There is a nice view here to the northwest toward Grandmother (6,369 feet) and Grandfather (6,306 feet) mountains. In July there's lots of beargrass in bloom, and in late summer huckleberries are ready for picking. It is but one mile further to Freezeout Saddle (5,900 feet) where the signed BLM Marble Creek Divide Trail #275 takes off for Grandmother Mountain (three miles) and Grandfather Mountain (five miles). This is a moderately strenuous ridgeline trail with views across Marble Creek Canyon eastward to Lookout Mountain at elevation 6,789 feet, the peak with the bare rock slab for its top. (The trailhead was recently reconstructed with help from Sierra Club volunteers. The trail is open not only to hikers and equestrians, but, unfortunately, off-road vehicles.)

Three miles past Freezeout Saddle is Hemlock Springs, where you can camp. There is another camping area with a pit toilet 1.7 miles further down the road. About 2.4 miles past Hemlock Springs is a turnout to the Crater Lake trailhead (see Crater Lake hike). From here it is about two miles to your destination. There is a turnout at 5,922 feet near Orphan Point. Here you will find

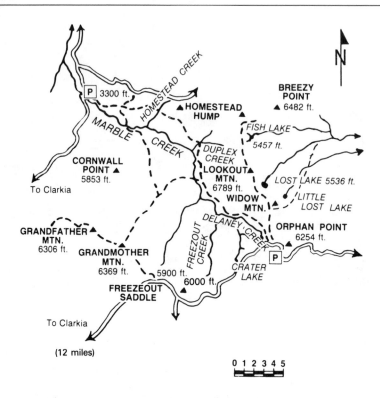

the Widow-Mountain trailhead (campsites, privy). It is by this trail that you'll locate the Marble Creek Trail.

The trail to Marble Creek from here is hard to find (although as of 1989 the Forest Service has long-term plans to do quite a bit of trail maintenance and reconstruction in the vicinity). Ignore the topo map which shows the trail starting from the road west of the parking area. Instead, follow the unsigned Widow Mountain-Lookout Mountain trail, which starts from the northwest end of the parking area. This trail climbs moderately at first through timber, through a small meadow, and back into timber. It then begins to switchback up the mountain and onto an open grassy ridge. It passes to the right of the 6,582-foot peak shown on your topographic map and drops into a saddle at approximately 6,500 feet.

To the east is an impressive lakeless cirque—one of the abrupt beginnings of Lund Creek—and views to the northeast of endless mountain ridges. From here the trail proceeds west across the ridge and begins to contour around Widow Mountain. As you begin to contour around Widow Mountain (at the 6,500 foot level), descend cross-country westward toward Delaney Creek. After dropping about 300 feet or so, you will meet the Marble Creek Trail—it's the first one you'll encounter. Head north and you're on your way.

You may be tempted to continue along the Widow Mountain-Lookout Mountain Trail. If so, you will find alpine country with crags, cirque lakes (Little Lost, Lost, and Fish lakes) and beautiful vistas from expansive meadows. You may want to climb Widow Mountain, hike 3.5 miles to the summit of Lookout Mountain, or hike 5.5 miles to a lakeside camp at Fish Lake.

The Marble Creek-Delaney Creek Trail contours Widow Mountain at 6,200 feet with spectacular views. It then drops through huckleberry patches and pockets of subalpine fir, then forks (not according to the topo map, however).

Take the left fork and begin to drop very steeply into timber. Shortly, the grade lessens, and you enter a grove of 80 to 100 year-old white pine and Douglas-fir. After a quiet walk in this pocket of old growth forest, you again start a sharp descent, and, before long, cross a small creek.

Then comes a wet area with numerous springs. The trail soon drops to a cliff edge viewpoint several hundred feet directly above Delaney Creek. At this point, you've dropped to approximately the 5,200-foot level in about 1.5 miles. The elevation loss continues as you parallel Delaney Creek, cross a small side stream with a beautiful little waterfall, and come almost immediately to the first of many small campsites along this trail. Upstream is a view of the ridge you just descended, and downstream you can see the canyon where Freezeout Creek and Delaney Creek join to form Marble Creek.

The trail gradually descends as it proceeds down the drainage. It then bears sharply right (north) into the canyon of Marble Creek. At this point you are three miles in, and for another three miles the trail drops through timber and huckleberry patches. A signed junction appears at mile six. Here the Delaney Creek Trail (#273) meets the Homestead Hump Trail #261 (i.e., the Marble Creek Trail). The left fork takes you on a side trip directly to cool, clear Marble Creek in a short, but steep, hundred yards. This trail fords the creek to campsites on the west side, then climbs to the top of Grandmother Mountain. The campsites probably get heavy use during the hunting season, but are otherwise mostly empty.

Marble Creek is a fairly large stream even this far up the drainage, and there are plenty of pools for fishing or swimming. The stream harbors native cutthroat.

From the trail junction, it is nine miles north on the Homestead Hump Trail to the Marble Creek Road. In general, the trail trends lower in elevation, except for periodic climbs out of the side stream canyons. This section stays well above Marble Creek but crosses numerous year-round streams. From the junction, the trail climbs through meadows and across two small streams—one of which has a campsite. It then enters a long stretch of quiet forest. Unlike the predominate subalpine fir found in the higher elevations, the conifer species vary markedly in the lower elevations. Along the route you'll see Douglas-fir, grand fir, larch, white pine, Englemann spruce, lodgepole pine, and red cedar (not necessarily in that order).

About nine miles in, you come to Duplex Creek (4,280 feet). Here, after crossing the creek, the trail climbs to 4,400 feet. After a short, level stretch, it climbs to 4,580 feet and crosses a small stream. Thereafter comes a half-mile of generally level hiking before you drop gently through a thick stand of larch and into an open area where Marble Creek once again comes into view. Next comes a steep drop of 650 feet in about 3/4 miles to the crossing of Homestead Hump Creek.

This is a fairly large stream coming out of an impressive side canyon with sheer rock walls visible upstream. You will find a small, but tempting, campsite on the left just after you ford the stream.

The trail now climbs an abrupt 280 feet and through a small saddle with a meadow at 4,030 feet. Shortly after, the trail splits. The right fork goes east up the Gold Center Trail to end one mile later at the Homestead Hump logging road. The middle fork continues to parallel Marble Creek to bring you to your eventual destination. The left fork drops straight down for some 480 feet in about half a mile to Marble Creek. The left fork offers a good side trip. It passes through forest and by some rusted mining equipment. It then meets the creek at the old splash dam. Although the dam has deteriorated greatly (thanks to Mother Nature), it's still obvious that it took a lot of manual labor to build. Marble Creek flows around one side of this structure of wood, rock, and soil. These old dams were used to form small, temporary reservoirs. The water could then be released to carry felled logs downstream.

About a .25 mile upstream from the dam is a secluded campsite beside the creek. The trail fords Marble Creek and eventually reaches the summit of Grandmother Mountain.

Back at the main trail, at about mile 14, you make a gentle climb and cross one stream. The trail then tops out and passes through a small meadow. It then begins a steep and steady descent through pine and fir westward toward Marble Creek, dropping over 500 feet along the left (south) side of Davies Creek. After .5 mile it crosses the creek and enters a large, tranquil meadow right beside Marble Creek. There is a streamside campsite here, but at this point you are just .5 mile from trail's end. The last half-mile includes a climb of about 280 feet, followed by just as sharp a drop back to Marble Creek and the Marble Creek Road—elevation 3,300 feet.

In total you will have walked 15 miles and lost over 3,000 feet in elevation from the starting point near Orphan Point. Of course, because of the two major trail junctions along the way, it is possible to plan other loop hikes. A good possibility for those without two vehicles would be to ford the creek at mile six, climb Grandmother Mountain, and return to the Freezeout Saddle road via BLM Trail #275.—*Don L. Crawford* □

Mallard-Larkins Proposed Wilderness

Overview

The large Mallard-Larkins roadless area of over 300,000 acres lies astride the long ridge dividing the St. Joe and Clearwater River valleys. Crossing the low grade Fly Hill Road, the area extends on eastward to the Montana border.

The idea of protecting this area as designated wilderness originated with Lewiston forester and sawmill designer Morton Brigham, who began visiting the region as early as 1938. In a 1973 article in *Living Wilderness*, Brigham shared his vision with a broader public, and the magnificent area has been included in every serious Idaho Wilderness debate since then.

Idaho conservation and hunting and angler groups now propose the establishment of a 265,000 acre wilderness. It would include the high lakes near Mallard Peak (see the Larkins Lake hike), the deep valleys of Buck and Foehl Creeks and that of the Little North Fork of the Clearwater River. On the south, the Elizabeth Lakes would be included as would the stunning sub-alpine scenery around Five Lakes Butte.

The wildest part of the wilderness lies to the east, in Chamberlain and Vanderbilt Creeks. Here, in a huge valley with the Bitterroot Range as an eastern border you can find deer, elk, moose, certainly wolves, and perhaps even an occasional grizzly be ar. Few trails enter this eastern section.

The Fly Hill, Smith Ridge, and Surveyor Ridge roads all provide good access to the Mallard-Larkins, even into the higher elev ations. Several out-fitters make their living in the area and they, along with hunters and an-glers, have been among its best friends.

Wilderness boundaries for Mallard-Larkins, as proposed by both the U.S. Forest Service and various Idaho politicians, have been uniformly poor, of-ten running on straight lines across cliffs. The boundary proposed by both Idaho and national conservation groups follows roads and valleys in an at-tempt to be both identifiable and ecologically sound. Strenuous legal efforts have, so far anyway, fended off the numerous logging road intrusions planned by the Forest Service and private companies.

In the 1983 congressional examination of Idaho wilderness, the Mallard-Larkins received more public support for wilderness classification than any other area. Despite that, government agencies and many Idaho politicians still wage an unrelenting war against the area as the 1990s arrive.—*Dennis Baird* □

HIKE 5 *LARKINS LAKE*

General description: A seven-mile hike into a mountain lake, from the Clearwater National Forest into the Idaho Panhandle National Forests* in north-central Idaho on the western slopes of the Bitterroot Range.

General location: About 80 miles northeast of Lewiston, Idaho, and 30 miles northeast of the small logging community of Pierce, Idaho.

Maps: Buzzard Roost, Mallard Peak, Sheep Mountain, and Thompson Point (7.5') USGS quads; and Clearwater National Forest map.

Special attractions: Late summer hiking in high mountain lake country with cutthroat trout fishing and a chance to see Rocky Mountain goats, moose, elk, deer, and an occasional black bear

Difficulty: Moderate.

Season: Mid-July to mid-October.

Information: Canyon Ranger District, Clearwater National Forest, Box 1702, (12730 Highway 12), Orofino, Idaho 83544; (208) 476-4541. Northfork Ranger District, P.O. Box 2139, Orofino, Idaho (208) 476-3775.

The hike: After the trek to Larkins Peak at 6,661 feet, hikers peer 500 feet down to Larkins Lake, a clear, cold, inviting gem in the Mallard-Larkins Pioneer

---

* The Coeur d' Alene, Kaniksu, and St. Joe national forests are now collectively managed as the Idaho Panhandle National Forests. The section of the Idaho Pan-handle Forests included in this hike is the St. Joe.

Area. It's a welcome sight. The trail along Goat Ridge is gently sloping and easy enough, but it took me five hours to hike it, and there's no water along the way.

The lake is 12 acres in size, oval in shape, and has four large camping areas. It's also home base for moose, cutthroat trout (which greedily grab at a dry fly), and goats which graze near the top of the steep face of Larkins Peak, visible from the lakeshore. It's a popular hike, mainly because of accessibility, so expect to see others on the trail, especially on weekends.

To get to the trailhead, drive to Greer, Idaho, on U.S. Highway 12. Then head up Idaho Highway 11 on the Greer "grade," a nine-mile-long steep, winding road which leads to Weippe, the largest of several small logging towns on the Weippe Prairie. Stay on Highway 11, passing through Pierce and Headquarters, Idaho. Just north of Headquarters, take a right and drive down a good dirt road for about 28 miles to the Aquarius Campground located on the North Fork of the Clearwater River. Turn left here and drive for about a mile, then turn right at Isabella Creek. Stay left on this winding dirt road for about nine miles until you get to the trailhead. The trailhead is hard to miss. A hitching post on the left, restrooms and Forest Service trail mileage signs on the right, announce that you've reached your destination on Smith Ridge. (The USGS quadrangles do not show this road accurately.)

The trail winds through white pine and Douglas- and grand fir forest for about two miles until it hits the boundary of the pioneer area. The trail condition is good, with only an occasional snag obstructing the way to the top. Ferns line the lower levels, giving way to colorful wildflowers, fruitful huckleberry bushes, and beargrass at higher altitudes. Further along (always staying to the right, except for the cut-off trail to Elmer Creek just under four miles from the trailhead, at which you should stay left), hikers can stop to catch a breath, eat some gorp, and view Mallard Peak to the east.

The days are warm in this area in mid-August—often hikers must cope with temperatures up to 90 degrees Fahrenheit. During August, the air cools off at night, but not much. This brings a problem: mosquitoes. They abound at the lake, which means campers must slip deep into their sleeping bags. To avoid becoming too uncomfortable, take mosquito netting and lots of insect repellent. At night, unless there's a strong wind, the mosquitoes are downright voracious.

Giardia and other forms of biological contaminants have been detected in the waters of the forest. However, there are several springs along the perimeter of the lake. The spring water is probably safer to drink than that of the lake proper. To be completely safe, boil all your water. (See the section on Giardia near the beginning of this book for more information on water treatment and Giardia).

The lake is not noted for large fish; it's too popular for that. But the fish that are here have a short feeding season and are hungry most of the time. Nearby, up out of the lake basin and about a mile further down the trail, lies the smaller Mud Lake to the north. To the east sits Crag Lake below 6,879-foot Crag Peak, and farther still is the 40-acre Heart Lake, known for its occasional larger cutthroat trout. These lakes dot the subalpine high country nestled in glacial cirques.

The Heritage Cedar Grove, located at the confluence of Elmer Creek and Isabella Creek, "is an outstanding example of several majestic groves of ancient cedars that survived the 1910 and later forest fires," according to a brochure

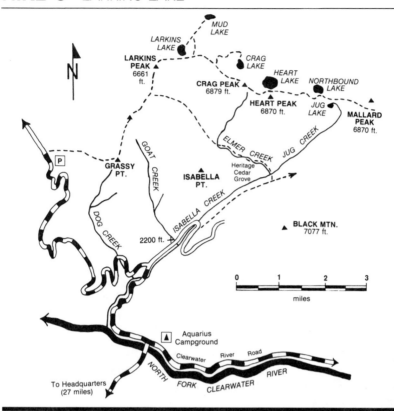

called "Mallard-Larkins Pioneer Area" published by the Clearwater and St. Joe national forests (May 1970). Although USGS and Forest Service maps show a connecting trail between Goat Ridge and Elmer Creek, I didn't hike it. If you care to do so, I'd check with the Forest Service first.—*Bill Francis* □

(Editor's note: The "pioneer" area designation is unique to the Mallard-Larkins roadless area made by the Region I [Northern Region] of the U.S. Forest Service. The hike described here lies within the pioneer area. Although this designation does provide protection similar to wilderness [no timber harvesting, recreational vehicles, or roads, etc.], it is a temporary administrative decision and does not carry the weight or permanence of a congressionally designated wilderness. Some feel the pioneer area was created to forestall or avoid the creation of the proposed 265-thousand-acre wilderness. At any rate, the 232 thousand acres outside of the pioneer area may be honeycombed with roads in the near future if it is not soon protected as wilderness.)

HIKE 6 *FORAGE LAKE*

General description: A hike past several lakes and along the top of the St. Joe Divide to a remote lake.

General location: About 90 miles northeast of Lewiston, Idaho, in a remote part of the proposed Mallard-Larkins Wilderness.

Maps: Bacon Peak, Chamberlain Mtn. (7.5') USGS quads.

Special attractions: Numerous lakes; fine views.

Difficulty: Moderate with some cross-country. Most of the trail was rebuilt in 1989-90.

Season: Early July to late September.

Information: This is a hike of six miles, traversing a lovely high lake basin, climbing a small mountain, and then following a ridge out to a little-visited lake hanging far above the St. Joe River.

The hike: To reach the trailhead, use the Fly Hill Road. This is passable in average snow years by early July. Its southern end has been "improved" for log hauling, but past Fly Hill it is slow and rough, but with only a few mud holes. The road's southern end is at Cedars campground on Forest Service Road #250 (the Pierce-Superior, Montana, road). From Cedars, the Five Lakes Butte trailhead is about 18 miles of slow, but lovely driving on FS roads #720 and #715.

The trailhead is often poorly marked (due to vandalism), but you will know you've gone too far when you cross the second bridge over the forks of Meadow Creek. Park just south of the southernmost bridge. The trail follows a partial jeep track for about 200 yards before becoming a trail in wet meadow.

Past the meadow the trail climbs fairly steeply for about 1.5 miles, crossing a small creek in the process. It finally levels out in a huge meadow where Tin and Copper lakes are barely visible to the north.

Leaving the meadow, the trail passes close to Silver Lake, which has several heavily used campsites scattered among huge boulders. From Silver Lake, the trail climbs about 250 feet in a half mile toward Gold Lake. A spur trail leaves, leading through the grass and berry bushes to this lake, which lies right at the foot of Five Lakes Butte.

Turning south, the trail quickly climbs another 250 feet to an open saddle near the top of the St. Joe Divide. From the saddle, the views are spectacular with the Nub and the valley of Skull Creek visible to the west. At this saddle, leave the trail which continues along the St. Joe Divide a short distance before ending. Climb the narrow ridge northeast for about .5 mile until you reach the summit of 6,713-foot Five Lakes Butte (an altitude gain of another 500 feet). Again the views are stunning, with the Bitterroot Range and the deep valley of the North Fork of the Clearwater River visible, plus the deep blue lakes in the basin below.

From the summit, contour down to the northeast (no trail) through low timber to nearby Heather Lake. Few people visit here and this lake also escapes the worst of the insects that sometimes plague the other lakes beneath Five Lakes Butte. Forage Lake is about two miles north of here. It is reached by climbing the 600 foot ridge just north of the lake. Just northeast of peak 6,859, a trail begins. Unmarked, but easy to follow, it follows the wide ridge leading northward, then northwestward.

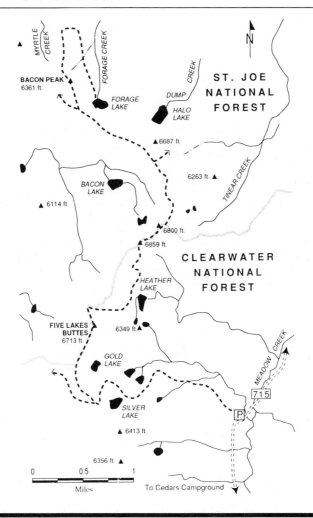

At about a mile a nice view is had of Bacon Lake, and the poor trail coming up out of Bacon Creek from the St. Joe River is crossed. Follow this trail until it begins to drop down the west side of Bacon Peak. Climb 100 feet to the top of Bacon Peak for a remarkable view of Forage Lake below and Needle Peak across the deep valley of the St. Joe River to your north. To reach the lake, contour down the north spur of Bacon Peak and then head back south to the lake. Expect good fishing and few visitors.—*Dennis Baird* □

Above, Forage Lake in the proposed Mallard-Larkins Wilderness. Dennis Baird photo.

Proposed Great Burn Wilderness

Overview

Fortunately, the Forest Service has recommended much of the Great Burn area for wilderness designation. Unfortunately, it hasn't recommended enough. The Kelly Creek drainage to the north and northeast has mostly been left out of the wilderness proposal, along with Cayuse Creek, a major tributary of Kelly Creek. Both of these nationally known trout streams are threatened by logging and road-building plans. The 260-thousand-acre Bighorn-Weitas Roadless Area to the west has been officially confirmed as occupied by the endangered Rocky Mountain gray wolf. Despite its wolves, however, Bighorn-Weitas will soon be heavily logged unless hard work continues to protect it from development. This vast wilderness surrounding Blacklead Mountain, at which the trail to the following hike begins, has been cut into several large pieces by a few primitive roads. However, to date, it remains the only expansive region of undeveloped wildland left in Idaho north of the Clearwater River. Your voice is needed in securing protection for these areas.

HIKE 7 *GOAT LAKE*

General description: A six-mile round trip to a secluded mountain lake in the proposed Great Burn Wilderness of Idaho and Montana.

General location: Approximately 28 road miles northwest of U.S. Highway 12 and the Powell Ranger Station in the Cayuse Creek drainage of the Clearwater National Forest.

Maps: Rhodes Peak (7.5') USGS quad.

Special attractions: A secluded and lightly used lake amidst 7,000-to 8,000-foot peaks; numerous trail connections to other lakes and the Bitterroot Divide.

Difficulty: Moderately easy.

Season: Mid-July to mid-September.

Information: Kelly Creek Ranger District, Clearwater National Forest, Box 1209, Orofino, Idaho 83544; (208) 476-4541. Northfork Ranger District, P.O. Box 2139, Orofino; (208) 476-3775.

The hike: The trail to Goat Lake starts at the very summit of Blacklead Mountain (7,318 feet) and drops 826 feet in three miles to the lake. The summit offers an outstanding view of the proposed Great Burn Wilderness of the Bitterroot Divide country. To the northeast is the divide, heart of the wilderness. To the north and northeast is the Kelly Creek drainage . To the south is Cayuse Creek, and due west is the Bighorn-Weitas roadless area.

From Lewiston, Idaho, drive about 164 miles east on U.S. Highway 12 to the Parachute Hill Road (Forest Service Road #569) which joins U.S. 12 from the north just east of the turnoff to Lochsa Lodge and the Powell Ranger Station. Drive north up this road for 2.7 miles to a fork. Take the left fork and drive 1.8 miles to another fork. Again, keep left. About 1.6 miles further is the signed Powell Junction. Proceed straight ahead on Forest Service Road #500 (The Lewis and Clark Trail) for another mile to Papoose Saddle. Continue straight ahead, and after about 3.9 miles you will pass a sign marking the Lost Lake Trail (#40). After 8.1 more miles, you arrive at Cayuse Junction. The stretch of road you have just traveled follows the approximate route of the Lolo Indian Trail used by Lewis and Clark to cross the Idaho mountains in 1805 and 1806. It is passable in passenger cars with good tires and drivers not anxious to exceed 20 miles per hour. However, in the opinion of the Forest Service, this is a four-wheel-drive road.

At Cayuse Junction, turn right onto Forest Service Road #581. From here it is about 8.2 miles to the turn-off (right) to Blacklead Mountain. This turn-off is marked by a sign which reads "Deer Creek Trail #513." This last steep mile of rutted, rocky jeep trail is not suited for sedans.

The trail begins as a jeep road traversing the ridgeline northward and losing elevation rapidly. After a quarter-mile and a drop of 240 feet into a saddle, the road ends near an old mine digging and a grave (simply a pile of stones with a worn wooden marker). Two trails appear here. The most obvious climbs the ridge toward the peak marked 7,514 on your topographic map, but it isn't the one you want. In fact, it's not even on the topo. The correct trail leads to the right and immediately begins to switchback down in a southeasterly direction from the saddle toward Silver Creek. The side ridge here is untimbered, and the valley below is pocketed with fir, pine, small meadows, and brush fields.

On the trail to Goat Lake in the proposed Great Burn Wilderness. Don L. Crawford photo.

After dropping another 280 feet in a quarter-mile, you'll come to a small, cold, clear spring which flows right out of the mountain to form Billy Rhodes Creek. Although you cross two more perennial streams before reaching the lake, this spring is probably your best bet for *safe* drinking water. After the spring, the trail drops less steeply. The next quarter-mile is easy to follow, but it's so lightly used that it can't be seen from the ridge above as it passes through a beargrass meadow and patches of lodgepole pine and alpine fir.

Shortly after the trail levels out at about 6,650 feet, it splits and gives you a choice—right, down Billy Rhodes Creek to Silver Creek and ultimately to Cayuse Creek; or left, towards Goat Lake. As you keep left, the trail levels as it contours around the ridge for about two miles to cross the two small streams. These flow out of two impressive cirques (which the topo indicates as lakeless). Numerous rock outcroppings begin to appear on the ridge above.

Here you come out onto a wide open stretch of ridge. To the southeast is a view across Silver Creek to Williams Peak (7,501 feet)—a gray slab dominating the skyline. On the eastern horizon is Rhodes Peak (7,930 feet). Goat Lake still can't be seen, because it is hidden by its own cirque wall which juts out in front of the trail.

The lake comes into view as you round the southern end of the cirque wall. Surrounded by the 180-degree wall which rises abruptly to a thousand feet above, this beautiful lake makes you automatically reach for your fishing rod. There are a couple of campsites at the trail's approach to the southeast shore.

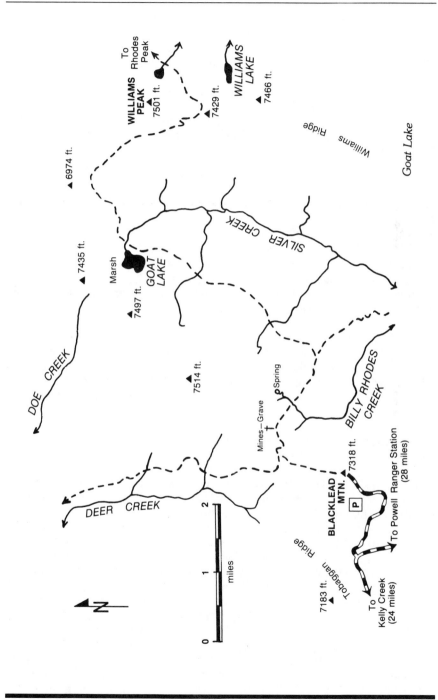

There is also a nice site on the other side of the lake. The outlet creek departs the lake at its marshy northeast side. The view of the lake and the wall are especially nice from this location.

An extra attraction for hikers here is the number of trail connections to other lakes, to Cayuse Creek, and to the Bitterroot Divide. A good extension from Goat Lake is the trail over Williams Peak (7,429 feet) and down to Williams Lake (7,005 feet). This trail ultimately reaches the divide via Rhodes Peak.

The return to the trailhead from Goat Lake is leisurely—mostly level, except for the last steep climb back to the top of Blacklead Mountain. From the top, you can look northeastward back across the proposed Great Burn Wilderness as you plan your next hike into this remote and magnificent region.—
Don L. Crawford □

HIKE 8 *STEEP LAKES LOOP*

General description: A five-day hiking and angling trip through the proposed Great Burn Wilderness on the Idaho/Montana border.
General location: In the Clearwater National Forest, northeast of Kelly Creek. Approximately 150 miles east of Lewiston, Idaho or 60 miles west of Missoula, Montana.
Maps: Bruin Hill, Straight Peak (7.5') USGS quads.
Special attractions: Outstanding angling in several sub-alpine lakes for diverse species including Westslope Cutthroat, Dolly Varden, and California golden.
Difficulty: Both the beginning and end segments of this 25-mile loop are easy. The segment following the Boundary Trail is moderate with some route-finding problems.
Season: July through October.
Information: North Fork Ranger District, Clearwater National Forest, PO Box 2039, Orofino, Idaho 83544; (208) 476-3775.

The hike: The proposed Great Burn Wilderness is located in the extreme northern range of the Bitterroot Mountain system. This large expanse of backcountry encompasses land in both Idaho and Montana.

The present day environment of the region was shaped by the Great Idaho Fire of 1910 (hence the name "Great Burn"). This catastrophic event burned huge areas of northern Idaho, even destroying several towns. Eighty years after the fire, much of the area proposed for wilderness is still quite open.

The Steep Lakes cirque is nestled at the headwaters of the North Fork of the Clearwater River. This lake basin, aptly named in its precipitous position below the ridge separating Idaho and Montana, is seldom visited. The only way to reach these lakes is on foot or by horse via the Boundary Trail.

Access to the trailhead is possible in a number of ways. The best route is from Superior, Montana west over Hoodoo Pass (a paved road), then downstream along Long Creek to its junction with Lake Creek. Both streams are tributaries of the North Fork. Another route is from Orofino, Idaho, following the North Fork of the Clearwater upstream to its headwaters.

HIKE 8 *STEEP LAKES LOOP*

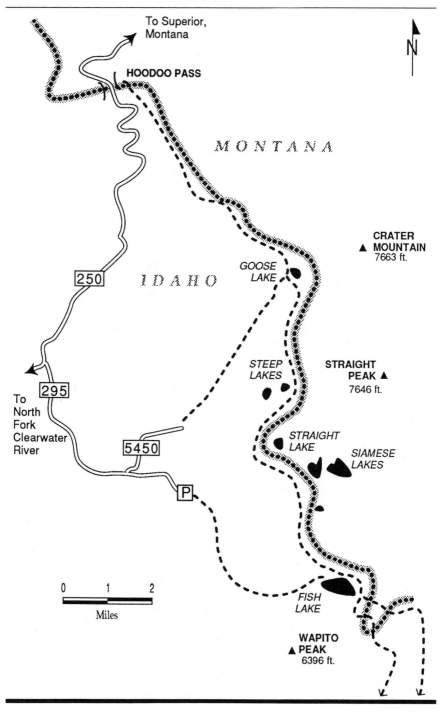

To Superior,
Montana

HOODOO PASS

M O N T A N A

I D A H O

250

295

5450

CRATER
▲ **MOUNTAIN**
7663 ft.

*GOOSE
LAKE*

*STEEP
LAKES*

**STRAIGHT
PEAK** ▲
7646 ft.

*STRAIGHT
LAKE*

*SIAMESE
LAKES*

To
North
Fork
Clearwater
River

P

*FISH
LAKE*

WAPITO
▲ **PEAK**
6396 ft.

N

0   1   2

Miles

A much more exciting drive is Forest Service Road #569 from U.S. Highway 12 at the Powell Ranger Station, up to and along Toboggan Ridge and to famed fishing stream Kelly Creek. This is an extremely rough and narrow road following ridgelines. A truck or a four-wheel drive vehicle is definitely needed, although in August of 1986, Jeff Smith and I negotiated the road in his subcompact loaded to the brim with camping gear, backpacks, and two Chesapeake Bay retrievers. We awoke the next morning on Kelly Creek to a flat tire! For specific instructions to this route see the Goat Lake Hike.

Proceed up Lake Creek on Forest Service Road #295 about seven miles to a barrier. The barrier is located on Lake Creek about 1.5 miles past its confluence with Goose Creek. Here there is a small parking area. The trailhead is undeveloped.

This 25-mile loop begins by following the closed logging road at the barrier. From the trailhead it is an easy five miles to Fish Lake. The old road track turns into a trail after a mile or two. Unfortunately at the present time dirt bikes and ATVs are allowed to travel to the lake. This is the source of numerous complaints, but wilderness designation would prevent this.

Special fishing regulations delay the opening day for Fish Lake and Steep Lakes until August 1. The reason is to protect the spawning of West Slope Cutthroat in Fish Lake and the California Golden trout in Steep Lakes. Because of the regulations, the fishing is quite good. However, if you prize solitude and quiet, do not walk to Fish Lake on August 1!

You reach the Boundary (or State Line) Trail just beyond Fish Lake, which is barely inside Idaho. Motorized travel is prohibited on this trail, which follows the Bitterroot Divide closely. The Boundary Trail begins a few miles north of Lolo Pass where U.S. Highway 12 crosses into Idaho, and it follows the state line for over 45 miles. The view from the trail is excellent into both states. Some 20 lakes are scattered along it on both sides of the divide.

Elk, moose, and deer are abundant in the area, making it a popular hunting destination in the fall. Isolated sightings of both grizzly bear and North Rocky Mountain gray wolf have occurred in recent years. The Franklin, or spruce grouse, is also quite common.

The section of the Boundary Trail from Fish Lake northward to Goose Lake is traveled infrequently. The route is moderately difficult in places as the trail disappears on some of the more rocky and open parts of the ridgeline. Finding the route is no great problem, however, as the ridgeline is the only logical route of travel. Most of the lakes below on either side of the ridge are reached only with off-trail hiking. There is no water on top of the Bitterroot Divide except for temporary snowmelt.

Before you reach the Steep Lakes, you pass the Siamese Lakes and Straight Lake, both of which are in Montana. The upper Siamese Lake is an excellent overnight camping choice after a first night at Fish Lake. Here fishing for cutthroat trout is excellent.

The country near Steep Lakes is appropriately named. Straight Peak, on the Montana side, is a sight to behold from the Boundary Trail, and the Steep Lakes Cirque has to be one of the most sublime locations in Idaho. The Steep Lakes are deep and dark blue set among rugged cliffs.

Fishing is the reason Jeff Smith and I ventured to the area. The lower Steep Lake supports a naturally reproducing population of California golden trout. The limit here for this rare fish is two. Carefully release all others so that once again the flash of crimson and gold may strike your dry fly.

From Steep Lakes, the Boundary Trail continues north four or five miles to the Goose Lake basin. The small, shallow, and fishless lake is a watering hole for moose and elk. Camping at the lake is possible, but the surroundings are quite marshy. A sign at the trail junction here should steer you down the Goose Creek Trail. It's about seven miles down this well-maintained and easy-to-follow trail to the Goose Creek trailhead. At the trailhead, we stashed our backpacks in the bushes and walked the remaining mile to our car.—*Phil Blomquist* □

Selway-Bitterroot Wilderness

Overview

The northern third of the great wild country of Central Idaho is largely contained within the 1.8-million-acre Selway-Bitterroot Wilderness.

Geologically similar to much of the River of No Return Wilderness country to the south, the Selway-Bitterroot sits atop the huge granitic bulge of the Idaho Batholith. Its rocky bones jut to the surface in the form of the Selway Crags in the wilderness' northwest corner and the towering Bitterroot Range to the east on the Idaho-Montana border.

Most of the Wilderness is steep country of ridges and canyons. The canyons center on the Selway River (a unit of the National Wild and Scenic River System) and its many tributaries. Much of the wilderness is forested with a larger variety of conifers that occur in Idaho south of the Salmon River.

Efforts by the timber industry and the Forest Service to dismember the old Selway-Bitterroot Primitive Area when it was administratively reclassified as a wilderness area in the early 1960s gave impetus to the efforts of conservationists to establish the National Wilderness Preservation System. These efforts were successful in 1964 when Congress passed the Wilderness Act providing for permanent protection of designated wildernesses by U.S. statute instead of by bureaucratic discretion.

The success of the Wilderness Act and of the classification of the River of No Return Wilderness in 1980, which restored wilderness protection to much of the area ripped out of the Selway-Bitterroot Primitive Area by the Forest Service in 1963, means that the Selway today runs clear and clean. The sandy soils derived from the granitic batholith often run like sugar when logging and road-building strip them of their protective cover of vegetation. Chief among the areas restored is the Magruder Corridor on the Selway-Bitterroot's south side.

Success was not obtained for the Lochsa Face on the north side. This unit of the National Wild and Scenic Rivers System is today threatened by logging on its steep slopes, much of it carried out by means of subsidies that make it artificially attractive to cut timber but end up costing more than the trees are worth.

In 1988 a wildfire burned a large area around Moose Creek. In your future travels, it will be interesting to observe the natural succession of revegetation.

HIKE 9 *SELWAY CRAGS VIA BIG FOG & LEGEND LAKES*

General description: A seven-mile round-trip hike into the Selway Crags of the Selway-Bitterroot Wilderness.

General location: About 32 miles from Lowell, Idaho, in the Nez Perce National Forest. The trailhead is accessed via the Selway River and Fog Mountain roads.

Maps: For Mountain and Fenn Mountain (7.5') USGS quads.

Special attractions: Ridgeline hiking to lightly used alpine lakes. Much of the trail traverses through old burns with picturesque snags and panoramic views.

Difficulty: Difficult.

Seasons: July through mid-October (snow keeps the Fog Mountain Road closed before July and after mid-October).

Information: Moose Creek Range District, Nez Perce National Forest, Box 464, Grangeville, Idaho 83530; (208) 983-2712.

The hike: From Lewiston, Idaho, drive approximately 97 miles up the Clearwater River on US Highway 12 to Lowell, Idaho. Here the Lochsa and Selway rivers join to form the Middle Fork of the Clearwater River. Turn right, cross the river at the confluence, and follow the Selway River road upstream. This road will take you to the Selway-Bitterroot Wilderness boundary and give you numerous choices of hiking trails in and adjacent to this vast wilderness including the Selway River trail, the Meadow Creek trail, and trailheads into the beautiful alpine country of the Selway Crags.

Follow the Selway Road upstream for about 17 miles. It is paved for the first few miles, but then turns into a well-maintained gravel road. This road is usually passable throughout the hiking season except for occasions during the peak days of spring melt (late May to early June) when the river may flood its banks and cover the road in places. Stay on the main road, keeping the river to your right. Just short of Selway Falls and directly after the Gedney Creek crossing, you will come to the Fog Mountain Road which meets the Selway River Road from the left (north). Take the Fog Mountain Road. If you miss this turn, you'll come to the end of the river road after another mile, at Race Creek Campground.

The Fog Mountain Road ends at Big Fog Saddle after a drive of about 14 miles with a steep climb of 4,100 feet! A sign at the bottom of the road warns that it's unsuited for cars with automatic transmissions. The brakes of such cars tend to overheat on the return trip. Indeed, the Fog Mountain Road is barely passable even by manual transmission passenger cars, for it is extremely steep and loaded with rocks aimed directly at your oil pan. Still, a careful driver can negotiate the road at about five miles per hour; so do not despair, for "slow and steady wins the race." At Big Fog Saddle there is ample parking but few good campsites. It you arrive too late to start your hike, you'll probably have to look around for an out-of-the-way spot, since this trailhead is heavily used despite the difficult access.

The Selway Crags are large in area, containing numerous alpine lakes hidden within deep cirques and surrounded by jagged peaks. The hiker who takes the trail described here avoids the crowds, which tend to conglomerate at just

Legend Lake. Don L. Crawford photo.

a few of the lakes, and finds real solitude amongst the crags. Big Fog Lake and Legend Lake lie in a beautiful basin to the south of the main peaks. They are reached by a strenuous hike across the top of Big Fog Mountain (7,122 feet). From this trail, the panorama of the Selway-Bitterroot Wilderness unfolds to the north, south, and east as far as the eye can see.

Three trailheads are located at Big Fog Saddle. The far left trail drops down in a northwestwardly direction to cross Canteen Creek. It then climbs six miles to the Cove Lakes. This is one of the most popular trails in the entire wilderness. The far right trail heads east and contours the south side of Big Fog Mountain, passes Parson Lake, and then joins the Three Links Lakes. These lakes lie directly below Fenn Mountain (8,021 feet) in the heart of the Crags.

The center trail heads northeast up and over Big Fog Mountain and then follows a high ridge north into the south side of the Crags. This is the trail to take. One should reconnoiter the trailhead choices carefully before starting out. The first time I hiked in the crags, I headed for the Cove Lakes (like most everyone else), took the wrong trail by mistake, and ended up at Legend Lake (with no regrets).

The Fog Mountain Trail is the only one that starts out with a stiff climb. It initially switchbacks from the 5,920-foot level to 6,880 feet in a distance of about 1.25 miles. Most of this area was once burned, and there are many snags. Once atop the ridge, you'll have an easier time as the trail climbs more gently to a high point at 6,920 feet. This is a good spot to rest and have lunch as you look northward across the glacier-carved canyon of Canteen Creek to its sheer white and grey rock headwall rising abruptly more than 1,500 feet to peaks as high as 7,623 feet.

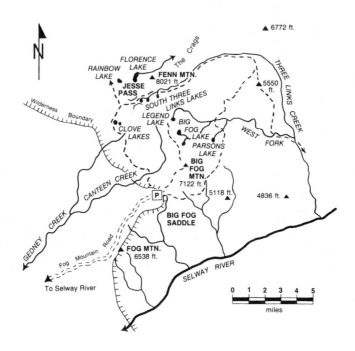

The trail continues east along the ridgeline and at mile two skirts the north side of Big Fog Mountain (7,122 feet). This is wide open country, where cross-country travel is easy and trails tend to disappear. From Big Fog Mountain you're mostly on your own. Don't continue eastward on the main trail, for it will drop down in a distance of two miles to a point (6,312 feet) above Parsons Lake. Instead, turn to your left at Big Fog Mountain and follow the sharp ridgeline north. The trail is generally good, but from this point on, you may find yourself mistakenly on animal trails that abruptly fade away to nothing. These "goat" trails are numerous and easy to take by mistake. One cannot go wrong, however, since the ridge drops off sharply on both the east and west. The ridgelines are beautiful in early September when the abundant buckwheat turns to a gold-brown.

This narrow ridgeline separates the Canteen Creek drainage (west side) from that of Three Links Creek (east side). Big Fog Lake and Legend Lake lie in cirques which form the headwaters of the West Fork of Three Links Creek. You'll drop from the 7,000-foot level to a windy saddle (6,795 feet) about .75 mile north of Big Fog Mountain. From here you look directly down on a small unnamed lake to your right (east). Continue to contour northward along the 6,800-foot line (refer to your topo); and after passing through a rocky, marshy area with crags above you to the left, you'll see Big Fog Lake well below you to the east. The entire lake is visible from above. It is often frequented by moose. Indeed, I have had the luck of seeing moose every time I've hiked in the crags; and at Big Fog Lake, a hiking buddy and I watched a cow moose feed in this rather shallow lake for half an hour one afternoon. She was finally alerted to our presence by her two calves, at which time they all beat a stormy retreat.

There is no trail to Big Fog Lake, but it's easy to drop down cross-country on the north side. No campsites are evident, but there is a flat spot above the lake on the northeast side (near 6,464 feet on your topo). This is a fragile site; make it a fireless camp if you choose to stay the night. Photographers will like this spot, especially in the early morning hours on clear days.

To hikers on the ridge above Big Fog Lake, the Selway Crags are visible to the northeast, especially the sharp ridge separating the cirque of Legend Lake on the south from that of the South Three Links Lakes on the north. As you continue northward and approach this massive wall of sheer rock and talus, there is but faint sign of any trail. After a half-mile of cross-country with abundant views, you drop down to the deep, blue waters of Legend Lake (6,800 feet). At this point you are about two miles north of Big Fog Mountain and some seven from the trailhead. There is a small, but nice, campsite at the west end of the lake.

There is no simple loop through the crags via Big Fog and Legend Lakes that does not require some backtracking. From Big Fog Mountain, you can continue east and connect with the South Three Links Lakes Trail via Forest Service Trail #693. From the upper of these three lakes (6,780 feet), you can climb by trail over Jesse Pass (7,200 feet) and then drop down to the Cove Lakes (6,320 feet). The Cove Lakes Trail then provides a route back to Big Fog Saddle. This is a strenuous loop with many ups and downs. But in reality, there are no hikes in the rugged Selway Crags that can be considered easy. All, however, can be considered infinitely worthwhile.—*Don L. Crawford* □

HIKE 10 *LOWER SELWAY RIVER*

General description: An easy, well-maintained trail gaining little elevation for about six miles.

General location: In the Selway-Bitterroot Wilderness, about 18 miles up the Selway River road from Lowell, Idaho.

Maps: Selway Falls and Fog Mountain (7.5') USGS quads.

Special attractions: Federally designated wild river in a forested canyon; good fishing (catch and release); early season accessibility; campsites under shady cedars or on sandy beaches.

Difficulty: Moderate.

Season: Early April to November.

Information: Selway Ranger District, Nez Perce National Forest, HC 75 Box 91, Kooskia, Idaho 83539; (208) 926-4258.

The hike: Due to its low elevation, this is one of the earliest accessible trails in northern Idaho.

From Lewiston, Idaho, follow U.S. Highway 12 up the Clearwater River approximately 97 miles to Lowell, Idaho. Here, the Lochsa and Selway rivers join to form the Clearwater River. Turn right at the confluence, cross the river, and follow the Selway River road about 18 miles to the trailhead. This road is paved for the first few miles, but then turns to gravel. It is usually passable throughout the hiking season, except sometimes during the peak of spring snowmelt (late May to early June), when the river may go over its banks and flood the road in places. Stay on the main road, always with the river on your right. There will be three bridges crossing the Selway; don't cross over them. Do stop for the view of Selway Falls, however. Continue past the falls and along the river for a mile or so to the road's end at Race Creek Campground. There is parking for 20 to 30 cars. If you arrive late, you could overnight at this small campground, which has pit toilets but no running water.

The trail begins at 1,780 feet elevation at the upstream end of the lower parking area, where you will see the trail register. The trail heads upstream (east) along the north side of the Selway. It sparkles with mica on sunny days as it winds along the river through a canyon cut out of decomposing Idaho Batholith granite. The first level mile and a half is outside the wilderness, but the Forest Service has banned trailbikes in this area.

You'll see the sign marking the wilderness boundary shortly after crossing Packer Creek, at about mile 1.5. This and other creeks flow steeply down from Fog Mountain (6,538 feet) to the Selway (1,785 feet). They roar with icy clear snowmelt during May and June, but they can be easily crossed on appropriately placed logs. Although the Selway also runs bank to bank in spring, it runs clear because it drains more than a million acres of pristine Selway-Bitterroot Wilderness. Alas, the fishing doesn't get really good until the water begins to recede (in some years, late July). All along the trail there are nice reststops. Take your choice—relax under a big cedar which will shade you on sunny summer days and keep you dry on drizzly days; or stop for lunch on one of the numerous sand beaches. This trail is perfect for leisurely weekend family hikes with children, but you should watch small children closely since the trail traverses ledges and cliffs that drop abruptly to the river.

About 2.5 miles in, you cross Teepee Creek; a half-mile further you meet the Otter Butte-Highline Lakes Trail. If you wish to take this trail, you must make a difficult (impossible in spring) ford of the river. Once across, you climb a steep 3.3 miles and 4,300 feet from the river level to Otter Butte (6,088 feet). Then the trail climbs Highline Ridge to the crest of Mink Mountain (7,260 feet and drops down into the cirque basin of the two Highline lakes. It is a strenuous hike but rewarding for those interested in panoramic views and mountain lakes less crowded than those of the Selway Crags further north. The Highline Lakes can also be reached, without such an extreme climb, from a trailhead at Indian Hill (6,810 feet).

The main river trail continues through mixed ponderosa pine, western red cedar, and Douglas-fir to Renshaw Creek. The forest here is young and vigorous, especially on the north-facing slopes across the river. Young timber is rapidly replacing a forest scorched by tremendous fire in the early 1900s. Numerous picturesque snags still stand as reminders of the devastation once wrought over several million acres of the Selway-Bitterroot during this conflagration.

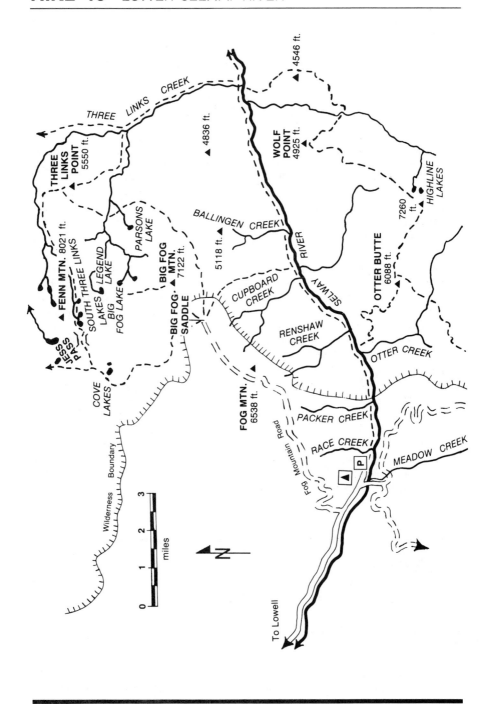

There are several nice campsites at Renshaw Creek; but, because this is only a little over 3.5 miles in, these sites are heavily used. Two are under old-growth cedar, and one is beside a beautiful little beach adjacent to where the creek empties into the Selway. If you find these sites full, which is likely on most summer weekends, and if you aren't ready to hike another mile or so upriver, there is another campsite a few hundred feet up the creek from the trail (east side of the creek). You will sometimes share this camp with deer or elk, and you may even find horses.

As with any hike, the further you get from a road, the fewer people you will encounter. On the Selway trail, you'll lose most day hikers at Renshaw Creek. From here the trail climbs about a hundred feet in a mile and then stays high for awhile. There are great views up and down the canyon, with occasional upstream glimpses of snow-capped mountain ridges. At about six miles, you'll reach Cupboard Creek and find several really nice campsites, a beach, and roaring rapids with a big drop. Cupboard Creek is a good goal for hikers out for a weekend trip. An unsigned side trail, #710, not on your topo, takes off from the river trail here and climbs about 4,100 feet from river level (at approximately 1,800 feet), to Big Fog Saddle (at 5,900 feet) and the terminus of the Fog Mountain Road, from which many hikers enter the Selway Crags.

For hikers interested in an extended trip into the Selway country, the river trail continues upstream, and there are side trails to take you into the high country. Your choices are basically limited only by your imagination (or by your stamina, if you choose to hike up out of the canyon). On the river trail, you can walk upstream all the way to the Magruder Road's crossing of the Selway and into the river's headwaters which are within the 2.4 million-acre River of No Return Wilderness.

A challenging one-way loop trip involving the lower Selway trail starts at Big Fog Saddle (see the next hike description for directions) and loops through the Selway Crags via the Cove Lakes, Jesse Pass, and the South Three Links Lakes; and then drops down to the Selway River via the Three Links Creek Trail. From here it is 15 miles downstream to the trailhead at Race Creek. The total distance is more than 30 miles, with lots of ups and downs. A week is needed to really enjoy the country. Logistics will require two cars, one to get you to Big Fog Saddle and one waiting at Race Creek Campground when you finish the hike.—*Don L. Crawford* □

HIKE 11 *WHITE CAP CREEK*

General description: A major excursion into the vast backwoods of the rugged Selway-Bitterroot Wilderness.

General location: 65 miles by road west of Darby, Montana.

Maps: Burnt Strip Mountain, Mt. George, Mt. Paloma, and Tin Cup Lake (7.5') USGS quads.

Special attractions: A trail along a primeval major tributary of the Selway River that climbs from 3,000 feet to 7,630 feet. Plenty of wildlife, especially deer and elk, with quite a few black bears.

Difficulty: Moderately difficult, once spring run-off recedes.
Season: The first several miles are accessible in late May. The Bitterroot Divide isn't open until mid-July.
Information: West Fork Ranger district, Bitterroot National Forest, 6735 Westfork Road, Darby, Montana 59829; (406) 821-3269.

The hike: This trailhead starts at the Paradise Ranger station, which is a 12-mile drive down the Selway River after you turn north off the Magruder Corridor Road. The corridor divides the Frank Church/River of No Return Wilderness from the Selway-Bitterroot Wilderness. Except for the corridor, designated wilderness stretches as far as the eye can see.

The corridor is a long, difficult stretch of road that you can enter from Elk City, Idaho, on the west, or Conner, Montana, on the east. (See Sheep Hill hike for access description).

The trail begins just past the ranger station near an outfitter's camp. From there is follows the north side of White Cap Creek, which, given its size, should be named the White Cap River.

Depending on the number of days you've allotted, your destination can be either Cooper Flat, Patzy Ann Falls, the Triple Lakes, or White Cap Lakes— the furthest being White Cap Lakes, about 27 miles from the trailhead. A major forest fire burned the south side of White Cap Creek some years ago, and its impact is still quite evident. The entire Selway-Bitterroot Wilderness is slowly being placed under a natural fire plan that allows naturally caused fires to burn themselves out when conditions are not extreme. Aside from the burn, this country is heavily forested.

The trail is well-maintained to Patzy Ann Falls, but in the early season, you can expect to cross winter deadfall. In the lower elevations, you might see rattlesnakes on the trail. Black bears are common; keep a clean camp and hang your food bag.

Cooper Flat, about nine miles from the trailhead, takes a day to reach. There's an old Forest Service cabin here, but it's not open to public use. Here, White Cap Creek is joined by a major tributary—Canyon Creek. A major trail crosses White Cap Creek here on a bridge, providing access to Cooper Flat. The trail heads up the narrow, timbered mouth of Canyon Creek. The narrow mouth is deceptive, however, as Canyon Creek widens considerable after 1.5 miles. This is a potential side-hike.

The second day you may want to hike to Cliff Creek, another nine miles distance, which has an excellent camping area. In June, however, both Paloma creek (2.5 miles past Canyon Creek) and Cliff Creek are high with run-off, and crossing may be dangerous. It is not unusual during spring melt for White Cap Creek to rise more than a foot by mid-afternoon. The trail to Cliff Creek is good except for early season deadfall and avalanche debris where timber may be stacked like Lincoln logs.

On day three your options double, for after 4.5 miles you reach a trail junction near fabulous Patzy Ann Falls. You can either climb 3.5 miles and 2,000 feet to Triple Lakes or contine up White Cap Creek on a fainter trail (not shown on the maps) to end at the White Cap Lakes. Triple Lakes have excellent fishing. The trail leads to the middle lake (the lower one to the west is well off the trail). The highest lake requires about a quarter mile of easy off-trail hiking. The visitor finds much alpine larch, which grows in Idaho only along

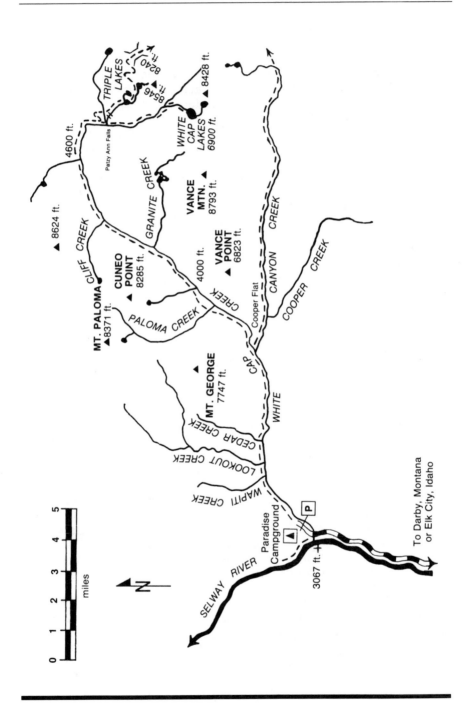

the Bitterroot Divide. From the lakes, the trail snakes over the Bitterroot Divide into Montana and down to large (and popular) Tin Cup Lake.

The trail fork to White Cap Lakes and Triple Lakes occurs near a small campsite. To get to White Cap Creek Lakes, follow the lower route across Triple Lakes Creek below Patzy Ann Falls. The trail has much deadfall and many detours made by animals and hunters. Keep your eye on the aged tree blazes. Do not cross White Cap Creek, stay on the east side for 4.5 miles, passing through huge subalpine forest choked with huckleberries.

At this point, you ford White Cap Creek. You are one-half mile from, and several hundred feet below, the lakes. The broad ford is shallow and easy even early in the season. After a bit more forest, the trail slants steeply upward through a meadow below a rock outcrop to lead to the outlet stream. A short travel upstream takes you to the White Cap Lakes. There are a couple of lightly-used campsites on the northeast side of the lake. Once to your destination, take pride in the accomplishment. Very few make it to this area.

The fishing in this large, relatively low elevation lake is outstanding and worth the 27 miles. California golden trout (Salmo aquabonita) were first stocked here in 1973. You should plan on at least three days to reach the lake from the trailhead and three days to hike out. Of course, you'll probably want a few extra days to explore the area.—*Philip Blomquist with Erik Fisher* □

Gospel Hump Wilderness

Overview

Born of controversy and compromise, the 206-thousand-acre Gospel Hump Wilderness is one of Idaho's most wild and least-visited places. It was established by Congress in 1978 after several years of legal and political battles. Lengthy negotiations between conservation and development interests preceded introduction of legislation. The final settlement, enacted by Congress as part of the Endangered American Wilderness Act (P.L. 95-237), not only established the wilderness, but also allocated roadless land along the South Fork Clearwater River to timber development. Still other roadless land was the subject of wildlife and fishery studies completed in 1982, and the 1983 Nez Perce Forest Plan made final decisions on the uses of the "study" lands. Neither the final wilderness boundary nor the final allocation of lands for development pleased all the interested parties, but the solution has so far stood the test of time.

Elevations within the wilderness range from 1,970 feet at the Wind River Pack Bridge on the Salmon River, to 8,940 feet at the summit of Buffalo Hump, a lovely and quite dramatic mountain. Vegetation types along the Salmon River breaks (southern) portion of the wilderness consist chiefly of grass and large-diameter ponderosa pine. The old wagon road (now a trail) leading east from the Gospels toward Buffalo Hump serves as a hydrologic divide for the wilderness. To the north, streams flow into the South Fork of the Clearwater in deep, but often wide, valleys. Lovely meadows predominate here, with fir species and lodgepole pine the most common type of trees to be found. Brush is thicker on this side as well, due to higher rainfall. Precipitation on the Salmon River side is as low as 18 inches a year but reaches 60 inches further north.

This climatic variation also affects visitor use. The Wind River and trails associated with it are often snow-free by March, yet trails leading into the Ten and Twenty Mile creeks country off the Sourdough Road don't open up until late June or July. The high country around Wildhorse Lake on the east edge of the wilderness is the last to open, although increased mining activity in the Buffalo Hump mining district, which was excluded from the wilderness, could mean earlier plowing some years.

The wilderness is rich in both fish and wildlife. Both resident and anadromous fish can be found in some streams, and most of the numerous lakes in the wilderness have fish as well. Several of the north side drainages are especially popular with moose, and there is evidence of elk migration back and forth across the wilderness, with large wintering populations found on the Salmon River side. Both goats and sheep are fairly common on the canyon breaks, especially in Crooked Creek. Cougars and black bears are both relatively uncommon species, but there is evidence of occasional gray wolf use of the wilderness. The large deer and elk populations make hunter camps a common autumn sight, especially along the Sourdough Road. Four outfitters operate in the wilderness, one using llamas for pack animals.

The road system leading to Gospel Hump trailheads is generally well kept and well marked. The Salmon River road to Wind River is a charming drive in itself, as is the road from Crooked Creek up to Wildhorse Lake, where the trail to North Pole Mountain begins. The Gospels Road, reached by driving east from the Slate Creek Ranger Station on U.S. Highway 95, is by far the most lovely road access route to the wilderness, offering dramatic views south into Wind River and across the Salmon River into the adjacent River of No Return Wilderness. The Sourdough Road, which begins just past Golden (on Idaho Highway 14) is in the process of a major relocation. So, for some years to come, it will be best to check at the forest supervisor's new office east of Grangeville on the status of this key route to the north edge of the wilderness.

Trails within the wilderness range from poorly kept to not maintained at all. As a result, the Gospel Hump Wilderness offers a superb chance to escape crowds and yet still enjoy fine stream or lakeside camping, hunting, and fishing. The rough country southwest of Buffalo Hump is by far the least visited part of the wilderness, but spring hikers in the Wind River and Crooked Creek country can also expect no crowds.

A management plan dated early 1983 offers guidance to the Forest Service on how to manage the wilderness and would make interesting reading for visitors as well. It also outlines several threats to the wilderness, including mineral exploration and development (chiefly for gold) among those parts of the wilderness that border the mining district exclusion; and potential development of a major resort on private land within the wilderness at lovely, historic Shepp Ranch. Let your congressional delegates know how you feel about such development within a designated wilderness.

A special Forest Service map of the Wilderness is available, but recent USGS topographic mapping of the wilderness at 1:24,000 scale (7.5′) is quite reliable for most uses.—*Dennis Baird* □

HIKE 12 OREGON BUTTE

General description: A three-mile hike with profuse wildflowers, solitude, fishing, and a spectacular vista of the Salmon River Canyon.

General location: 50 linear miles southeast of Grangeville in the obscure Gospel Hump Wilderness. Advised assess is by 4-wheel drive; if not, the hike is eight miles longer.

Maps: Buffalo Hump (7.5') USGS Quad.

Special attractions: Mining ghost towns and glory holes. Solitude amid spectacular scenery.

Difficulty: Moderate.

Season: Mid-July through August.

Information: Red River Ranger District, Nez Perce National Forest, HC 01 Box 23, Elk City, Idaho 83525; (208) 842-2255.

The hike: The Gospel Hump area, just north of where the Salmon River runs through the maze of the Salmon River Mountains, is characterized by pronounced glacial features on the north and east side of the ridges and by fairly gentle south and west slopes.

The trails typically wander along the more gentle slopes through subalpine fir, whitebark pine, and Englemann spruce combined with numerous open parks and meadows. The meadows are wet most of the year and display many kinds of wildflowers such as alpine heather, shooting star, pinks, and lupine.

Mountain goats and a few bighorn sheep inhabit the heights, while mule deer and elk are common on the lower slopes. Moose migrate from lake to lake and are particularly common in Jumbo Canyon. Because of the excellent big game population, many hunters frequent the area in September and October.

Oregon Butte lies about seven miles southeast of one of the most unusual features of the Gospel Hump Wilderness the Buffalo Hump. You'll pass this granite exfoliated dome named for its east-west profile, which resembles a buffalo. The area near Buffalo Hump is difficult to reach due to the long (six-hour) drive from Grangeville that ends with a rugged four-wheel-drive trail. But the reward is spectacular scenery, solitude, and big, smart trout.

Your journey begins in Grangeville on Idaho Highway 14, the Elk City Road. Follow this winding paved road up the scenic South Fork of the Clearwater River to the Crooked River Road. This is a well-marked gravel road 42 miles from Grangeville. Here, cross the South Fork and proceed 13 miles toward Orogrande, a turn-of-the-century mining town which is now just a cluster of summer homes. Watch for moose along the Crooked River in the overgrown tailings ponds left by old mining activity.

One mile past Orogrande, you leave the main road and turn right onto the Orogrande-Summit Road (#233). This is where the gravel ends, but the granite soils of the Idaho Batholith nevertheless provide a good, well-drained rock base for this unsurfaced road. The Orogrande-Summit Road is maintained as soon as the snow melts in July and is passable by sedan. It climbs steadily through dense conifer woods to Orogrande Summit, the watershed divide between the Salmon and Clearwater rivers. Here you'll find another prominent intersection. The right fork deadends at Wildhorse Lake. The left fork goes to your destination—Jumbo Canyon.

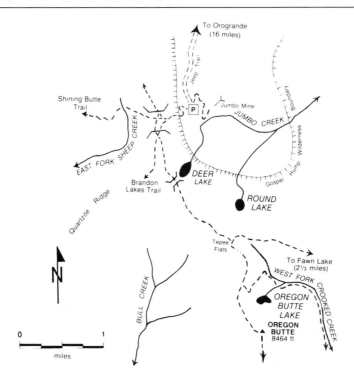

Just past this intersection, the road deteriorates as it descends into Lake Creek. The next three miles are negotiable by truck, but tough for a sedan. In several places, water flowing across the road has exposed large rocks which will high-center a sedan. Don't try to get past the summit in a car unless you are an experienced mountain driver and have an older vehicle you don't mind beating. up.

One-half mile past Lake Creek Campground, the road becomes passable by four-wheel-drive vehicles only. If you park here, you have an extra eight miles to hike to the trailhead at Jumbo Canyon.

This road is badly washed; water flows over it even in the summer. In several places it climbs steep ledges of bedrock that are challenging even to a four-wheel-drive. Plan to average five miles an hour or less through this section. Where the road tops out near Hump Lake, three miles past Lake Creek, there is a spectacular view of the Buffalo Hump plus a much improved road. If there's time, you can take a right turn for a half-mile side trip to Hump Lake—a high lake lying at the base of the Buffalo Hump.

Back at the intersection of Orogrande Summit, the left fork continues through alternating subalpine fir and alpine heath past a private airstrip on the old Calendar Mine property. One-half mile before you reach the airstrip, a road turns off to your left, climbing to a ridge overlooking Bear Lake. Day hikes into Bear, Crescent, and Ruby lakes can be made from this point. Although they are close to the road, Bear and Ruby lakes have generally good fishing for 12- to 14-inch trout. One mile past the airstrip, the road drops gradually into the headwaters of Jumbo Creek and your trailhead at the end of the road near Jumbo Mine.

You'll find plenty of room to park and camp at the trailhead, with a convenient source of water in nearby Jumbo Creek. However, the water will need to be purified since, like all of the meadows in the Hump country, those in this area are grazed by sheep.

You can take an interesting short hike during the trip into the historic boom town of Calendar. In its heyday in the 1880s, the Buffalo Hump Mining District was home for over five thousand miners. Calendar is the only Hump country ghost town where the remains of buildings are still visible. To find Calendar, look for a Forest Service sign about one mile past the Lake Creek Campground. An obvious trail leads down from the road to Calendar. About 100 yards past where the trail crosses Lake Creek, you will encounter old rotting timbers and rusting machinery.

Up until the mid-1960s, several buildings were still standing in Calendar, and old bottles and antiques were easily found. Since then bottle diggers and other scavengers have thoroughly picked through the bones of the settlement, and heavy winter snows have brought the last buildings down.

If you have a little extra time and are interested in old mines, the Jumbo Mine is a half-hour hike from the trailhead at Jumbo Canyon. To find the mine, follow the Jumbo Canyon trail (#230) down a steep granite slope to where it reaches the valley floor. On the way down this hill, you can see the mine buildings on your left and to the north. Cross Jumbo Creek on the trail and shortly thereafter you will see old mine tailings near the trail. Follow them uphill less than a quarter mile from the trail and you will come upon the old mine and mill buildings. Heavy machinery for processing is still evident at the mill site. How could such equipment possibly have been brought in with no road the last half-mile? One old-timer in Grangeville explains that the machinery was skidded in from Grangeville in the middle of the winter over an old trail that followed the Clearwater-Salmon Rivers Divide. An elaborate wench and pulley system was devised to get the machinery down the cliffs in Jumbo Creek. As with so many other human artifacts that are hauled into the wilderness, these were abandoned when no longer useful.

The trail into Oregon Butte Lake (#201) begins in a wet meadow in the headwaters of Jumbo Creek. After a boggy creek crossing, the trail switchbacks steeply for a quarter mile to a low saddle between Jumbo Creek and the East Fork of Sheep Creek. Here you'll find a seemingly confusing system of trails and shortcuts. Stay left to go to Oregon Butte Lake.

If you are interested in a short day hike into Shining Lake, which is slow fishing for big fish, go straight and stay on Trail #201. The junction for the trail into Shining Lake (#228) is about a half mile past the junction for the Oregon Butte trail. The Shining Butte Trail is hard to find, as it has been almost obliterated by sheep grazing. If you lose the trail, remember that the lake is about the same elevation as the saddle. It lies in an indistinct glacial cirque one mile due north of the saddle. It has a perennial outlet stream, and if all else fails, you can follow the outlet up to the lake.

The trail into Oregon Butte (#202) climbs slowly from its junction with Trail #201, staying on the ridge between Sheep Creek and Jumbo Canyon. One-half mile from the junction, an angler's trail leads down from a saddle into Deer Lake. This trail is easy to follow into Deer Lake.

About one mile past the junction, you will find a sign marking an old trail into Brandon Lakes. The trail is infrequently used and hard to find in places. The Brandon Lakes lie in two adjacent east-facing cirques on Quartzite Ridge. Both of the lakes basins were burned over in 1969 in the Elk Creek Fire, which caused evacuation of Oregon Butte Lookout. Quartzite Ridge is very rugged and supports a small population of mountain goats.

From the Brandon Lakes junction, the Oregon Butte Trail (#202) climbs moderately for 1.5 miles to a saddle, then drops steeply into Tepee Flats. You can make camp at Tepee Flats and use it as a base to hike into Round, Oregon Butte, and Fawn lakes. About two hundred yards before the trail levels off above Tepee Flats, a rather indistinct angler's trail goes to Round Lake. The trail follows a small perennial stream down into a cirque, crosses the stream to avoid a bog, then drops through dense old growth spruce to Round Lake. The lake is hard to find if you lose the trail. Round Lake has excellent fishing for big fish.

At Tepee Flat, another trail follows Drumlumen Ridge out to Fawn Lake. The first half-mile of the trail crosses a meadow and is indistinct. However, the trail is easy to find once it leaves the meadow if you stay on top of Drumlumen Ridge. The fishing at Fawn Lake is not as productive as at other lakes in the vicinity, but it often has moose.

About a half-mile past Tepee Flats, Trail #202 forks into two well-defined paths. The right fork climbs to a saddle that switchbacks to Oregon Butte Lookout for a superb view of the Salmon River Canyon. The left fork drops fairly rapidly into the West Fork of Crooked Creek. About a half-mile down the West Fork Trail, a distinct angler's trail leaves the main trail and continues on to Oregon Butte Lake. Oregon Butte Lake is rarely fished and even less frequently stocked. It has a few large fish (16 to 20 inches) that are hard to catch. However, it is highly scenic and the hike is well worth it.

The Gospel Hump Wilderness is little used. The summer one of us was stationed at the Oregon Butte Lookout, there were no visitors to Oregon Butte, and only two parties visited Round Lake.—*Dan and MaryAnn Green* □

Frank Church-River of No Return Wilderness

Overview

The story of how the River of No Return Wilderness came to be is not quite as romantic as its name. But it's sure to arouse passion and nostalgia in the hearts of the many who put their minds, mouths, and money into this labor of love. Although many concessions were made, this was a victory to which every environmental group contributed.

At 2.4 million acres, this is the largest wilderness area in the lower 48 states. Its birth as official wilderness in 1980 was breathtaking in that several decades of effort could have been lost. The Central Idaho Wilderness Act was passed in August 1980. In November 1980 its most important sponsor, Senator Frank Church, lost his bid for reelection. A scant three months' delay in passage could have sunk the whole ship.

Several years later, after his death, the name "River of No Return Wilderness" was modifed by Congress with his name added. A man of great achievement in American history, his name on the wilderness area may be remembered when other deeds have been forgotten.

The River of No Return is the Salmon River, declared unnavigable by explorers Lewis and Clark back in about 1804. It remains that way except for recreational navigation: it provides some of the best whitewater boating in the world. The wilderness itself is comprised of the former Idaho and Salmon River Breaks Primitive Areas and adjacent wild lands previously unprotected.

The need to protect the wild country of central Idaho was recognized way back in 1931 when the Forest Service established the Idaho Primitive Area. This administratively protected area included a million acres of rugged Salmon River Mountains out of an area of wild country four times that size existing in one vast mountain fastness.

A Primitive Area was a temporary classification, however, and in the late 1930s the Forest Service began to study and reclassify the various primitive areas around the nation into the permanent status of wilderness. Unfortunately, rather than keeping a bit of America wild forever, the reclassification often turned out to be a method of stripping an area of all potential merchantable timber and "protecting" the rest—the rocks. "There will be no logging above timberline," assured one regional forester.

Conservationists began to seek a more reliable form of protecting the wild country than the old method of administrative decree. Although many Forest Service leaders were strong proponents of wilderness, something stronger was needed—something that would be difficult to rescind. The answer was to pass a law—land guaranteed as wilderness permanently by U.S. statute.

For many years, the battle to create a national wilderness system was fought in Congress. Progress was slow, but in 1964 a federal bill creating the National Wilderness Preservation System was signed into law. Senator Church was a co-sponsor and leading supporter of the Wilderness Act.

In 1963, the year before the Wilderness Act, the Forest Service had, by administrative fiat, reclassified much of the 1.8-million Selway-Bitterroot Primitive Area, just north of Idaho Primitive Area. While the resulting

1.2-million-acre Selway-Bitterroot Wilderness was the largest in the nation at the time, hundreds of thousands of acres of forest, canyon, and mountain meadow had first been torn from the primitive area: Elk Summit, the Magruder Corridor, Meadow Creek. Twenty years later, the Magruder Corridor was made part of the Selway-Bitterroot Wilderness, and conservationists still battle to keep Elk Summit and Meadow Creek off the chopping block (We describe a hike along Meadow Creek elsewhere in the book).

Conservationists redoubled their efforts after passage of the Wilderness Act. The National Wilderness Preservation System only included those areas already classified as wilderness by the Forest Service. However, additions could be made. The remaining unreclassified primitive areas were to be studied for wilderness classification over a ten year period. Recommendations for their future were to be made to Congress. Among the areas in Idaho, this review included the Idaho and Salmon River Breaks primitive areas.

In 1972, the 200,000-acre Sawtooth Primitive Area was successfully reclassified as the Sawtooth Wilderness, but the great Idaho Primitive Area and its neighbor, the Salmon River Breaks Primitive Area, totalling 1.4 million acres, were saved for last.

In 1974, the Forest Service began to solicit public opinion to determine their future. Options ranged from preserving the entire 1.4 million acres of the two primitive areas down to preserving nothing at all. Losing any part of the official primitive areas seemed, in the words of one Idaho conservationist, like choosing which of your children would live and which would die.

But the future of the paper primitive areas wasn't the only worry. These areas were surrounded by another million acres of orphan wild land that had been protected only by their inhospitality to development. Environmentalists had a brainstorm, a brainstorm which would save both. All the existing wildlands in Central Idaho, those with pedigree and those without, should be protected

This idea became the 2.3-million-acre River of No Return Wilderness Bill. The bill was drawn up and presented in public meetings. From one end of the state to the other, in public hearing halls packed to the rafters and hot with debate and histrionics, the contenders made their case—the 500,000-acre "roadless recreation area" proposed by the Boise-Cascade Corporation versus the 2.3 million acre bill for a River of No Return Wilderness, along with the middle-of-the-road Forest Service option of 1.4 million acres. Environmentalists turned the tide. When the results were in, the 2.3 million acres were over-whelmingly endorsed by the citizens of Idaho.

Finally then, in 1980, this public support convinced enough politicians, so that almost all of the 2.3 million acres (over 3,500 square miles) formally became wilderness.

The individual victories in the bill's passage were many. Among lands now protected, in addition to the former primitive areas, were the headwaters of Camas Creek and Warm Springs Creek. The airy upper reaches of Loon Creek were included as a detached portion of the wilderness. Sulphur Creek and Elk Creek, important spawning streams for salmon, were saved from below cost logging. Marsh Creek and lower Bear Valley Creek were included, making the headwaters of the Middle Fork of the Salmon sacrosanct from ORVs and other internal combustion intrusions. Poker and Ayer meadows, slated for noisy auto campground futures, were instead kept for the elk and sandhill crane.

Another Idaho resident out for a backcountry expedition. Harry Engels photo.

The entire watershed of the Middle Fork, both inside the wilderness and out, was withdrawn from dredge mining.

Bitter compromises were made, too. The lower portion of the Big Horn Crags and the Panther Creek breaks were made part of the wilderness, but cobalt mining was declared the dominant use. This came after a Canadian mining company, in a fit of altruism, no doubt, mounted a public relations campaign to reduce the risk that the United States would run out of this "strategic" mineral. Subsequent to this concession, the foreign firm lobbied for a government subsidy to make cobalt mining profitable. To date no mining has taken place.

Small miners were allowed to continue their low-value diggings in Big Creek, the Middle Fork's main tributary. Mining was allowed on Thunder Mountain adjacent to the west boundary of the Wilderness. Since that time several bad spills of mining waste have found their way into adjacent wilderness streams. The country above the Dixie Tail (familiar to those in northern Idaho) was not protected, and now timber sales in the top part of the Salmon River Canyon are planned—sales that cost the taxpayer more than the timber is worth. Ironically, most of the environmentally damaging timber cutting in central Idaho is done at an absolute economic loss, made possible only because the Forest Service furnishes road-building money courtesy of the U.S. taxpayer.

With the exception of the subdued topography of Elk Creek on the south end of the wilderness and the vast plateau called Chamberlain Basin, the wilderness is a sea with waves of one steep mountain ridge after another. The major canyons of the Middle Fork and main Salmon twist through the mountains, in places almost 7,000 feet deep! This is deeper than the Grand Canyon.

Long ago a vast body of molten rock pushed up under central Idaho. It never reached the surface as lava. Instead, it cooled and crystallized into in a complex of granitelike rocks—a batholith. Millions of years later, this batholith was exposed to the elements, carved by wind, water, thawing and freezing, and glaciers into mountains and canyons. The rocks of the Idaho Batholith, one of the world's largest such igneous intrusions, underlie much of Central Idaho, including the River of No Return Wilderness. When roads are blasted into its mountains, the soft, coarse-grained rock washes into the rivers, choking them with sand.

Most environmentally aware citizens are familiar with the Idaho Batholith. What is not so well known is that most of the southeastern part of the wilderness, as well as Big Creek, is instead a pile of volcanic rock, part of the vast Challis volcanic field. These mountains too are fragile with erosion after disturbance. Here the result is cloudy water as devastating to fish as the clear, but sand-clogged, streams from disturbed batholithic soils.

The undisturbed mountains and canyons of the wilderness are rich in wildlife, including elk, bighorn sheep, mountain goats, mule deer, mountain lion, black bears, and a few moose and whitetail deer. Lynx, fishers, wolverines, and wolves exist in smaller numbers. There is an occasional unconfirmed grizzly bear sighting. The abundance of wildlife is due not to the area's fertility as much as to its untouched nature, especially the deep canyons that provide rare undisturbed winter range for wild animals.

Trout fishing in the wilderness is excellent for rainbow, dolly varden, and especially for rare westslope cutthroat. Small numbers of salmon and steelhead (sea-run rainbow trout) still spawn in the pure wilderness waters after having run the gauntlet of dams all the way up the Columbia and Snake rivers.

Twenty-eight major trailheads enter the River of No Return Wilderness. Most take you on lonesome trips where you can spend a week without encountering another human soul, but busier trails, such as those in the Bighorn Crags, are also available.

The wilderness can be hiked almost 10 months of the year; for, while the highest peaks are almost 10,500 feet, large portions of the major canyons are 4,000 feet in elevation. Some are as low as 2,200 feet, thus gathering little snow in the winter, while the high country is inaccessible most of the most of the year. In the spring, the wildlife on the canyon breaks is a scene of almost Pleistocene grandeur.

Many parts of the wilderness are so remote that a hard three- or four-day trek is needed to reach them. However, there are a number of primitive landing strips allowing Idaho bush pilots to cater to a different, albeit more expensive, use of the wilderness. Numerous outfitters and floating guides operate in the area, offering fine pack trips, fishing trips, gourmet float trips, and quality fall hunts, as well as keeping the area's economy prosperous

You could spend every summer for a decade in the River of No Return Wilderness and still not walk every trail.

HIKE 13   *CHAMBERLAIN BASIN*

General description: A 55-mile trip ascending out of Big Creek into the Chamberlain Basin, across its rolling expanse, and down again to meet the Salmon River. The entire area is within the Frank Church/River of No Return Wilderness.

General location: About 55 miles northeast of McCall.

Maps: Frank Church-River of No Return Wilderness, North Half, Forest Service map; Big Creek, Lodgepole Creek, Wapiti Creek, Devil's Teeth Rapids, Waugh Mountain, and Square Top Mountain (7.5) USGS quads.

Special attractions: The ultimate in solitude, offering glimpses of elk, deer, bear, moose, and coyote. Fantastic views of the heart of the wilderness area from two abandoned fire lookouts.

Difficulty: Difficult.

Season: Mid-June through September.

Information: Big Creek Ranger District, Payette National Forest, McCall, Idaho 83638; (208) 634-8151. McCall Ranger District, P.O. Box 1028, McCall, Idaho 83864; (208) 634-0400.

The hike: "With each passing day, as nature draws me deeper into her realm, I become calmer, thoughts become clearer, and I begin to open myself to the simple yet complex environment around me. I am always called back to this unfettered mode of living, for here the questions which occupy my mind so are either answered or don't matter."—(*From a wilderness journal, 21 Aug. 1981.*)

The hike described here is ideal for those seeking the solitude of the more remote reaches of Idaho. There are many trails through the Chamberlain Basin. Our chosen route led us over 55 miles of wilderness in five days, with an initial elevation gain of 5,000 feet in five miles and subsequent gains and losses averaging 2,000 feet each day. The trail begins at Big Creek at 3,400 feet, quickly ascends to Ramey Ridge at 8,400 feet, then eventually falls to 2,800 feet at the Salmon River.

The Chamberlain Basin is really a high plateau, bound on all sides by the river canyons of the South Fork of the Salmon (west), Main Salmon (north), Middle Fork (east), and Big Creek (south). Consequently, any access requires a major ascent on foot. Hikers must be in good physical condition. Compass and topographical maps are essential. This hike will take you through a wide range of landscapes from ridge to subalpine fir forests to lovely high meadows, and from dry, savannah-like sidehills dotted with ponderosa pine to lush creek bottoms.

A shuttle vehicle is required for this hike. You can start from either end (see map). If you choose to start from Disappointment Bar on the Salmon River, see the Garden Creek hike for access instructions. From Garden Creek, it's about another 20 miles to the end of the road at Corn Creek. Then you'll have to hitch a ride with a raft across the river. Don't count on crossing at the pack bridge at Horse Creek which is shown on the Square Top Mountain topographic quad but not the Frank Church-River of No Return Wilderness map— that bridge washed out a long time ago.

Should you start at the Ramey Ridge end on Big Creek, note that road access to Big Creek can take several routes, but your main objective is to get to Yellow Pine. At Yellow Pine, your route turns due east (right) up the East Fork of

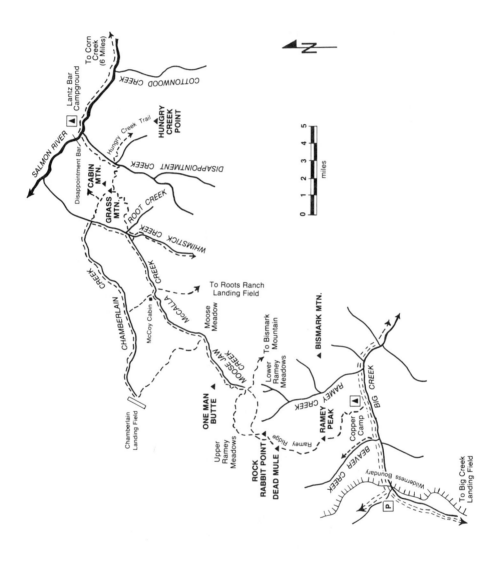

the Salmon River and follows this small stream for about three miles to the intersection with the Profile Gap-Big Creek road. Profile Gap is a high pass closed by heavy snow drifts, sometimes until the first of July. It is about 12 miles from Profile Gap to the trailhead.

An alternative approach to Ramey Ridge is to walk through the Bighorn Crags and over the Middle Fork of the Salmon via the Big Creek pack bridge, then along Big Creek to the Ramey Ridge trailhead. This makes for about a 55-mile trek. See the Reflection Lake hike for a partial description of this access.

Assuming that you start the hike from the Ramey Ridge end, your trail up to Ramey Ridge trail takes off left (north) from the Big Creek trail about five miles from the trailhead at Smith Creek. This first section follows an old mining road.

The trail ascends through a Douglas fir-pondrosa pine forest to Ramey Ridge, where elevation and an active fire history have produced stands of subalpine fir and lodgepole pine. After about five miles, just when you begin to worry about water, look for the remains of a small cabin just off the trail. Near here someone has thoughtfully diverted water from a spring through a section of pipe. Although not in keeping with the wilderness setting, it's a welcome relief nonetheless.

Keep following the ridge for another five miles until the trail branches to the right, leading to Rock Rabbit lookout at 8,360 feet. There is an abandoned log structure here—a breathtaking spot for a late lunch. From this vantage point, note the marked difference in texture on hillsides where new-growth lodgepole pine has reseeded after a fire and how the sunlight renders closer features in great detail while a layer of haze veils distant ranges.

About one-half mile from the lookout, the trail divides. The left branch follows Big Ramey Creek to Upper Ramey Meadows. Stay on the right branch for three miles to Lower Ramey Meadows and find a well-established campsite in the trees at the edge of the meadow. Look for pine siskins (tiny dark finches with a touch of yellow on the wings and tail) to greet you from a nearby lodgepole pine.

The second day will find you descending Moose Jaw Creek through a series of meadows. The mood here is one of tranquility, quite unlike the exhilarating mountain vistas of the day before. The creek is aptly named—we encountered a moose cow and calf just off the trail here.

After 5.25 miles, at Moose Meadows, a trail branches to the right toward the Root Ranch and Whimstick Creek. Stay to the left and follow McCalla Creek, noting its transformation from a meandering brook to a swifter torrent rushing over boulders on its journey to the Salmon River. A most convenient campsite lies near the McCoy Cabin, a total of 12 miles from lower Ramey Meadows. This is an outfitter's camp.

Continue down McCalla Creek for just under three miles to its junction with the Whimstick Creek trail. Follow Whimstick Creek south for several hundred yards to an obvious trail to the left that leaves the creek and heads east and north toward Grass Mountain. As you ascend from the creek, you'll be traversing a drier sidehill shaded by towering ponderosa pines and softened by knee-high grasses which wave golden in late summer. There is a spring off to the left just after the trail crosses Root Creek.

Just 2.25 miles and 800 feet after trail leaves Whimstick Creek, it branches to the left. This left branch leads about one-half mile to Grass Mountain. It's really worth the extra effort to take the side-trip to Grass Mountain, for a 6,252 feet, it offers a 360-degree view. To the southwest, over 20 miles away, is the long outline of Ramey Ridge. With binoculars you can see Rock Rabbit lookout, your lunch spot of two days ago. McCalla Creek drainage shows clearly, and to the east lies Disappointment Creek, which will be your route to the Salmon River. To the north is the Salmon River Canyon, which is now about eight miles away. Grass Mountain is completely exposed, as the cabin and lookout itself burned down long ago, so you won't tarry if you're already hot and thirsty.

From the lookout, retrace your steps to the main trail, and follow it for two miles across the south-facing slope. Sections of the trail are badly eroded from horse traffic but are still passable. The trail switches back steeply for one-half mile down to Disappointment Creek. One-half mile further there is a satisfactory campsite in a grassy opening just off the trail at its junction with the Hungry Creek Trail.

From this campsite, it's a short three miles down Disappointment Creek to the Salmon River. The lower trail, overgrown with mountain alder, huckleberry, thimbleberry, and hawthorne, follows the creek bottom. Stay on the main, or upper, tail along the west bank for a drier walk and a better view of the surrounding country. There is a campsite and orchard at Disappointment Bar, but you must eventually hitch a ride across the river with a passing river raft to pick up the Salmon River trail. It's best to get across the river as soon as possible and spend the remainder of the day sunning and swimming at the sandbar on the river's north bank.

As the sun sets and the canyon begins to cool, walk up the trail one-half mile to Lantz Bar and camp there. Although this is a popular campsite, it is quite large. I recommend camping there rather than along the river. If you must camp along the river itself, do so with minimum impact.

Get an early start the next morning. The Salmon River canyon is notoriously oven-like in the summer; even at dawn you feel yesterday's heat emanating from the rocks. The trail is rocky, with occasional patches of poison ivy. However, it is maintained and in good condition. Rattlesnakes abound, so be on your guard. Watch also for bighorn sheep spying on you from the rocks above. The trail ends 12 miles from Lantz Bar at Corn Creek, which is a favorite launching point for rafters. You should have little trouble getting a ride out to the town of Salmon during the summer.—*Anna Elizabeth Hammet* □

HIKE 14 *CRIMSON LAKE AND WEST YANKEE FORK*

General description: A three- or four-day round trip to a beautiful lake basin set amid high orange-red and gray peaks.

General location: About 15 miles northeast of Stanley. The lakes are in the River of No Return Wilderness, but most of the hike is in a roadless area that was left out of the wilderness designation.

Maps: East Basin Creek, Knapp Lakes, Mt. Jordan, and Sunbeam (7.5') USGS quads.

Special attractions: A variety of scenery from lush, central Idaho stream valley to glaciated colorful peaks hedged by cirque lakes. Abundant wildlife.

Difficulty: Easy up the West Yankee Fork to Cabin Creek, except for a steep but short climb at the trail's beginning. Moderate to the head of Cabin Creek. Moderately difficult to Crimson Lake due to the climb and a rocky trail.

Season: Mid-July to mid-September.

Information: Yankee Fork Ranger District, Challis National Forest, HC 67 Box 650, Clayton, Idaho 83227; (208) 838-2201.

The hike: I first wondered about this area when I was in the Sawtooth Range, weary of the streams of people pas sing by on the trail. I noticed that across the Stanley Basin and to the northeast a clump of jagged peaks rose that looked a lot like the Sawtooths and, I thought, seemed a lot less crowded. These peaks didn't seem to have a name, and I couldn't find any one who had been there. But during the hearings on the River of No Return Wilderness, people began referring to them as the Tango Peaks since many of them cluster about the head of Tango Creek.

Years later, now familiar with the area, I, along with others, helped push the headwaters of Loon Creek and Tango Creek into the wilderness classification. Included in this addition were the Crimson Lake and the Knapp Lakes basins, even though they do not drain directly into the Middle Fork of the Salmon River (which was the official justification for including the headwaters of Loon and Tango Creek in the Wilderness). The colorful Crimson Lake area, however, contains mineralized rock. The mining lobby, therefore, helped carve out room for an open pit mine at the head of Cabin Creek.

Drive 13 miles east of Stanley on Idaho Highway 75; or, from the other direction, drive 44 miles west on Highway 75 from Challis. In either case, turn off at Sunbeam to head northward up the Yankee Fork of the Salmon. Drive on this road (paved to the mine tailings, then good gravel), watching for speeding mining trucks as you pass spooky-looking mining camps where you may see shotguns propped against the trees.

Turn left onto a dirt road at the ghost town of Bonanza a cluster of log cabins 7.5 miles north of Sunbeam. Pass a Forest Service guard station on this road (muddy when wet) to the end at the West Fork Campground after 1.5 miles. You'll pass a sign marking the trail one mile from the guard station, but it's handier to park at the campground and then angle up the hill to the trail, which is easy to find from the campground.

The trail quickly climbs 300 feet up the mountainside to avoid a short gorge that constricts the West Fork, then it quickly drops down to the floor of this canyon, which, by central Idaho standards, is quite lush. After the climb and descent of the first mile, the trail is easy all the way to the confluence of Cabin Creek, about 4.5 more miles. As soon as you descend to the West Fork of Yankee Creek, you'll find places to camp in the pine grass under the conifers. Good camping spots continue up the canyon as well as up Cabin Creek.

At the bottom of the descent to the West Fork, the Deadwood Creek trail leaves to your left, crossing the river. Continue up the canyon along the West Fork Trail to reach a lava cliff and a small meadow after a mile. The trail wanders around the base of the cliff. I camped here one night in late July. It had been a warm day, but that night it froze about one-third inch of water in my water bottle. The frost at the base of the bluff in the shade did not leave the meadow until 10:30 a.m. Although only at 6,600 feet in elevation, the Yankee Fork and vicinity collect cold air from the sea of surrounding mountains at night. Be prepared for the cold.

Just beyond the cliff, a trail leaves to the right up Lightning Creek. Lightning

Crimson Lake in the Frank Church/River of No Return Wilderness. Ralph Maughan photo.

Creek is best waded, although I jumped—only one boot filled completely with water. The West Fork Trail continues upstream for two more miles, passing through forest and willow thicket and occasional meadows that give views of pink-colored Red Mountain ahead. The willows look like a good place to meet a bear. Black bears do frequent the West Fork.

Turn right at the Cabin Creek Trail and head up Cabin Creek. (Alternatively, a hike to the head of the West Fork is certainly pleasant as well.) The trail up Cabin Creek soon crosses the creek to its west side and heads up a linear meadow. About .75 mile from the start of the Cabin Creek trail, the path disappears under avalanche debris. Cross to the east side of the creek here, where you'll pick up the trail again. As you continue up the canyon, each open area gives you a closer view of the rugged gray mountain at what looks like the head of Cabin Creek. Actually, Cabin Creek bends to the west and then to the south to where it begins at Crimson Lake. The gray mountain is really a wall of the canyon. As you reach its base, a side trail leaves to the left to a mining camp. Scattered around in the trees is debris left by mining operations.

Staying on the right, cross the stream (the North Fork of Cabin Creek), and begin to climb. At the west edge of the bend in the big switchback, the Crimson Lake Trail leads to the left. The main trail continues to the right, climbing 1,400 feet to drop into Pioneer Creek. Climb to the left up Cabin Creek on the rough Crimson Lake Trail. Soon you'll hear the creek crashing below you in a gorge. A short step off the trail gives a good view of the gorge, the north side of Red Mountain, and down Cabin Creek. I spooked an elk here once.

The trail continues in its rough-hewn fashion, crossing over rockslides and through sparse forest with fine views of the rugged and increasingly colorful mountains. Soon you pass into the River of No Return Wilderness and drop down to Cabin Creek, cross a tributary and labor the last .3 mile and 600 feet up to Crimson Lake. This lake, large, deep, and full of cutthroat trout (some of them quite large), rests on top of crimson-colored rock. Rough, jagged peaks of reddish orange rise above the lake, with the two-toothed spires of Cabin Creek Peak providing a contrasting gray color. As I climbed between the two teeth of the peak, a large billy left the other mountain goats and watched me for a half-hour.

The unnamed lake at elevation 8,565 feet, above and southeast of Crimson Lake is also full of large cutthroat. However, the lake in the small cirque above and southwest of Crimson is windswept and barren. From this barren lake, however, you can walk to the top of the mountain for a grand view of Knapp Lakes below. There are over 20 of these lakes, all barren and completely pristine except the largest and lowest lake, which is full of rainbow trout. Beyond are the typical endless ridges of the River of No Return. A descent to Knapp Lakes from this mountain requires an exciting ride down a moving talus slope.

There are a number of campsites around Crimson Lake. Please use the less-used sites in order to give the stomped-out ones a chance to heal over.—*Ralph Maughan* □

Note: The Forest Service has logged the area around the old informal trailhead and created a new one with hitching post, horse loading ramp, and john. It is downhill and to the west of the old trailhead near the top of a clearcut of lodgepole pine. To reach the new trailhead, follow the instructions as before, but bypass the campground and take the road signed "Bonanza Cemetery". Pass by this cemetery, and don't take

HIKE 14 *CRIMSON LAKE AND WEST YANKEE FORK*

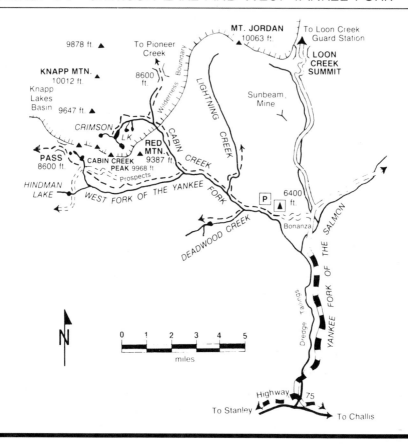

the road to "Boot Hill Cemetery". This is a second cemetery further up the hill. Follow the road signs for the trailhead instead.

Unfortunately the new trailhead is not at the end of the new road, but this road has a closed gate at the trailhead.

Park and hike down this road. After a short distance the road splits. Either fork will take you to the bottom of the canyon and to the pack trail. The right fork of the road leads first to a gravel pit. It's about .3 mile from the trailhead to canyon bottom.—*Ralph Maughan*

HIKE 15 *REFLECTION LAKE*

General description: A long trip into the Bighorn Crags area of the River of No Return Wilderness.

General location: In the southern part of the Bighorn Crags, 37 miles due west of Salmon.

Maps: Hoodoo Meadows and Mt. McGuire (7.5') USGS quads.

Special attractions: A beautiful basin full of lakes just below the crest of the crags' divide between Wilson Creek and the Middle Fork of the Salmon River. Good fishing, wildlife, and fewer people than in the northern part of the Crags.

Difficulty: Moderate.

Season: Early July to late September.

Information: Cobalt Ranger District, Salmon National Forest, Box 729, Salmon, Idaho 83467; (208) 756-2240.

The hike: To reach the trailhead, follow the same directions as for the Ship Island Lake hike. This hike begins similarly to the Ship Island hike. Start at the Crags Campground near Golden Trout Lake and climb the ridgeline, passing by Cathedral Rock and continuing to the junction with the Clear Creek and Waterfall trails at five miles. On this trip, however, continue to the left, down the Waterfall trail.

You'll immediately begin to switchback down into Wilson Creek through a forest of lodgepole pine. After dropping 400 feet in one-half mile, cross a tributary of Wilson Creek. This is the first water you'll encounter beyond the trailhead. Most of this trail portion is severely eroded due to fragile soils. Past the tributary, the trail's grade slackens as you wander through the woods, across some rocks, and past several meadows.

At 7.3 miles from the trailhead, you come to a trail junction. The path to the right leads either up into a tight cirque basin that shelters Harbor and Wilson lakes on over Fishfin Ridge and down to Birdbill and Gentian lakes (see the Ship Island Lake hike). You should go left, following the sign to Welcome Lake. Welcome Lake is surrounded by peaks nearly 10,000 feet high. This shallow, but beautiful, lake basin is filled with lush grass and marsh. It has plenty of campsites but is usually devoid of fish due to winter-kill. Mosquitoes can be a real threat here in the early summer, so by prepared to fend them off with repellent. As you approach Welcome Lake, a trail junction marks the way to Reflection Lake. This trail is not on USGS quadrangles.

The trail switchbacks six times in one-half mile up the steep ridge to the southeast to climb to an elevation of 9,000 feet. Follow the ridge to drop down a moderate grade through timber. The trail takes three long switchbacks down, totalling nearly three miles in length. The mammoth basin below to the west is a beautiful timbered margin along the celebrated Bighorn Crags ridgeline. Eight lakes dot the nappy pine quilt of trees—Skyhigh, Turquoise, Echo, Reflection, Twin Cove, Fawn, Doe, and Buck. It is also alive with wildlife, primarily deer, elk, goats, and bighorn sheep.

At mile 11, cross Skyhigh Creek, descend, and gently switchback through the basin. Cross another small creek and follow the trail uphill to Reflection

67

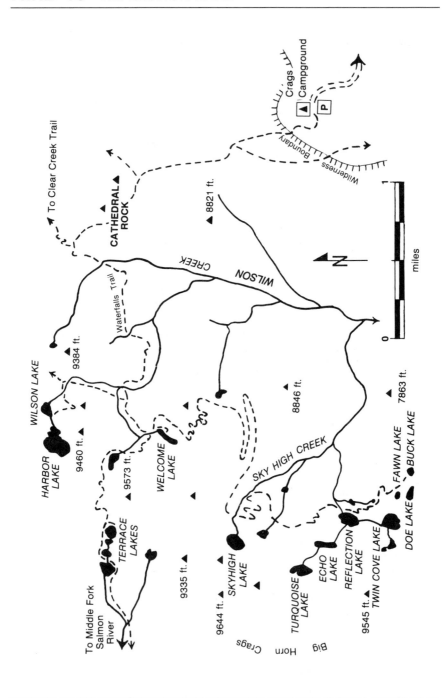

Harbor Lake. Ernie Day photo.

Lake at 13 miles. Reflection Lake is a good basecamp. It contains numerous cutthroat and rainbow trout. The trail continues for another mile to Buck Lake. Someone, in a fit of imagination unique in Idaho mostly to the River of No Return area, named this lake, along with two others, as a nuclear family—Doe Lake, Buck Lake, and Fawn Lake. From here the country is as wild as any in the West—a frontier in a sea of civilization. You can reach more lakes via cross-country ridge travel.—*Philip Blomquist.* □

HIKE 16 *SHEEP HILL*

General description: An up-and-down hike along a ridge that gains 1,200 feet and loses 2,000 feet in 10 miles. 14 lakes nestle beneath the ridge. In recent years, forest fires burned several segments near this trail.

General location: 75 road miles southeast of Grangeville, Idaho, and 45 miles west of Conner, Montana, on the northern rim of the River of No Return Wilderness.

Maps: Sabe Mountain, Sheep Hill, and Spread Point (7.5') USGS quads.

Special attractions: Mountain lakes and fishing, overviews of both the River of No Return and the Selway Bitterroot Wilderness.

Difficulty: Moderate.

Season: Mid-July to mid-September.

Information: Red River Ranger District, Nez Perce National Forest, HC 01 Box 23, Elk City, Idaho 83525; (208) 842-2255.

The hike: If you are looking for high jagged peaks, this isn't the trip for you. None of the high points are above timberline. Spruce, alpine fir, and whitebark pine cover most of the ridges. However, if you enjoy wildlife, wildflowers, mountain lakes, and high-rent vistas in an area that receives moderate use, this trip is worth the difficult road access. Bighorn sheep, black bears, elk, deer, and golden-mantled ground squirrels are common. Grizzly bears and timber wolves have been sighted in recent years but are very rare. In mid-July and early August, the open ridges are literally covered with wildflowers. The most common are beargrass, mountain pinks, penstemon, lupine, Indian paintbrush, heath, and shooting stars.

Road access is over the Magruder Corridor (also called Montana Road). It connects the Red River Ranger Station on the west with Conner, Montana, on the east in a slow, one-lane road that is passable by car. All major points along the road are well marked, perhaps as a preventive measure against years of conservationists' attempts to close it. If this closure had come t o pass, the Selway Bitterroot Wilderness and River of No Return Wilderness would have been joined in a continuous wilderness of mind-boggling size: over 3.5 million acres.

The Montana route leaves U.S. Highway 93 at Conner on a paved road that leads up the West Fork of the Bitterroot River. Be sure to top your gas tank, as this is the last chance for many mountain miles. The road crosses over two major rivers and two mountain ranges before reaching the trailhead. The road is paved over Nez Perce Pass where it crosses the Bitterroot Divide. A high-standard gravel road leads down from the pass to Magruder Crossing, where the road bridges the Selway River. There is a large, developed campground here and a popular put-in for kayakers. The way to the other side of the mountain is a long one, and the road becomes one-lane although with a good, rock base. Due to its long grades and narrowness, it is not recommended for trailers. From Magruder Crossing, the road climbs over 3,000 feet as it skirts Salmon Mountain, then traverses Sabe Creek to your trailhead at Dry Saddle. An outstanding view of the Bitterroot Divide and deep forest are the redeeming qualities of this passage.

The route from the west follows State Highway 14 south out of Grangeville. Where the American River joins the South Fork near Elk City, turn right to follow the sign to the Red River Ranger Station. One mile past the station is a large sign warning the public of the hazards of driving the Montana Road. Check your gas gauge and turn left onto the road, following the sign to the Magruder Ranger Station. The road climbs steadily up the Salmon River-South Fork Divide to Mountain Meadows. This area was scheduled for a controversial timber sale that would have destroyed some prime elk summer range and caused untold damage to the pristine watershed of Meadow Creek—the largest tributary of the Selway River. This sale was dropped due to an administrative appeal led by the Idaho Environmental Council.

From Mountain Meadows, the road gradually drops into the headwaters of Bargamin Creek at Poet Creek Camp. This Forest Service-maintained camp is an ideal place to spend the night before beginning your hike in the morning. Poet Creek Camp is only about seven miles from the Dry Saddle trailhead and is a far better place to camp. At Dry Saddle, a road that is little more than two wheel tracks leaves the Magruder Corridor and meanders about one-quarter mile out along a ridge to the trailhead.

One final warning: the Magruder Corridor is a high-elevation road that can receive snow any month of the year. Take along chains and don't go in October or June unless you have a four-wheel-drive vehicle. In years of heavy snowfall, *the road isn't passable at all*. Check with the Forest Service before you go.

The trailhead is large, with a horseloading area, a john, and a small camping area with no water. These emblems of civilization belie the fact that this was the last place in the lower 48 states to be mapped by the U.S. Geological Survey and that good topo maps only became available in 1979.

The main trail follows the watershed divide between Bargamin Creek and Sabe Creek to the Sheep Hill lookout. The Forest Service recently reconstructed portions of the trail to contour from saddle to saddle along the ridge, so the grades are not steep. The trail is heavily used by pack stock in the hunting season. It is very well defined, and all intersections are signed.

Beginning with a slow drop into a saddle overlooking the Trilby Lakes, the first mile of the trail goes through timber. Trilby Lakes is a popular, although not especially good, fishing day hike; so expect to see other people.

At the Trilby Lakes junction, the trail climbs a moderate 350 feet to Spread Creek Point. Just before the final pitch, an unmarked fishing trail into Spread Point Lake meets the main trail at a high saddle. Spread Point Lake, a large lake, lies on the west side of the ridge. Several meadows at its outlet provide good big game conditions; I have often seen elk near the lake.

From Spread Creek Point on, the trail rises into the open and becomes more scenic. Spread Creek Point, once a Forest Service fire lookout, provides a good, 360-degree view of the surrounding country.

From Spread Creek Point, the trail stays on top of the divide for about a mile to where the main ridge meets a spur coming up from Sabe Creek. Here two side trails leave the ridge. The Ring Creek Point Trail leads down into Sabe Creek, 5,000 vertical feet below the ridge, and into some beautiful country that rarely sees anybody. The other is a trail for anglers that climbs down towards Saddle Lake and peters out. Saddle Lake is good fishing for 10- to 12-inch trout. Camping is very limited at the lake. I would suggest that you camp on one of the benches overlooking the lake near a perennial stream that you cross on the way to the lake.

HIKE 16 *SHEEP HILL*

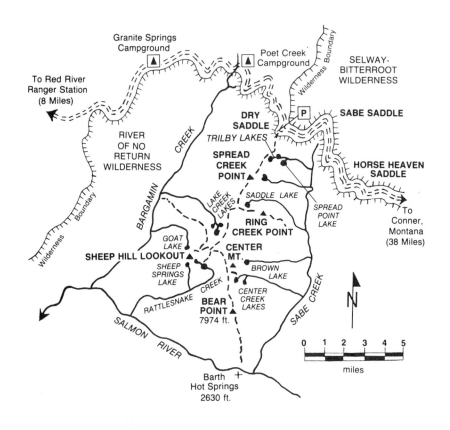

At the Ring Creek Point trail junction, the main trail begins its descent into Lake Creek Lakes. On some maps, these lakes are identified as the Sheep Springs Lakes. This climb is the longest on the hike, but is well graded. Carefully observe the location of the three lakes on your way down if you plan to visit them as they're in thick forest with no connecting trails. At the bottom of this grade is a sign marking an angler's trail that leads one-quarter mile down to the upper lake. If you plan to camp here, stay on the main trail and hike about one-quarter mile further to find an excellent camping place near a perennial stream. This is more scenic and less subject to mosquitoes than lake campsites.

Lake Creek Lakes are heavily used, and you can expect to meet other parties. The upper lake generally produces the largest fish while the lower lake, which has good natural reproduction, is the easier lake in which to catch fish. Because it is located in a meadow, fly anglers can get a backcast anywhere around the lake. I have never fished the middle lake with any real determination, because it has never been as good as the other two. Lake Creek Lakes make a good basecamp for the other seven lakes located on the Bear Point and Sheep Hill ridges.

At the Lake Creek junction, the main trail climbs 300 feet to a low saddle dividing Lake Creek from Rattlesnake Creek. Don't let the name throw you; all the rattlesnakes are at Rattlesnake Creek's lower elevations.

At the saddle, the hiker meets trails leading to three destinations: Bear Point to the left, Sheep Hill to the right, and Rattlesnake Lake in the middle. It is the trail to Rattlesnake Lake which is confusing. It starts out as a very well-worn track that leads directly into an outfitter's camp. There is a salt lick in this camp that generally attracts elk in the early morning. Although the camp has lots of "improvements", I suggest avoiding it because it is assigned to an outfitter on a special permit and because the water may be contaminated by stock.

From the outfitter's camp, the trail becomes very faint. You'll have to pay close attention to blazes cut into the trees. It contours along an east-facing slope to end with a 150-foot drop to the lake. Be cautious not to lose your elevation as you walk along the east-facing slope. It you do, you'll drop down into Rattlesnake Creek and end up headed toward the Salmon River. Once you get to Rattlesnake Lake, you may wish to explore Upper Rattlesnake Lake. To do so, follow the inlet on the northwest side of lower Rattlesnake Lake for about one-half mile.

The Bear Point trail climbs through open parks and clumps of whitebark pine to a saddle overlooking Ring Creek. Just past the saddle is a sign marking an angler's trail to Brown Creek Lake. This trail too is faint and hard to follow in places. It continues around the face of Center Mountain, then generally follows the inlet down to the lake.

One-half mile past the Brown Creek Lake sign, a well-marked trail leads down to Center Creek Lakes. These also are hard to find, but you can improve your odds by setting down your pack and walking an extra couple hundred yards out the Bear Point Ridge to where you can see them both.

After Center Creek Lakes, it is an extra two miles to Bear Point. Bear Point offers a spectacular view of the Salmon River 6,000 feet below. The area around Bear Point burned heavily in 1989, giving this vantage point an eerie feeling amid the twisted black tree snags. A visit to Bear Point in 1990 found the canyon filled with smoke again as a large fire burned across the Salmon River Canyon in Chamberlain Basin and smaller fires burned in the bottom of Sabe Creek just below the point to the east.

Back at the forks near Lake Creek Lakes, the right fork is the main trail and heads toward Sheep Hill. It climbs gradually for one-half mile along a ridge to Deadman's Saddle, where it meets a side trail dropping into Bargamin Creek. From Deadman's Saddle, the trail climbs 400 feet to Sheep Hill Lookout. Near the lookout are a salt lick and spring that are sometimes frequented by bighorn sheep. From the lookout you can see four small lakes surrounding Sheep Hill. All of these lakes have fish, but they aren't as productive as some of the larger lakes. A good trail leads from the lookout down to Sheep Springs Lake; but you should ask the lookout for directions about the best route into Goat Lake, which does not have a trail.—*C.P. Stokes.* □

HIKE 17 *SHIP ISLAND LAKE*

General description: A 22-mile round trip into the famous Big Horn Crags of the Frank Church-River of No Return Wilderness. This is one of the most spectacular areas in this vast wilderness.
General location: 36 linear miles west of Salmon.
Maps: Maggipah Mtn., Hoodoo Meadows, Mt. McGuire (7.5') USGS quads.
Special attractions: Stunning views of Ship Island Lake and onward into breaks country of the Middle Fork of the Salmon River. Very rugged granite mountains with spires, knobs, and huge monoliths. Many lakes with good fishing. The north and west sides of the Crags are especially noted for bighorn sheep.
Difficulty: Strenuous.
Season: Early July to mid-September.
Information: Cobalt Ranger District, Salmon National Forest, Box 729, Salmon, Idaho 83467; 208/756-2240.

The hike: Milton's words in *Paradise Lost* best describe this popular hiking and horse packing area—Heaven's high towers. It is a must for those who enjoy major excursions.

There are two possible routes to reach the Big Horn Crags Campground and trailhead.

Those coming from the north will go south through the town of Salmon to take the Williams Creek Road. This good, 12.2-mile, route climbs over the Salmon River Range for about 3,000 feet to the junction with the Panther Creek Road. From the junction, drive up Panther Creek until you reach Porphyry Creek and turn right.

If coming from the south, continue past Challis for nine miles on U.S. 93 to the signed Morgan Creek junction. Turn left and follow the Morgan Creek Road for 19.6 miles (pavement, then good gravel) to Morgan Creek Summit where the road becomes the Panther Creek Road.

From Morgan Creek Summit drive north down Panther Creek for 14 miles to the signed turn-off at Porphyry Creek. The Porphyry Creek road is graded and climbs over 2,500 feet in about 16 miles to the road junction to the Crags Campground trailhead (to the right) and Yellowjacket Lake road (to the left). From the junction, it's a couple more miles to Crags Campground. Once the road has climbed out of Porphyry Creek, it keeps near an 8,500 foot elevation ridgetop just 300 feet outside the Wilderness boundary. The new Blackbird Mountain USGS quad is useful for identifying sights from this impressive, sometimes "white-knuckled" road.

The campground is large, requires a fee, and is developed, but we advise bringing your own water (none of the taps when we visited were working except ours). There is, however, a stream flowing down the hill above the campground. This water requires treatment. There is a loading area for horses. Due to elevation, plan on cold nights.

The hike to Ship Island Lake can be very demanding, depending on which route you take. If thunderstorms threaten, it's better to take the Waterfalls Canyon Trail than the ridge route (more on this later). The trail begins by climbing 500 feet along the ridge overlooking the basin of Golden Trout Lake, where cutthroat have displaced the California goldens. The climb continues for 0.8

Ship Island Lake. Ernie Day photo.

miles and 500 feet, then descends for 1.2 miles to a fork. From this ridgeline you can see in the distant south the 9,045 foot granite Sugarloaf monolith. The trail to the south leads some four miles to Yellowjacket Lake. Take the trail which heads northwest: the trail to the northeast is the horse route.

Once on the trail, you climb again 300 feet to the ridgeline. Below, on the left, is the deep Wilson Creek drainage. In the distance ahead is the Crags divide. The trail winds this 8,900 foot ridge, passing among granite spires.

At 4.1 miles, you reach the base of another monolith called Cathedral Rock. Here a sign reads "Cathedral Lake" and points to the right. This cutoff leads to a possible first night destination if you plan to take the ridge route. The lake is reached by a 0.3-mile route. Besides campsites at the lake, there is an excellent view of Cathedral Rock. Fishing is good for rainbow and cutthroat trout.

Continuing on the main trail, begin a mile-long contour along the top of Wilson Creek Canyon. After this, five miles from the trailhead, you reach the junction of the Waterfalls Canyon and Clear Creak trails. (Clear Creek is a large, pristine drainage, heavily fought over by the timber industry before it was included in the River of No Return Wilderness.) The Waterfalls Canyon Trail, the easier of the two, although one mile longer, does have two water sources.

Assuming that you take the ridgeline trail (take lots of water), you'll briefly climb straight up and will reach a saddle at 8,600 feet. Clear Creek is the drainage to the northeast. Don't drop into this. Instead, take the trail that

75

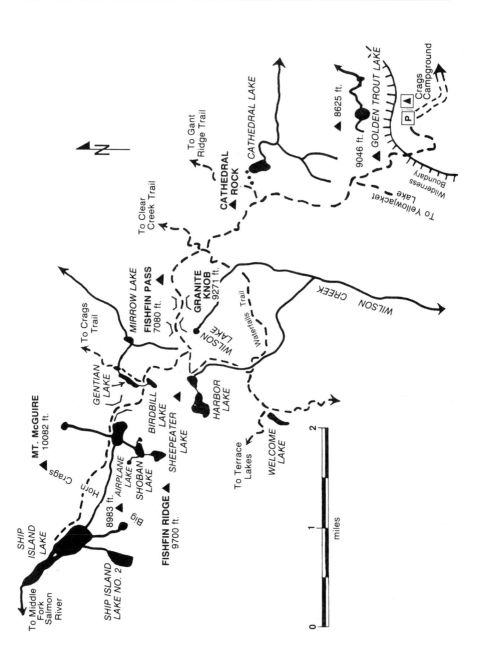

continues climbing along the ridgeline. This trail is not on the 1962 Mt. McGuire USGS topographic map or the Salmon National Forest map. It is, however, shown on the map available at the trailhead. Following this new trail, climb up and around a granite knob of over 9,200 feet, then drop to a small saddle. From here you traverse over to Fishfin Pass. After six hard miles, you stand on a divide looking down 1,000 feet to Mirrow and Gentian lakes.

If you decide to take the Waterfalls Trail, you descend in a long grade to Wilson Canyon which is timbered with ponderosa pine. In about one-half mile you come to the first and biggest stream. This is the best place to camp. Although the map shows a second perennial stream in another one-half mile, this one was almost dry in mid-August in a year of normal precipitation.

You hike about 1.5 miles west through forest cover then turn north to head up Wilson Canyon. The fork in the canyon in which one trail leads west to Welcome and Heart Lakes is not quite where it is shown on the Mt. McGuire map. It is actually at the fork of Wilson Creek and the creek emptying Heart and Welcome Lakes. You do not cross the creek as shown on the map. Wilson Creek is just a little trickle of a meandering meadow stream. The left fork is much bigger and has a bridge over it. You will be ascending to the headwaters of Wilson Creek. The trail gains about 400 feet as it tracks along the canyon rim about 100 feet above the creek (unlike the map which shows it in the creek bottom). Follow the trail through this high alpine forest where it gets lost a little way north of peak 9,460. The trail, once found, is broad and obvious, leading to Harbor Lake. Because we ignored the map available at the trailhead, we continued up the canyon bottom and to the waterfall from Wilson Lake as it spills 120 feet over the cliffs—hence the name—Waterfall Canyon. It trickles into a lovely meadow, strewn with large boulders. All around the headwall of the canyon are spires and crags. Rather than make the mistake we did, stick to the Harbor Lake trail which will take you up to Fishfin Pass.

The trail down Fishfin is along a vertical cliff and quite narrow. It spirals down about 280 feet on the right side of the canyon, then crosses to the left side. We could smell the carcass of a horse which had fallen from the pass. There is not enough room on Fishfin for hikers and equestrians to pass safely. At the bottom, you cross to the other side of the canyon, just above the creek, and gain about 80 feet to contour along the trail cut in the rock. From the pass you can look down into Mirrow Lake but cannot see Gentian and Birdbill lakes until rounding the bend and rising to drop down the rocky saddle into these lakes. The lakes have good fishing for small rainbow.

Near Gentian Lake is an outhouse and a hitching post. The campsites in this high lake basin are beaten-down to hardpacked dirt. This site is a major trail intersection. The northern route, recommended for horse traffic, from Cathedral Rock up the Clear Creek drainage, comes in here.

After Gentian Lake it is a climb of some 160 feet on a low, slow, horse trail and traverse over the ridge into the huge Ship Island basin. At the top of the ridge you can see both Airplane and Ship Island Lakes and the massive granite cliffs backdropping Ship Island Lake. It's about 2.5 miles to the eastern shore of Ship Island Lake and a 1,000-foot drop from the pass. The trail in places is very eroded, exposing bare bones of rocks. This makes for tougher going than one would expect. The descent, outside of the 400 feet to Airplane Lake, is in heavy forest (horse traffic is not allowed beyond Airplane). There are many good campsites at Airplane but nothing like the stupendous views at Ship Island. Both lakes offer excellent fishing for rainbow and cutthroat. From Airplane Lake, you can cut cross-country to Shoban and Sheepeater lakes. It's a quarter mile and 200-foot climb to Shoban, and another half mile and 250-foot climb to Sheepeater. Both have excellent fishing.

At Ship Island there is a heavily used campsite right to the east of the inlet from Airplane Lake. The view of the lake is enough to take your breath away for a couple of months. This end of the lake is boggy and, other than this one spot, is too wet, uneven, or exposed to the wind for camping. Better camping spots are located after you wade through Jenny's Bog. One is about .25 mile down on the east side of the lake on a point protected from the wind by a cove. There is a stream with good water just before this large campsite. There is another big campsite about another .25 mile from the first. From Ship Island Lake, you can climb to Ship Island Lake No. 2 which retains a few California golden trout.

The basin holding Ship Island Lake is large and beautiful, hemmed in by rugged ridges of nearly 10,000 feet. You can hike down and around the east side of Ship Island Lake to its outlet. All told, it is about one mile to the lake outlet. The trail is at times faint, not maintained. The going is somewhat slow due to a huge amount of deadfall, the faintness of the trail, and the crossing of a boulder field.

The country on the right of the outlet is very rugged and the trail, such as it is, through the smooth sheets of granite is marked only by an occasional cairn. Stay to the right side on the rocks up here while you drop some in elevation to round the bend to the view down Ship Island Creek Canyon. At the outlet of the lake, immense granite spires line the canyon walls, and here Ship Island Creek begins to tumble down a steep, trailless canyon. It drops 4,500 feet in five miles to the Middle Fork of the Salmon River. Few have ever descended this canyon. The route out from Ship Island and back to the trailhead is pretty much what has already been described. You may spot bighorn above Wilson Lake on Fishfin Ridge. (A couple of climbers we met from Seattle saw three bighorn at Wilson Lake in the morning coming down for a drink; one young one and two not yet in full curl.)

Be prepared for foul weather at any point along the hike. This is high country and we encountered some heavy rain and light snow in August.—*Jackie Johnson Maughan and Phil Blomquist* □

HIKE 18 *SLEEPING DEER MOUNTAIN*

General description: A scenic area of small lakes trapped in cirque basins near Sleeping Deer Mountain.

General location: At the end of a long improved dirt road deep in the Frank Church/River of No Return Wilderness about 45 road miles from Challis.

Maps: Sleeping Deer Mountain (7.5') USGS quad.

Special attractions: Fine primitive scenery and fishing in subalpine lakes. A very scenic, inspiring road trip to the trailhead.

Difficulty: Moderately easy to Cache Creek Lakes except in the early summer. Moderate to the more distant West Fork Lakes.

Season: Mid-July to mid-September.

Information: Challis National Forest, HC 63 Box 1671, Challis, Idaho 83226; (208) 879-2285.

The hike: This is a strikingly beautiful area exciting, rugged, and not heavily used. The access road is equally impressive, perched as it is on a wilderness ridgetop for 24 of its slightly more than 40-mile length. The boundary of the Frank Church/River of No Return Wilderness is just 300 away feet on either side of the road. Sleeping Deer is one of the highest mountains in the Wilderness and the highest in this area.

One of the great victories of the political fight to establish the River of No Return Wilderness was to include not just the area from Sleeping Deer Mountain westward to the Middle Fork of the Salmon River, but also all of the canyons to the east of this striking mountain. The Forest Service felt this addition was "just too much wilderness". However, this area, of over a half million acres to the east and south of the old Idaho Primitive Area, was just as wild and primitive as the primitive area itself and did indeed become part of the River of No Return Wilderness. The access road gives you a magnificent view of this pristine country, all of which drains into the Middle Fork.

The road is improved dirt for over 30 miles, suitable for trucks without four-wheel drive, but marginal for sedans and unsuitable for RVs and horse trailers. It takes at least three hours to get from Challis to the trailhead.

Begin on Main Street of the town of Challis. Turn right (northward) from Main Street onto the Challis Creek county road. Follow this paved road through farmland in lower Challis Creek canyon. It eventually becomes a gravel road. Soon thereafter, take a right turn onto the improved dirt Bear Creek Road (FS #086). The road passes through some recreational homesites, then climbs 3,200 feet to a pass at 9,190 feet elevation between the cone-shaped Twin Peaks which rise to well over 10,000 feet . There is an active fire lookout on the southern peak.

From the pass, the road follows a ridgeline to the trailhead. You pass a number of trailheads which lead down into the wilderness canyons three to five-thousand feet below. There are also a number of primitive vehicle campsites along the road (no water). The road was improved to Spider Creek helispot in 1989 in order to facilitate fire fighting equipment, but is still a 15 mile-per-hour drive. The last 12 miles beyond the helispot have a number of rocky spots, but do not require four-wheel drive. At times, the road is so narrow that one must back up several hundred feet to a half mile if another vehicle is encountered.

The trailhead, located at the end of the road and perched on a ridgetop high above Rock Lakes at 9300 feet, has room for about four vehicles. If it is full, you must go back a half-mile and park. The trailhead usually has space available. There is a hill side outhouse, but no water.

Like many routes in the Salmon River Mountains, this one takes you up and down, up and down, from pass to basin, from basin to pass. In all you'll cross four passes, two of which are notable Sleeping Deer and Woodtick. None of these are long "pulls". In fact, the trailhead is the highest elevation of the trip. The distance from the trailhead to the West Fork Lakes, your final destination, is seven or eight miles.

From the trailhead, the trail immediately swings around a ridgetop and contours high above Cabin Creek to Sleeping Deer Pass just southeast of beautiful Sleeping Deer Mountain. The views, framed by contorted whitebark

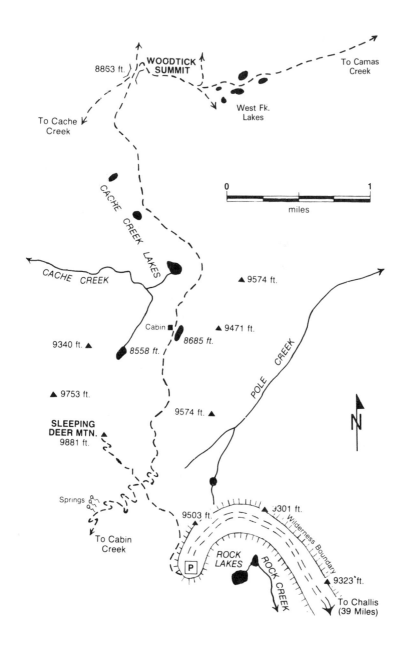

8853 ft.

**WOODTICK
SUMMIT**

To Camas
Creek

West Fk.
Lakes

To Cache
Creek

CACHE CREEK LAKES

CACHE CREEK

▲ 9574 ft.

0   1
miles

Cabin ■

9340 ft. ▲

8558 ft.

8685 ft.

▲ 9471 ft.

POLE CREEK

▲ 9753 ft.

9574 ft. ▲

**SLEEPING
DEER MTN.** ▲
9881 ft.

N

Springs

To Cabin
Creek

9503 ft. ▲

▲ 9301 ft.

Wilderness Boundary

**ROCK
LAKES**

ROCK CREEK

P

9323 ft. ▲

To Challis
(39 Miles)

pine, are outstanding. At the pass, a trail fork to the left takes one quickly thousands of feet down into Cabin Creek. Straight ahead a trail climbs to the abandoned lookout tower on Sleeping Deer Mountain. (We did not attempt this day hike due to thunderstorms on both our entry and exit days). You take the trail to the right which descends in seven switchbacks to the cirque just below Sleeping Deer Mountain at the head of Pole Creek. This descent is fairly easy except early in the summer when snow makes it dangerous without an ice axe.

At the bottom of the switchbacks is an intersection, with the trail to the right leading down Pole Creek Canyon. Stay to the left. The trail traverses the rocky head of Pole Creek Basin (directly below the cliffs of Sleeping Deer Mountain) to the easy pass between Pole Creek and Cache Creek. This section (from the trailhead to the top of Cache Creek) gets a lot of weather because it is high and exposed. It is dangerous during thunderstorms due to the possibility of a lightning strike. In addition to keeping an eye on the weather, however, do also be looking for bighorn sheep. They frequent the area.

From the divide you descend 400 feet on a rocky, eroded trail to the first of the four trail-accessible Cache Creek Lakes. The most scenic campsite is near the lake's inlet on the right side near a pretty, little spring. Despite its beauty, in July it might be too mosquito-ridden to be habitable, since it is flanked by an extensive wet meadow. There are also several big camps often used by horse parties. One is at the top of the meadow above the lake. Another is by the cabin below the lake outlet. Although we saw little wildlife here in late August, we did observe a good deal of bear and coyote scat on the trail between Cache Lakes and Woodtick Summit. We did see and hear many pika and marmots, as well as a lot of grouse in the wooded areas. The grouse whortleberries (the smallest of the blackberries) were ripe.

We found the fishing here good for brook trout (6-12 inches). Our nine-year-old nephew caught the biggest one on his third cast with a barbless hook on a spinner.

The trail drops down past the cabin and continues north. Losing little elevation, it passes three more lakes. They lie about a hundred feet below the trail on a shelf above dramatic Cache Creek Canyon. The second lake is the largest. The third one loses much of its water by mid-summer and so contains no fish. The fourth lake is within the burned area of the Battle Axe Fire of 1988. There are six more Cache Creek Lakes scattered about the area. Access requires cross-country hiking.

Just past the third lake, you enter the Battle Axe Burn. Here you must look carefully for the trail junction to the right which takes you to Woodtick Summit. (If you find yourself descending to the lake, you've missed the junction.) The junction is obscure because the trail sign burned in the fire and, at the time we visited, was additionally hard to see due to a fallen, burned tree. You can spot the trail up on the flank of Woodtick ahead.

From the junction, the trail climbs over a corner of peak 9,488 to Woodtick Summit at 8,863 feet. The elevation gain is only about 300 feet. This entire portion of the route lies within the Battle Axe Burn. The area near the trail has burned twice now in the last 40 years, so it ought to remain a generally open slope providing fine views of Sleeping Deer Mountain and the basin at the head of Cache Creek.

Woodtick Summit is not notable for the presence of ticks. At the summit is a trail junction. Take the fork to the right which descends two steep switch-backs and then contours across the head of Woodtick Creek. From here you have fine views down heavily-forested (and unburned) Woodtick Creek. After a mile or so, this rocky trail leads to a grassy divide between Woodtick Creek and the West Fork of Camas Creek. From the divide you get a good view of three of the West Fork Lakes. At the trail junction on the pass, take the one that descends into the West Fork. The descent of 500 feet is steep, and the trail at times worn and rocky.

Once at the bottom, you're on the north side of the largest of the West Fork Lakes. Take the right fork of the trail here and walk until you've crossed over the stream which is the inlet. Here you'll find a scenic, although heavily-used, campsite. We found this largest of the lakes to be the only one to have fish—a few large trout we were unable to catch. There was plentiful elk sign and much pika activity. One of our party photographed a bighorn while climbing the unnamed peak behind camp.

The lowest of the West Fork Lakes has recently increased considerably in size due to beaver which have dammed the outlet. Their large lodge is visible in the lake. The lake shore has an eerie quality—swamped, dead timber, marsh grass, and half-submerged trails.—*Ralph and Jackie Maughan* □

HIKE 19 *STODDARD LAKE*

General description: A week-long backpacking vacation into rugged parts of the River of No Return Wilderness.

General location: Seven miles from the end of the Salmon River Road just below the mouth of the Middle Fork of the Salmon River.

Maps: Butts Creek Point, Cottonwood Butte, Long Tom Mountain (7.5') USGS quads.

Special attractions: Spectacular vistas of the Middle Fork of the Salmon River's Impassable Canyon and the Bighorn Crags across the Middle Fork's canyon.

Difficulty: Very difficult due to a climb of 5,400 feet in one day.

Season: The lower part of the trail is accessible as early as April, but it is early July before you can easily make to to Stoddard Lake. Snows come to the high country about October 1.

Information: Salmon National Forest, Box 729, Salmon, Idaho 83467; (208) 756-2240.

The hike: Stoddard Lake is no weekend hike. Although it is situated on the edge of the Chamberlain Basin—a gentle 300-thousand-acre plateau in the middle of the giant, 2.4-million-acre River of No Return Wilderness—getting there is a physical challenge. You begin by climbing out of one of the world's deepest canyons in just one day. The trailhead is at the Stoddard Pack Bridge, 3,000 feet in elevation. It climbs to no less than 8,800 feet, and most of the climb (over a mile in altitude change) happens the first day.

To reach the trailhead, drive north from Salmon on U.S. 93 to North Fork. Leave the highway here and follow the Salmon River Road west from North Fork for about 40 miles to the mouth of the Middle Fork of the Salmon River.

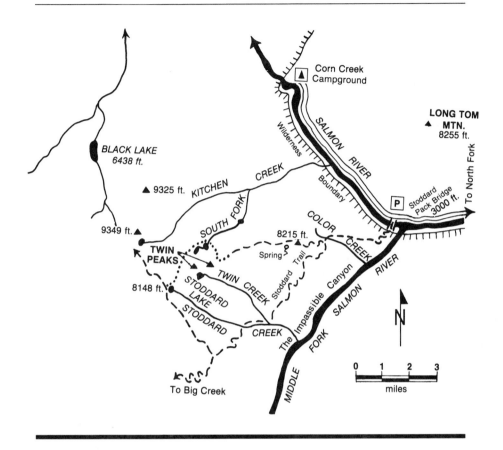

Here, where the Middle Fork flows out of the Impassable Canyon into the Main Fork of the Salmon, there used to be a sign that read, "Yonder Lies the Idaho Wilderness." It was removed during the battle over reclassifying the old Idaho Primitive Area into the River of No Return Wilderness. The dark humor at the time was that the sign would be replaced reading, "Yonder lies 4 billion board feet of sawtimber." Happily, that issue was resolved in a different fashion, but the old sign was not returned.

The pack bridge is one-half mile downstream on the Main Fork from the confluence of the Middle Fork. Cross the bridge, carrying plenty of drinking water. The trail immediately begins climbing up the face of the Salmon River Canyon. In 12 switchbacks, you climb from the river's 3,000 feet to an elevation of 4,613. At this point, you round a ridge and continue climbing in the company of excellent views of the Middle Fork Canyon, with the river chewing its way ever deeper into the bedrock of the Idaho Batholith.

The trail is now above the breaks of the Middle Fork Canyon, and you continue to climb, but less steeply. At an altitude of 5,800 feet, you reach a saddle; and here the trail crosses a small, grassy park. Here is an excellent stop for a rest, with a very photogenic view of both the canyon and the Bighorn Crags on its opposite side.

At Color Creek, five miles from the trailhead and 6,414 feet in elevation, stop and refill your water bottles. Just a quarter-mile past Color Creek, watch for the cut-off trail leading to the right to Nolan Mountain. Take this cut-off trail; it is unmarked but fairly easy to find. Here you leave the well-built Stoddard trail, leaving it to wander along the side of the Middle Fork's canyon. (The Stoddard trail leads ultimately to Stoddard Lake but it's a two-day horse ride.)

Now on the trail to Nolan Mountain, you'll have to switchback steeply uphill. As you near the top (a climb of about a thousand feet from Color Creek), the trail worsens. It has not been cleared in years. The deadfall may be thick, although the Act of Congress creating the River of No Return Wilderness optimistically commands that all trails are to be kept cleared. At various times, Nolan Mountain becomes prominent on the skyline and before too long you are on top of the mountain next to its abandoned lookout tower.

Follow the trail downhill to a spring. You may want to camp here. After all, you've climbed 5,200 feet and hiked about seven miles. This is a good campsite, one used by hunters in the fall.

From the spring, the trail runs along the top of the ridgeline. However, its path deteriorates and is easily lost in the deadfall. This is no great matter, however, as you are on a high ridge with only one way to go: west towards the 9,000-foot-plus Twin Peaks. Soon you'll find the trail again; however, just as it seems to improve, it ends. It ends just as the topographic map suggests—at a magnificent saddle which certainly looks like the bighorn sheep country it is. The best, and really the only way to go, is onto the saddle and straight up the mountain. It is not difficult, but you'll have to contend with loose rocks.

Walk along the ridge just before the first of the Twin Peaks, and two lakes will appear below in the South Fork of Kitchen Creek. Descend steeply for a thousand feet to the lakes. Camping is just fair at the lakes, and there is a lot of deadfall, but the cutthroat trout fishing more than makes up for this.

On your third day, follow an outfitter's trail that starts near the outlet of the upper of the two South Fork of Kitchen Creek Lakes. This trail switchbacks steeply up a ridge radiating from Twin Peaks and goes over to Stoddard Lake.Cutthroat fishing is good at Stoddard Lake.

From Stoddard Lake, trails follow deep into the primal wilderness to Papoose Lake, Cottonwood Lake, Basin Lake, Black Lake, and the vastness of Chamberlain Basin.

You can follow the Stoddard trail to make a loop back to the trailhead, but count on at least two hard days. If you are tempted to take any other route back to the Salmon River's main fork other than that which crosses the Stoddard Pack Bridge, remember that you'll have to swim across this major river to get back to the Salmon River trail. There are no other bridges within hiking distance.

For those who start back on the Stoddard trail but end up at dusk on the side of the Middle Fork Canyon, there are a few marginal spots to bivouac next to the trail.—*Philip Blomquist* ☐

Note: This trail was largely closed for reconstruction during the summer of 1989, as were parts of the entire trail along the Middle Fork of the Salmon River. Construction of portions may continue in 1990. Therefore, check with the Salmon National Forest before planning a trip.—Ralph Maughan

HIKE 20 *UPPER LOON CREEK LOOP*

General description: A three- to four-day hike on 32 miles of good trail, with side trips for fishing and plentiful camping sites.
General location: In the Salmon River Mountains of Central Idaho, about 40 road miles north of Stanley.
Maps: Casto, Knapp Lakes, Langer Peak, and Pinyon Peak (7.5') USGA quads.
Special attractions: Half of the loop lies in the River of No Return Wilderness. Subalpine lakes and wildlife are abundant.
Difficulty: Moderately difficult.
Season: July to October.
Information: Middle Fork District, Challis National Forest, Clayton, Idaho 83227; (208) 879-5204.

The hike: This is one hike where you'll never need to worry about drinking water. (However, because of the presence of horse parties, water should always be treated.) There are two major climbs, one of 3,000 feet in nine miles and the other of a 1,000 feet in six miles. The country covered by this loop is right on the edge of the River of No Return Wilderness. Although the terrain itself is not difficult, the length of the loop puts it out of the league of the novice.

Sunbeam is about 10 miles east of Stanley. Both towns are outdoor recreation outposts, and the area is a sort of contemporary legend popularized in part by minstrels Muzzie and Gary Braun in the tune "Yankee Fork" and the "prose" of Gino Sky Clay in his book *Appaloosa Rising*. This country is not only worth writing about, it's also certainly worth visiting.

From Sunbeam, proceed north on a Forest Service road that follows the Yankee Fork of the Salmon River. The road is paved for about five miles, then turns into all-weather gravel. This area is a real piece of history, so take your time and enjoy it. There is a developed campsite about one mile north of Sunbeam at Flat Rock and another near Bonanza on the West Fork of the Yankee Fork. When the pavement ends, you can't help but notice big piles of river rock on both sides of the road. These are remnants of gold dredging that occurred in the 1930s and 1940s. About 10 miles up this road on the left you'll find the Yankee Fork dredge. The bulk of machinery is now a Forest Service exhibit, and the principles of dredge mining are explained here in detail. Shortly after the dredge, the road forks. One mile down the right fork in the mining ghost town of Custer; this too is a historical site complete with museum. Stay on the main fork of the road which leads 20 miles to the trailhead at Loon Creek Guard Station.

At roughly the 13-mile point, the active Sunbeam Mine appears on your left.

From the mine the road switchbacks steeply seven miles to Loon Creek Summit.

On the other side of summit, the wilderness flanks both sides of the road. (The road itself, of course, is redlined out of the wilderness since a wilderness, by definition, has no roads.) It's 10 miles downhill from the summit to Loon Creek Guard Station. The entire road is passable by sedan, but it has its serious moments with uphill grades and rocks. Check with the Yankee Fork Ranger District for road conditions. (An alternate approach of approximately the same driving distance is Forest Service Road #172 via Idaho Highway 21, 15 miles northwest of Stanley. This scenic road requires four-wheel drive.)

When you reach the guard station, turn left and proceed through the center of the complex. Behind the buildings, you'll pass through a gate into an open field used as a heliport. Continue down this jeep road, bending left and following a fence on the right for about 100 yards. Another gate, posting notice of closure to ORVs, marks the beginning of the trail. The trail starts as a jeep road on the south side of the gate. You can park either in the field before the gate or back at the guard station.

The Upper Loon Creek Trail begins as a jeep road that winds flatly through sagebrush cover containing a few Douglas fir and lodgepole pine. At about .3 mile, you'll come to trail signs pointing straight ahead (south) to the Loon Creek Trail which you'll take, and right (southwest) to the Trail Creek trail, on which you'll return. At one-half mile, the jeep road continues straight ahead, but a sign directs you to a pack trail on the left. Follow the pack trail which then climbs gently through forest along a ridge above Loon Creek. At 1.2 miles, No Name Creek intersects from the left. Along this section we saw ruffed grouse, tasty game birds often found beneath bushes next to the trail. Not known for their intelligence, these birds usually don't notice human presence until it's more than obvious.

Talus slopes begin on your left at about the two-mile mark. The loose rocks on these slopes provide habitat for the pika, a small, squirrel-sized animal whose short, clarion squeaks scold your approach. Just after the talus slopes, the signed Pioneer Creek-Cabin Creek Trail comes in from the left. The Loon Creek Trail crosses Pioneer Creek, which was still running high on Labor Day when we were there. A few yards upstream is a good log crossing.

In another quarter-mile, still heading south, you'll cross to Loon Creek's west side. Note that this crossing does not agree with the USGS or Forest Service maps. Such discrepancies occur often on this hike, due primarily to trail rerouting since publication of the maps. Again, there are good crossing logs a few yards upstream. The trail, climbing moderately at times, now skirts a ridge of habitat similar to that on Loon Creek's east side. Oregon grape, salmonberry, paintbrush, and a variety of other wildflowers bloom in this area. The noisy chirps of red tree squirrels can be heard along this and most other sections of the trail. In less than .1 mile, the trail crosses back to the east side of Loon Creek and climbs gently, but steadily, through a lodgepole pine forest for a mile. Occasionally the forest canopy opens into areas where aspen have colonized following a rockslide or avalanche.

Seven miles from the start of the hike, you'll cross Loon Creek for the third and final time. After a half-mile climb, you'll see a sign which points out the Fish Creek Trail on the left. In spite of the sign, the trail is not acknowledged

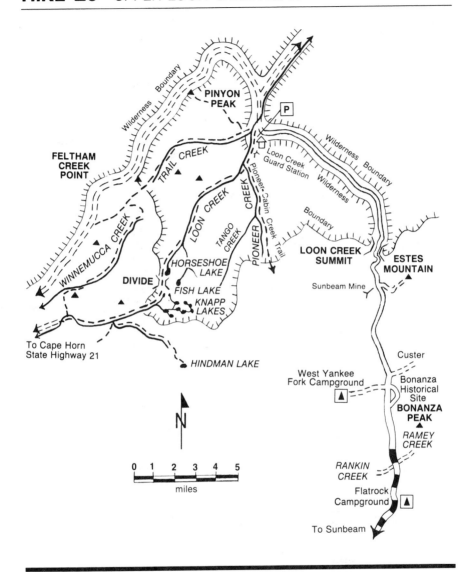

on the USGS Knapp Lakes, Challis Forest, or River of No Return Wilderness maps. It looks like about a two-mile hike following the stream around the back of a ridge to Fish Lake. Fish Lake reportedly contains 13-inch trout. From the Fish Lake side trail, the main trail now climbs through forest, gaining a thousand feet in 1.7 miles. At nine miles you arrive at Horseshoe Lake (8,000 feet), having now climbed 2,200 feet from the trailhead.

Horseshoe Lake is typical of many shallow, subalpine lakes in the Sawtooth and Salmon River mountains. Pan-sized trout can be caught in the lake. Most land areas abutting the lakeshore are rocky, although good campsites exist on the north end and on the land between the legs of the horseshoe. Mosquitoes are abundant. We saw black bear tracks and scat near the lake, also ducks and kingfishers. Vegetation changes here: whitebark pine, Engelmann spruce, and subalpine fir—all species that favor high elevations— now dominate the forest community, along with some lodgepole pine.

It's .8 mile and a steep, hairpin ascent from Horseshoe Lake to the Knapp Lakes Divide (8,600 feet), the highest point of the hike. At the divide is an excellent view of Horseshoe Lake and the adjacent, towering mountains.

From the Knapp Lakes Divide, the Knapp Creek Trail descends toward Knapp Lakes. At roughly the 10-mile point, the trail leads into an area where a forest fire left only lodgepole snags. Ground squirrels, if not seen, are at least commonly heard in this area. At 10.4 miles a sign points to Knapp Lakes. Although there is no trail, it's just a short hike over to these lakes and their small trout. Knapp Peak (10,012 feet) is prominent to the northeast of the lakes. (*Editor's Note:* Knapp Lakes were included in the wilderness due to a request by Ralph Maughan. Squeaky wheels do get greased on occasion.)

The trail descends rather steeply from the Knapp Lakes sign and crosses Knapp Creek at 11.2 miles (note difference from USGS map). At this point you have descended a thousand feet from the divide. In less than a quarter-mile, you'll cross Knapp Creek to the southern side and continue a moderate descent in a southwest direction through a spruce-fir forest. In about a half mile, cross Knapp Creek for the last time. The trail soon opens into a sedge meadow with showy daisies, asters, and other wildflowers. The trail turns into a jeep road at 12.8 miles, and at the 13-mile mark, a pack trail from Valley Creek and Hindman Lake intersects the Knapp Creek Trail. Several changes in scenery are very noticeable now that you've temporarily left the River of No Return Wilderness.

For the next three miles you'll descend gradually along the jeep road, first through sagebrush rangeland and then through young lodgepole forest. The jeep road runs close to Knapp Creek, where good campsites are abundant.

At about 16 miles, the road crosses a dry creekbed. It continues straight here along Knapp Creek and eventually leads down to Cape Horn and State Highway 21. Just after crossing the creek bed, take the faint trail to the right (north) that leads over to Winnemucca Creek. The trail goes through sagebrush and then climbs somewhat through lodgepole pine before leveling off and descending toward Winnemucca Creek. It's 1.5 miles over to the Winnemucca Creek trail. The closed forest overstory affords few views. At 17 miles, the trail descends into a boggy meadow. It crosses Winnemucca Creek to lead 10 yards up to another jeep road. A sign marks the jeep road-pack trail junction. Proceed right (east) on this road to begin the Winnemucca Creek trail.

For the next 1.3 miles, the road winds northeast through meadows interspersed with tracts of lodgepole. There are several good campsites here, but ORVs are not uncommon. At 18.5 miles, the road again turns into a pack trail. After passing a bog on the right, climb gently for three miles through forest with sagebrush meadows. Good campsites are present a few yards off to the right. We enjoyed listening to elk bugle in the evening and morning at one of these sites. At the 22-miles point, cross the dry bed of Winnemucca Creek, and begin a climb to 7,800 feet. Again, note the change in the plant community that is, the reappearance of spruce and fir.

If you're tired now, you'll get a brief reprieve as the trail levels and skirts a ridge on the left, heading toward Beaver Creek. It climbs steadily for a quarter-mile before beginning the descent to Beaver Creek. At 23.5 miles you cross Beaver Creek. Shortly, you'll reach the junction of the Beaver Creek and Winnemucca Creek trails in a grassy meadow. Take the Beaver Creek trail to the right and head north, noting the Forest Service sign posted on a tree.

The trail winds north through a meadow and takes a sharp right turn across a small creek. Be careful not to get lost here! The Beaver Creek trail climbs steadily, at times steeply (one mile, 400-foot elevation gain), to the top of the Trail Creek drainage (25 miles). This is a good spot to take a break, as it's a long seven miles downhill to Loon Creek Guard Station from here. The mountain on the upper left is Feltham Creek Point, also a Forest Service lookout station. The top of Trail Creek demarks your return to the River of No Return Wilderness.

After a switchback descent of about one-half mile, you'll hear Trail Creek a few yards off to the left. Roughly a mile from the start of the Trail Creek trail, you cross the creek to the left (northwest) side. Shortly, the trail opens into meadows with willows dominating the stream side. Soon you'll come to a camp with a fire ring and horse hitches. Look to your left and follow the trail blazes on the trees, crossing Trail Creek to your left. It's important to make this crossing or you'll have to slog through a wet meadow.

After leaving the bog meadow, the trail ascends for a few yards, then descends steeply before rounding a ridge above Trail Creek. At about 28 miles, it turns due east to head for Loon Creek Guard Station. A large marsh appears on the right, where you can see the work of beaver and some beautiful algal blooms.

Continuing along the trail, notice that Douglas fir is the only major tree species. The dry, south slope on the left consists mostly of sagebrush and bitterbrush, with some mountain mahogany high on the ridge. This slope provides excellent mule deer habitat.

At 30.4 miles, cross Rabbit Creek, and .3 mile later, Packer Gulch. Now it's less than 1.5 miles to the end of the loop. At 31 miles you'll come to a trail that leads up to the Pinyon Peak lookout tower. Straight ahead are the fields of the Diamond D Ranch, one of a number of private inholdings conceded to in order to obtain wilderness classification. Look to your right for a trail sign. Follow the sign direction and continue along Trail Creek. In .7 mile, you'll reach the end of the hike.—*Craig Groves and Julia Corbett* □

Note: An August 1994 thunderstorm ignited the Pioneer Creek fire, which eventually burned 9,700 acres before being controlled by firefighters and autumn weather. This fire burned approximately 3 miles of the Loon Creek trail upstream from the Loon Creek Guard Station.—Ralph Maughan □

HIKE 21 *UPPER VANITY LAKES*

General description: A short cross-country hike into a basecamp at one of two high mountain lakes.

General location: 15 air miles northwest of Stanley in the southern portion of the River of No Return Wilderness.

Maps: Langer Peak (7.5') USGS quad.

Special attractions: Side trip to cross-country ridgeline hike affording fantastic views of Vanity Lakes and the Knapp Lake country. Solitude.

Difficulty: Moderate; requires competence with compass and map over a short distance.

Season: Mid-July to October.

Information: Challis National Forest, HC 63 Box 1671, Challis, Idaho 83226; (208) 879-2285.

The hike: No marked trails lead to any of the 12 lakes draining into Vanity Creek. The two lakes described here are the closest to the road and the easiest to get to; yet because they are trailless, they still get little use. Once at the lakes, you can navigate up onto a ridgeline which can be hiked for about 1.5 miles. Although short, this hike should not be under taken without the Langer Peak USGS quadrangle, plus knowledge and possession of a compass.

To reach the starting point of this hike, turn north off of Idaho Highway 21 at the Forest Service sign indicating Lola Creek Campground and Seafoam area. Follow Forest Service Road #008 leading to Vanity Summit and Seafoam Area. This dirt road is marked and passable by sedan. Continue to follow it for about eight miles as it climbs to top out at Vanity Summit. Park off the road in the wider area directly on top of the summit.

It is about one mile round-trip, with a minimal elevation gain, to the first of the Upper Vanity Lakes. Begin hiking on the east side of Vanity Summit and head in a direction just a hair south of due east. You will gradually climb through trees. Occasionally, you will have to climb over some rocky areas. As long as you do not drop off to the left (north) or climb the rocky cliffs to the right (south) and as long as you continue a course of gradual elevation gain, you will eventually break out of the trees and reach a small lake. Another lake is located a quarter-mile beyond to the east. The two are connected by a stream that you can follow. The third lake, to the south, also empties into the firs via an annual stream. The total distance to the first two lakes in not much more than a half-mile.

Camping sites are available on the lakeshores, but to minimize environmental damage, you'll want to get back in the trees. Campsites directly abutting the lake can turn green, grassy areas into dirt and dust. At the time I visited them, the lakes showed no signs of camping. To keep it that way, do all your cooking and sleeping in the trees; and, for those times of personal contemplation, you can visit the edge of the lake.

Since the hike to the lakes is short, you are in a good position to make a side trip. The slight saddle to the southeast of the lakes is a scramble through trees for about 800 feet until you reach timberline. From here it's about 40 more feet to the saddle. This ridgeline can be followed to the north and northeast to oversee the main Vanity Lakes sprinkled among the trees. Behind you to the south you will see the magnificent Sawtooth Range.

HIKE 21 *UPPER VANITY LAKES*

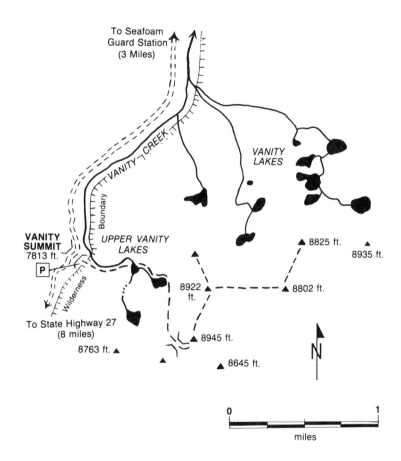

Below the ridge, you will also catch a glimpse of a road in the Beaver Creek drainage to the east. The road leads to Felthman Creek Point and on to Pinyon Creek Lookout to the northeast. This road was the topic of a conversation I once had with a woman at a gathering of people working to protect the River of No Return Wilderness. Her late husband had spent a good number of years at the Pinyon Creek Lookout with an eagle's view of the River of No Return country. Like so many others, he had become enchanted with the area. He felt that, because the Pinyon Creek Lookout could also be reached by driving up Loon Creek, the primitive road up Beaver Creek should be closed. He envisioned a chunk of wild country extending from Vanity Lakes across to the east into the beautiful, rugged, Knapp Lakes area. Such a boundary in the southern portion of the River of No Return Wilderness would have created an unbroken expanse of rocky ridges and crags, and sweeping drainages dotted with crystalline lakes.

As it is now, however, the Vanity Lakes area is isolated by roads into a finger of wilderness averaging four miles across. The old ranger's dream of an unbroken Vanity-Knapp lakes territory was another casualty among the many concessions necessary to gain passage of the River of No Return bill.— Ron Watters □

Note: In order to find the first lake quickly, be sure to hike near the creek once you have intercepted it after walking from Vanity Summit. I visited the area in 1989 for the first time and arrived at the lower lake in just twenty minutes.

Hikers must have listened to Ron Watters' injunction contained in the first edition. I found no fire rings at the lakes.—Ralph Maughan □

HIKE 22 *BLUE BUNCH MOUNTAIN*

General description: A day hike to the top of Blue Bunch Mountain in the Frank Church-River of No Return Wilderness.

General location: About 50 road miles North-Northwest of Stanley.

Maps: Blue Bunch Mountain (7.5') USGS quad.

Special attractions: Excellent views of the River of No Return Wilderness, the Middle Fork of the Salmon River, and surrounding country. Wildflowers and regeneration after a forest fire.

Difficulty: Moderately difficult if done in one day. Moderately easy if done as an overnighter.

Season: July through September.

Information: Lowman Ranger District, Boise National Forest, HC 76, Box 3020, Lowman, Idaho 83637; (208) 364-4250.

The hike: Blue Bunch and nearby Cape Horn Mountain stand near the headwaters of the Middle Fork of the Salmon River. The hike to the summit ridge of Blue Bunch Mountain gives a splendid view of the Dagger Falls portion of the Middle Fork canyon, the expansive Poker and Bruce meadows and Bear Valley Creek to the west, rugged mountains of the Soldier/ Langer Lakes area to the east, and of Cape Horn Mountain to the south.

The trail to the top of Blue Bunch is not difficult. It involves a moderately-paced climb of 2,000 feet and can be done easily in a day by those who are in fairly good shape. You can also camp on the mountain. The best camping spots are in the vicinity of Cy Springs near the top of the ridgeline.

From Idaho Highway 21, turn onto a well-marked gravel road a few miles east of Banner Summit that leads to Dagger Falls and Bruce Meadow. This road is improved and maintained but also often badly wash-boarded and subject to heavy recreational traffic leading to and from the popular Middle Fork put-in at Dagger Falls. Be alert for vehicles with horse trailers, boat carrying rigs, and buses.

Follow this road for about 12 miles until you see the sign and the side road for Fir Creek Campground. If you break out of the timber into Bruce Meadows, you have gone too far. The trailhead is about a half mile down the side road mentioned. Proceed straight down it to the bank of Bear Valley Creek, and don't take the right turn to Fir Creek Campground. There is plenty of parking room at the trailhead and a fine bridge over beautiful Bear Valley Creek. The wilderness boundary is immediately on the other side of the creek.

After crossing the bridge over Bear Valley Creek, turn left. The right fork of the trail leads down Bear Valley Creek but is unbridged, crossing this small river several times. It's a difficult wade even in mid-August.

You walk upstream just briefly. The trail then makes a right angle turn and begins to climb the mountain. It is a steep trail at first, but it soon levels out only to steepen and level repeatedly. You soon reach occasional burned trees from the Deadwood Fire of 1987, but most trees remain green. The lower mountain saw only a ground fire. As you climb higher, most lodgepole pine are charred and dead. The large Douglas fir, however, are only blackened at the bottom; their thick trunks protected them. I found the wildflower display subsequent to the fire dazzling, but as I climbed higher there were numerous spots where the fire burned hot and little revegatation was present two years later.

As you near the top of the ridge, you reach Cy Springs, a good water source. There are places to camp in the springs' vicinity. Just above the springs, you find a rough cabin. It was reported that a holy man lived here during the early 1970s.

The trail becomes faint near the springs, but just climb to the top of the ridge and you will find it again. Walking the ridgetop trail is fairly easy, but keep an eye open for gathering thunderstorms.

The fire burned to the top of Blue Bunch Mountain but stopped for lack of fuel on its east-facing slope. There are many burned whitebark pine on the ridgetop. From the ridge the view to the immediate east is over green, undulating cirque basins with a few small ponds, then further east across the partially hidden canyon of the Middle Fork of the Salmon. These basins are a good place to spot elk. You also have a view of Cape Horn Mountain to the south and the Bruce Meadows area to the southwest. In 1989 I climbed the mountain the day after the large central Idaho forest fires broke out (the Red Fire, Warm Lake complex, Whangdoddle, etc.). Large plumes of smoke rose in the southwest, west, and northwest. I continued until the trail reached the north end of the ridge for a fine view across the Dagger Falls area and down the Middle Fork canyon.

Location of the wilderness boundary on the banks of Bear Valley Creek and the inclusion of Blue Bunch and Cape Horn Mountain was a great environmental victory. The Forest Service had recommended putting the boundary about ten miles to the north and developing the Bear Valley area, Poker, and Ayers Meadows, as "staging areas" for recreationists heading for Dagger Falls and the Middle Fork. Idaho environmentalists wanted to include Blue Bunch Mountain, Cape Horn Mountain, and the Bear Valley Mountain area to the west (called then the "Sulphur Creek" roadless area) in the River of No Return Wilderness, but even they had given up the lush meadow area between as "lost".

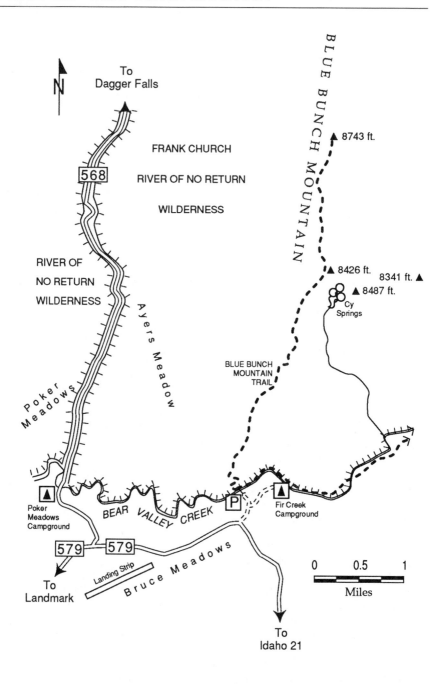

In the summer of 1980, I was sitting in Washington D.C. with Andy Weissener, then the majority counsel to the House Subcommittee on Public Lands, helping draw the boundaries for the River of No Return Wilderness. Together we drew in about 500,000 additional acres on the south and southeast sides of the old Idaho Primitive Area; environmentalists felt that preservation of these acres was important. Andy asked me, "Why Blue Bunch Mountain but not the meadows below it?" I said there was no reason except the Forest Service would go nuts. He took a red pen and placed these two large, wildlife rich meadows inside the wilderness, putting the boundary down the middle of Bear Valley Creek for a number of miles and only 50 feet on either side of the lengthy road leading to Dagger Falls.

The additions, including the meadows, quickly gained the approval of John Seiberling, the subcommittee chair, and of Senator Frank Church who only asked us to delete 25,000 acres of proposed additions in the Furnace/Camas Creek area near Challis. This was so that the entire River of No Return Wilderness package would be 2.24 million acres, and thus could not be rounded off to 2.3 million acres (the reported total size of Idaho environmentalists' proposal). In delicious irony, official recalculation of the size of the Frank Church/River of No Return Wilderness years later revealed its actual size to be almost 2.4 million acres.

Today signs along the Dagger Falls road inform visitors that they are privileged to drive through a "wilderness corridor" which flanks the road all the way from Bear Valley Creek crossing to Dagger Falls. One is led to think the Forest Service originated the idea.—*Ralph Maughan* ☐

HIKE 23 *SOLDIER LAKES/PATROL RIDGE LOOP*

General description: A three-day loop covering about 22 miles in the Frank Church-River of No Return Wilderness.
General location: In the Salmon River Mountains of Central Idaho, north of Stanley.
Maps: Greyhound Ridge, Chinook Mt. (15') USGS quads.
Special attractions: Good fishing in numerous subalpine lakes. Views down into the Middle Fork of the Salmon Canyon and many distant peaks.
Difficulty: Moderately easy to Soldier Lakes. The entire loop is moderately difficult.
Season: July to October.
Information: Yankee Fork Ranger District, Challis National Forest. HC67,Box 660, Clayton, Idaho 83227 (208) 838-2201.

The hike: This hike covers a popular area of lake and high ridge country in the southern part of the Frank Church-River of No Return Wilderness. The hike ranges from forest to near the alpine zone at 9,000 feet. The trail begins at 7,100 feet at Josephus Lake in Float Creek and passes by, or near, over a dozen lakes and goes along a high ridge with a tremendous views as it traces a rough horseshoe shape. Most of the lakes are fishable and have cutthroat trout.

The lakes are in two groups—the Soldier Lakes and the Cutthroat Lakes.

Both lie in large basins beneath a long ridge that sports numerous rugged, but short, peaks, called Patrol Ridge. The ridge is unnamed on most maps. The most popular and perhaps the more scenic of the two groups of lakes is the Soldier Lakes, nestled beneath Patrol Ridge at the headwaters of Soldier Creek. Each of the Soldier Lakes is named after a military rank, but in a somewhat arbitrary fashion. The Cutthroat Lakes are generally unnamed (except one large one named Cutthroat Lake). They lie under Patrol Ridge at the head of Muskeg Creek.

The north side of Patrol Ridge, which overlooks the lakes, is precipitous. Its opposite side is steep but smooth, plunging several thousand feet into the Middle Fork Canyon. The trail on the ridge keeps close to the top and offers outstanding views of both sides.

Drive northward from Stanley on Idaho 21 for 18.6 miles and turn off the highway onto a gravel road (#008) that goes up Beaver Creek. The road is in good condition until you begin the climb to Vanity Summit. From Vanity Summit down to Float Creek, the road narrows, is steep, and has tight blind curves. It is passable to a small sedan, however, since it isn't rocky or badly rutted. Sixteen miles from where you turned off Idaho of 21, you arrive at the junction with the road up Float Creek. It is five miles and a modest 1,100 foot climb to Josephus Lake, the trailhead. The condition of the Float Creek Road is similar to the one down Vanity Creek you have been following.

Scenic Josephus lake is actually two lakes separated by a short stream. It is heavily used by anglers and campers but has space to park only about seven vehicles. There is an undeveloped (no water) campground south of the lower lake.

The trail leaves from the right (north) side of Josephus Lake, crosses an open slope with good views and then heads into deep forest. The wilderness boundary is quickly reached. The trail climbs steadily through forest and a few openings to reach pretty Helldiver Lake after two miles. There are a few springs along the trail to Helldiver Lake early in the summer. Mushroom Springs, about a mile from the trailhead usually flows all summer. Float Creek remains far below the trail. Helldiver Lake has just a few campsites, mostly near the trail.

Past Helldiver Lake, a climb of 400 feet in .75 mile puts you on a pass between Float Creek and the Soldier Creek drainage. There is a fine view if you climb 30 yards up the north slope from the pass. This pass also marks the spot where Greyhound Ridge joins Patrol Ridge.

The trail drops steeply, but briefly, down from the pass and past a pond to a trail junction. At the junction, follow the Soldier Lakes trail to the left. The trail soon breaks into the open as it begins to cross the head of Soldier Creek Canyon whose thickly-timbered bottom spreads below you. After a mile, drop down to the first of the Soldier Lakes—First Lieutenant. The best campsites are on the far end. Next, one quickly comes to Colonel Lake and a trail junction. Right goes to more of the Soldier Lakes and to the Cutthroat Lakes. Left goes to more Soldier Lakes and then to the top of Patrol Ridge. Most people end their trip in the vicinity of this junction and begin fishing and relaxing.

On the Patrol Ridge Trail, you quickly come to a pretty blue-green lake called The General. From the General, an unmarked trail climbs briefly to the biggest of the lakes, the Captain. Best camping here is at the lake's inlet,

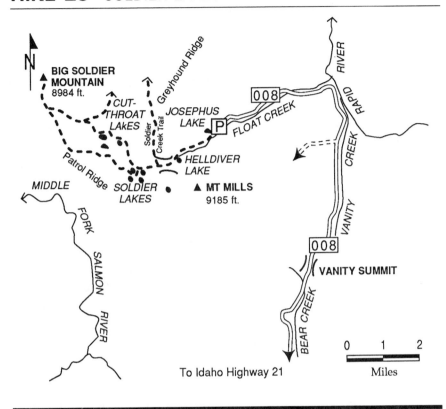

toward the base of the ridge. The main trail circles the General, then circles a lake with no fish called the Major, after which it begins a steep 400 foot ascent to the top of Patrol Ridge.

Once on the ridge, views are few at first and the trail is quite narrow, but both conditions soon improve and after a half mile the trail follows the very top of the ridge, offering dramatic views of the Soldier Lakes below and down towards the Middle Fork in the opposite direction. In July the ridge is covered with flowers between the scenic clumps of whitebark pine.

As the trail follows the ridge, it gradually climbs. One gains views of the Cutthroat Lakes below and finally (to the south) the headwaters of the Middle Fork where Marsh Creek and Bear Valley Creek run together. You see not just the canyon, but the actual river. You also see the results of the huge Deadwood Fire of 1987. This fire burned through the Elk Creek, Sulphur Creek, and Bear Valley Mountain area of the Frank Church Wilderness. It blew down Boundary Creek to the Middle Fork and forced campers into the river. A change of wind blew it back up Boundary Creek, burning it twice (notice how black the drainage is still), but probably saved lives.

The trail reaches its highest point (about 9,000 feet) as it bends northward and traverses under Peak 9,107. Here, as you cross the head of Lincoln Creek (which bears a lake far below you), the trail grows quite narrow with a very steep slope down into Lincoln Creek. It is not so treacherous, however, to prevent its use by horses (which, prudently, should be walked).

Soon there comes a saddle that may appear to be the one on the map showing the loop trail dropping eastward off Patrol Ridge to begin the loop back to the Soldier Lakes. This is not the case. The correct saddle is a quarter mile farther north. This saddle is broader than the first (wrong) one. There may or may not be a sign marking the trail (called the Muskeg Creek trail), but the track is obvious if you walk to the edge of the saddle-top meadow. Before continuing the loop, however, you will probably want to make a side-trip by continuing along the ridge to its terminus at Big Soldier Mountain. This is a three mile round trip. An abandoned lookout tower sits atop Big Soldier Mountain, from which you have views of all of the southern part of the Frank Church Wilderness. You can't see the actual Middle Fork from the lookout. However, you can see it on your way to the lookout. One can even see the Dagger Falls put-in point on the river.

Back on the loop, the trail leaves the saddle to contour directly under the cliffs of Patrol Ridge. For about a mile, as it contours around the head of a tributary of Muskeg Creek, the trail is rocky, narrow, and somewhat difficult. Soon, however, it begins to ramble through forest and meadow as it approaches the Cutthroat Lakes. For the last mile before reaching Cutthroat Lake it descends 900 feet.

Cutthroat Lake is at the base of Peak 8,996 on Patrol Ridge. There are campsites on both the east and west ends of the lake, but the west side is overused and near a bog. A small cascade tumbles into the lake on its west side. At a junction a half mile above Cutthroat Lake, a fork leaves to the left down Muskeg Creek, to Soldier Creek and eventually the Middle Fork of the Salmon River.

From this junction to Colonel Lake, the trail you follow is called the Cutthroat Trail. The Cutthroat Trail generally climbs, sometimes steeply, and fails to go close to most of the Cutthroat Lakes. You have to seek them out. Two miles past Cutthroat Lake, the trail drops into the Soldier Creek drainage and soon you pass by two beautiful and large Soldier Lakes—Staff Sargent Lake and Sargent Lake. Soon thereafter the loop is completed at the junction at Colonel Lake.—*by Ralph and Jackie Maughan* □

Lick Creek Mountains

Overview

The Lick Creek mountains are a portion of the vast Salmon River mountain range lying east of Long Valley, which contains the towns of McCall and Cascade. It is generally conceived that the canyon of the South Fork of the Salmon River marks the east side of the Lick Creek mountains.

The igneous rock of these scenic peaks has been intensely carved by ice-age glaciers into a variety of peaks and cirque basins. About 150,000 acres of this area burned in the fire summer of 1994, including much of Hike 25, Box Lake, and just to the northwest of Loon Lake, Hike 27. A small portion of Hike 29 near Lava Ridge may have been affected.

HIKE 24 *BOULDER LAKE/LOUIE LAKE LOOP*

General description: An easy day hike or overnighter to either lake. The loop is a slightly more difficult day hike. Close to
McCall, providing good access to high mountain scenery and fishing.
General location: Ten linear miles southeast of McCall.
Maps: Paddy Flat (7.5') USGS quad.
Difficulty: Easy to reach each lake, moderate for the six mile loop (1,400 foot elevation gain).
Season: Mid-June through September.
Information: McCall Ranger District, Payette National Forest, Box 1026, McCall, Idaho 83638; (208) 634-2255.

The hike: This is a popular area with routes to two different lakes that can put you in some very beautiful country after about 1.5 miles either way. A loop trip is also possible with a connecting trail between the lakes. Use can be heavy on weekends. There is a primitive campground just before the Boulder Meadows Reservoir.

Drive south from McCall on Idaho Highway 55. One mile south of this resort community, turn left (east) onto the Farm to Market Road. Follow the curves that bend at one-mile intervals for four miles until the road crosses Lake Fork Creek. The main road curves right, but you should go straight on the Boulder Creek Road which is marked by a small Forest Service sign.

There are several roads straying to the left and right; stay on the main road, which eventually becomes gravel. The last mile or so suffers from water erosion after a rain. You may want to park at the Louie Lake trailhead, just below Boulder Meadows Reservoir. The trailhead for Boulder Lake is at the reservoir, less than one-quarter mile up the road. To get to Boulder Lake, start on the north side of the reservoir, following the well-used trail, which parallels

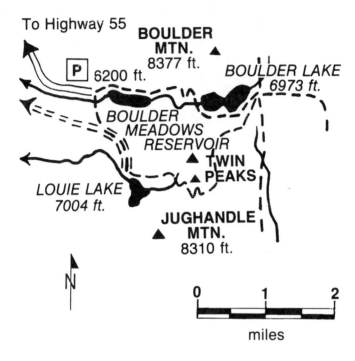

it. Most of the wet areas have been recently bridged by trail maintenance crews. This area, including the trail section to Boulder Lake, hosts the western-most extension of grand fir (Abies Grandis).

At the end of the reservoir, the trail climbs about 500 feet to a granite bowl. There are numerous switchbacks, sometimes with alternate routes, but the trail is generally well marked. The rocky stretches minimize dirt bike use. In early June heavy run-off from the still ice-covered lake can make the upper part of the trail a significant channel for Boulder Creek.

Boulder is a natural lake, but a small dam has been built at the mouth by an irrigation district for water storage. Fishing can be good for stocked rainbow, depending on the season. There are numerous camping spots around the lake.

The meadow east of Boulder Lake is awash with flowers in late spring. Even in midsummer you can find a riotous flood of color with yellow composites, white phlox, blue penstemon, and red monkeyflower (mimulus) covering the hillside. Wildlife in the area includes marmots, mule deer, black bears, pikas, mountain chickadees, and red-breasted nuthatches.

The trail skirts to the south side of the lake, and just beyond the lake is a trail junction giving access to other lakes and fine views from the top of Boulder

Mountain and from Buckhorn Summit. Before this trail junction is a cairn-marked trail to the right, leading to Louie Lake. This trail is shown on the Paddy Flat USGS quadrangle map; however, it has been removed from the Forest Service trail inventory. The ridge it follows, just east of Twin Peaks, alternates between forest and meadow, offering some of the best views on the Payette Forest. Some of the meadows have, unfortunately, been heavily grazed by sheep. (During the summer of 1989, the Northern Rockies Chapter of the Sierra Club, with the help of the Payette National Forest, began a two year project to restore this nearly three mile trail connecting the lakes.)

After a gradual climb of nearly 700 feet, you cross over the ridge. A tenth of a mile later, a small lily-covered lake appears about 100 yards to your left. Numerous views of Jughandle Mountain (8,310 feet) and Louie Lake can be seen as the trail drops 700 feet to Louie Lake and the jeep road which accesses it.

Louie Lake is a tarn (glacial lake) set in a granite-ringed cirque. Cliffs at the backside of Jughandle rise precipitously from the clear lake waters. This is a beautiful spot despite the fact that it is open to off-road vehicles. Once again, a small dam has increased the level of the lake. The lake shore is not as adversely affected by draw-down of the water as it is at Boulder Lake. Take a short side trip down the east side of the lake to an aspen grove which beautifully decorates the area in the fall. Here is a view of Jughandle across some small islands. Return to your car by walking one mile on the jeep road and then making a right turn onto the prominent trail which may or may not have a sign. A half-mile on this trail takes you to a log crossing of Boulder Creek and the trailhead.

The hike to just Louie Lake, or to Boulder Lake, is worthwhile by itself, but the nearly six mile loop is the better choice.—*Jerry Dixon with update by John Allen* □

HIKE 25 *BOX LAKE*

General description: A beautiful day hike or overnighter that climbs over a mountain pass to descend to Box Lake.
General location: 12 road miles northeast of McCall.
Maps: Fitsum Summit and Box Lake (7.5') USGS quads.
Special attractions: High-quality wilderness replete with wildlife, a large subalpine lake, and high mountain scenery.
Difficulty: Moderate; elevation gain of 1,600 feet in three miles.
Season: Late June to early September.
Information: Payette National Forest, Box 1026, McCall, Idaho 83638; (208) 634-0700.

The hike: Long Valley, in which the town of McCall is located, hosts 16 pairs of nesting osprey. Some of them nest in crags along Payette Lake near McCall. From Payette Lake to Box Lake, it is 10 miles as the osprey flies. River otters, which slide on their bellies, have been known to make it from the north end of Payette Lake to Box Lake in one day. When a biped with auto wants to get to Box Lake, the easiest way is to drive close to the Lake Fork Campground and walk a short distance.

When Idaho Highway 55 reaches Payette Lake from the south, it makes an

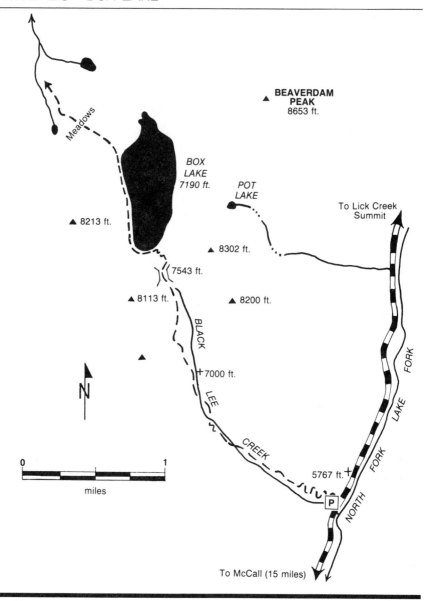

abrupt left turn. This is downtown McCall, where you'll part with Highway 55. Make a right turn here and stay on the main road for about one-half mile while it doglegs through east McCall to finally take a definite right (east) turn at the McCall Municipal Golf Course. There will be a sign here indicating the Lick Creek Road. About two miles east of the golf course begins the all-weather gravel Lick Creek Road, marked by a sign. This road follows the north shore of Little Payette Lake for about 2.7 miles (although you can't see the lake from the road), and gradually heads north along Lake Fork Creek. All told, the scenic drive to Lake Fork Campground and the U.S. Forest Service guard station is about eight miles northeast of McCall. Another four miles or so north is the Black Lee Campground. From here, the Box Lake trailhead is the distance of about three city blocks farther up the road. Although the trailhead is not developed with running water or pit toilets, it is marked. There is parking space for about four vehicles and room for several campsites.

This hike provides a good introduction to the Lick Creek Mountains, which form part of the western portion of the massive Idaho batholith, one of the largest bodies of intruded granite in the world. The batholith covers the vast core of central Idaho, extending northeasterly from Boise some 200 miles to the Bitterroot Mountains of the Montana border. The batholith was formed about 70 to 90 million years ago during the Cretaceous period. Range after range of steep mountains and narrow valleys furrow this region as if a gigantic rake had been dragged over it. This has frustrated generations of road builders—no road has ever been blasted completely through it.

Glaciers once filled the valleys in the Box Lake area during the Pleistocene (Ice Age) era and left many tarns, or glacial lakes, when they receded. These mountains are also characterized by steep river breaks with shallow soils.

The trail goes northwest from the trailhead and immediately begins to switchback up a steep slope into the canyon of Black Lee Creek. This first mile is a zigzag climb of 800 feet up a fir and pine slope which parallels the creek. The trail then meanders through several meadows after a ford of Black Lee Creek. Here yellow columbine, red Indian paintbrush, blue penstemon, and yellow composites all flower in August.

Although the temptation to shortcut the switchbacks can be great, try not

Box Lake. Nelle Tobias photo.

to. Other offenders have already caused erosion and gullies. Trail rehabilitation costs money that is better spent on other projects.

After another 800-foot climb, the trail levels out and you'll top a rise (7,543 feet) giving you a grand view of the surrounding mountains, with Box Lake 400 feet right below. Camping spots can be found along most of the perimeter of this mile-long body of melted snow. However, ethics, and sometimes the law, require that you camp 200 feet from a lake shore and 100 feet from a stream. Domestic sheep often graze this country, so water should be purified.

From the topo maps, it looks possible to proceed north-northwest to marshy Heart Lake (two miles), Brush Lake (2.7 miles), or Pearl Lake (4.5 miles). You could extend the hike further west to the junction with Wagon Creek Road (seven miles) or five miles along the road in the Pearl Creek drainage. This should bring you out at the North Fork of the Payette River. You'll need the Granite Lake 7.5 minute quadrangle to route this part of the hike, plus a shuttle vehicle, since you'll come out at a different trailhead.

The Lick Creek Mountains west of the South Fork of the Salmon River have been recommended for wilderness by the Forest Service. The area includes Box Lake. It would, or course, be preferable if all of the Lick Creek Mountains, both east and west of the South Fork, were protected as part of the National Wilderness System.

The Idaho Wildlands Defense Coalition has proposed a 441-thousand-acre Payette Crest Wilderness, which includes the western section. The Lick Creek mountains in the eastern section have been proposed as a 90-thousand-acre South Fork of the Salmon River Further Planning Area. However, even with Forest Service support for wilderness for the western Lick Creek Mountains, we cannot hope to see them so preserved without the active persuasion of those who use them.

Upon your return to the Lick Creek Road, be sure to stop near the top of the first set of switchbacks on the trail and look southward down the classic U-shaped valley of the North Fork of Lake Fork Creek. To the right is Slick Rock, an 800-foot-high vertical slab of granite. From here, looking down this canyon that now has a road in it, you can imagine how truly wild this country once was. Within your field of vision, the rare gray wolf was sighted in 1979. Quite possibly, wolves still roam these mountains.—*Jerry Dixon* □

HIKE 26 *WEST FORK, BUCKHORN CREEK*

General description: A 7.5-mile hike following a creek through wild, forested country to a lake stocked with rainbow trout.

General location: About 57 road miles and 17 linear miles east of McCall in the country between the north and south forks of the Salmon River.

Maps: Teapot Mountain and Fitsum Peak (7.5') USGS quad.

Special attractions: A hike through several habitat zones starting with steep river breaks, through ponderosa pines, to granite ridges flanked with subalpine fir and dotted with lakes.

Difficulty: Somewhat difficult. The trail to Buckhorn Lake includes a 3,100-foot elevation gain and a bushwhack for the last half-mile.

Season: Late June through September.

HIKE 26 *WEST FORK, BUCKHORN CREEK*

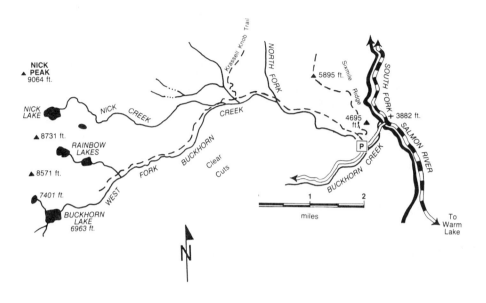

Information: Krassel Ranger District, Payette National Forest, Box 1026, McCall, Idaho 83638 (208) 634-0700.

The hike: Starting east from McCall (see instructions to Box Lake in the preceding hike description), travel over Lick Creek Summit, down Lick Creek to the Secesh River, and along the Secesh until you come to the South Fork of the Salmon River. This is a total of 35 miles from McCall by road. Turn right and head up the South Fork of the Salmon, passing its east fork and a number of campgrounds, until you come to Buckhorn Creek after 11 miles. Turn to the right (west) up Buckhorn Creek. After only about a half-mile you come to the West Fork of Buckhorn Creek. There is no developed trailhead, but you can pull off the road and park right at the West Fork's mouth. There are a few places to park. The dirt road continues up Buckhorn Creek for several more miles, but it has been closed above due to a disastrous landslide caused by building this timber access road over unstable soil.

 ' The hike begins on the east side of the road bridge over the West Fork. Following the stream, the trail is in good condition as it winds through ponderosa pine-blue bunch wheatgrass habitat. A side trail soon takes off to the right to climb up Sixmile Ridge and points beyond. Sixmile Ridge and similar south-facing river breaks are critical wintering areas for elk and deer.

About 2.5 miles from the trailhead, Krassel Knob trail takes off to your right. It travels north for about 7.5 miles to intersect with the Fitsum Creek Trail. Along the way, in about four miles, it crosses the North Fork of Buckhorn Creek. Stay to the left here and continue up the creek. In the next one-third mile, you will cross two small tributaries. The second drains from Nick Lake. This lake rests at 7,691 feet on the front (southeast) side of Nick Peak. The 9,064-foot Nick Peak, which dominates t he landscape, can be seen due east from downtown McCall. About two miles further up the trail is another tributary joining from the right. It drains Rainbow Lakes, which, at 7,435 and 7,205 feet, are set in tarns in the spiny granite ridge of the Lick Creek Mountains. As with Nick Lake, there is no trail to the Rainbow Lakes.

This is both mountain goat and cougar country. Perhaps the best place to see a mountain goat is on the drive in, on the Lick Creek road. Near Lick Creek Summit, look eastward high on the rocky cliffs. Your chances of seeing a cougar are slim because they are solitary animals. Cougars will follow humans but will not harm them. Feel secure that even though they are invisible to you, they are present.

It is 1.5 miles from the second tributary to Buckhorn Lake. The lake is a turquoise aqueous eye reflecting the azure western Idaho sky. It was stocked with rainbow trout in 1982. The last push to the lake includes a scramble over a small ridge as you navigate through the trees. A compass may be advisable, although you can follow close to the sound and sight of the creek. The trail seems to have been swallowed by the trees, but the best places are often the ones that have no trails.

Plans are in the works for timber cutting in this area. You may want to do something to prevent yet another marginal timber sale which destroys the country for short-term economic gain, or even a loss. If we want to have salmon in the Salmon River again, road building into the unstable soils of west central Idaho for timber cutting access must stop.

The soil, formed exclusively from decomposed granite, has the texture of fine sand. This smothers the eggs in the salmon redds (nests).— *Jerry Dixon* □

HIKE 27   *LOON LAKE AND BEYOND*

General description: A relatively easy hike in the eastern edge of the Lick Creek Mountains to a beautiful lake with opportunities for extended hiking. A loop trail in mid-summer, when the Secesh River is low enough to ford otherwise an out-and-back hike.
General location: 24 miles northeast of McCall.
Maps: Box Lake, Loon Lake, and Victor Peak (7.5') USGS quads.
Special attractions: A variety of scenery, rugged mountains, a relatively large, low elevation mountain lake.
Difficulty: Moderately easy to Loon Lake. Moderate above.
Season: Mid-June through September.
Information: McCall Ranger District, Payette National Forest, Box 1026, McCall, Idaho 83638; (208) 634-0700.

The hike: February 1943. A four-engine bomber on a routine flight from Nevada to Idaho's Mountain Home airbase is lost in the snow above the rugged peaks of the Salmon River Mountains. Searching for a radio beam coming out of Oregon, the pilot sees he will soon run out of gas, and he starts to nose the plane down. Through the swirling clouds, jagged glacier-carved peaks reach up, locked in winter's grip. Surely landing the bomber in the rugged terrain is impossible. The pilot is not even sure where he is—somewhere over central Idaho in the dead of winter.

Suddenly, the canyon opens up and, miraculously, a field one-half mile in diameter lies below. It is surrounded by an expanse of trees, and mountains loom at one end. The pilot edges the bomber around and makes a once-only-and-forever approach with the wheels up. The lumbering plane drops into the opening and skids across the field—a frozen lake. It slides into the lodgepole pine on the far side, tearing off the wings. The fuselage careens through the trees and stops. One aviator suffers a broken leg; no one is killed.

How the aviators escaped from these mountains in winter with no winter gear, snowshoes, food, or information on their position has become a local legend. That they got out, after several of them walked overland for days without snowshoes across mountain passes buried 12 feet deep in snow, attests to their determination and courage.

The patch of snow that appeared out of the mountain vastness and saved their lives is Loon Lake. The wreckage can still be seen near the lake, although for 45 years hikers have carved their names in it and carried off souvenirs like a band of army ants.

To approach Loon Lake from McCall, turn north at McCall onto the Warren Wagon Road (Forest Service # 22), and drive towards Burgdorf. This "wagon road" is paved for 31 miles north of McCall to the Burgdorf junction. Turn right at the junction and continue eight miles east until you cross over the Secesh River. Shortly after the crossing, on the right, you'll see a sign for Chinook Campground. Turn here onto a road that is dirt for the last mile to the campground.

The trail to Loon Lake can be done as a loop, although completion of the loop is possible only after the Secesh River has receded enough to wade in mid-summer. Assuming that you take this hike in mid-summer, ford the Secesh one-half mile above the campground. It is a wide, gentle stream at this point. The trail gradually climbs up the side of the canyon and away from the immediate vicinity of the river. (If the Secesh is too high to ford, you can head southeast along the river's east side for about 3.5 miles. There you'll find a bridge across the river. Then you can head west along the trail to Loon Lake. See the map.)

The name "Secesh" has an interesting origin. During the Civil War, when Warren (12 miles to the east) was one of the largest towns in what was to become Idaho, the people in the area were deeply divided in their loyalties. The town of Warren physically divided itself. Part called itself Washington, and part belonged to the secessionists. Some of the rebels moved to the river, which became known as the Secessionist River or Secesh.

The five miles of trail to Loon Lake is mostly lodgepole pine and huckleberry habitat—excellent for deer and elk. It's also a fine place to see Wilson's warbler, cassin finch, spotted sandpiper, Hammond's flycatcher, rough-winged swallows, pine siskin, chipping sparrow, dark-eyed junco, and the yellow-rumped warbler.

Two miles before Loon Lake, a trail leaves to the right (northwest) up Willow

Admiring the view from Loon Lake. Nelle Tobias photo.

Basket Creek. It is well-maintained, wandering up a clear stream and across verdant meadows to end at Ruby Meadows. (Unfortunately, by the time this book goes to press, a foreign corporation might be gouging Ruby Meadows for gold. These valleys are just now recovering from the effects of mining done a hundred years ago. Let your elected representatives know your opinion on letting foreign interests exploit this area.)

Just past the junction of the trail to Ruby Meadows and a second trail which leads up Victor Creek, you'll cross Victor Creek over a bridge. Then it's about 1.5 miles over hill and through meadows to Loon Lake. Just before Loon Lake, you'll meet a trail in a meadow that heads down the Secesh River. This is the trail you will take back to Chinook Campground. Still another trail leaves from the edge of the same meadow, heading southeast to Split Creek.

Loon Lake sits at the bottom of a large meadow. The mountains in the Loon Creek drainage above the lake rise in a manner reminiscent of Switzerland. There are occasional loons at Loon Lake. Loons are birds with legs located so far back on their bodies they cannot stand on the ground like ducks. On land, a loon can only push and slide on its belly, so they build their nests close to the water. They are adept swimmers that dive for their food, and they are graceful fliers. Listen for their piercing, haunting cry—truly the call of the wild.

You can head down to the Secesh River from Loon Lake and complete the loop in five miles. You'll drop 250 feet in 1.5 miles from the lake to the river which is bridged. Of course, for a longer excursion, you can continue up the Loon Creek drainage. Circle to the right around the lake on a trail that is clearly-marked and easy to follow. You'll pass through numerous forest habitats while climbing to the source of Loon Lake—forest lodgepole pine, then Douglas fir, followed by spruce, and finally, subalpine fir. Up the drainage, avalanche corridors have torn loose whole hillsides of trees and piled them like matchsticks on the valley floor below. In some places the trail is cut through trees stacked four feet high.

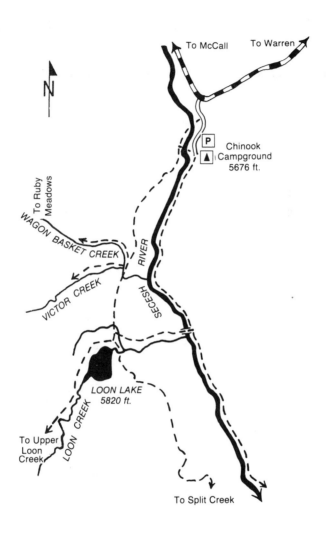

You'll encounter only one crossing of Loon Creek. After mid-June, you should be able to cross on log jams or ford. Near Loon Creek's headwaters the trail passes beneath South Loon Mountain. It and its neighbor, North Loon just to the east, are the highest peaks in the South Fork of the Salmon River drainage.

In January of 1980, with Ron Watters and Greg Eames, I attempted a winter ascent of North Loon (9,322 feet). During one 48-hour period, we had 40 inches of snow dumped on us which collapsed our tent. The only structures that could withstand the heavy snow were igloos. After four days, we retreated in waist deep snow. The passes out of Loon Creek remain thus locked in white until late June.—*Jerry Dixon* □

HIKE 28 *THIRTYTHREE LAKE*

General description: A short but rigorous weekend hike to a high mountain lake.
General location: In the Lick Creek Mountains, 18 miles northeast of McCall.
Maps: Box Lake (7.5') USGS quad.
Special attractions: A very deep lake in a cirque basin containing mackinaw (lake trout) and rainbow trout.
Difficulty: Difficult, due to the need for some route-finding.
Season: Late June to early September.
Information: Payette National Forest, Box 1026, McCall, Idaho 83638; (208) 634-0700.

The hike: Thirtythree Lake is named for its size of approximately 33 surface acres. It sits in a high mountain basin on the headwaters of the North Fork of Fitzum Creek. Fitzum Creek is a tributary of the South Fork of the Salmon River. This lake was stocked with mackinaw by pack train countless years ago. These have naturally reproduced since the initial planting. The lake also contains numerous rainbow trout.

Drive 18 miles northeast of McCall on the Lick Creek Summit road (see Box Lake hike description for directions to the Lick Creek Summit road). Approximately three miles before Lick Creek Summit, the road makes a switchback. There is a parking turnout that will accommodate about five vehicles, but otherwise the trailhead is not marked.

You'll need a topographic map for this hike, although the trail is not shown on the map. There is a sheep trail of sorts at the beginning of the hike; unfortunately, the Forest Service allowed grazing during the summer of 1982 which resulted in degradation of the drainage and a once pristine mountain meadow beneath the saddle overlooking the lake.

Near the turnout, just north of the small creek emptying the drainage, you'll find the beginning of the trail. After about one mile the trail disappears, although cairns in strategic locations mark the final portion of the route. You'll climb continually through pine forest paralleling the creek but keeping far enough north to maintain high ground. When you come to the lush meadow, it's best to circle a little farther north, as the meadow is usually wet. The creek forks in the meadow. Continue on the north side of the forks to arrive at an

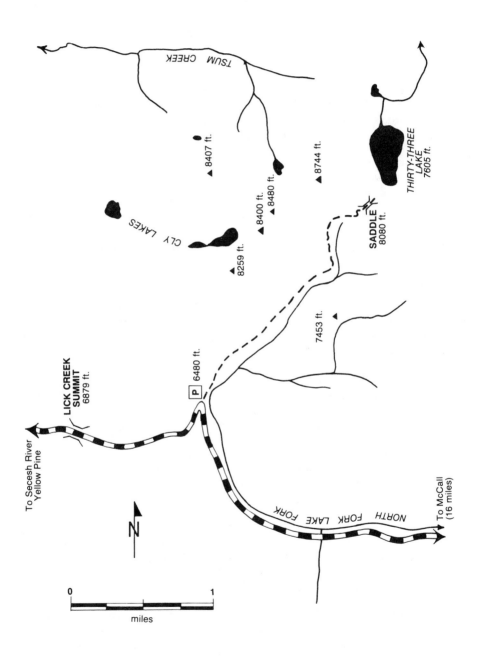

open slope of bitterbrush, sagebrush, and deer browse. This is a fairly steep ascent of several hundred feet.

Upon reaching an open alpine meadow, the best route is up the middle of the draw and then towards the right to a rock terrace. You must use caution, for the going is very steep and there is no trail. The last 500 feet up is marked by cairns but still requires scrambling with both hands and feet for balance.

From the saddle you can see Thirtythree Lake. Notice the extreme depth of the lake and the large boulders in it and on its west slope. You'll drop down from the saddle 500 feet to the western end of the lake. Although the descent is steep, you can pick your way down through enormous boulders.

Campsites are not abundant. There are several overused sites on the west shore, but it's better to follow the lake to the east shore and near the outlet to establish your camp. Be sure to check out the view from the outlet of the lake. Thirtythree Lake is perched at the top of the North Fork of Fitzum Creek. From this vantage point, you can gaze down the deep canyon and beyond to the Salmon River Mountains that stretch to the east as far as you can see.— *Philip Blomquist* □

Salmon River and Clearwater Mountains

Overview

If you can imagine a continuous mass of mountain ridges and canyons 300 miles long and 100 miles wide, you'll see the Salmon River Mountains. This continuous mass comprises most of central and northern Idaho. Here, three great wilderness areas have been designated—the River of No Return, the Selway-Bitterroot, and the Gospel Hump. More wilderness still should be designated. This continuous rugged stretch of ridges has largely precluded human habitation and development and has cut northern Idaho off from southern Idaho both economically and socially. Only now, with timber cutting fueled by taxpayer subsidies, are these mountains yielding to the bulldozer.

The mountains north of Boise to where the Main Fork of the Salmon River cuts directly through the mountains from east to west are generally called the Salmon River Mountains. North of the Salmon River they are called the Clearwater Mountains, although there is really no scientific distinction. This huge mountain fastness is largely made of granite and granitelike rocks formed out of one of the largest batholiths in the world—the famous Idaho Batholith. A batholith is an enormous intrusion of molten rock that cools before it reaches the surface as lava. It is then gradually exposed by weather, water, and uplift.

These mountains are not easily subdivided into lesser mountain ranges. Names such as the Lick Creek Mountains, the Big Horn Crags, the Tango Peaks, or the Grandmother Mountains are only names attached by history to certain spectacular portions of indefinite extent.

All of the major wildlife species of the Northern Rockies inhabit these mountains, with moose being limited largely to the Clearwater Mountains portion.

The lower elevations are accessible as early as April, since the canyon bottoms are as low as 2,000 feet. The heights of the mountains reach up to 10,000 feet. Strangely, the highest portion of these mountains surround the low areas of the Middle, South Fork, and Main Fork of the Salmon River. This is due to isostacy, wherein the removal by erosion of the mountain mass that once filled these enormous, 5,000 -foot-deep canyons actually caused the adjacent land to rise.

The number of hiking and backpacking trails in this 30,000-square-mile region sometimes seems to be almost infinite. This boo k describes only a small representative portion of these trails. □

HIKE 29 *PARTRIDGE CREEK—LAVA RIDGE LOOP*

General description: A difficult 15-mile loop trail into the forest primeval and ridge country of a little-known, unprotected wilderness north of McCall.
General location: 25 linear miles northwest of McCall in the Salmon River Mountains.
Special attractions: American wilderness in the first person; old-growth Douglas fir, tamaracks, and ponderosa pine; spectacular views and immense solitude; access to nearby mountains lakes.
Maps: Patrick Butte, Hershey Point, and Hazard Lake (7.5') USGS quads.
Difficulty: Difficult due to stream crossings, elevation changes, route finding.
Season: Late June through September.
Information: New Meadows Ranger District, Payette National Forest, Box J, New Meadows, Idaho 83654; (208) 347-2141.

The hike: This is a beautiful, but tough, loop hike that takes three or four days. You'll travel in deep old-growth forest and over Lava Ridge, where you'll find sublime views of the surrounding forest, canyons, and mountains. The loop is in the 120,000-acre French Creek Roadless Area a very wild piece of country that the Forest Service should have recommended for wilderness classification but has not, due to pressure from timber companies.

To reach the trailhead, drive west on Idaho Highway 55 from McCall toward New Meadows. Turn right at the Brundage Mountain turnoff and drive toward the Brundage Mountain Ski Resort. Stay left and turn onto a well-maintained gravel road at the junction with the ski resort road. Drive north on this, the Goose Lake road, for about 15 miles. You pass side roads that lead right (east) to Hazard Lake and Big Hazard Lake, but the main road is distinct. The road ends at the Clayburn trailhead, where there are rest facilities, a turnout, and a sign showing trails, lakes, and prominent features.

Put on your gear and head north past the sign to follow a forest road that has been effectively closed to vehicles by ditching. The Forest Service has done a good job of keeping four-wheel-drive vehicles off this abandoned road.

In two miles you climb about 300 feet through forest and meadow to Warm Springs Saddle. The two-lane footpath ends at the saddle, where a small meadow provides a good place to camp if you get a late start. Trails leave the saddle to go south, west, and north. A sign marks this junction. Take the north trail across the meadow. The trail is not visible in the meadow, but go past a small spring (good drinking water) and you will pick the trail up again.

At the saddle, an impressive slab of granite towers above the forest to the west. This is Hard Butte (8,600 feet). Some years, snowfields cling to its skirts throughout the summer. On the summit are the ruins of an old fire lookout.

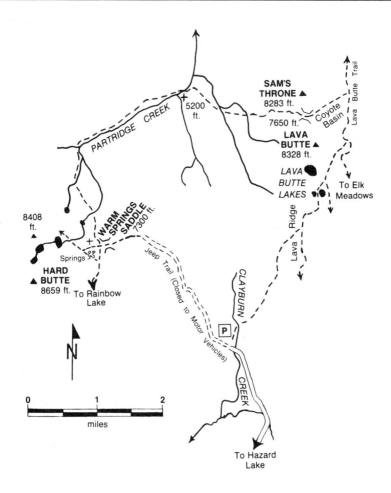

Just north of Hard Butte is a basin with several small lakes. The Forest Service is considering converting the lookout to an unattended interpretive center with maps showing major features of the area.

The trail descends from the saddle into the headwaters of Partridge Creek by dropping 1,300 feet in two miles. Wind downward through verdant forest of Douglas fir. Calliope hummingbirds swirl through the air and mountain chickadees call from the lofty branches of fir trees.

After two miles the trail makes a right angle turn with the canyon. The canyon broadens a bit and becomes less steep, although you drop another 700 feet in the next two miles. The deeper you plunge into this forest primeval, the higher and darker the forest seems to become. Majestic yellow pines and

Douglas fir grow here; some of them are older than our nation. Tamaracks reach diameters of three feet. Watch for deer and elk in the dense foliage. Old-growth forests like this one host the goshawk, which can live in no other kind of habitat.

Here, four miles from Warm Springs Saddle, the trail crosses Partridge Creek. Instead of continuing down the canyon, take the faint trail (mostly blazes) that parallels the creek a short distance and then starts a steep climb out of the canyon to a notch between Lava Butte and Sam's Throne. Look carefully for the blazes. You will cross several streamlets; however, the blazes are always visible on the other side of the crossings. The trail climbs 1,500 feet in one mile to the pass. This is a good place to stick close to the trail to avoid getting off-route. The trail ascends to a bench above Partridge Creek. This ascent involves a contouring around the toe of a lava slope. From the bench, cross two streamlets and pass through meadows where the flowers and perennials are chest high. The last half-mile of trail grinds up an almost 80 percent slope to a pass, but the view is well worth the climb. It's even better if you scramble up Sam's Throne to the north or Lava Butte to the south. The basin with the wet meadow below you is Coyote Basin, although some call it Mosquito Basin.

From the top of Lava Butte, nature in all its glory stretches out before you. Westward you look across probing fingers of lava to the fortress of Patrick Butte. This area is unique as it represents an overlap of Columbia River basalt and the central Idaho Batholith. To the northwest is the Salmon River country. Partridge Creek drops out of sight below you as it runs north into the Salmon River and the summer time sunset. Gospel Hump and Buffalo Hump, visible to the northwest, are protected by the Gospel Hump Wilderness Area created in 1979. Due north, the Salmon River seems to melt into the chasm below. From here you can tell that this canyon is deeper than the famous Grand Canyon. Elk Meadows lies due east, as do the clearcuts in Elkhorn Creek— the only evidence of human intrusion in sight.

French Creek runs northward just east of Elk Meadows. The prominent faces of Storm Peak and North Loon stand out in the Lick Creek Mountains to the southeast. Bruin Mountain and Blacktip lie south of Lava Butte at the headwaters of French Creek. Rejoice—there is still country wild enough to get lost in!

After crossing the pass, descend to the north edge of Coyote Meadows. The trail is marked with cairns. Proceed eastward to the meadow's outlet. Here you will see a rock field to the north. Cross the outlet here and look for the trail on the east side. Another half-mile brings you to a junction. Take the right fork. The left fork trail goes to Hershey Point and eventually the Salmon River.

The trail climbs about 200 feet over the shoulder of Lava Butte then descends to the basin of Lava Butte Lakes. There are several good camping spots here.

The continuing trail passes between the two lower Lava Butte Lakes and then climbs abruptly up onto Lava Ridge. In August, fields of flowers await you here. Hike southward along the ridge until another marked trail comes up from the east from Heather Basin. Here you must head west, away from the edge of the ridge. A sign on top says "Goose Creek Road 2.5 Miles" but this will put you down the road several miles from your vehicle. Instead find the trail that leads west. It's evident about 100 feet from the ridge crest. This trail winds down the back of the ridge to the Clayburn trailhead. The beautiful purple flowers between the large areas of bare ground are lupine—a poisonous

Patrick Butte landmark in Partridge Creek drainage. Nelle Tobias photo.

member of the pea family. They spread when an area is overgrazed. Until just a few years ago thousands of livestock were herded through here each year. The loss of topsoil and the lupines are reminders.

Partridge Creek is an area as wild as all America once was. It should be kept that way if only as a memory of our heritage.—*Jerry Dixon*☐

Note: Several miles of the trail in Partridge Creek burned in the Warm Springs fire of 1992 and still more in the giant Corral Creek fire of 1994. Fall 1994 found the trail in poor condition, but hikable. Horse use is not recommended. There are plans to reconstruct the trail sometime after 1996. Most of nearby French Creek also burned in 1994. With luck, salvage logging will be limited to areas that are not fragile or roadless.

HIKE 30 *HAT CREEK LAKES*

General description: An excellent location in the Hat Creek Lakes Basin for an isolated weekend of high mountain lake fishing.
General location: 28 road miles north of Challis on the divide of Morgan and Panther creeks.
Maps: Wards Butte, Taylor Mountain, and Black Mountain (7.5') USGS quads.
Special attractions: An obscure trail (not shown on the maps) to a lake basin with excellent cutthroat trout fishing.
Difficulty: Moderately difficult.
Season: Mid-July to mid-September
Information: Cobalt Ranger District, Salmon National Forest, Box 729, Salmon, Idaho 83467; (208) 756-2240.

The hike: Hat Creek Lakes Basin is situated in the Salmon National Forest just east of Morgan Creek Summit. The hike in is about four miles—unless

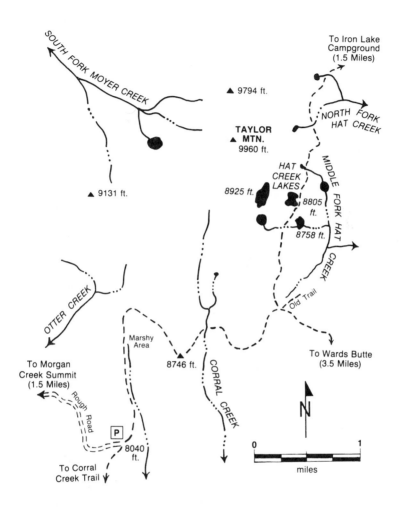

you're driving a sedan, in which case it's better not to try to drive the last 2.5 miles of jeep road. Hat Creek Lakes basin has good fishing for cutthroat. The more ambitious and skilled can try their luck for Arctic grayling after a cross-country trek to a lake emptying into the South Fork of Moyer Creek.

This hike provides an alternative route to the basin and is less crowded than the more commonly used route from the Iron Lake trailhead. To reach the trailhead, drive nine miles north of Challis on U.S. Highway 93 to the Morgan Creek turnoff on the left. This is a good all-weather gravel road. Follow it approximately 19 miles to Morgan Creek Summit. Just past a sign indicating the summit's elevation of 7,578 feet, turn right on a rough dirt road. This four-mile-long road climbs to over 8,000 feet. It is in poor shape, sporting large ruts, rocks, and projecting tree roots. Unless you have a four-wheel-drive vehicle, you'll need to stop within about 1.5 miles and start hiking.

Proceed to an undeveloped trailhead. Here a trail to Corral Creek begins to the south. The road to Hat Creek Lakes climbs to the northeast where it soon becomes a trail. One mile from here, the trail temporarily disappears in a marshy meadow. Cross the meadow and creek. The trail continues on the east side but is not obvious until you cross the bog. Continue climbing through the forest along the creek. Soon you will reach a ridge where you can look down into Otter Creek. The trail cuts back in a southeasterly direction and climbs to 8,746 feet. From this vantage point you can see down both forks of the mostly heavily forested Corral Creek.

Next the trail descends a hundred feet in one-half mile to Corral Creek. You'll find good camping sites here in this lush meadow with tall grasses.

Follow the trail and begin climbing again. In another half-mile, you'll climb around another forested ridge to 8,946 feet. From here the trail continues north to a saddle, where you'll encounter a junction of trails. The trail to your right leads south along the ridge to Wards Butte. The trail on your left leads to Hat Creek Lakes. This junction is deceptive. An old trail drops immediately down the saddle from the junction to dead end in a large meadow. Don't follow it. Instead, backtrack 25 yards and follow a trail to the left that climbs slightly and stays at an elevation of 9,060 feet through large pine trees.

Once you find this trail, it's an easy mile to Hat Creek Lakes Basin. The trail first passes above a small nameless lake, marked on the topographic map simply as "8,758" (feet). Continue for another half-mile to lake 8,805. There are many good places to camp at this lake, or you can climb west to an even larger lake that also has good camping sites. Both lakes contain an abundance of cutthroat for excellent fishing.

If you wish to explore further, you can climb the steep, rocky saddle south of Taylor Mountain. On the other side of this cross-country side trip is the South Fork of Moyer Creek and a lake draining into it. Here you'll find slow fishing for Arctic grayling.

If you prefer to take the usual route to Hat Creek Lakes Basin, you can hike in from the north from Iron Lakes. The Salmon River road leads to Upper Iron Lake and a forest campground. A four-mile-long trail crosses several saddles nearly 9,000 feet in elevation. If you prefer, however, to avoid other hikers, you should take the Morgan Creek route.—*Philip Blomquist* □

HIKE 31 *MEADOW CREEK TRAIL*

General description: A shady streamside retreat, in the early stretches, in one of the most quietly beautiful places on earth. This trail rises to cover, in total, 15 miles.

General location: 20 miles from Lowell, Idaho, in the Nez Perce National Forest.

Maps: Selway Falls, Anderson Butte, Vermilion Peak, and Sable Hill (7.5') USGS quads.

Special attractions: Lovely, fern-covered, narrow stone walls in a shady walk along sizable Meadow Creek to climb to the Meadow Creek Ranger Station, available to public use by reservation. First portion makes a good family hike.
Difficulty: Easy for first three miles, difficult for one mile, then moderate.
Season: Early April to November.
Information: Selway Ranger District, Nez Perce National Forest, HC 75 Box 91, Kooskia, Idaho 83539; (208) 926-4258.

The hike: Fifteen miles up the Meadow Creek drainage of the Selway River system is the Meadow Creek ranger station, available until hunting season for public use if reservations are made. The first three miles along Meadow Creek are easy, making this a good day hike.

The Meadow Creek area is contiguous with the western side of the Selway-Bitterroot Wilderness but is not part of the designated wilderness. Conservationists lobbied hard to have the Meadow Creek Roadless Area, particularly its east side, added to the Selway-Bitterroot Wilderness in 1980 when Idaho Sen. Frank Church was guiding the River of No Return Wilderness bill through Congress. While Sen. Church ultimately did agree to make some significant additions along the southern edge of the Selway-Bitterroot (along the Magruder Corridor), he was never convinced to add Meadow Creek. For political reasons, most likely having to do with satisfying timber interests in nearby Elk City, Idaho, Senator Church ignored the pleadings of conservationists, even though he understood the need to preserve this pristine, but fragile, area.

As of 1990, the Meadow Creek drainage is still largely roadless, and the Nez Perce National Forest plan for the area is to leave it mostly as is, at least for the next few years. Still, concerned citizens may yet have to fight to save Meadow Creek fro m bulldozers and chainsaws. For its part, the Forest Service has recently been working to upgrade the Meadow Creek Trail, and, recognizing its beauty and popularity, has included the trail as part of the National Recreation Trail System. Let us hope that future generations of Forest Service decision makers continue to recognize the importance of Meadow Creek as de facto wilderness. Better yet, perhaps someday we will see this magnificent area added to the Selway-Bitterroot Wilderness.

From Lewiston, Idaho, follow U.S. Highway 12 up the Clearwater River about 97 miles to Lowell, Idaho, where the Lochsa and Selway join to form the Clearwater (known as Three Forks). Cross the bridge at the confluence and follow the Selway River road (#223) approximately 17 miles to Selway Falls.

The road is paved as far as the Fenn Ranger Station, four miles from the confluence, where information and a telephone are available. Campgrounds with and without water are located on both beach and hill side of the road.

Selway Falls is a magnificent sight during the spring. At dusk, osprey fish here as well as at other sites along the river. The simple, old Selway Falls ranger station gives a taste of timelessness.

Cross the Selway on the one-lane bridge just above the ranger station and begin following Meadow Creek along a narrow, but good, dirt road. Roads first to Elk City and then to the Indian Hill Lookout take off from either side of this stretch.

HIKE 31 *MEADOW CREEK TRAIL*

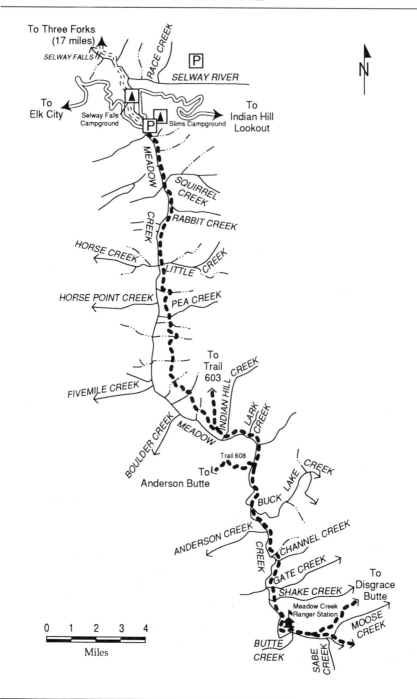

Two camping areas, Selway Falls and Slims Campground, are located along the two miles between the bridge and the trailhead. Both have water and pit toilets. Slims Campground has two or three sites, ample parking, and facilities for pack animals.

Perched to the right of Meadow Creek under graceful pines, these sites are more beautiful than those at Selway Falls. However, the stock bedded here also draw flies and give that intimate odor of the stable. Flies are prevalent along the trail too but seem to be the type which merely annoy rather than eat humans.

To begin the hike, park at Slims Campground and find the trailhead at the south (upstream) end of the area. (Note the sign which reminds you that, currently, fishing season begins on July 1 for Meadow Creek.) The trail begins at 1,800 feet and continues with virtually no change in elevation for the first three miles. The canyon of Meadow Creek is narrower than that of the Selway and has a tree canopy which provides a welcome retreat from the heat which can build up in these low elevation canyons in July and August. Ferns and lichen-covered rock walls add to the coolness. Mica glitters in the mostly dirt surface of the trail.

Crystalline Meadow Creek quietly rushes over boulders and log jams or pools in the shade of old growth cedars. While the bank is mostly rocky, there are some pockets of sand. The trail offers opportunities to slip over to creek's edge to rest or fish. The rainbow and cutthroat always seem to be biting. While you will release a lot of small ones, there is an occasional 10- to 12-incher.

A little over a mile up the trail, you will encounter Squirrel Creek, the first of several charming rivulets which bubble and churn into Meadow Creek. Rabbit Creek follows a half mile later. Squirrel Creek has a bridge and Rabbit Creek is narrow enough to be stepped over.

The third, Little Creek, marks the end of the easy part of the trail. Forest Service maps and trail signs indicate that a trail to Horse Point branches off to the west side of Meadow Creek here, but I was unable to locate it. Rangers at Fenn Station say that the Horse Point Trail has not been maintained. Just on the other side of the bridge which crosses Little Creek is a large cleared area which has been used as a camping site. However, this is not a designated site and so has no fire rings or toilet. Extreme care should be taken to preserve the health of this pristine location by making sure your latrine is at least 200 feet from the margins of both Meadow and Little creeks.

Whether you stay or not, a ramble through the brush to Meadow Creek's edge is well worthwhile. Horse Creek tumbles out of the steep west wall of the canyon into a pool where fish laze. Here there are also some beautiful, deep pools. You can stand on boulders and look straight down into clear water 10 to 20 feet deep. Looking upstream, you will see the canyon narrow into a trailless gorge of cliffs and white water.

The next stretch of trail brings a half mile of switchbacks, not indicated on the USGS map, which ascend from Little Creek along the steep hillside to an elevation about 800 feet higher. The trail then stays at this level for about five miles before dropping back down to Meadow Creek. Replenish your water supply before leaving Little Creek because Pea Creek, the only one indicated as permanent on the USGS maps, is a mere trickle in July. This trickle veils the mouth of a cave I didn't have the nerve to inspect.

As the trail traverses the hillside, the timber opens up on this fairly dry west-facing ridge to expose the vast timber stands to the south and west. This is a view of one of the most remote, fragile sections of this de facto, undesignated, central Idaho wilderness.

The trail drops quickly to where Indian Hill Creek joins Meadow Creek. Just before the creeks is the junction with trail #603. The trailhead is on the road near Indian Hill Lookout. This is 3,000 feet higher and 4.5 miles away but makes a 13-mile loop with vehicles at either end an interesting possibility.

A mile beyond Indian Hill Creek and just beyond the Lark Creek bridge is another trail junction. Trail #608 fords Meadow Creek and climbs west to Anderson Butte. The Meadow Creek Trail continues six more miles, crossing Buck Lake Creek, Channel Creek, Gate Creek, and Snake Creek, none of which require fording, before arriving at the Meadow Creek Ranger Station.

The Meadow Creek Ranger Station offers cabin accommodations for eight, including six beds and mattresses. There are also pit toilets and a woodshed. The kitchen has indoor plumbing and a propane-powered refrigerator and is equipped with dishes and pot s and pans for six. A newly-built corral and barn accommodate livestock, but grazing is not allowed in the station area. The cost (as of 1989) is $25 per night. Reservations can be made by contacting the Selway Ranger District of the Nez Perce National Forest.

The Meadow Creek Recreation Trail can be a peaceful excursion in midsummer, but after mid-September, the area is heavily used by hunters.— *Charmaine Wellington with Don Crawford* □

HIKE 32 *RED MOUNTAIN LAKES AND LOOKOUT*

General description: A day hike or weekend backpack through subalpine meadows and woods to several trailless lake basins.

General location: Northwest of Lowman, between the South Fork of the Payette River and Bear Valley, in the proposed Red Mountain Wilderness.

Maps: Cache Creek and Miller Mtn. East (7.5') USGS quads, and Boise National Forest map.

Special attractions: Easily accessible and close to Boise; terrific views of the Sawtooth Mountains and most of the Boise National Forest.

Difficulty: Moderately difficult due to some cross-country route finding.

Season: Early July into October.

nformation: Lowman Ranger District, Boise National Forest, HC 77, Box 3020, Lowman, Idaho 83637; (208) 364-4250.

The hike: The proposed 100,000 acre Red Mountain Wilderness is a magnificent land. In the south, this wildland is deeply dissected by steep ponderosa canyonlands; to the north it is high and rolling, heavily forested with lodgepole pine, subalpine fir, and Englemann spruce. It has excellent elk summer range and plenty of mule deer; it also has high quality habitat for mountain goat. There are a number of well established elk calving and rearing areas, and, along the border with the South Fork of the Payette, lies key elk winter range.

Anchoring this extensive wildland on the west is Red Mountain itself. At 8,772 feet, it is the highest mountain in this portion of the Boise National Forest— the summit was topped by a lookout for many years, now dismantled

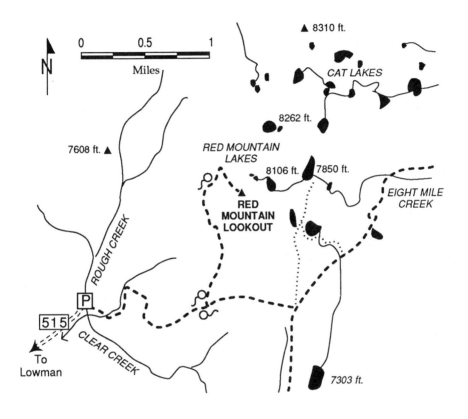

and overgrown with raspberries. Fanning out to the north and east in four different drainages lie the Lost Lakes, Cat Lakes, Red Mountain Lakes, and Clear Creek Lakes. These lakes provide the trout fishing and spectacular camping to ease many a winter night's dreaming and to invigorate many a summer weekend.

Leaving Lowman and Idaho Highway 21, turn north on the Clear Creek Road (Forest Service #582) and head toward Bear Valley. At 12 miles leave this thoroughfare for the road less taken, bearing east on #515. This road is passable to most passenger cars as long as one is willing to move the larger rocks out of the way. At about 4.5 miles you'll encounter the Red Mountain Transfer Camp with its picnic tables, a firepit, shady tentsites, and lots of parking.

From here motorized vehicles should be left behind. Hike the last half mile of road #515 through sunny meadows and beside Clear Creek to the trail register. The trail proper immediately crosses Rough Creek on a bridge then travels up a small tributary canyon, satisfyingly verdant and cool. The tributary in the summer is easily forded with a couple of quick steps. Next comes the steepest pull of the hike along a west-slope sidehill through lodgepole and Douglas fir. The trail then veers east into the open and the first views of the Sawtooths. At about two miles and 1,000 feet of elevation gain, the trail comes to a junction with the lookout trail (on the left, leading northeast) near a small spring.

The detour is highly recommended—pitch the packs and head on up for 1.3 miles and 1,300 feet of switchback and contour through mostly open forest. Keep a sharp eye out for elk that frequent this slope in the summer. The trail is heavily eroded from years of horse-packing to supply the lookout.

The summit arrives before one expects, with views in all directions: from Schafer Butte right behind Boise to the White Cloud Peaks poking up beyond the Sawtooth Range. At one's feet (plus several hundred more feet) the Red Mountain Lakes spill downward and east.

Back on the main trail (which leads east and is shown on the Boise National Forest map as trail #145), one travels through lush and ungrazed (by livestock anyway) meadows strewn with flowers in July and buzzing with hummingbirds. Then there is a stretch of subalpine forest to finish the first three miles. Here one comes to a junction with the Kirkham Ridge Trail (#144) and a choice. One route to Red Mountain Lakes takes you a half mile eastward on the Kirkham Ridge Trail. Just past the wet meadow on the left and a trickle across the path, turn left to go cross-country through the woods and climb two open slopes to reach the Clear Creek Lake (not named on the Miller Mtn., East, map). If you don't find it too beautiful to just stay, hike around the lake on the west side and veer left through a small, rocky saddle ahead (a small tarn in the saddle reassures that you are in the right place) in order to drop down to the middle (7,850 feet) of the three biggest Red Mountain Lakes. The alternative route heads straight up the meadow from the trail junction on a tiny footpath which soon peters out—stay along the edge of the ridge and keep the saddle ahead, once it becomes visible. Below on the right, Clear Creek Lake will appear, partially obscured by trees. It is possible to traverse along the slope to visit this lake if so desired.

The lowest of the Red Mountain Lakes has great fishing, but not the best camping—for this, stay at the middle lake. If the Cat Lakes catch your fancy, the easiest way to get started in this drainage is to pop over the low ridge at the north end of the middle Red Mountain Lake, just below the (fairly) red face that gives this mountain its name.

Extensions? You name it: 9.5 miles along the Kirkham Ridge Trail to Bull Trout Lake, 11.5 miles over Eight-Mile Mountains to the Warm Springs trailhead, or 15 miles of meander on the broad slopes of Miller Mountain to Road #558 above Lowman.

Red Mountain has been proposed in its entirety by the Idaho Wildlands

Defense Coalition for wilderness designation. Its preeminent character has been recognized: the Boise National Forest has recommended 93,000 acres for wilderness; unfortunately, important winter range for elk has been omitted in the Fivemile and Kettle Creek drainages in order to allow timber harvest. The McClure/Andrus Idaho Forest Management Act, first put forth in 1988, protects Fivemile and Kettle Creeks proper but omits the entire eastern third of the proposed Red Mountain Wilderness. This omitted portion contains over two-thirds of the wilderness' trail miles. This strange mistake appears to have been a concession to off-road vehicles—which currently have over three-quarters of the trail miles of the Boise National Forest. Adding together timber harvests, ORV soil damage and wildlife harassment, not to mention recreation conflict, the conclusion must be that all of Red Mountain should be saved.—*Erik Fisher* □

Lemhi Mountains

Overview

Over 100 miles long as the crow flies, longer still with the kinks stretched out, the Lemhi Range rises out of the arid lava of the Snake River Plain and advances northwest to Central Idaho.

These mountains, which form a high, nearly continuous ridge, are relatively arid in their southern reaches despite the fact that numerous peaks thrust upwards above 11,000 feet. Towering Diamond Peak, for example, reaches 12,197 feet, making it the third tallest in Idaho. Nevertheless, one can climb it without the use of ice axe in late June.

The Lemhi Mountains lie in a rain shadow, and the moisture of Pacific storms is dissipated first by the many mountain ranges of Central Idaho. In the southern Lemhis the precipitation that does fall percolates rapidly down through the limestone and dolomite that constitute the mountains' vertebrae. There is a general absence of lakes and creeks.

One ought not be misled by arid beauty of the southern Lemhis, however. June storms can dump as much snow as a winter blast and summer thunderstorms can be violent. In 1987 a tornado touched down in Sawmill Canyon.

Northward these mountains shrink to a "mere" 10,000 to 11,000 feet but compensate as their girth spreads to 15 or 20 miles. Here the sedimentary rock formed under ancient seas gives way to harder rock. As you travel from south to north, dolomite first appears then changes to an assortment of quartzites through which a number of mineral-bespeckled intrusions have pushed. Adding color, the quartzites of the northern Lemhis are covered in places by the chocolate, red, black, brown, gray, and maroon of the younger Challis volcanics, the result of a vast outpouring of volcanic activity 25,000,000 to 50,000,000 years ago. These volcanics washed over and cover large parts of east and south Central Idaho.

Thanks to the harder rock, water stays on the surface in the northern Lemhis. Cirque lakes huddle beneath peaks and permanent creeks run down almost every canyon.

Despite years of prospecting, sporadic timber cutting, and little official attention to recreation, the Forest Service has identified almost 500,000 acres of roadless land in these mountains suitable for wilderness designation by Congress. Most of the roadless land is in two large blocks. In the southern Lemhis, there is a 187,000 acre roadless area. The larger, in the northern Lemhis is over 300,000 acres.

Idaho environmentalists are proposing that Congress designate 130,000 acres in the south and 180,000 acres in the north as the Lemhi Wilderness. The southern roadless area is sometimes referred to as the Diamond Peak proposed wilderness in reference to the giant pyramidal peak that rises five miles west of the gas stop/store/cafe called Lone Pine. The Forest Service did propose a small wilderness in the north during the late 1970s, but under pressure changed its mind. None of Idaho's present major politicians are proposing that these mountains be protected as designated wilderness.

Four great high desert valleys flank the Lemhi Mountains. To the north are the Pahsimeroi and Lemhi valleys, lying on the west and the east sides of the Lemhis respectively. To the south is the Little Lost River Valley on the southwest side and the Birch Creek Valley on the southeast. The streams draining down these valleys flow into the volcanic rock of the Snake River Plain and disappear.

These four valleys support the majority of Idaho's pronghorn antelope. You may see them as them speed with seemingly little effort over the desert and open mountain slopes. With massive lungs they sometimes will race alongside your vehicle and even overtake it on a gravel road to pass in front of you. In addition to antelope it is common to see deer and even elk patrolling the valley floor and foothills. Even black bear are sometimes seen in the valleys. Here truly, the deer and the antelope play.

The typical Lemhi Range hike proceeds like this: A dirt road leaves the highway and gradually deteriorates into a jeep track near the mouth, or a little way up a canyon. Intelligence gets the best of inertia and you park. Wearing your pack now, you follow as the track deteriorates further, and then you set out cross-country. This usually isn't difficult for in many places these mountains, like the nearby Lost River and Beaverhead Mountains, have little underbrush.

Be sure to take the prescribed topographic maps from the U.S. Geological Survey along. Most of the Lemhi Range and adjacent valleys are covered by a new set of these in the 7.5 minute size. The maps are usually as much for navigating the maze of dirt roads in the valleys as to orient yourself once in the mountains. Shovels will prove a useful accessory too as you engineer your way over the big alluvial fans that have been built by thousands of years of runoff spilling from canyons to desert. Minor washouts are frequent on these unmaintained roads.

Nights are cold in the area until after July 4. Once spring is past, storms are brief but can be violent: wind with lots of dust, heavy rain, lightning (and remember much of this is open country). The sometimes numerous mosquitos of June fade to be replaced by biting flies the rest of the summer.

Dirt bikes and all-terrain vehicles are becoming more common, especially on weekends. You will rarely find them far back in the mountains, although they are penetrating the Northern Lemhis to a greater distance than in the South. One very bad spot, however, is Eightmile Canyon and the South Fork of Pass Creek on the Targhee National Forest near Lone Pine. Here they have destroyed all the esthetic beauty of the Eightmile Canyon with uncontrolled hill climbing.

Lack of water can be a problem hiking the Targhee National Forest (southeast) side of these mountains. The South Fork of Pass Creek is the only reliable creek, although scenic Rocky Canyon often has a small creek until midsummer. The southwest side has small creeks in most of the major canyons and water is common in the northern part of the range.

In addition to the deer, elk, and antelope mentioned, there are quite a few black bear, cougar, bobcat, a growing herd of bighorn sheep from a transplant, and a large mountain goat population. Moose were recently transplanted into the Sawmill Canyon area. Occasionally an endangered Northern Rocky Mountain wolf may wander through, but there seems to be no reproducing population.

Public interest in the Lemhi Mountains has grown throughout the 1980s. We are hopeful the day is near when politicians will be required to direct the Forest Service and the Bureau of Management to manage these superlative mountains and valleys for recreation and wilderness rather than subsidized grazing and logging.

HIKE 33 *BIG CREEK—TIMBER CREEK LOOP*

General description: A glorious 40-mile, five-day loop.

General location: 110 miles north-northwest of Pocatello. 95 miles northwest of Idaho Falls, and ten miles west of Leadore in the IWDC proposed Lemhi Range Wilderness.

Maps: Big Creek Peak, Iron Creek Point, Sheephorn Peak, and Yellow Peak (7.5') USGS-quads.

Special attractions: Big mountains and high meadows, spacious views, opportunities for adding to the basic loop.

Difficulty: Moderately difficult due to some faint trail portions and the considerable length of the total loop.

Season: Late June to late September.

Information: For the Big Creek and Snowbank Trail portions: Challis Ranger District, Challis National Forest, Box 337; Challis, Idaho 83226; (208) 879-4321. Big Timber Creek portion: Leadore Ranger District, Salmon National Forest, Box 180; Leadore, Idaho 83464; (208) 768-2371.

The hike: This is a tremendous loop that takes from four to six days to backpack. This is in a mountain range that has few trails, much less loop trails. If you can't spend most of a week, you will also enjoy hiking portions of the loop. In total, the loop has 12,500 feet of total relief. You hike over three divides and through a variety of mountain scenes. You will not encounter many other people, but the area is better known now than when described in the first edition of this book. All of the loop is within the proposed Lemhi Range Wilderness except the Snowbank Trail portion. Unfortunately, the area is being discovered by dirt bike and all-terrain vehicle jockeys; and they are pushing for "improvements", damaging some meadows, and opposing wilderness classification.

Commonly seen are deer, elk, mountain goats, antelope, coyote, and black bears. Moose were recently introduced in the general area. Cougar are fairly common but seen only rarely.

There are three principal ways of getting onto this loop. The one described in detail in this book is that from the junction of the North and South forks of Big Creek with road access from the Pahsimeroi Valley. The other good access points are from the Iron Creek Trail in Sawmill Canyon and the Big Timber Creek Trail with access from Leadore (pronounced "lead ore").

The Iron Creek Road is gravelled and located just two miles up Sawmill Canyon beyond the Mill Creek road (see the Mill Creek hike for directions).

To reach the Big Timber Creek Trail, go west from the town of Leadore on the Lee Creek road for a mile. Turn left onto Forest Service Road #105 and go 7.5 miles to a junction signed "Timber Creek Reservoir". Continue left here on #105. The road ends near Big Timber Creek in about four more miles. A mile back from the end of #105 is the best place to park for horses since there is an unloading ramp and a wide turnaround for trailers, while at the trailhead there is limited parking.

To get to the Big Creek trailhead, drive to the small town of Howe. Turn off the highway and follow the county road that goes up the Little Lost River Valley all the way to valley's end at Summit Reservoir. Cross the low divide here and drop down into the Pahsimeroi Valley. About 57 miles north of Howe, a sign reads "Big Creek Trail". Take the dirt road here and drive 3.5 miles to Big Creek Camp, a small campground near the forest boundary where Big Creek forms from its north and south forks. The road can be bad after a heavy rain but is suitable for automobiles.

You can head up either fork right from the campground to begin the loop. The first part of the south fork trail is faint and an alternative beginning for it exists a third of a mile back up the road on the bench above the canyon. The alternative beginning for the south fork trail is signed. It's often called the "high trail". To me, however, the faint trail leading upstream from the campground, which keeps close to the river for a mile, was acceptable.

If you plan to hike during high water (June and early July), it's prudent to begin the loop by going up the North Fork of Big Creek. The most difficult stream crossing is several miles up this canyon. If you can make this ford, you can make all of the rest on the loop. I describe the loop from this clockwise direction.

It's seven miles from the trailhead to the Park Fork of Big Creek. The trail leaves the trailhead campground and goes east along the right bank of the North Fork. For a mile it's a rocky trail through conifer and aspen with some mountain mahogany present. Near the mouth of trailless West Fork of Big Creek you reach the first of two fords of the North Fork. There are two places to make this ford. The lower, mostly for horses, is the more difficult. The hiker's crossing is slightly upstream.

Once across, you make a steady climb for another mile to the second crossing. The best place is about 200 yards upstream from where the trail drops into the river. The bottom is uniform-sized rocks, but expect high water and a temperature in the low 40 degree range until snow melt is past.

There is a small meadow at the second crossing and two more in the next two miles. These are good places to camp, but there are no grand vistas here.

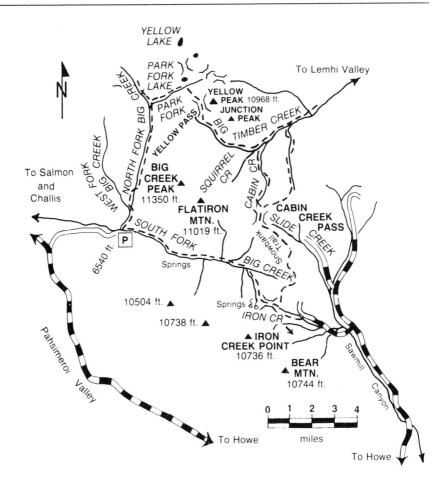

Up-canyon past the meadows, the trail climbs what appears to be a large, low glacial moraine, and it stays on it for about a mile. You ford two small tributaries as you cross over talus and glacial cobblestone stretches. Glimpses of large unnamed peaks up-canyon reward your efforts.

The trail approaches the North Fork closely as you near the Park Fork. You can ford the Park Fork where the trail crosses (it's about twelve feet wide), or you can search upstream for a log. The trail then leads between the Park Fork and the North Fork for about one-eighth mile leading to their confluence. Here the left fork of the trail continues up the North Fork giving access to Yellow Lake and Big Eightmile Creek on the Salmon National Forest. Take the right fork here and head up the Park Fork of Big Creek. It's 3.5 miles and 2,000 feet of relief from the bottom of the Park Fork to Yellow Pass at the top.

The first half-mile of the ascent is a steep, switchbacking climb, paralleling the Park Fork, which thunders down the mountain in June. The gradient then declines and resembles the previous hike along the North Fork.

Scout the mountain slopes on the left (north) for mountain goats as you listen to the pika calling from the talus slides. The trail goes through fir forest interspersed with huge boulders left by glaciers.

The trail keeps to the north side of the creek until you are about a mile below Yellow Pass. After the jump of Park Fork, the trail turns southward. Just before reaching this spot, you have the opportunity to make a cross-country hike to Park Fork Lake. Head to the northwest and climb 300 to this small lake located at 9,300 feet elevation in a glacier-cut bowl of intruded igneous rock of the Park Fork Stock.

After crossing the Park Fork, you climb quite rapidly toward Yellow Peak (10,968 feet) which probably was named from the slightly yellow quartzite boulders on its slopes. After just a quarter mile, the trail forks. The left fork soon forks again, with one fork leading over to Park Fork Lake and then to Yellow Lake. The second fork goes to the Middle Fork of Little Timber Creek and the third goes to Rocky Canyon (a tributary of Big Timber Creek). Ignore all this unless your destination is not Yellow Pass and take the trail to the right.

The trail becomes a bit faint, but just head southward to the obvious pass and stay close to the bottom of the draw as talus makes walking on the sides somewhat difficult.

At Yellow Pass (9,760 feet) you are rewarded with a spectacular view of Flatiron and Big Creek Peaks to the southwest. An extra hour will allow you to scramble to the top of Yellow Peak for a panorama of mountains grander still.

At Yellow Pass you cross the crest of the Lemhi Range and enter the Salmon National Forest. The trail drops steeply and is faint in places until, after a descent of a thousand feet in a distance of a mile, you reach Big Timber Creek Canyon. From here the trail is good, easy, and you seemingly roll down the canyon for about four miles until you reach Cabin Creek, which you will go up to continue the loop. Many elk and mule deer frequent this large drainage. The low whistles and grunts of the elk add to the wilderness atmosphere in this land of striking high mountain scenery and sub-alpine meadows that break up the stands of quaking aspen and conifer.

After passing four major side drainages which drop off of Flatiron Mountain and Big Creek Peak (11,350 feet), you enter a large meadow which lies directly below Junction Peak and is opposite the Cabin Creek side canyon. Posts in the meadow help you locate this important junction. As of 1988, a sign read "Squirrel Creek Trail, Leadore 19 miles." Be sure to head up Cabin Creek here, not Squirrel Creek, although Squirrel Creek is a very scenic side loop (a recently improved trail goes up Squirrel Creek, over a divide, and then down Falls and Prospect Creeks to Big Timber Creek, making a five-mile loop). To be sure you go up Cabin Creek, go to the east as soon as you cross Big Timber Creek until you encounter a creek. This is Cabin Creek.

The trail that continues down Big Timber Creek from the junction described above is a good alternative access trail to and from the Big Creek—Timber Creek loop. It is 5.9 miles down Big Timber Creek from Cabin Creek to Forest Service Road #105 that comes from the town of Leadore.

The climb to Cabin Creek Pass is 1,600 feet. The trail stays close to Cabin Creek for the first mile and a half, then the grade increases and the trail follows a fork of Cabin Creek to the pass, which is a small saddle at 9,282 feet. At the pass a trail drops steeply down the other side into Slide Creek. Avoid this trail. Walk westwardly along the divide and you will soon find yourself on the Snowbank Trail.

Cabin Creek Pass marks the southern boundary of the wilderness proposed by Idaho environmentalists. Southward you will see a proliferation of logging roads and the scar of the Little Lost fire that burned 9,000 acres in the head of Sawmill Canyon during the drought summer of 1988. Despite this, the Snowbank Trail is picturesque, especially the first several miles past Cabin Creek Pass. The Snowbank Trail contours high above Sawmill Canyon giving inspiring views of that canyon. You gain excellent views of Bell Mountain and Diamond Peak far to the southeast and also of the unnamed and rarely visited symmetrical peaks and cirque basins to the south of the South Fork of Big Creek. High marshy meadows intermingle with well-weathered conifers as the trail bumps along just below the ridgeline.

This ridgeline, unlike the others visited while hiking this loop, is composed of colorful volcanic rocks rather than quartzite, dolomite, or limestone.

You'll follow the Snowbank Trail for seven miles to its junction with the Iron Creek trail (another good access trail onto the loop). There are some high elevation camping spots about a mile past Cabin Creek Pass.

The trail drops off the ridgeline and rolls through a few small side drainages to Redrock Creek, named for the color of the rock in the area. You can camp here; or if you don't mind carrying water up a hill, you'll find a great view and an adequate campsite just south of Redrock Creek.

About a mile south of Redrock Creek, you cross an area clearcut about 15 years old. A volcanic column looms here.

Continue contouring around the upper slopes of Sawmill Canyon and one of its major tributaries, Iron Creek. Massive Bear Mountain (10,744 feet) and pointed Iron Creek Point (10,736 feet) dominate the view as you round a spur and head generally southwest around the top of Iron Creek. From the spur, an easy mile-and-a-half brings you to a four-way trail junction. Take the trail that goes upward over the pass to the west. This is the South Fork of Big Creek Trail. Heading down is the Iron Creek Trail. Continuing along toward Iron Creek Point is an extension of the Snowbank Trail. The climb out of Iron Creek into the South Fork is about 400 feet. If the trail is faint due to the "trail-eating" meadows, just head for the obvious divide above you.

Switchback down into the South Fork of Big Creek canyon through a mixture of ancient, fire-ravaged ghosts of whitebark pine and new growth. Iron Creek Point rises behind you and the trail's grade decreases as you come to a place of multiple springs, the birth of the south fork of Big Creek.

The canyon remains narrow, and you'll cross the creek perhaps 10 times in small jumps as it descends through thick fir forest. The need to cross talus slopes occasionally slows you down. After crossing a tributary from the north, the trail remains on the right side of the stream.

A major tributary (incorrectly named the "South Fork of Big Creek" on older maps) flows in from the north about three miles from the trail junction back at Iron Creek. At this spot it is seven more miles to the end of the loop.

Still the canyon remains narrow, and the hike can be laborious as you cross talus piles and sidehills. Some interesting avalanche chutes spill from the high unnamed ridge to the south of the creek. The trail is blazed in places, directing you through marshy streamside meadows. If you want to keep your feet dry, obvious alternate routes border the willows and the talus slides.

Some two miles above the wedding of the forks to become Big Creek, you reach a wide green area supported by upslope springs and kept in place by beaver dams. There are good camping sites here. From here you descend down into a narrow canyon. The trail seems to disappear into a cliff just before reaching the trailhead. In fact, it skirts the cliffs for a few hundred feet before popping out at the campground and trailhead.—*by Ralph Maughan* □

HIKE 34 *BUCK AND BEAR VALLEY LAKES*

General description: Two clusters of cirque basin lakes amidst the grandeur of the northern Lemhi Mountains.
General location: About 25 miles due south-southeast of the city of Salmon, Idaho, and 50 miles by road.
Maps: Lem Peak (7.5') and Lemhi (15') USGS quads.
Special attractions: Pyramidal Lem Peak (10,985 feet). Excellent fishing in both trailed and trailless lakes. Abundant wildlife, including mountain goat.
Difficulty: Moderate to the trailed Buck and Bear Valley lakes.
Season: July to late September.
Information: Leadore Ranger District, Salmon National Forest, Box 180, Leadore, Idaho 83464; (208) 768-2371.

The hike: Both the Buck Lakes and the Bear Valley lakes nestle in the heart of the proposed Lemhi Range Wilderness. They are situated at the north end of the high Lemhi Peaks.

From Salmon drive 39 miles south on Idaho Highway 28. Then, about a mile north of the unincorporated crossroads of Lemhi, turn to the west (right) onto a paved county road leading up Hayden Creek—a large creek that boils downhill in early summer toward its union with the Lemhi River. After 3.5 miles, the road turns into gravel. This occurs at the junction with the Basin Creek road (go to the left here). The Hayden Creek road then gradually narrows, as does the canyon, and keeps about a hundred feet above the stream on a cut in the steep canyon sideslope. Just beyond the sign marking the Salmon National Forest boundary, there is a fork in the road. The Hayden Creek road (#008) leads left. To reach the trailhead, take the right fork (#009).

Remain on #009 all the way to the trailhead. It's a generally good dirt road as it climbs and winds tortuously above Bear Valley Creek, crossing several creeks finally to end at the well-developed trailhead just past tributary Short Creek. Here are horse loading facilities, a latrine, and a water pump.

The trail begins 100 yards below the parking area. Here you cross over a good bridge and start up the canyon. The High Trail, which is faint, leads up the mountainside right on the other side of the bridge. The Bear Valley Creek Trail keeps to the canyon bottom quite near the thundering (in early summer) creek and keeps to the right side.

Here Bear Valley Creek, as well as Hayden Creek back down the canyon,

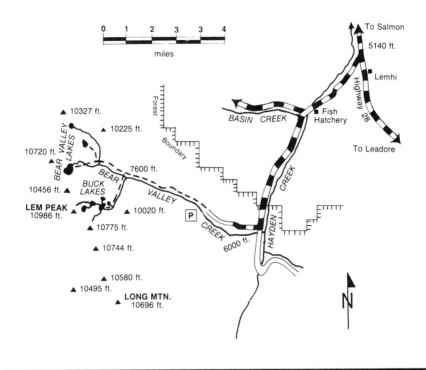

look like fine trout fishing streams. Oddly, they are very poor fisheries for resident fish but are important spawning streams for anadromous fish which still come all the way from the Pacific Ocean via the Columbia River. Most of these spawn at the fish hatchery not far from Highway 28.

The first portion of the Bear Valley Creek trail is fairly level and traverses open country, but soon enters forest. Here, just inside the forest, in 1989 Ralph surprised a young cougar at close range.

After 2.2 miles you come to Buck Creek Canyon, visible through the forest to the left. There is a trail up Buck Creek and a sign indicating the trail, but we found that this sign is often taken down in the winter, and in early summer might not be re-erected.

The Buck Lakes trail (#081) is not on the USGS topographic quadrangle. It leaves the Bear Valley Creek trail at 7,680 feet after you have begun to climb steeply and have partially passed the mouth of Buck Creek Canyon. The ford of Bear Valley Creek may be difficult until early or mid-July, but generally one can scramble across the creek on a large fallen log above the trail crossing. Once on the other side, the route becomes obvious: it switchbacks through the forest, keeping to the west side of Buck Creek.

After a mile, you'll cross a small creek, the outlet of the first Buck Lake. This is really just a pond 400 feet above you on the mountainside. Next, the trail climbs up to lake 8,474 where there are numerous campsites and fishing for medium-sized trout. The next lake is only a half-mile above lake 8,474, but it's a steep 500-foot, cross-country pull through timber and deadfall. The route is to follow the inlet creek up the mountainside. Camping here is limited, but the fishing is good.

The highest Buck Lake sits at 9,456 feet, with its back to the base of rubble-strewn Lem Peak, which is almost 11,000 feet high. It's a difficult task to get here, but Phil was rewarded with a catch of two 17-inch grayling in 1988 and one of equal size in 1989. In addition to such near record grayling, the lake has a cutthroat trout fishery and has been restocked with smaller grayling. Not only is the route difficult to this prize lake, but there is not more than one marginal spot for a tent.

The Bear Valley Lakes occupy the large cirque at the head of Bear Valley Creek. Continue past the exit of the Buck Lakes Trail and continue to climb, rather steeply in places, up the Bear Valley Creek Trail. About a mile past Buck Creek, the trail becomes not only steep, but rocky. Not quite four miles past the trailhead, one arrives at a trail fork. There was an identification sign here in 1989. From this spot the High Trail (#178) leads to the ridgeline and eventually back to the trailhead, making a loop trip possible. We did not walk this trail, but it is reported to have been recently recut.

About 4.2 miles past the trailhead, you come to another fork in the trail. The right fork leads to the two Upper Bear Valley Lakes. On the right fork, it is a mile and a 400 foot climb to the larger upper lake. The left fork of the trail continues on to Bear Valley Lake, the largest, 5.4 miles from the trailhead. First, however, and just past the High Trail's exit, a third trail leaves, this time to the left to climb to the pass just north of Lem Peak to meet a jeep trail in Allison Creek.

Camping is good in the vicinity of the main lake as well as the upper lakes, and visitors enjoy fine views of Lem Peak to the south from the upper lakes.

Fishing is good for large rainbow trout in Bear Valley Lake. The two upper lakes are cutthroat fisheries. In 1989 the smaller upper lake provided the best angling.

Both the Buck Lakes and the Bear Valley Creek trails are open to dirt bikes. They rarely are seen on the Buck Lakes trail, but you can expect them at Bear Valley Lakes from time to time.—*Philip Blomquist and Ralph Maughan* □

HIKE 35 *BUNTING CANYON*

General description: A day hike giving an impressive close-up view of the high southern ridge of the Lemhi Mountains.

General location: In the southern end of the Lemhi Mountains, 100 miles north of Pocatello, 60 miles northwest of Idaho Falls, and 25 miles north of Howe, as the crow flies.

Maps: Badger Creek, Fallert Springs (7.5') USGS quads.

Special attractions: A huge, shallow, mountainside cavern, nearby mining camp ruins, and early season hiking.

Difficulty: Easy to the bend in Bunting Canyon. Moderate cross-country above.

Season: Late May to mid-October.

Information: Lost River Ranger District, Challis National Forest, Mackay, Idaho 83251; (208) 588-2224.

The hike: When you stand in the middle of the arid Little Lost River Valley and look, for the first time, at the jagged, forbidding outline of thirsty gray rock forming the Diamond Peak masiff, you wouldn't expect to find a canyon glen of green softness nestled at its base. Here, Badger Creek and its tributary, Bunting Creek, bubble toward the valley, watering canyon bottoms of meadow, marsh, cottonwood, water birch, and quaking aspen. These riparian zones contrast with the mountain slopes of rock filigreed with grass, sage, mountain mahogany, and a few fir.

To reach the trailhead, drive through the agricultural village of Howe and head north on the main road. This is a county road which varies yearly in consistency of pavement, chuckholes, new asphalt, and gravel. At 23.5 miles north of Howe, turn right at a small gravel pit. There are two dirt roads leading from the pit. Take the rightmost road which climbs toward the Lemhi Mountains following a fence. The road climbs at a gentle grade (but with numerous small rocks) for four-and-a-half miles up Badger Creek Bar (a huge alluvial fan) to the mouth of Badger Creek Canyon. Some old mining scars mark the mountains near the canyon's entrance. Antelope commonly patrol the area from the gravel pit all the way to the rising Lemhi Mountain slopes.

You leave BLM land at the canyon entrance to cross into the Challis National Forest. Here you climb briefly into what appears to be a brushy canyon on a poor dirt road. The road is passable by sedans driven with care. In just a half mile, however, you arrive at a pleasant meadowy area of grass and marsh, half encircled by deciduous trees. Badger Creek runs through the meadows, in many places as a deep slot in the sod, although livestock grazing has served to widen it at spots. The road is easy here but crosses Badger Creek twice over creaky old bridges which I expected to collapse a decade ago (they still were passable in 1989). You find numerous camping spots near the edges of the meadows.

Ahead lie the forks of the canyon—exactly 1.7 miles from the boundary of the Challis National Forest. To your right is Bunting Canyon, your destination. On the left, a mucky jeep track goes toward a old mining camp. The track soon disappears, but you will find a trail leading to a number of badly deteriorating, bramble-filled log cabins of a long ago era. Badger Creek rises

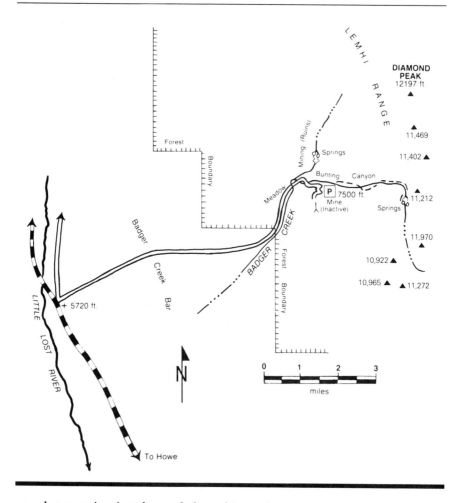

as a large spring just beyond the cabins. Above the spring, Badger Creek Canyon widens, and after a walk of about a mile you can gain a view of 12,197-foot Diamond Peak—the third highest summit in Idaho.

Bunting Canyon, the right fork, has a good dirt road (and one dilapidated bridge), for a short distance. After a half mile, the road switchbacks a now impassable route up the mountainside to some old mining sites. Drive a hundred feet or so past where the road starts up the mountain to arrive at the "parking lot" on the edge of Bunting Creek.

Starting up the trail, you immediately hop across Bunting Creek. The path then winds its way through an intimate forest of babbling brook, tall Douglas fir, hemmed in by dark rugged cliffs of dolomite (calcium magnesium carbonate), a close relative of limestone.

The hike is fairly easy on a faint trail. First-timers are likely to think they are walking up a box canyon because dead ahead a continuous ridge of convoluted rock rises 3,000 feet to an altitude of over 11,000 feet. Actually, the canyon turns southward at a right angle when you get to the very base of the ridge. From time to time, you glimpse a huge hole in the side of the ridge ahead. Apparently this 75-foot-high, 100 foot deep cavern was formed when a slab of the limestone mountain broke away.

You will lose the trail at the bend, near the spring-fed source of Bunting Creek. There is no water beyond this point, making this area the best campsite. There are a few spots to pitch a tent on the right (west) side of the creek just past the canyon bend.

The intermittent and faint trail does continue past the bend. It is located on the right side of the canyon. Here you walk through open fir forest to the head of the canyon. The sight of the rugged, twisted ridge on your left is astonishing all the way to the top of Bunting; at the head, rugged mountains also rise on the canyon's right side.

There are a few small cutthroat in both Bunting and Badger Creeks. The presence of cattle in the lower (roaded) portion of Badger Creek can reduce your car camping pleasure. You might want to check with the Lost River Ranger District to plan your hike before (or after) the cows are in the canyon. This hike is just perfect in late June. Another especially pleasant time is mid-September when the aspen have turned gold.—*Ralph Maughan* □

HIKE 36 *EAST FORK, PATTERSON CREEK*

General description: A comfortable two-day hike crossing the crest of the Lemhi Range to a subalpine lake.
General location: In the north part of the Lemhi Range, 42 miles southeast of Salmon and 98 miles northwest of Idaho Falls, in the proposed Lemhi Range Wilderness.
Maps: Patterson (15') or the new Patterson, Yellow Peak (7.5') USGS quads.
Special attractions: Rugged mountains, alpine meadows, wildflowers, and a beautiful lake.
Difficulty: Moderate with a short cross-country segment at the end.
Season: July through mid-October.
Information: Challis Ranger District, Challis National Forest, HC 63 Box 1669, Challis, Idaho 83226; (208) 879-4321.

The hike: Here's a beauty of a lake nestled in the crest of the Lemhis. Good fishing for cutthroat, with little competition, awaits you after a three-mile hike that climbs 2,000 feet. This is a nice weekend hike if you start early. The driving time from Idaho Falls or Pocatello is three to four hours.

If approaching from the south or the east, drive to Howe, then drive along the only road going up the Little Lost River Valley. Follow this county road to its end. Continue past Summit Reservoir into the Pahsimeroi Valley to the ghost town of Patterson. Patterson is approximately 60 road miles north of Howe. Alternately, you can drive from Challis or Salmon on U.S. Highway 93 to the paved county road going south through the Pahsimeroi Valley past the little burgh of May. Then continue 12.2 miles further south to Patterson. At Patterson, a gravel road turns off the paved road and heads east right up into the V-shaped mouth of Patterson Creek.

Patterson Creek is a big stream for the Lemhi Mountains and likewise drains a big canyon that is 2,000 to 3,500 feet deep as soon as you enter it. In the 1940s and 1950s, the lower part of the canyon was horribly corrupted by tungsten mining at the Ima Mine. The ore was deposited around the edge of the Ima stock, a pillar of igneous rock that rose from the depths of the earth intruding into the ancient quartzites above it. The diggings into the mountain left quartzite tailings of white sand all over the canyon, choking the streamside zone and spilling into the water for the first 1.5 miles to the mine. There have been preliminary attempts recently to reopen the mine. Hopefully, the new operators will abide by modern day mining ethics and show some environmental concern.

Above the mine, the road narrows and trees form a shady patchwork of canopy overhead until you come to the bridge over Patterson Creek. This bridge washed out in June 1983, and it may or may not be replaced. At this point, the main fork (called the "North Fork" on some maps) of Patterson Creek verges to the left. This is not your destination. The canyon is about eight miles long, and the trail appears to be brushy and isolated with many bushwhacks.

As you continue eastward up the East Fork, the road deteriorates. The next .6 mile can be navigated in a small car or light truck if you're careful. Then you'll come to a ford of the creek. You'd best stop here and park if the water is high with snowmelt, even if you have a four-wheel-drive vehicle. The velocity of the spring runoff could turn over even a steadfast jeep.

Once it crosses the creek, the old mining road switchbacks and climbs 400 feet in the next mile, leading to a miner's cabin. Another old mining road leaves this one just before the cabin and climbs high up the south side of the canyon. This road is a sidetrack.

Near the headwaters of the East Fork of Patterson Creek. Ralph Maughan photo.

HIKE 36 *EAST FORK, PATTERSON CREEK*

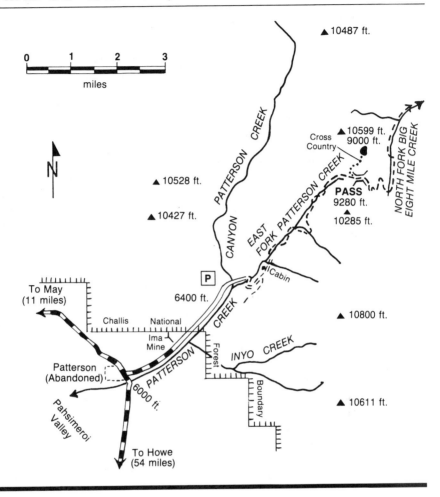

The trail itself begins at the cabin. It quickly comes to another crossing of the East Fork. Until snowmelt is over, this is a torrent. It's impossible to wade until July, although one year, on June 27, I jumped the 11 feet over it. My heart, seeking altitude no doubt, leapt into my throat.

This ford used to be bridged, which accounts for its steep banks. All four-wheel-drive vehicles and most trail machines stop here even after the water recedes. Hopefully, the ford will retain this useful function until the area is classified as wilderness.

Once across the creek, the trail is good. It heads up the left side of the creek as it putters through brush growing on the edges of rockslides. The rockslides are littered with the bodies of trees shattered by avalanches.

The canyon grade flattens out a bit after one-half mile, and you'll enter a grove of Douglas fir. There are places to camp here. At last inspection, there were log bridges at the two creek crossings in this fir grove.

Just past the grove, you'll cross a tributary. Early in the season, crossing this requires another running jump. The trail then begins a broad coiling climb up a gray rockpile. This mass of gray quartzite is called a moraine; it was brought down by the glacier that once flowed down from the broad side canyon to your right.

The broad trail, at one time a wagon road, climbs 700 feet up and off the moraine. Mid-way, it enters aspen and Douglas fir. Once the climbing is done, the canyon again levels out a bit. This time, instead of rocks, you are greeted with strings of meadow that break up the forest. In mid-July they color up with wildflowers. Even in late June, hardy buttercups and globeflowers push through the shallow patches of snow.

The trail, as is often the case, becomes faint in the meadows, but it continues its obvious route upward until you reach the pass on the crest of the range. Here, at 9,300 feet, the trail drops steeply down into a fork of Big Eightmile Creek. Instead of following it, walk along the crest northward a brief distance until you can see the lake ahead to your right. Walk cross-country and drop down to the lake. There are plenty of places to camp in this pristine environment. The lake has no generally accepted name nor any obvious trail. Cutthroat trout swim out generally unmolested lives in the lake's clear water.

The reddish gray siltite rock of the crest zone here was deposited by very ancient waters in what geologists call the Precambrian period—before there was any life on earth. If you look carefully, you can find mudcracks and ripple marks preserved in this, the Apple Creek Formation. They are a billion years old. Some people find rocks boring, but they're the only way I know of that mortals can actually touch a piece of eternity.—*Ralph Maughan* □

Note: The Patterson Creek road has deteriorated since 1984. It would be prudent to drive a truck. A four-wheel drive vehicle is not needed, yet. The washed-out bridge at the junction of East Patterson and Patterson Creek has not, and will not, be replaced. The effect of this is to add a mile or so to the hike. Late in the summer some dirt bikes and all-terrain vehicles ford the creek here and go up the trail. Use by off-road vehicles of the trail is not heavy yet, although some damage has been done to the meadows near the crest of the range.

Efforts to reopen the Ima Mine so far have not been successful. —Ralph Maughan

HIKE 37 *NORTH FORK, LITTLE MORGAN CREEK*

General description: A rough, cross-country hike typical of the wildest portions of the Lemhi mountain range.
General location: 35 miles south of Salmon City in the north part of the Lemhi Range, mostly in the proposed Lemhi Range Wilderness.
Maps: May (15'), or the new May Mtn., Ennis Gulch (7½') USGS quads.
Special attractions: Mountain goats and extreme wildness, route-finding, solitude.
Difficulty: Difficult due to an elevation gain of almost 3,000 feet and a route over rockslides and deadfall.

Season: July through September.

Information: Challis Ranger District, Challis National Forest, HC 63 Box 1669, Challis, Idaho 83226; (208) 879-4321; Salmon District Office, Bureau of Land Management, Box 430, Salmon, Idaho 83467; (208) 756-2201.

The hike: No one except an occasional hunter goes into this wild country of rock, high peaks, and struggling timber. It is included here as an example of one of dozens of similar such opportunities to really get out on your own devices, a way from even the sparse number of backpackers found in the Lemhi Mountains. The scenery is spectacular, and you work to earn it. It's a fine place for a Fourth of July or a Labor Day weekend trip, when other mountain play-grounds of Idaho are full of tourists.

Drive south from Salmon on U.S. Highway 93, and turn south onto the paved road at Ellis that heads up the board Pahsimeroi Valley. It's 7.1 miles to the Little Morgan Creek road (mislabeled "Morgan Creek" on most maps). The BLM may have put up a sign at the turnoff onto this dirt road.

Alternatively, you can drive to Howe and from there go up the Little Lost River Valley on the county road. Go all the way to valley's end at Summit Reservoir then continue on, dropping gently down into the head of the Pahsimeroi Valley. Keep going northward until, 80 miles north of Howe, you reach the Little Morgan Creek road (to the right). Don't be fooled by a signed turnoff 1.4 miles before the correct one. This first turnoff leads to an impassable, unbridged crossing of the creek far downstream of where you begin to hike.

Drive for two miles to mouth of the canyon on this rough road. Continue on through a mixture of BLM and private land, being sure to close the gates. If you don't have a four-wheel-drive, park just before the junction of the North and East forks of Little Morgan Creek (there is no south fork). With a jeep, you can ford the creek and drive a little way up either the North Fork or the East Fork. The prominent mountain you can see from time to time as you drive to the forks is May Mountain, 10,971 feet, one of the highest peaks in the northern Lemhis.

Drive about one-half mile up the North Fork and park under cottonwood trees about 200 yards past the boundary sign of the Challis National Forest. There are lots of camping places here by the stream.

Don your gear and follow the trail up the North Fork beside cottonwoods, willow, birch, and a few fir. After one-half mile, the creek makes a right-angle bend. Keep to the right side of the creek. Now you'll walk under a canopy of conifers, following one of the numerous game trails. The way is fairly easy. After about .75 mile, however, you arrive at an avalanche chute where you have to struggle across its debris. Next, you descend to the first of many (almost continuous) rockslides. Walk on these quartzite boulders; it's a lot easier than thrashing up the damp, overgrown area next to the stream that is full of hidden rocks in the bush.

Red Point, composed of hard blackish-red quartzite, rises on the north side of the canyon (the rock is reddish but is spotted with the growth of black lichens). Look for mountain goats on its face and for the rest of the way up the canyon.

The rockslides continue for two to 2.5 miles. The rocks are large enough to step on with little fear of their rolling. Finally you enter the forest after a struggle through some deadfall, over an occasional boulder, and over several mossy tributaries.

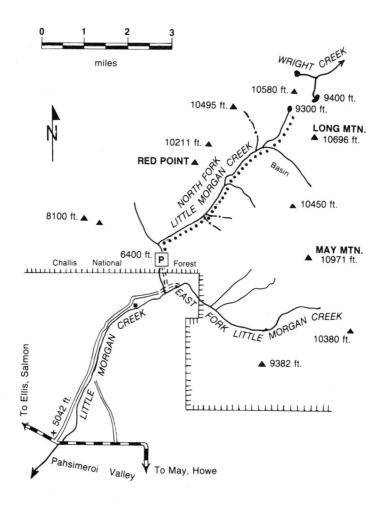

Fortunately, after about one-half mile, the streamside begins to open up. Flowers bloom everywhere along the stream. Small seeps and numerous springs provide places to stop and rest. Campsites appear.

If you follow the first major tributary you come to, you'll climb about 900 feet to a small lake set right at the base of an unnamed, 10,580-foot peak of olive pink quartzite. There are campsites here by a flower-banked stream that emerges below the lake and splashes downhill. This lake is full in July but dries up by late August. It has no name. In fact, no feature up here has a name except 10,696-foot Long Mountain which rises just south of the lake. From the lake you can look toward the south and southwest at a huge cirque from which flow the headwaters of the North Fork. Steep mountains with a dark red hue block the basin's head.

You can scramble to the high divide between peak 10,580 on the north and Long Mountain on the south for a view of a permanent lake just over the crest. It is at the head of a tributary of Wright Creek. Lying on the north side of Long Mountain as it does, the lake still had a large snow drift the first week of September in 1982. It's obviously not a likely place to fish. You can get down to the lake by descending Long Mountain.

Years could be spent visiting the unnamed lakes, basins, and peaks of the Lemhis. Here, unknown to most outdoor enthusiasts and probably all of the politicians who will make a judgment on protecting the Lemhis, is some of the wildest country in the west. When you visit this area, decide for yourself whether it deserves protection; then let the decision-makers know your opinion.—*Ralph Maughan* □

HIKE 38 *MILL CREEK LAKE*

General description: A day hike or overnighter to a mountain lake that opens up in early summer.
General location: 100 and 125 miles northwest of Idaho Falls and Pocatello respectively, in the Lemhi Mountains.
Maps: Gilmore (7½') USGS quad.
Special attractions: June access to a mountain lake in an alpine like setting. The trailhead is close to many other hiking areas in the Lemhi Mountains.
Difficulty: Easy to the lake; moderate to Firebox Meadows due to a trail that becomes increasingly faint.
Season: Mid-June to mid-October.
Information: Lost River Ranger District, Challis National Forest, Box 507, Mackay, Idaho 83251; (208) 588-2224.

The hike: When winter's ice still grips most high mountain lakes, Mill Creek Lake, in the rugged Lemhi Mountains, is usually quite suitable for a hike and overnight camping.

Dammed by a landslide, the lake lies in a short, rocky canyon. The rocks and cliffs enclosing the lake may cause you to think the surroundings are more alpine than they really are.

An increasingly faint trail above the lake leads to Firebox Meadows and Firebox Summit. This beautiful meadow and forest country, important elk range, contrasts sharply with the lake environs below.

To reach the trailhead, drive north in the Little Lost River Valley on the county road for 38 miles after leaving the cowtown of Howe. At 38 miles, a generally well-signed gravel road exits to the right (east) for Sawmill Canyon. Follow this road across Mud Flats for about seven miles. The road is in good condition. It will lead you into Sawmill Canyon, a large, southward-draining stream valley, and into the headwaters of the Little Lost River. Head past the Forest Service's Fairview Guard Station and continue for two more miles. Here, turn right (east) on the road which leads up Mill Creek, at a meadow which blazes with larkspur and wyethia in June. Go one mile to the end of the road.

Here you'll find the trailhead and a few picnic tables, with three or four places to camp under a forest canopy. They are right by Mill Creek, the only source of water. There are also plenty of undeveloped campsites nearby.

Look down the canyon from the Mill Creek Road, and you can see Bear Mountain (10,744 feet) rising on the west side of Sawmill Canyon.

You will easily find the trail. It is obvious, marked with a sign that reads, "Closed to Motor Vehicles." Set out into the forest for the peaceful, 2.5-miles, 1,200-foot climb to the lake.

At first, you'll walk easily through a gentle, open forest. Then, after a half-mile, you'll ford Mill Creek. The ford is fairly easy, except in June, when the

Mill Creek Lake. Ralph Maughan photo.

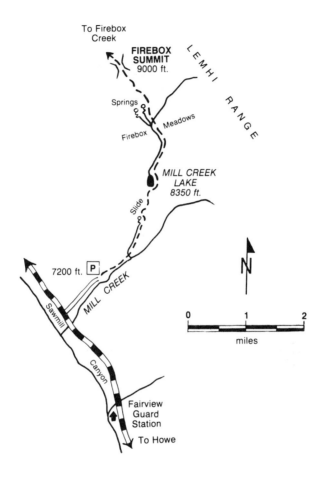

creek is wide and cold. Even then, you won't find it really difficult or dangerous.

Shortly after fording Mill Creek, you approach and enter a small canyon. The trail begins to climb with the increasing grade of the canyon, keeping about 50 to 75 feet above rushing Mill Creek. After about .75 mile, you come to the base of a big rockslide that has filled the canyon. The trees thin out as the trail switchbacks up the slide. Below you, Mill Creek pours as a full-blown stream out of the slide's base. The hard rock of the rock slide is quartzite, part of the Kinnikinic Formation.

A few big old Douglas fir have struggled to make a living out of the harsh conditions of the slide. These trees are hundreds of years old. Their ancient branches frame the view down the canyon of the Lemhi foothills and, farther to the west, Idaho's highest mountains, the Lost Rivers.

When the switchbacks end, there's a brief reprieve through a level section. Here, in early summer, you pass a small lower lake (not on the map) and the small meadow stream that flows over the top of the slide to feed it. These waters are the children of spring and disappear as the season progresses. From this spot, there is one more steep pitch to the lake.

Mill Creek Lake's water level varies, being highest after a winter of heavy snow. At the west end of the lake, some construction work has been done to try to retard seepage of water out of the lake. Despite changing water levels, Mill Creek Lake supports a good population of fat cutthroat trout. I've been most successful with wet flies and streamers.

You'll find campsites at both ends of the lake, but the north and south sides of the lake are too steep to camp on. Much of the time, you'll find a spring flowing just below a rockslide that rests above the lake's east side.

If you wish to hike beyond the lake, walk around to the inlet (east side). Here, a trail climbs at a gradual rate up Mill Creek Canyon, which soon broadens out and opens into a forest interspersed with meadow. In these meadows the trail fades, as is so often the case in such country, but it can be followed by carefully watching for blazes on the trees. There are many camping places here in the headwater rivulets of Mill Creek. You can scramble to the crest of the Lemhi Range from here as well. In the mid-reaches of this lengthy mountain uplift, the crest undulates from about 10,000 to 10,500 feet.

Firebox Summit is about three miles from and 750 feet above Mill Creek Lake. The general name for the country just south of the summit is Firebox Meadows, although there is no one particular meadow by that name. North of the summit, the faded trail continues down into Firebox Creek.

The 1957 Gilmore (15') USGS quad shows a trail going from Firebox Meadows back to the Mill Creek trailhead. Thus, you might think a loop trail hike is possible. However, while this old trail can be located at the trailhead, you can't find it in the Firebox Meadow area. The trail has been obliterated by downed timber and lack of maintenance.—*Ralph Maughan* □

HIKE 39 *ROCKY CANYON*

General Description: An moderately easy, early to mid-summer, two or three-day hike.
General Location: On the east side of the southern portion of the Lemhi Range, 60 miles northwest of Idaho Falls and 80 miles southeast of Salmon.
Maps: Diamond Peak, Nicholia (7.5') USGS quads.
Special Attractions: Rocky Canyon is the longest in the southern Lemhis. There are large cliffs towering over lovely meadows, mountain goats, and a spectacular view of Diamond Peak.

Difficulty: Easy to Rocky Canyon's forks; moderately difficult cross-country above.

Season: Mid-June through September—best around July 1.

Information: Dubois Ranger District, Targhee National Forest, Dubois, Idaho 83423; (208) 374-5422.

The hike: This hike is fairly easy, yet brings you into very spectacular mountain scenery. The only drawbacks are the presence of too many cows in midsummer and increasing damage to the meadows by dirt bikes and ATVs. The best time for this hike is the two week period from early to mid-July. Later you may have to carry all of your water.

From Idaho Falls, Pocatello, St. Anthony, or Rexburg, drive across the desert on Idaho Highway 28 through the town of Mud Lake and turn right (still on 28) at the highway junction just west of town. From here drive up into the Birch Creek Valley between the Lemhi Mountains on the left and Beaverheads on the right. At 7.7 miles north of the unincorporated gas/cafe spot named Lone Pine, turn left off of the highway onto a dirt road leading directly toward the Lemhi Mountains. A sign here in 1989 indicated "Coal Kiln, Mammoth, and Meadow" canyons, but not Rocky Canyon.

After about four miles this dirt road deteriorates, and you'll come to a number of junctions which change from year-to-year in this high, open rangeland country. Be sure to take the new 7.5' Nicholia USGS quadrangle to help navigate your way to Rocky Canyon. The dirt road to the canyon rim is deeply rutted and requires four-wheel drive. For those lacking such a vehicle, park about a half mile back. It's an easy and pleasant walk to the canyon in early summer.

Another route to Rocky Canyon is an unsigned dirt road 7.5 miles north of Lone Pine on Highway 28. You'll recognize this because it heads toward a microwave facility. Pass the facility and travel 1.2 miles further on a level, but high-centered, road and park on the approach to the rim of Rocky Canyon. Simply park near the canyon rim and hike down into the shallow lower reaches of Rocky Canyon.

The high desert (elevation 7,000-7,500 feet) around the canyon rim is especially beautiful in the early summer when wildflowers are abundant and the grass is green. Here, too, many large peaks are visible, particularly 12,197-foot Diamond Peak, lord of the southern Lemhi mountains. Eastward across Birch Creek Valley, the high cluster of peaks in the Beaverhead Mountains are the Italian Peaks (see Webber Creek to Divide Creek hike). The mountain in the Beaverheads to the northeast with radiating spurs is Eighteenmile Peak, the highest mountain on the Idaho/Montana border.

Drop down into the shallow lower portion of Rocky Canyon. Small cliffs with colorful rock variations line the upper edges of the canyon. There is an intermittent trail which eventually becomes definite by a large spring. Above the spring the trail follows a brook (although this dries up by late summer). The canyon gradually deepens, and about three miles from the start of the hike you come to the big meadow in the middle of the canyon. This is a good destination for a base camp.

Scenic rocky mountains rise on both sides of the big meadow, but especially impressive is Diamond Peak which looms over unnamed peak 10,994 at the head of the Left Fork. The face on Diamond Peak you see is its most difficult.

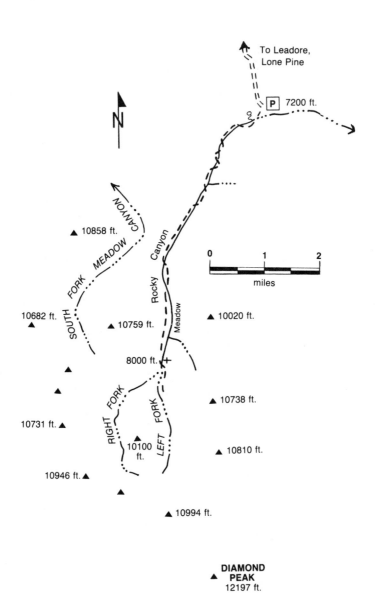

The best route for climbing it is on the west side, out of Bunting Canyon. We failed in an attempt to climb it from Lone Pine in 1988, after reaching cliffs with too many "portable" handholds.

Antelope are common in the lower reaches of Rocky Canyon and the adjacent Lemhi Mountain foothills. You are likely to se mountain goats on all of the high mountains surrounding the canyon. For the novice, a careful look is necessary for what later appears obvious. Goats often look like dingy-white, movable rocks or patches of late snow. We saw about 15 on our trip to the canyon. On a later helicopter flight over Diamond Peak we saw about 50 goats.

Bighorn sheep too are expanding their range in the area after being transplanted into Uncle Ike Creek, which is about 12 miles to the south on the other side of the mountain range. Elk and deer are abundant as well as cougar and black bear. Hang your food.

Rocky Canyon is frequently used by hunters, as evidenced by two well-used camps. Otherwise, few people use this canyon. The cattle allotment, which has been the source of complaints from hikers, is occupied beginning in mid-July.

Increasing damage from off-road vehicles in the meadows should be reported (hopefully with photographs) to the Dubois Ranger District of the Targhee National Forest.

Once at the meadow, the hike becomes an easy cross-country "stroll". The route to the canyon forks is obvious. We hiked up the Right Fork, which is more difficult, found its head to be a very scenic elk pasture but were eventually forced back by a mid-June snowstorm.

Parts of Meadow Creek and South Meadow Creek, the canyons just the other side of prominent peak 10,759 on Rocky Canyon's north flank, have been designated as a Research Natural Area. These canyons are ecologically similar to Rocky Canyon. You may camp and hike here too, but water is more difficult to find.—*Ralph Maughan* □

HIKE 40 *SOUTH CREEK*

General description: A late spring to early summer one or two-day hike into the southernmost part of the rugged Lemhi Mountains.
General location: Just east of the small town of Howe, 75 miles northwest of Pocatello, and 55 miles northwest of Idaho Falls.
Maps: Howe Northeast and Tyler Peak (7.5') USGS quads.
Difficulty: Easy about halfway, then moderate due to a faint trail.
Season: Mid-May through October.
Information: Lost River Ranger District, Challis National Forest, Box 507, Mackay, Idaho 83251; (208) 588-2224.

The hike: The stark, rough, southern end of the Lemhi Mountains rises abruptly from the Arco Desert near the sleepy town of Howe (population 20). The first peak in the range is 10,810-foot Saddle Mountain a chunk of limestone rising 5,500 feet (over a mile) above the floor of the Little Lost River Valley and the desert to its east.

South Creek, the only live stream flowing from the slopes of Saddle Moun-

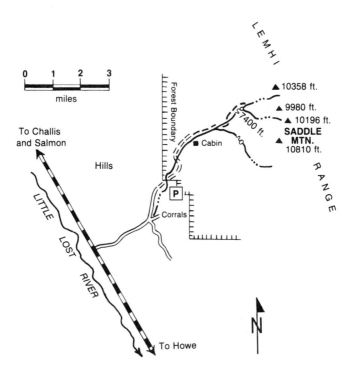

tain, provides a green pathway into the mountain range as early as May 15.

Drive to Howe and take the county road that goes through the town and heads northward up the Little Lost River Valley. About 7.5 miles north of Howe, turn off of the pavement onto a good gravel road that leaves to the east (right). The road heads straight toward the rough, sere mountains. After about 2.5 miles, you come to a complex of corrals. Here, turn to the left onto a less-improved dirt road. Drive a mile or so to its end right at the mouth of South Creek Canyon. Here you'll find several small grassy spots amid the sagebrush in which you can camp.

A jeep road continues up the canyon. Head up the road on foot. This old track seems to be in the process of abandonment and slow decay, having been partially blocked to traffic by a diversion of South Creek. The jeep trail keeps close to the bubbling creek, weaving in and out of the small streamside forest of river birch, cottonwood, and quaking aspen. Small groups of increasingly

Picturesque sod-roofed cabin near South Creek. Ralph Maughan photo.

rugged cliffs jut from the canyon walls, which are vegetated with sagebrush and short grass. Pink, white, and chocolate are the colors of these quartzite cliffs, contrasting with the gray limestone core of the range.

You'll cross the creek a number of times, but it's always just a short jump over one or two inches of water. The jeep track ends about 100 yards past an ancient sod-roofed cabin, about two miles from the beginning of the jeep trail. Here the old four-wheel track turns into an intimate path leading through an increasingly damp riparian forest. The trail is faint, but it's easy walking. It emerges from the tiny forest onto the grassy sagebrush hillslope and then goes back into the trees several times. The trail stays on the left (north) side of the creek the entire distance, with one short exception.

You'll find many places to camp in the 2.5 miles from the cabin to trail's end in a grassy meadow, where South Creek flows out of the ground. From this spot you can climb Saddle Mountain's rough slopes, or you can continue without a trail to the very end of the canyon. Above the meadow and spring rise a number of lesser peaks (all unnamed) to form the crest of the mountain range north of Saddle Mountain.

South Creek has a major fork about a mile downstream from the end of the trail. No trail follows this fork but it's an easy cross-country walk once you've bushwhacked through the thicket of forest where this fork flows into South Creek. Up the fork, you'll find a short stream that also bubbles up in a meadow. Choose a pristine campsite here in full view of Saddle Mountain, but please—leave no fire rings.

The best season for hiking South Creek is from about the second week of June to early July.—*Ralph Maughan* □

Note: Public access to South Creek was blocked in 1991 by a locked gate just beyond the corrals. However access is still fiarly easy by driving to the old mines in Camp Creek, a mile or two to the north. From here walk south through hilly open rangeland until you drop into South Creek canyon. The Challis National Forest is working to develop a new public access trailhead. Meanwhile, the new Challis travel plan permanently closes South Creek to full-sized motor vehicles.—Ralph Maughan □

HIKE 41   *YELLOW LAKE*

General description: A good weekend trip to a lake in the center of the proposed Lemhi Range Wilderness.
General location: About 58 road miles south of Salmon.
Maps: Sheephorn Peak, Yellow Peak (7.5') USGS quads.
Special attractions: A particularly spectacular view of Yellow Peak. Solitude at an alpine lake in a large, grassy, cirque basin. A chance to encounter mountain goats.
Difficulty: Moderately difficult due to the climb.
Season: Early July through September.
Information: Leadore Ranger District, Salmon National Forest, Box 180, Leadore, Idaho 83463; (208) 768-2371; or Challis Ranger District, Challis National Forest, Box 337, Challis, Idaho 83226; (208) 879-4321.

The hike: Yellow Lake sits at 9,500 feet in a grassy cirque dotted with struggling clumps of fir. Mountain goats graze the glacial basin of the lake and wander over the high, rounded crest of the Lemhi Range here. Some people call this lake Golden Trout Lake, although it is full of rainbow trout instead. On the Patterson USGS quadrange, it is given no name at all.

The best route to Yellow Lake is from the east, via the Lemhi Valley and Idaho Highway 28. From Idaho Falls or Pocatello, drive up the Birch Creek Valley and over Gilmore Summit to Leadore, a ranching hamlet in the Lemhi Valley with a population of 114. From Salmon, drive south, going up the Lemhi Valley for 46 miles to Leadore. The Leadore Ranger District office of the Salmon National Forest at Leadore can give you current information about the hike and about many other nearby hikes.

In Leadore, turn off the highway and go west on the Eightmile Road, which is marked by a Bureau of Land Management sign. This road has been a source of confusion in the past but is now marked with signs, and the Leadore topographic quadrangle is accurate. The BLM recently improved the road with gravel.

The trail lies just past the Timber Creek Reservoir in the Middle Fork of Little Timber Creek, approximately 10 miles west of Leadore. You'll begin in an open area used by cattle and sheep. Here a sign designates the trail to "Golden Trout Lake". Follow the trail across a small creek and begin climbing amid thick timber. In this beginning part of the hike you'll encounter a lot of dead-fall timber, but the Forest Service generally maintains the trail well. Continue up the Middle Fork of Little Timber Creek Canyon for about

HIKE 41 *YELLOW LAKE*

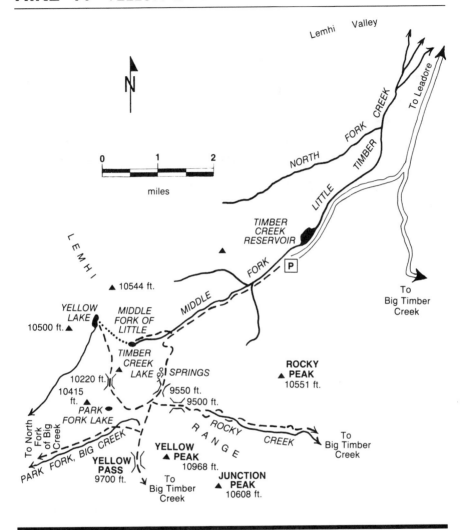

3.5 miles, then the trail swings to the south to climb steeply to an open park and then to a pass just under 9,600 feet high. The pass is about four miles from the trail's beginning, a 1,900 foot gain in altitude.

On the pass you look down into the beautiful Park Fork of Big Creek with magnificent Yellow Peak rising to nearly 11,000 to your left. (See the Big Creek/Big Timber Creek Loop hike description for more information about the Park Fork).

Below, you'll notice a trail junction. A large tree with a sign indicates the route to Yellow Lake, and the trail swings back to the north to climb absolutely straight up the ridge in a grueling haul that gains 800 feet of elevation in a mile. Far below, you'll see little Park Fork Lake. In the far expanse to the

The Yellow Lake cirque. Philip Blomquist photo.

west are Mt. Borah and the Tremendous Lost River Mountains.

When you reach the rubble-strewn summit, look down to the lovely Yellow Lake cirque. The glacier-created basin is large, perhaps 80 acres in size. A cliff and rubble ridge drops into the lake's west side, while the cirque curls northward beyond the lake. You'll descend on the trail toward the lake over a talus slope and then through a meadow punctuated by clumps of pine. There are plenty of places to camp, although right next to the lake it is mostly wet and marshy. The rainbow trout are usually very hard to catch, due to the lake's clarity and open aspect.

On my last trip to Yellow Lake, I saw seven mountain goats on the ridge to the northeast and east of the lake. This is a good alternate route to return to the Middle Fork of Little Timber Creek. Climb just 200 feet to the ridge east of the lake and drop down to Middle Fork of Little Timber Creek Lake on the other side. It's a steep downhill haul to the lake in a short drop of 550 feet, but there's a newly constructed trail at the lake that will take you down the canyon to rejoin the trail you began on, making a loop hike. In 1981, the junction to this new trail was not marked.

Occasionally a few trail bikes are found in the vicinity of Yellow Lake, but they are not common. In addition, the crest of the range here is sometimes grazed for a short period in the summer. Check with the Forest Service for dates if you don't want to risk sharing Yellow Lake with sheep.—*Philip Blomquist* □

Note: Our revisit to Yellow Lake in 1989 found it full of large golden/rainbow trout hybrids. Angling success was good.—Philip Blomquist

HIKE 42 *BELL MOUNTAIN CANYON*

General description: An easy and beautiful early summer day hike or overnighter.

General location: On the east side of the Lemhi Range, 65 miles northwest of Idaho Falls, 100 miles north-northwest of Pocatello, and 75 miles southeast of Salmon.

Maps: Bell Mtn., Coal Kiln Canyon (7 1/2') USGS quads.

Special attractions: Glacier-sculpted peaks visible throughout the easy five-mile hike. Wildflowers.

Difficulty: Easy to moderately easy.

Season: Early June through mid-October—best from mid-June to mid-July.

Information: Dubois Ranger District, Targhee National Forest, Dubois, Idaho 83423; (208) 374-5422.

The hike: At 11,612 feet, Bell Mountain is the second highest peak in the Lemhi Mountains. Its most beautiful side faces the east. Bell Mountain Canyon was sculpted to its present form by a glacier that flowed from its northeast slopes.

This hike is a five-mile loop that rambles through meadows, past a spruce-fir forest and back through meadows. It is exquisitely beautiful from mid-June (when the annual growth is green and wildflowers bloom) until the time cattle are put in the area (about mid-July).

From Idaho Falls, Pocatello, or Rexburg, follow Idaho Highway 28 to the town of Mud Lake. Continue on Highway 28 at the highway junction just west of town and drive up into the Birch Creek Valley. Drive past the store and gas station at Lone Pine. Look for an improved, dirt side road to the left of the highway, 13.2 miles past Lone Pine. Here a sign reads "Charcoal Kilns Historical Site, 6 miles". If you are coming southward from Salmon, this road is 10.3 miles south of Gilmore Summit.

The side road heads almost straight toward the Lemhi Mountains. At 4.8 miles there is a junction. Turn left here onto a primitive dirt road (passable to two-wheel drive vehicles most of the time). After .4 mile there is another junction. Keep to the right.

The dirt road winds around and up toward Bell Mountain and Mammoth canyons. After 1.2 more miles you cross a fence marking the Targhee National Forest, and the road forks right leading steeply downhill. Go down the hill and park (or park on top if it looks too steep).

Magnificent Bell Mountain and a similarly-shaped unnamed peak in front of it rise before you.

You can begin the hike by heading up the faint, grassy jeep track in the canyon, or, better, climb the end moraine (hill) at the mouth of the canyon and walk along its rolling surface. There are outstanding views from the moraine. After a mile, you come to the beginning of the end moraine and drop down into the broad canyon bottom. Here are meadows and patches of trees.

Follow the track up the canyon (or hike cross-country). Eventually you come to the forks, which are separated by a low, timbered hill. Hike up either fork about a mile and then cross over into the other fork on a low, non-forested pass.

Elk, deer, and antelope are common in this easily accessible, but wild canyon.

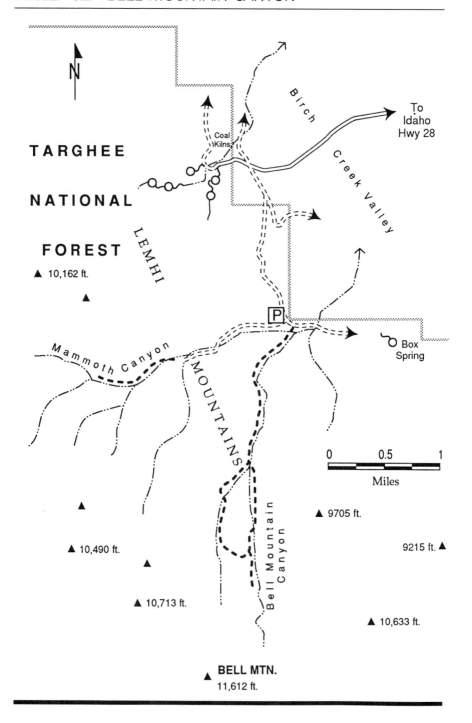

This open country could easily be damaged by off-road vehicles. Hopefully the machine jockeys will leave it alone as it was in the summer of 1987 when I visited.

There is no water. You must take a quart for each person for a day hike.

Mosquitoes can be bad from mid-June until July unless the previous night saw a hard freeze.—*Ralph Maughan.* ☐

HIKE 43 *NEZ PERCE LAKE*

General description: A relatively short, but steep, trail into the Lemhi Mountains near Leadore. Ideal for a day or overnight trip.

General location: Seven linear miles southeast of Leadore beneath 10,465 foot Sheephorn Peak.

Maps: Purcell Spring, Sheephorn Peak (7.5') USGS quads.

Special attractions: Nez Perce Lake offers solitude and the chance to catch Arctic grayling, a rare species in the Rocky Mountains.

Difficulty: Moderate as a day hike due to the climb.

Season: July to late September.

Information: Leadore Ranger District, Salmon National Forest, Box 180, Leadore, Idaho 83464; (208) 768-2371.

The hike: Nez Perce Lake is seldom visited, but is attainable by a short hiking trail (closed to machines). The trail is steep, but not difficult to follow. The most difficult part of this hike is reaching the undeveloped trailhead. Follow these instructions carefully.

Drive southward on Idaho Highway 28 from Leadore. After six miles, turn west on a well-maintained gravel road. Here a BLM sign indicates the route to Timber Creek and Cold Spring. At one mile the road crosses Texas Creek (the headwaters of the Lemhi River) and then swings south again. Three miles later, you reach Cold Springs. Located at the end of the maintained road is a small ranch house and assorted buildings. Turn to the right on a rough road immediately before you arrive at the ranch.

The road climbs a short distance through a gap between the edge of the mountain range and a small butte near the ranch. It is yet another 3.5 miles to the trailhead. A pickup truck, or better yet, a four-wheel drive is needed. Near Purcell Spring the route is two tire tracks through the sagebrush, and the road is extremely rocky. The forest boundary is marked by a swinging gate. A sign indicating the direction of Nez Perce Creek is located on the gate. The end of the track is another half mile. It is a steep and potentially hazardous way.

In contrast to the road, the Forest Service has cut a new trail to the lake. It is 2.5 miles and a climb of about 1,200 feet on the easily followed new trail.

The lake basin is a small cirque, rocky with somewhat limited overnight camping. As of 1989 there were no fire rings; please use your backpack stove! Deer and elk are frequently seen in the area, and, if you are fortunate, a mountain goat may be spotted on the flank of Sheephorn Peak.

Nez Perce Lake was stocked with Arctic grayling in 1982. By 1989 some were quite large. In the past, trout in this small lake sometimes were winter-killed.

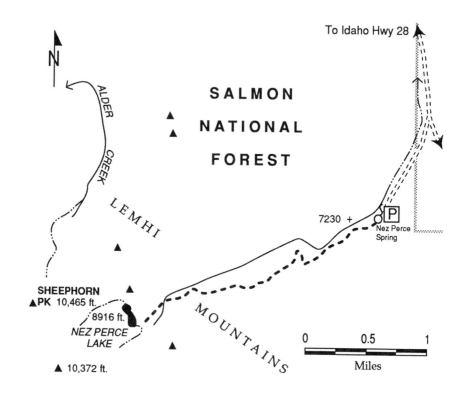

To Idaho Hwy 28

S A L M O N

N A T I O N A L

F O R E S T

ALDER

CREEK

L E M H I

7230 +

P

Nez Perce
Spring

SHEEPHORN
▲PK 10,465 ft.

8916 ft.

*NEZ PERCE
LAKE*

M O U N T A I N S

▲ 10,372 ft.

0   0.5   1

Miles

Grayling are hardier and by 1989 had also survived two years of drought. Much to my surprise, Nez Perce Lake is filled with freshwater shrimp. This is good for growing fat fish, but it makes hooking a grayling more difficult. —*Phil Blomquist* □

Lost River Mountains

Overview

A range of contorted sedimentary rock, the Lost River Mountains are by far Idaho's highest. Running from southeast to northwest, they parallel the neighboring Lemhi Mountains, separated from them by the broad Little Lost River Valley and by the Pahsimeroi Valley.

Borah Peak at 12,622 feet and 12,228-foot Leatherman Peak, Idaho's first and second highest peaks, grace the middle part of the range. Only the nearby Pioneer Mountains and the Lemhi Range have 12,000 footers (and then only one such summit each). Besides Borah and Leatherman, the Lost Rivers sport seven others over 12,000 feet. They are: 12,247 (the north spur of Borah); 12,140 (Mt. Breitenbach); 12,078; 12,023; 12,010 (estimated); and 12,003 (estimated). As you see, most of Idaho's highest peaks are unnamed, and some are not even measured accurately!

Although the colorful Challis Volcanics have buried the low northern end of the range and have also washed up on the mountain's east side, the high core of the Lost Rivers is relentlessly limestone—ancient sea deposits compressed into rock and then pushed up over two miles above sea level, warped, folded and broken to stand in the dry, cold air of southeast central Idaho.

The Lost River Range has still fewer hiking trails than its longer neighbor, the Lemhi Range; and, other than climbers seeking the summits of Leatherman and Borah, a few hunters in the fall, and stray recreationists, these heights see only cowhands.

The west-facing side of the Lost Rivers rises very abruptly, presenting a bold and austere mountain front towering 5,000 feet above some of the largest alluvial fans in the West. Many people travel U.S. Highway 93, which follows the bottom of the Big Lost River Valley here, but few folks reach the mountains, since the access roads are poor and the canyons rough, rugged, and choked with brush.

The east-facing side of the range, on the other hand, has long canyons. These harbor much more flowing water, some hiking trails or easy routes, and a few lakes near the crest where the altitude and snowmelt overcome the tendency of water to drain into the limestone. These lakes are rare, but they are among the most beautiful in Idaho.

While the parallel Lemhi Mountains have no low passes, the Lost Rivers are split into four sections by low passes. The first section begins southeast of Arco near Howe. Often called the Arco Hills, these "hills" rise to 9,045 feet at Jumpoff Peak. There are no hiking trails, absolutely no water, but many interesting cliffs and rock formations. It is a rarely visited area. A low pass (Arco Pass) separates the Arco Hills from the first section of the real mountains.

King Mountain is the first big mountain in the range. At 10,612 feet, King Mountain is one of the few named peaks in what has become known as the 95,000-acre King Mountain Roadless Area. Despite a nameless high point of 11,081 feet in the King Mountain portion, even here there is scarcely any water. Instead, you'll find unknown country of big mountains, canyons lined with incredible cliffs and rock fins, caves, and other geological oddities.

A good dirt road that goes over Pass Creek Summit (only 7,600 feet) marks the next division of the Lost Rivers. North of this division, the really high Lost Rivers begin. This middle portion of the range was proposed for classification as the 115,000-acre Borah Peak Wilderness by the Forest Service as a result of RARE II. Though the area contains no commercial timber, no minerals, no damsites, no proposed ski areas, and the highest mountains in Idaho, still, anti-wilderness die-hards will make wilderness classification difficult. Your voice is needed in the campaign to protect this area.

North of the Borah Peak proposed wilderness, a deep trough cuts across the range. Here, at Doublespring Pass (8,318 feet), another good dirt road crosses the mountains. It leads from the Big Lost River Valley over to the Pahsimeroi Valley. The last and northernmost portion of the range is often called the Pahsimeroi Mountains. It, too, is a little-traveled area of high limestone peaks and little water. Just north of Grouse Creek the range fades and is buried by Challis Volcanics, taking on a rolling rather than rugged appearance.

View of the Lost River Mountains from the White Knob Mountains. Ralph Maughan photo.

From south to north, the major canyons in the Lost Rivers include Ramshorn, Cedarville, Cabin Fork and North Fork of Cedarville, Van Dorn, Basin Creek, Elbow, Pass Creek, Wet Creek, Big Creek, Lower Cedar, Upper Cedar, Long Lost Creek, Dry Creek, east and west forks of the Pahsimeroi, Mahogany Creek, Willow Creek, Doublespring Creek, Christian Gulch, and Grouse Creek. Roads fill Pass Creek, Willow Creek, and Doublespring Creek, leaving little room for hiking. The rest of the canyons offer good, but sometimes rough, hikes—mostly either on a jeep trail or cross-country. Reliable water can be found in Basin Creek, Big Creek, Lower and Upper Cedar, Long Lost and Dry creeks, and the forks of the Pahsimeroi; and Mahogany and Grouse creeks.

By and large, road access to the canyons is plentiful but of poor quality. Drive carefully; carry maps, a shovel, and a spare tire.

Wildlife in the Lost Rivers is varied but not particularly abundant. Most common are antelope, deer, and elk. A reintroduced herd of bighorn sheep is faring well. Mountain lions and bobcats are common, but rarely seen. As with the Lemhi Mountains, the se mountains have been managed for livestock use rather than multiple uses, unlike the law dictates. The prevalence of rock, however, keeps the absolute number of cattle down.

On October 28, 1983, the earth at the base of Borah Peak split, leaving a fault scarp 10 miles long from north to south. The earthquake was the biggest (7.3 on the Richter Scale) in the lower 48 states in 24 years. Those exploring the range will most certainly find new rockslides and some rearrangements of the trails. As the earthquake caused the valley to drop, the Lost River Range's relief may be 15 to 20 feet greater than before the quake.

HIKE 44 *BEAR CREEK LAKE*

General description: A day or weekend hike to a small lake tucked amid towering mountains.
General location: 12 miles northeast of Mackay, 90 miles northwest of Pocatello.
Maps: Mackay (15') and Methodist Creek (7.5') USGS quads.
Special attractions: Access to gigantic mountains after a relatively short hike.
Difficulty: Moderate. A fairly steep but short hike on a faint trail.
Season: Late June through September.
Information: Lost River Ranger District, Challis National Forest, Box 507, Mackay, Idaho 83251; (208) 588-2224.

The hike: The biggest problem with hiking in the Lost River Mountains is finding a passable road to the point you begin the hike. Happily for those without a jeep, the Bear Creek trail is an exception. The road is not great, but a small car can make it to the trailhead. An uncrowded trail ascending quickly to stunning mountain scenery rewards you for your efforts. The trail leads to small, barren, but beautiful Bear Creek Lake in 2.5 miles with a climb of about 1,500 feet.

Turn off of U.S. Highway 93, eight miles south of Mackay (or 19 miles north of Arco) at a clump of houses called Leslie. Here a gravel road travels northward for about two miles and then heads northeast toward a low spot

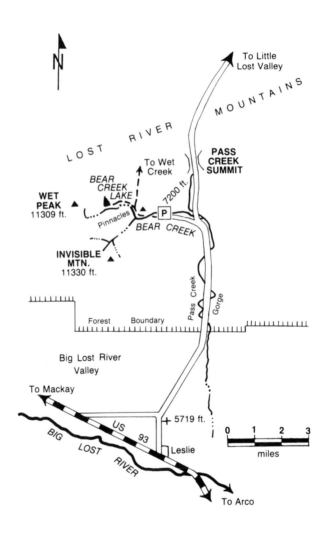

(an obvious canyon) in the Lost River Mountains. The road enters this tight canyon called Pass Creek Gorge. Here, the rugged scenery of looming limestone walls lasts for two miles. Suddenly, the gorge opens into an open canyon where cows graze the pastureland. About two more miles brings you to the Bear Creek side-road (to the left). This road is 9.5 miles from the highway exit at Leslie.

This road heads northward over stream gravel toward a canyon with impressive walls. Bear Creek Canyon, a tributary to the canyon of Pass Creek through which you are driving, begins abruptly with cliffs that rise 600 vertical feet. The road passes through scrubby aspen, goes past the informal, undeveloped Bear Creek Campground, and passes into open forest. The trailhead is 1.2 miles from the start of the Bear Creek side-road. Watch out that you don't take a road to the right (it goes right down to the creek) at about the one-mile mark. I did my first time in Bear Creek and spent an hour wading through stinging nettle, cow pies, and swamp. Keep left, drive up a small hill, and park where the road ends in the shade at a trailhead that also serves as an informal camping spot. There is room for three or four vehicles.

The trail strikes out straight ahead up-canyon. The trail is lightly used but well blazed—easy to find and follow.

The map shows the trail crossing the creek several times. In fact, it only crosses it once. Instead, follow the trail for about one-half mile on the left side of the creek. Suddenly, the trail drops down to the creek and crosses it on two logs lashed together. Now on the creek's right side, you'll walk through level, open forest a short distance to the forks of the canyon—Methodist Gulch to the left and Bear Creek to the right. Huge peaks appear up Methodist Gulch, but their full magnitude is frustratingly hidden by nearby trees and the bend of Methodist Gulch.

At the forks, the trail climbs almost straight up the mountainside on the right. An unmapped, misleading trail here stays lower down. Ignore it. Climb about 300 feet in one-quarter mile through a Douglas fir forest growing on the dry, rocky mountainside. Next you'll break out into the open. Here, across Bear Creek, you can see the decaying remains of an old horse road once used to log part of the canyon. After puffing for a total of about a half-mile and climbing 500 feet from the forks, you come to a sign that points uphill, reading "Wet Creek." Here is the place for some easy route-finding. Don't continue uphill on the obvious trail you've been following. Instead, leave to the left, walk into the trees, and keep about 50 yards from the creek until you find the faint trail continuing up-canyon. It's marked by faint blazes, and it does not appear on the Methodist Creek USGS quadrangle. It is shown on the older Mackay quadrangle, however.

Soon you see Bear Creek's waters disappear into the limestone rubble of the creek bed as you keep on climbing up the canyon. You cross the now-dry bed of the creek just after an open spot, cleared by ancient horse logging and now kept clear by avalanches. Continue up Bear Creek, crossing the creek bed every now and then. Look for the numerous faint blazes on the trees that mark the route. After a waterless half-mile, you'll be happy to find that the creek reemerges. Then, just past a small, startlingly green meadow, the trail climbs straight up the hillside to Bear Creek Lake. It's about .3 mile and a tough 300-foot climb to the lake. You may find that the trail disappears completely, but it doesn't matter. You will find the lake. Keep your eyes on the giant peak ahead and just angle to the right.

Like "taffy from a giant's kitchen," the twisted pinnacles near Bear Creek Lake flow upward toward the sky. Ralph Maughan photo.

Just before you come to the lakeshore, you'll reach a beautiful green, flat meadow (a pond in early June). This is a fine place to camp. A few yards beyond the meadow shimmer the jade waters of Bear Creek Lake. Sorry, no fish.

The giant peak toward which you've been heading now rises as a wall behind the lake. Above the wall, however, you can see even higher peaks, indicating that the wall is but a small ornament on the crest of the Lost River Range.

From the lake, as you look toward the southwest, you'll see astounding pinnacles rise. This is the south wall of Bear Creek. These twisted rocks flow toward the sky like taffy from a giant's kitchen. These pinnacles, similar in appearance to the much-photographed, much-climbed Dolomites in the Italian Alps, guard a green alpine meadow where Bear Creek begins its tumbling descent in the grass and boulders. From this meadow beneath the crags you can see the lofty heights of the Wet Peak masiff at the very head of Bear Creek Canyon.

Northeast of the lake, a long talus gulch slides down from a pass. You can scramble up the gulch for access to Wet Creek (no water!), or you can use it as a scrambling route to the crest of the mountain range. At the pass lies an interesting area of grassy limestone plateau, complete with wildflowers and ephemeral ponds, all high above timberline.

I found just one fire ring near the lake. Will you keep it that way?—*Ralph Maughan* ☐

Note: Reportedly, as of 1990, the upper portion of the trail is much more visible than the decade previous.—Ralph Maughan

HIKE 45 DRY CREEK

General description: A one-day to several-day hike up a spectacularly broad, open canyon in the proposed Borah Peak Wilderness.

General location: 105 miles northwest of Pocatello, 88 miles northwest of Idaho Falls, and 15 miles north of Mackay in the Lost River Mountain.

Maps: Hawley Mtn. (15'), Leatherman Peak and Massacre Mtn. (7.5') USGS quads.

Special attractions: Gorgeous 12,000-foot peaks. Good fishing in lower Dry Creek for brook trout and at Swauger Lakes for cutthroat.

Difficulty: Easy, if you can get your vehicle close to the end of the road.

Season: Late June to mid-October.

Information: Lost River Ranger District, Challis National Forest, Box 507, Mackay, Idaho 83251; (208) 588-2224.

The hike: Dry Creek, ironically, has plenty of water. It is one of the most scenic hikes in eastern Idaho, with emphasis on views of large, rugged mountains with complex folds in their rocks. Dry Creek also has good fishing for brook trout in the first part of the hike. A side trip to Swauger Lakes, which lie on the divide between Dry Creek and Long Lost Creek, brings you to a pleasant cutthroat fishery.

As with so many hikes in this portion of the book, first drive to Howe at the southern end of the Little Lost River Valley. Drive up the Little Lost Valley for 28 miles to an abandoned white school house called "Clyde." Here is a signed road junction where you turn to the left (west) and head across sagebrush flats for a few miles until you come to Wet Creek. Wet Creek is a foothill, rangeland stream that sometimes has pretty good fishing. After you cross Wet Creek, a drive of not quite two miles brings you to the turnoff for the Dry Creek Road. The turnoff is just before a second crossing over Wet Creek. The Dry Creek Road is not great, but it's not a jeep road either. It's rutted and often sports six-inch rocks. Bounce along at five miles per hour for about seven miles in a land of high, bare hills—antelope heaven—and you'll come to what is shown on some old maps as Dry Creek Reservoir. There is no reservoir, however, because the dam was dynamited years ago in a water war. There is good fishing in the hole just below where the water spills over the wreck of the dam.

Unless you have a four-wheel-drive vehicle, park here. The road descends a rockslide that requires four-wheel-drive to go back up. A beautiful view of the high peaks at the head of Dry Creek pulls you on. You cross small Long Lost Creek (a poor road heads up its canyon to your left) and then you cross Dry Creek. The road continues on for about a mile as the scenery improves. The road ends where a sidehill blocks large vehicles. There is plenty of room to park here.

The massive core of the Lost River Mountains is made up of limestone—sediments deposited under ancient seas and then raised up to become the incredible peaks you see. On this side of the mountains, in addition to limestone, more recent volcanic rocks, called collectively the Challis Volcanics, have washed up over the base of the limestone into high, colorful foothills.

You'll start up Dry Creek Canyon, walking along a good trail through open Challis Volcanic country—high, reddish hills with numerous springs but little

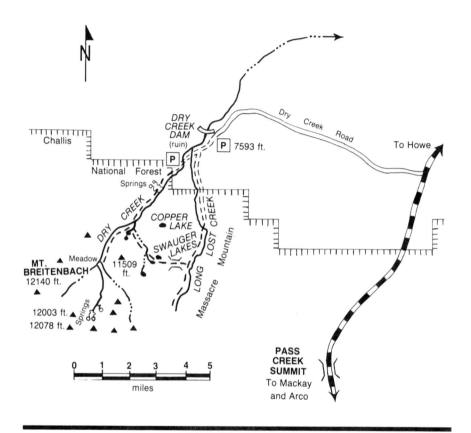

timber. Birch and willows cling to the broad canyon bottom. Here and there stands a clump of aspen and even a Douglas fir or two. The creek is full of brook trout. There are quite a few camping spots all along the canyon floor; these are fine except when livestock are present. Check with the Forest Service to plan a trip before they're in the canyon.

About two miles up the trail, you'll find a pretty waterfall on Dry Creek, Unfortunately, there are no fish above the falls.

A large triangular mountain dominates the view as you continue up Dry Creek. This 11,509-foot peak is the first of the big limestone peaks in Dry Creek. As you approach its base, the trail drops down to and crosses Dry Creek; then it heads up a steep rocky side-canyon to Swauger Lakes. This is a thousand-foot, two-mile climb. The lakes are small but beautiful, lying in meadow country where the volcanic formation meets the rugged limestone peaks.

These lakes offer tranquil camping, where you can sit by a small lake at a meadow, staring at the rocky crag of an 11,509-foot peak rising right before you. From the lakes, you can also continue on to the south, following the trail down into Long Lost Creek—a canyon similar to Dry Creek in its structure and scenery.

As an alternative, you can elect not to climb up to the lakes from where the trail crosses Dry Creek. On the hill just across the creek, a spring feeds a pretty pond. Near the pond, you can pick up a faint trail that continues up Dry Creek. As you follow this easy trail, passing through small patches of conifer and meadows, more and more rugged mountains appear, mostly up-canyon and on the north (right) side of the canyon. The largest is 12,140-foot Mt. Breitenbach on the upper northside of the canyon . Every point on the giant wall at the very head of the canyon is over 11,400 feet, and some of its points top 12,000 feet; yet not a single peak has a name.

The trail peters out at a nice meadow just at the confluence of the three forks which feed into Dry Creek at the canyon's head. This is a good place to camp and spend a day doing some rugged cross-country exploration of Dry Creek's forks. Look for elk, deer, and coyotes in the canyon.

You'll find the Dry Creek hike both inspiring and relatively painless. The most difficult part is the drive over the Dry Creek road to the start of the trail. (Note: Hunters present during the big earthquake of October 1983 reported a large rockslide in the head of Dry Creek.)—Ralph Maughan ☐

Note: Since the first edition of this book, off-road vehicles have discovered the Swauger Lakes, and they have done some high altitude hill-trashing. They have also developed a trail that leads directly to Swauger lakes via Copper Lake. This is not shown on any map. The Challis Forest Plan was appealed by various conservation groups in hopes of eliminating these ma chines from the proposed Borah Peak Wilderness. There is some possibility that the number of ORVs in this drainage, and others, will be reduced or eliminated in 1991 or 1992.—Ralph Maughan

HIKE 46 *MERRIAM LAKE*

General description: A short hike to a stunning high mountain lake. It would be an overnight trip were it not for the time-consuming road access to the trailhead.
General location: In the crest of the Lost River Range in the proposed Borah Peak Wilderness 16 linear miles northwest of Mackay and 75 miles south of Salmon.
Maps: Burnt Creek, Elkhorn Creek, and Leatherman Peak (7.5') USGS quads.
Special attractions: One of Idaho's most beautiful lakes set in a large cirque basin, dominated by an unnamed 12,065- foot peak.
Difficulty: Moderate. A short, steep hike.
Season: Mid-July to late September.
Information: Challis Ranger District, Challis National Forest, HC 63 Box 1669, Challis, Idaho 83226. (208) 879-4321.

The hike: The permeable limestone core of the Lost River Range is hostile to the formation of lakes, despite the mountains' great height. The few lakes

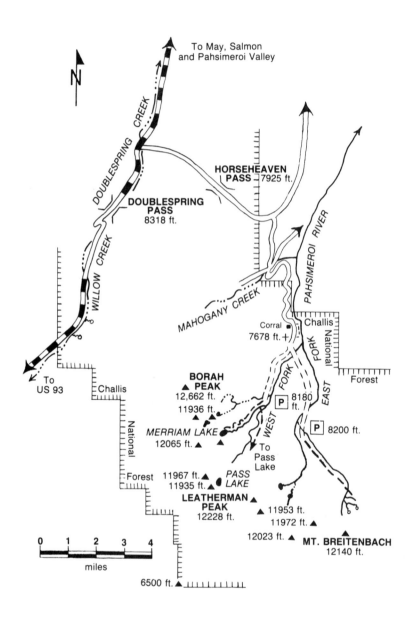

To May, Salmon
and Pahsimeroi Valley

N

DOUBLESPRING CREEK

HORSEHEAVEN
PASS 7925 ft.

DOUBLESPRING
PASS
8318 ft.

WILLOW CREEK

PAHSIMEROI RIVER

MAHOGANY CREEK

Corral   Challis
7678 ft. +

To
US 93   Challis

BORAH
PEAK
12,662 ft.
11936 ft. ▲

National

MERRIAM LAKE
12065 ft. ▲

WEST FORK

EAST FORK

P 8180 ft.

P 8200 ft.

To
Pass
Lake

Forest   11967 ft.▲
11935 ft.▲

PASS
LAKE

Forest

National

LEATHERMAN
PEAK
12228 ft.

▲ 11953 ft.

11972 ft. ▲

0 1 2 3 4
miles

12023 ft. ▲ MT. BREITENBACH
12140 ft.

6500 ft. ▲

that do exist in these crags are both fertile and scenic. Merriam Lake is possibly the most beautiful. Set in a glacier-carved cirque at 9,600 feet, Merriam reflects the image of picturesque peak 12,065 at the basin's head. The lake is flanked by mountains over 11,000 feet on both sides.

Like most accesses to the east side of the Lost Rivers, the road to the trailhead is long and bad. Moreover, it has deteriorated since the first edition of this book. You must take a high clearance vehicle, and a four-wheel drive is recommended. Access is from the Big Lost River Valley or the Pahsimeroi Valley.

From the Willow Creek Valley, drive south along U.S. 93 from Challis, over Willow Creek Summit, and then 7.8 more miles to the May-Patterson (Doublespring Pass) Road to the left of the Highway 93. From Mackay, drive northward on U.S. 93 about 22 miles to the turnoff. At 2.4 miles onto the May-Patterson Road, there is a picnic area and interpretive displays describing the effects of the great earthquake of 1983. This is near Mt. Borah, the highest mountain in Idaho, and adjacent to part of the earthquake scarp. Drive five more miles on a fairly good gravel then dirt road to Doublespring Pass. Continue over the pass down broad, dry Doublespring Creek Canyon for three more miles. Turn right at the sign indicating Horseheaven Pass.

For the Pahsimeroi Valley access, drive to the almost ghost town of May, then cross over the valley to the county road that goes up its west side. This road leads up into Doublespring Creek, and 35 miles from May it comes to the Horseheaven Pass turnoff.

Drive up a short steep hill and follow the dirt road to Horseheaven Pass which is really a broad rangeland divide between the Lost Rivers and an outlying mountain. You are likely to see pronghorn antelope in the general area.

Seven miles past the turnoff from the May-Patterson Road, you'll reach a junction. The road to the left leads to the Pahsimeroi Valley. It's a rough alternative route which we won't describe here. You should keep to the right. In another mile, you'll come to a four-way junction just before Mahogany Creek. Continue straight ahead at the junction, and drop down to cross Mahogany Creek. Go up the creek for .1 mile, then turn onto the road at the left to go up a steep, short hill. The road then makes a broad 180-degree turn around the hill and enters the broad valley which is the headwaters of the Pahsimeroi River.

After about 2.5 miles on an increasingly rocky road, you come to a line shack and a corral. Just beyond, the road forks. The left fork follows the East Fork of the Pahsimeroi. You can see amazing cliffs and rock folds up this fork (see the hike description for the East Fork, Pahsimeroi River).

Continue to the right up the valley of the West Fork of the Pahsimeroi. About three miles of the twisting and rocky road brings you to the trailhead, where there is room to park several vehicles, and several camping spots. The only good thing we can say about the road is that it's no worse in a rainstorm.

The trail begins at the end of the road as a wide gravel path on the right side of the left fork of the creek. Be sure not to cross the left fork of the creek and be careful not to get too high to the creek's right side either. About .25 mile into the hike, the correct trail turns to the right and crosses a meadow. Blaze marks can be seen if you look carefully. Beware, as a trail to Pass Lake that does cross the creek here looks deceptively like the correct one.

The trail climbs moderately for 1.5 miles, gaining 625 feet altitude. For the last half mile, though, it climbs 750 feet quite steeply, switchbacking to the

Merriam Lake and the crest of the Lost River Mountains. Ralph Maughan photo.

lake outlet. The trail always stays on the right side of the creek. At the lake's right side, both near the outlet and near its top side, there are some campsites. Unfortunately, they are overused. Above the lake, however, you'll find pristine camping spots in a rock garden and alpine meadow setting. Please keep them in this condition and use a stove rather the scavenging the meager woods for a campfire.

The huge peak that dominates the view up the basin is 12,065 feet high and remains nameless, although a surprising number of visitors think it's Borah Peak. Borah is a good two miles to the north and not in sight.

If you follow the lake's inlet stream upward, you will pass delightful cascades, wildflower-filled meadows, and a few small ponds. Eventually you reach an upper lake, jade-colored, set in an alpine rock basin at 10,220 feet. Here there are no fish. The sharp peak rising to the lake's north is 11,936 feet high, and as is usual in these mountains, nameless.

From Merriam Lake you can also climb the ridge to the lake's northwest. From the top one looks straight down to a no-name lake in a nameless canyon. To the southwest you look across 11,000 foot high side ridges of bare rock with the high point of Leatherman Peak in the distance. This ridge is a good location for hunting fossils (Paleozoic coral).—*Donna and John Pinsof* □

HIKE 47   *MILL CREEK TO SHEEP PEN BASIN*

General description: A day or overnight hike to a large rock stream that flows down a cirque basin in the northern part of the Lost River Mountains.
General location: 20 miles east of Challis, 55 miles south of Salmon in the Pahsimeroi Mountains of the Lost River Range.
Maps: Grouse Creek Mtn., Mahogany Hill, Meadow Peak (7.5') USGS quads.
Special attractions: An early season hike to the base of an 11,000-foot peak, with a huge rock stream in Sheep Pen Basin at the foot of the peak.
Difficulty: Moderate due to elevation gain and a faint trail.
Season: Early June through October.
Information: Challis National Forest, HC 63 Box 1669, Challis, Idaho 83226; (208) 879-4321.

The hike: North of the Doublespring Pass, the Lost River Mountains are often called the Pahsimeroi Mountains. Both names are printed on the topographic quadrangles.

The core of this area consists entirely of high limestone peaks and ridges, broken by two major canyons Grouse Creek and Christain Gulch. Although there are a few tarns and springs hidden in the recesses of this rugged, remote area, only Grouse Creek and its tributary, Mill Creek (described here), have perennial streams. You won't be bothered by human company in these mountains. The Forest Service estimates only 400 vistor-days per year for this roadless mountain range.

Getting to Mill Creek involves either driving over Doublespring Pass from the Big Lost River Valley, up from Howe from the Little Lost River Valley, or southward from Salmon and up the Pahsimeroi Valley.

Let's assume you start at the tiny town of May in the Pahsimeroi Valley. Drive south from May on the paved county road for 1. 5 miles. Here, turn right onto Hooper Lane. Drive 2.8 miles to the end of Hooper Lane, crossing the Pahsimeroi River (good fishing) in the process. At the end of Hooper Lane, turn to the left (toward the southeast). Then, after 1.5 miles, turn off on a dirt

Grouse Creek Peak and Sheep Pen Basin. Ralph Maughan photo.

road on the right that gives access to both Grouse Creek and Meadow Creek.

You bounce slowly toward the mountains up a big alluvial fan, gaining elevation at a rate of about 160 feet per mile. After you've gone straight for 2.9 miles, a road leaves to your right, going to Meadow Creek. Keep left. Finally, in about 1.5 more miles, you drop into Grouse Creek and easily ford it at 1.9 miles past the Meadow Creek junction. Drive carefully up the lower part of the Grouse Creek Canyon, fording the stream several times. Lastly, after 2.4 more miles, you come to the Mill Creek side-canyon. Ford Mill Creek and turn left. You can drive a small car about a mile up Mill Creek on the grassy track that serves as a road. The seldom-visited canyon of Grouse Creek (eight miles long and two or three thousand feet deep) which you leave behind is accessible only by four-wheel drive.

Try to park your vehicle a bit off the grassy road bed when the going gets tough. Don your gear and start to walk. It's three miles and a 1,900-foot climb to Sheep Pen Basin.

The track leads you along for about a mile through aspen, a few fir, and a lot of brush. The hillsides are covered with sage, grass, and more brush. Mill Creek leaps down the canyon following a fault, a geological weakness that opened the way for water to carve the canyon. The hillside on your right is the upthrown side of the fault and is composed of what geologists call the Grand View Dolomite. The steep hillside on your left is on the downthrown side. The pinkish gray weathered rock is the area's ubiquitous limestone.

After about a mile, you enter fir forest, and the track turns into a number of parallel game trails along which you make your way quite easily. In about one-half mile, the canyon bends to the west (following an intersecting fault).

HIKE 47 *MILL CREEK TO SHEEP PEN BASIN*

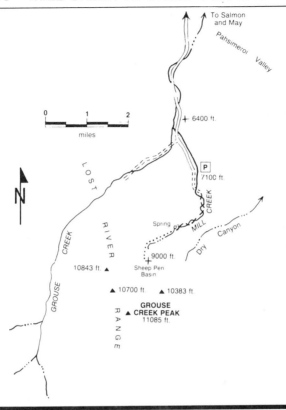

The trail, somewhat faint here, stays near the creek under heavy forest canopy. Another half-mile brings you to a nice spring, the source of Mill Creek. This water, so rare on the surface of these sponge-like mountains, bubbles up where two faults intersect. If you're camping, this is a good spot—on the grass and sage bench on the south side of the creek.

Deer come to water here early and late in the day. In later summer, livestock do too, making the area less desirable. As you sit and admire the scenery, especially the crown of unnamed peak 10,843 up-canyon, you might feel tempted to get up and take a brief hike over the pass to your southeast, following cow trails.

About at the source of Mill Creek, the canyon narrows and the forest becomes dry. The trail climbs 800 feet in a mile over increasingly rocky ground. Eventually you'll step onto a huge rock stream that is slowly moving downhill. This is Sheep Pen Basin—a square mile of gradually moving rock. A few whitebark pines dot its gray expanse. Ahead and to your right rise the dark gray, fluted cliffs of Grouse Creek Peak and lesser summits. At 11,085 feet, this peak is the second highest in the northern part of the Lost River Mountains. Except for bursts of wind, silence is total in this land of rock and sky.—*Ralph Maughan* □

HIKE 48 EAST FORK, PAHSIMEROI RIVER

General description: A short, scenic hike to the base of Mt. Breitenbach.
General location: In the proposed Borah Peak Wilderness 15 miles northwest of Mackay and 77 miles south of Salmon.
Maps: Burnt Creek and Leatherman Peak (7.5') USGS quads.
Special attractions: A 1,500-foot high limestone wall with towers, nearby mountain meadows, and complexly folded cliffs.
Difficulty: Moderate.
Season: Late June through September.
Information: Challis National Forest, Box 337, Challis, Idaho 83226; (208) 879-4321.

The hike: The hike to the end of the East Fork of the Pahsimeroi and to Mount Breitenbach greets you with a high meadow, springs, and one of the most rugged sights in the mountain range.

To reach the trail's beginning, take the same route as for Merriam Lake (see the Merriam Lake hike description for instructions). However, when you pass the corral and the range line shack, take the left fork of the road. The right fork goes to the trailhead for Merriam Lake and Pass Lake (the West Fork of the Pahsimeroi). The road you take briefly runs close to the right fork of the road. Then it drops down and fords the West Fork of the Pahsimeroi and travels over into the broad canyon of the East Fork of the Pahsimeroi, keeping to the East Fork's right side. As you drive up this U-shaped valley lined with contorted cliffs, you will occasionally glimpse the mighty face of Mount Breitenbach.

After 2.5 to three miles, the poor road finally gives up and ends. Park your vehicle and walk on vague trails for 100 to 200 yards. You will break out of a thick grove of trees and find a well-defined trail going up the right (west) side of the canyon. Walk to the trail and simply follow it along the creek and across large grassy meadows separated by strips of lodgepole pine forest. To your left (east) you'll admire the lengthy slopes of pastel talus. The avalanche chutes and talus attest to the harsh work of snow, cold, and gravity on the friable limestone strata.

Wander up the canyon until it narrows to only about 50 yards wide. Stay high on the banks here. Happily, this constriction reopens almost immediately, and you reach your goal. Here lies a small upper valley where springs lace the hillside to create a meadow of moist beauty. Higher up this small valley is a campsite that is both flatter and drier than the spring area. Meltwater is commonly available at the camping area. In the summer of 1982, there was but one small fire ring here. Let's keep it that way!

The small valley is still wild, visited only be a few climbers and cowhands each year. Deer and mountain goats frequent the valley and the mountains above.

The hike is only about three miles long, gaining about a thousand feet. There's nowhere to go from the valley except to climb or scramble up the mighty peaks. Just to walk to the valley's head and back is well worth it. Mount Breitenbach, which pens in the valley, was named for Jake Breitenbach, who died on the 1963 American Mt. Everest expedition.—*Jerry Johnson* □

HIKE 49 *RAMSHORN CANYON*

General description: An easy, short hike, open in early season, into the little-known rugged southern end of the Lost River Range.

General location: 22 miles southeast of Mackay, 70 miles northwest of Pocatello.

Maps: Ramshorn Canyon, (7.5') USGS quad.

Special attractions: Exceptionally impressive rock formations. Lots of solitude for an area close to various small towns.

Difficulty: Easy to the end of the short trail from there a cross-country hike of medium difficulty.

Season: May through October.

Information: Lost River Ranger District, Challis National Forest, Box 507, Mackay, Idaho 83251; (208) 588-2224.

The hike: Despite its obvious rugged beauty, the southern end of the Lost River Range, like the northern end, is almost totally overlooked by hikers. South of the Pass Creek-Wet Creek road, which crosses the Lost Rivers, the mountains thrust to "only" 10,000 or 11,000 feet, compared to the many peaks over 11,500 or even 12,000 feet in the range's middle reaches.

Extended hiking in the heights and crags of this part of the mountain range isn't easy due to an almost total lack of surface water and trails. Despite considerable winter snowfall, the limestone that makes up the awesome cliffs and peaks of the Lost River's southern end sucks up water like a sponge.

There is a short trail up Ramshorn Canyon, however providing an easy, scenic introduction to this part of the mountains.

To get there, turn off of U.S. Highway 93 at Darlington. Head straight east on a good gravel road for 2.9 miles straight toward the mountains. At 2.9 miles, you come to a north-south gravel road called Hill Road. There is also a fence here with a gate that opens to a dirt road continuing eastward toward the mountains and the big canyon (Ramshorn) ahead. This is the road you take. Carefully drive up this dirt road 3.9 miles to the undeveloped trailhead. If the road seems too rutted, go south about 1.5 miles on the Hill Road. Here there is a second, slightly better, dirt road that goes to the canyon.

Ramshorn Canyon, though big, is not too impressive at first. It's a wide, dry, steep-sided canyon, often full of cows and dust, and covered mostly with sagebrush. There are some nice views of 10,612-foot King Mountain, however. This is the first mountain in the Lost Rivers, rising some five thousand feet above the Big Lost River Valley to the west. Don't get discouraged. At about 3.5 miles, the canyon makes a 90-degree turn to the north. The scenery quickly changes. The road ends at the base of a steep slope. This slope marks a dramatic change in the canyon.

Park your vehicle at road's end and hike up the steep jeep road into a patch of mountain mahogany. The jeep track quickly turns into a good trail. The climb is brief and leads you into a pretty defile filled with old-growth Douglas fir. Soon you'll come to a small meadow. The trail crosses the meadow and heads into a shallow canyon, cut into the huge main canyon. The trail becomes fainter, climbs to the edge of a grassy, rolling bench, and ends. On the bench, you'll be overwhelmed by the rows of fanlike cliffs that line the west side

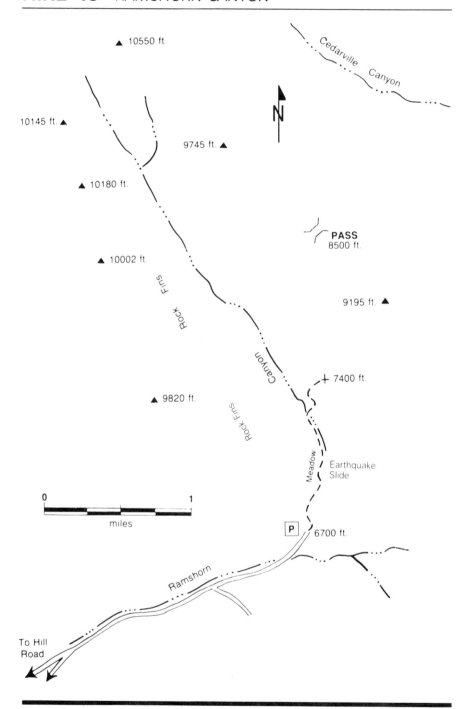

▲ 10550 ft.

Cedarville Canyon

N

10145 ft. ▲

9745 ft. ▲

▲ 10180 ft.

PASS
8500 ft.

▲ 10002 ft.

Rock Fins

9195 ft. ▲

Canyon

+ 7400 ft.

▲ 9820 ft.

Rock Fins

Meadow

Earthquake
Slide

0   1

miles

P 6700 ft.

Ramshorn

To Hill
Road

of the canyon from bottom to top—like armor on the back of some ancient dinosaur.

You can hike from here cross-country with only moderate effort along this bench until the dry creek bottom rises to meet you. From that point, further hiking is hard going—over rocks, slides and through brush to the head of the canyon. An obvious alternative is to hike for the obvious low spot (a pass) on the northeast side of the canyon. A not-too-difficult thousand-foot climb allows you an inspiring view into rarely visited Cedarville Canyon, a big canyon on the range's eastern side.

The prime season for this short trail (or for more extended cross-country hiking) is about June 5 to July 1. If the weather has been dry enough to dry out the dirt access road, May 10 is a reasonable time for the first hike. In the dry year of 1976-19 77, I walked a good way up Ramshorn in early April. — *Ralph Maughan* ☐

Note: I hadn't been up Ramshorn Canyon for at least ten years. Returning in 1989, it seemed somehow different. When I came to the small meadow mentioned above, the meadow was smaller still half buried in a landslide. A gigantic slide of boulders and dirt was shaken from the east ridge of the canyon during the 1983 Borah Peak earthquake. The trailhead is unchanged, but the trail now detours around the edge of the slide and is slightly more difficult than the original.

Another change is in nearby Cedarville Canyon, which can be viewed from the pass in Ramshorn mentioned above. It burned in August of 1989 —Ralph Maughan

HIKE 50   *MOUNT BORAH*

General description: This is quite a mountain, beautiful and bodacious. The peak, Idaho's highest, giving a eagle's view of the surrounding high country and high desert valleys, can inspire reverence, fear, and ecstasy. Expect to spend twelve hours on the mountain. It is worth the effort.

General location: About 55 miles southeast of Challis and 20 miles north of Mackay.

Maps: Borah Peak (7.5') USGS quad.

Special attractions: Idaho's highest mountain at 12,662 feet. It also harbors Idaho's only glacier.

Difficulty: Difficult and strenuous due to the relief and a knife ridge (with exposure) at 11,600 feet.

Season: May and June for the lower slopes. July and August for the summit.

Information: Lost River Ranger District, Challis National Forest, Box 507, Mackay, Idaho 83251. (208) 588-2224.

The hike: Don't believe much of what you've heard about Mt. Borah as there are a variety of views; but Borah is primarily a climber's mountain, but with one route (described here) that is accessible to the advanced hiker.

The hiker's route up Borah has worn its way into becoming an obvious, but steep, trail. This path ends at about 11,600 feet and the last mile and 1000

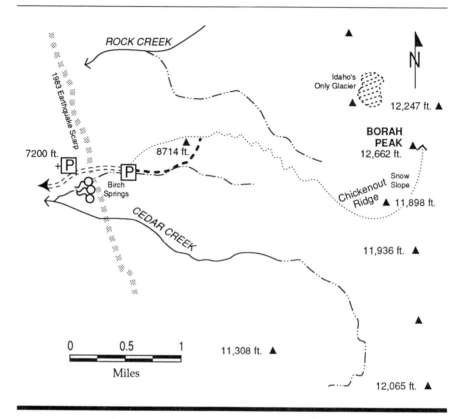

feet of relief is a scramble along a knife ridge (some call it "Chicken-out Ridge"), then up loose rock, solid inclines, and small cliffs. Hikers with no fondness for vertical exposure can get far enough up the mountain to gain a tremendous view and feel a sense of accomplishment.

July and August, when the snowfield on the saddle of the 11,898 foot southern spur is the lightest, are the best months for the hiker to try the summit. By July most of the grass in the Big Lost River Valley at the base of the Lost Rivers is brown. May and June would be pleasing times to try a partial climb of the Borah or nearby mountains.

Turn off of U.S. 93 about 55 miles southeast of Challis or 20 miles north of Mackay. The turnoff sign reads "Birch Springs Access to Mt. Borah." The road is good, but unimproved dirt. It slowly climbs about three miles through the high desert toward the base of the Lost River Range.

Most two-wheel drive vehicles will have to stop where the 1983 Borah Peak earthquake fractured the road. This continuous line of exposed dirt and rock bisecting the foothills is the quake's fracture line (called a "scarp"). Camping here among the sparse trees and big sagebrush near Birch Springs is dry and not particularly attractive. Birch Springs emerges farther downhill away from the road. The intermittent stream above the springs is usually dry by summer.

However, in July there were many yellow and orange columbine in bloom near the streambed.

Those in four-wheel drive vehicles can continue another half-mile into the mouth of the canyon where there is forest cover and heavily-used campsites. This too is likely to be a dry camp.

Until July you can count on melting snow on the mountain during the climb, but this is a poor source even in June. Each climber should be sure to take a gallon of liquid for a one-day round trip to the top. Carbonated drinks should be avoided as their containers are likely to explode at altitudes near the summit.

There are several places to camp on the mountain, such as the one on the saddle at 10,632 feet, but all are dry and exposed to wind, rain, snow, and lightning. To use these camps, you will need a stove, fuel, and extra water. Users have built small rock windbreaks at several campsites for meager protection.

The more heavily-used access route up the mountain begins at the end of the road. The trail stays in the canyon bottom (as shown on the USGS quadrangle). It then climbs at an angle northeast up a talus gulch, gaining 280 feet. Then it follows the treeline, gaining another 200 feet, to reach a forested pass just east of rock knob 8,714.

A less steep route leaves from the road about 600 yards past the scarp and goes northward briefly before starting up the mountain slope. Once on the mountain, climb, gaining about 800 feet, toward the rock knob 8714. If you angle to the right when about halfway to the knob, you should locate a trail, which then follows the ridgeline on the edge of the big canyon to the south.

The trail is obvious and steep, steep, steep. From the scarp it is a 5,422-foot gain in just 3.5 miles to the summit. That's over a vertical mile to the top. Most will need to begin the hike at dawn.

The trail nears knob 8,714, circles just to its north, then drops to a saddle losing 100 feet. Here the route from the canyon joins. Just past the saddle, the trail starts a very steep climb through open forest to timberline. After gaining about 1,200 feet, it levels out just before point 10,632.

As you advance above timberline, the round, gray summit of Borah looms to your left and the striped double-peaked spur at 11,898 feet punctures the sky ahead. Between the two is a short, nearly permanent snowslope. Due to the telescoping effect of distance, the long ridge to the spur looks more foreboding than it is.

Above timberline the trail continues, growing fainter until about 11,400 feet, where it ends. To your left is a continuous cliff which drops about 800 feet to a huge basin of a tributary to Rock Creek. To the right, a talus field slopes gradually down into Cedar Canyon, and above Cedar Canyon rises peak 11,308, a ruggedly beautiful gray and orange. At Cedar Canyon's head thrusts peak 12,058, and as you near the 11,400 foot mark, similarly beautiful Leatherman Peak, Idaho's second highest, rises to the left of 12,058. Look for rock cairns for guidance as the trail fades.

At about 11,600 feet, the scrambing begins. Keep near the ridgetop, which quickly becomes knife-edged. There is exposure here, and some may want to rope up. Stay on the ridge until you must climb down a short cliff onto the snowslope. Early in the season you will want an ice axe and crampons.

On the other side of the snowslope, a faint trail goes to the left (west) of the top of spur 11,898. It quickly leads to an easy saddle between 11,898 and Borah's summit. The east side of the saddle drops precipitously into a startling lake basin.

Soon you begin the last 800 feet up Borah, another scramble. By keeping near the ridgeline you will avoid more loose rock than if you drift to the west. As you approach the summit, you stare almost straight down into lake 10,204, nestled in the seldom-visited east cirque of Mt. Borah. There is a smaller lake below 10,204; and in wet years (or in early season), a third gleams further downslope on the east.

The summit register was placed by the Mazamas hiking club. Plan on an hour so you can rest and take in the view. Here you can see all of the rest of the 12,000 and near 12,000 foot peaks in Idaho. Keep an eye on the weather, however. The hike down requires staying on the ridgetop until you have descended 1,000 feet. The summit is over 2,000 feet above timberline.

As we neared the bottom of the mountain, the fading sunrays slanting against the forest edge, two red-tailed hawks rode the thermals. They soared in broad circles, emitting a slurred "keeer-r, keeer-r", One saw us, dipped its head for a look, then gave a slight push to resume its four-foot wingspread and continue to glide over the sunset sky. —*Ralph and Jackie Maughan* ☐

White Cloud, Boulder, and Pioneer Mountains

Overview

The "Salmon River Mountains" is a nonspecific name applied to a 30,000-square-mile of maze of high ridges and deep canyons in central Idaho. On the edges of this mountain fastness radiate other mountains, identifiable as separate ranges.

One such string of mountains, consisting of hundreds of 10,000 to 11,000 foot peaks, runs southward from the Salmon River Mountains to form the east side of the Sawtooth Valley; then it humps further south past Ketchum, Hailey, and Bellevue to end in the basalt of the Snake River Plain.

Although this is one continuous mountain range, over the years the string has been broken into three separate groups in people's minds. On the north, against the Salmon River Canyon and Salmon River Mountains, they are known as the White Clouds. This was originally a local name, limited to just one magnificent ridge of high, often white, peaks. Today, all mountains between the Salmon River Canyon on the north, Germania and Pole Creek on the south, and the East Fork of the Salmon River to the east, bear this name.

The next on this string are not pearls but boulders. The Boulder Mountains are perhaps the least known and visited of the three mountain groups. Finally, the most southerly and highest group is the Pioneer Mountains. In average elevation, they are the second highest range in the Gem State. One peak, Hyndman Peak, just tops 12,000 feet. The Boulders, it is generally agreed, end at Trail Creek Gorge. Here, the Pioneers more than take up the slack of the colorful Boulders with their glistening gray peaks, speckled tarns, and gorges thundering with cascades.

The White Clouds became celebrities in the late 1960s, when a group of hikers found the then lonesome Willow Lake, the first of the Boulder Chain Lakes, under siege. The waters of the lake are normally perfectly clear, reflecting the rainbow colors of a nearby peak. But the hikers found the waters full of "mud" from a driller's bit. One side of the lake had been stripped bare of trees to make room for the mining exploration. One of Idaho's most famous conservation battles ensued. Before the dust would settle, there'd be a new

The Boulder Mountains from Idaho Highway 75. Ralph Maughan photo.

conservation-minded governor in the statehouse (Cecil Andrus) with a whole new outlook, and the political clout to back it.

When the hikers protested the destruction, the now-famous retort was, "Don't worry, when we're done there won't be a lake. Hell, there won't even be a mountain!" The mountain they were referring to was none other than Castle Peak—at 11,810 feet the highest by far of the White Clouds, ruler of the range. This giant is now one of the best known mountains in Idaho. Back then, however, Castle Peak was pretty obscure in spite of its exciting, towering beauty. It just didn't tower over any highways—or dirt roads for that matter.

Dedicated Idaho conservationists and the public were not convinced by talk of temporary jobs from the proposed mine, or of the "critical" need for molybdenum in the economy—a metal that is now in extreme surplus.

Persistence led to creation of the Sawtooth National Recreation Area. This not only withdrew the White Clouds, most of the Boulders, and the Sawtooth Mountains from the filing of further mining claims, but also provided the means to clean up the subdivisions sprouting like mushrooms in a cowpie in Stanley Basin. It also reclassified the old Sawtooth Primitive Area into the new, larger Sawtooth Wilderness.

Ironically, while the White Clouds heralded the victory for many other successful battles, they themselves still lack wilderness designation. There are still little stakes of wood stapled with engraved metal and tied off with florescent banners marking the mining company's valid claims at the base of Castle Peak. The White Clouds are not wilderness. Plans to civilize the Sawtooth National Recreation Area need to be fought down every now and then like a patch of crabgrass, as does mining exploration. The other ranges in this threesome also remain unprotected as wilderness.

Both the White Clouds and Pioneers are punctuated with many alpine and subalpine lakes, full of fish. Consequently, they see the most visitors. Various wildlife species roam these mountains—elk, deer, mountain goats, bears, mountain lions, a greatly reduced herd of bighorn sheep; and, of course, coyotes. The comparatively lakeless Boulders offer rugged cliffs, booming waterfalls, colorful rock, and plentiful wildlife.

As for wilderness, the Pioneer Mountains were selected as a 105,000 acre proposed wilderness in the Forest Service's Roadless Area Review Inventory (RARE II) study, although the crucial southern part, south of Copper Basin, was dropped under pressure from mineral interests and off-road-vehicle clubs.

The White Clouds and part of the Boulders are a congressionally mandated Wilderness Study Area. Idaho conservationists propose a 450,000-acre White Clouds-Boulder Wilderness. This is one of the largest remaining unclassified roadless areas (literally and legally) in the United States. We're lucky to have it, but Idaho's present congressional delegation doesn't see it that way. This delegation, financed by every moneyed special interested group in the alphabet (from AMAX to Zinc), thinks that the wilds of Idaho are a mote in the eye of humanity. But the decision is up to Idaho and U.S. citizens. We shall see.

Efforts to protect the vast White Cloud/Boulder Mountain roadless area as designated wilderness have not gone well in the years since the first edition of the book.

In 1989, Idaho Senator James McClure introduced a bill that would protect only a third of the 450,000 acre roadless area. Moreover, that third would be broken into three parts by means of two designated motorcycle corridors: one in Germania Creek, the other in the South Fork of the East Fork of the Salmon.

The core of the White Clouds is presently closed to motorized vehicles, but access trails are open, requiring long hikes before reaching vehicle-free areas. The vehicle closure is also commonly violated. Forest Service enforcement has been nil. Germania Creek itself is also degraded in its lower portions by excessive grazing of livestock.

In the Pioneer Mountains, the McClure bill would fail to designate Fall Creek and its tributaries, the scenic core of Idaho's second highest mountain range, as wilderness.

In a bright note, the long-standing access blockage in the East Fork of the Salmon is being corrected. The Forest Service is building a new road that by-passes the private land in question. Its completion should take place by the end of the summer 1990. This will provide easier hiking access to over a 100,000 acres of the White Cloud and Boulder Mountains, reducing the congestion from the trailhead at Livingston Mine.

HIKE 51 *BOULDER CHAIN LAKES*

General description: A heavily used and absolutely beautiful trail to a string of lakes with many small rainbow trout.

General location: In the Sawtooth National Recreation Area (White Cloud Mountains) about 35 miles southeast of Challis.

Maps: Boulder Chain Lakes and Livingston Creek (7.5') USGS quads.

Special attractions: Fishing, peak-bagging, and generally fantastic scenery for the duration of the hike.

Difficulty: Moderate.

Season: Mid-July through October.

Information: Sawtooth National Recreation Area, 2647 Kinbly, Twin Falls, Idaho 83301. (208) 737-3200.

The hike: The Livingston Mill trailhead is decidedly crowded by Idaho standards. I counted about 30 vehicles there. However, you lose about half the traffic early on, when the trail forks to Big Boulder Lakes. This hike will confirm everything you may have heard about the beauty of the White Clouds and Castle Peak. It has just about every lure for the outdoorsperson except wildlife deep, cool forests, bubbling mountain springs, lakes for the spinner or fly fisher, mountains to climb, and a conservation battle to get you out of your armchair. (See the White Cloud, Boulder, and Pioneer Mountains overview.)

The only lake we fished without results on this hike was Frog Lake. ORVs are allowed on the trail until just after Frog Lake, which no doubt accounts for the paucity of good fishing there. Frog Lake was the only one in the Boulder Chain that had that stomped-to-death look more common in national parks.

For road access to the trailhead, see the following Wickiup Creek to Castle Peak hike description. The total length of this trail, if you follow it to the end of the line to a high basin overlooking Shallow and Scree lakes, is about 13 miles. The best camping is at the lower Boulder Chain lakes themselves, since the high lakes are colder, and Frog Lake is too busy. However, after the eight-mile haul up over Red Ridge, you may well want to spend the night at Frog Lake. The first half-mile of the trail is an old jeep road that ascends Big Boulder

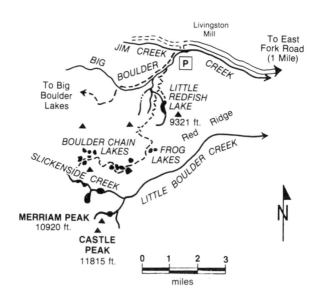

Creek Canyon. After the road disappears in a slide, you'll pass briefly through a lodgepole pine and spruce forest. The trail is good throughout the hike, and you should have no navigation problems. After the section of forest, you'll come out in the open into a willow flat. Here you cross a bridge over Big Boulder Creek. Shortly thereafter, the trail forks. The right fork leads to the Big Boulder Lakes.

The left fork, which is the one you follow, immediately leaves Big Boulder Creek and begins the long climb over Red Ridge, which involves about four miles and a gain of 1,800 feet of altitude. The trail was rebuilt a generation ago to accommodate horse and ORV traffic; therefore, it has many more switchbacks than appear on the topographic quadrangle map, dated 1964. While there are not a lot of great views from the trail, there is one good viewpoint after you've climbed about a quarter of the way to Red Ridge. Here you look out over Big Boulder Creek's timber, its meadow, and the high peaks that reign it all in.

After this heart-stopper view, you're stuck with the rest of the long switchbacking pull to Red Ridge. The trail's too gentle to make you pant, but long and steep enough to wear you down while making slow progress.

Lake 8,978 in the Boulder Chain Lakes. Keith Kemphski photo.

Three miles from the trailhead and about a third of the way to Red Ridge, a signed trail leaves to the left for Little Redfish Lake, about a mile away. There is camping there, plus a trout population. The main trail continues straight ahead.

Finally you reach the pass. Big Boulder Creek lies behind you, creating a magnificent view. Below Railroad Ridge to the northwest, not quite in sight, is the Livingston Mill, where you left your vehicle.

On the other side of the pass, Cattle Peak rises ahead, just perfect for a picture, framed by the ridge's wind-lashed whitebark pine. Below are the two Frog lakes in a meadow of marsh grass.

The trail descends toward Frog Lakes in seven long switchbacks. Along the third switchback is a spring. This is welcome because, despite the scenery ahead and behind on Red Ridge, this high slope is dusty, sagebrush country. Below the switchbacks, you reach a spring basin (boil the water). We camped here to avoid the mosquitoes at Frog Lakes. Further along the trail, after you've rested your feet and dumped your pack, you can walk down the trail through the woods to come out at the lake and try your luck at fishing. When we were there in late afternoon, the only things jumping were frogs, although the lake is full of big cutthroats that abide out in the middle.

From Frog Lakes you can see the northeast face of Castle Peak and, in front of it, Merriam Peak (10,920 feet). Merriam Peak is named after Dr. John Merriam, an economist who was extremely influential in saving the White Clouds and establishing the Sawtooth National Recreation Area. Upon his death in a hypothermia-drowning incident on the Palisades Reservoir in the mid-1970s, Merriam Peak was named after him as a fitting tribute to this man who did so much for the mountains.

You'll leave Frog Lake as the trail turns in a westerly direction to traverse a sagebrush hill. An excellent view accompanies you as you walk along into the Little Boulder Creek drainage below. You'll see, in miniature, the abandoned mine buildings that are, hopefully, only a memory of mining days.

The hike from Frog Lake on is pure joy. After the brief trek through sagebrush, you'll enter forest and lake country. The trail crosses the outlet of Willow Lake, where the forest has mostly reclaimed itself after the debacle that first aroused concern for this area (see overview). Just past the lake outlet is a trail junction. The left fork leads down into the Little Boulder Creek drainage, which is legally accessible at its beginning for the first time in 15 years beginning in 1990.

After Willow Lake, the trail climbs steadily from lake to lake, each one jumping with little trout. We camped at the fourth lake, which is about two miles from Frog Lake. For lack of a better name, this lake is known only by its elevation—lake 8,978. We spent the rest of the day fishing, wading, dozing, and climbing around on the decaying ridge to the south. The next day we started off, *sans* packs, to ascend to the head of the drainage. Upon passing lake 9,008, we saw some young boys diving off a cliff into its waters.

Follow the stream between lake 9,008 and the upper lakes for about a mile and a 400-foot elevation gain through moist forest. Each of these upper lakes is filled with stunted rainbow. We didn't bother to fish for them, being more intent on climbing the pass to Slickenslide Creek. As you turn south to skirt the edge of Hourglass Lake, the country begins to look more alpine. The next lake up is lake 9,643. To your south you'll see a boulder slope that you will ascend to get to the pass. From the lake, as is often the case, it looks more difficult to climb than it is. Once you start up the trail, it's easy and obviously marked.

The pass welcomes you with a great view. If you walk a few hundred yards beyond the pass, you'll get a wonderful view of Serrate Ridge as it merges with Castle Peak. The nameless peak on the east side of the pass is called number 10,296. I scrambled the 500-feet-plus to its top. I had in mind a traverse along the ridgeline, but the rock looked too rotten. From here I could look down on the boulder field we'd just crossed and see my friend as she descended. She had flown in from Michigan for this hike and had a touch of altitude sickness. Lowlanders, keep the altitude in mind!—*Jackie Johnson Maughan* □

HIKE 52 *WICKIUP CREEK TO CASTLE PEAK*

General description: A trail to the famous, majestic Castle Peak; less attractive but much less beaten than the trail to the popular Boulder Chain Lakes route.

General location: In the Sawtooth National Recreation Area (White Cloud Mountains) and straddling the Challis and Sawtooth National Forests; about 35 miles southeast of Challis.

Maps: Bowery Creek and Boulder Chain Lakes (7.5') USGS quads.

Special attractions: Direct access to a free climb of Castle Peak and a cross-country scramble to Castle Lake.

Difficulty: Moderately difficult to Castle Peak; difficult to Castle Lake.

Season: Mid-May through October (cross-country portion to Castle Lake: mid-June through mid-October).

Information: Challis Ranger District, Challis National Forest, HC 63 Box 1669 Challis, Idaho 83226; (208) 879-4321.

The hike: This is a climber's as well as backpacker's route to Castle Peak. The lower section of the trail stump s through a long, hot section of sagebush, but the upper portion leads right to the base of Castle Peak. The trail gains approximately 1,800 feet in 6.5 miles.

From Challis take U.S. Highway 93 about one mile south to its junction with State Highway 75. Follow this highway about 16 miles south to where it bends right to lead to Clayton. Here you turn off the highway onto the East Fork of the Salmon road, which is paved for about six miles; after this then becomes a well-graded dirt road. It is a total of about 20 miles from the highway to the marked Wickiup Creek trailhead. You will pass the Livingston Mine-Boulder Chain Lakes trailhead turnoff about three miles before the Wickiup Creek trailhead. About one mile beyond the Livingston Mine turn-off, the road used to be posted as closed , with a gate to enforce it. In 1990 the Forest Service built a new road around the closure.

There is no formal trailhead at Wickiup Creek. About a quarter-mile before the trailhead, there is a large flat with a clump of shrubs and trees near the East Fork. You can park here, and your vehicle cannot be seen from the road.

From the road, the trail leads up the left bank of Wickiup Creek. It gains elevation quickly, then it levels out and passes intermittently through Douglas fir canopy and open rangeland above the creek. You'll have to carry water here, especially in mid-summer; exposed south-facing slopes create mighty thirsts when temperatures soar into the 90s. But it's quite a pleasant walk in early autumn, when golden aspen dot the landscape in colorful contrast to the muted gray-green of sagebrush. After about five miles the trail again steepens and passes a large, open south-facing slope. The trail stays on the left bank of the creek. Although not always clearly marked in the openings, the trail is easily found again in the trees.

Another 1.5 miles find you going through a small saddle in the forest. Here the trail swings south for about one-half mile to its poorly marked junction with the upper end of the Boulder Creek Trail. It is easy to lose the way at this point, but you should be able to get oriented by the east face of Castle Peak, which is visible across a drainage skirted by rocky bluffs and cliffs. Take the right fork and follow the Boulder Creek Trail north (right) for only about a quarter-mile; then to reach Castle Peak, you must drop to the left (west-northwest) off the trail. If you don't wish to make the precarious climb to Castle Lake, there are ample places to camp off the trail at the base of the peak. This area is lightly used.

You should be able to pinpoint Castle Lake, though you can't see it. It's flanked by a cirque of bare rock, which forms the north face of Castle Peak. Getting there is more a matter of resolve than expert route-finding. You must pick your way up the cliffs, which are dotted with interesting rock outcroppings and an occasional precariously perched Douglas fir. Your efforts will be rewarded when you reach the rim of the cliffs and stand above Castle Lake, which at 9,400 feet, boasts clear, cold water and a fine stocking of trout. To the east lies the Little Boulder Creek drainage. Towering above all is impressive Castle Peak—a jumble of granitic rock whose jagged edges pierce the skyline.

HIKE 52 *WICKIUP CREEK TO CASTLE PEAK*

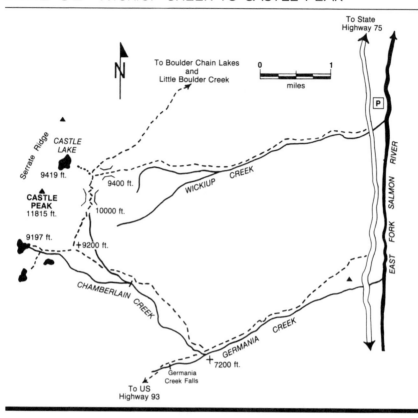

Castle Lake makes a fine setting for a campsite. However, the ground is hard and rocky, and you will be hard pressed to dig the obligatory six inches with your trusty plastic trowel; consequently, the farther away from the lake, the better. Campfires are out, as firewood is scarce to non-existent.

I won't go into detail here about the Castle Peak climb, since there are several routes to its summit. Basically, it's a free climb (when free of snow) up to the north face in the shadow of Serrate Ridge, with two false summits before you reach the marked summit at 11,815 feet. The summit view is spectacular, to say the least.

To make a loop of the hike, return to the Boulder Creek trail and follow it south past the east slope of Castle Peak. The trail is a bit rocky, with fairly steep switchbacks to the high pass dividing the Boulder Creek drainage to the northeast and the Chamberlain Basin to the southeast. As the trails drops to the Chamberlain Lakes, you find yourself once again in open sagebrush country. You are now in the Sawtooth National Forest; here, if the ground cover looks a bit matted and the sagebrush stunted or dead, it is evidence of heavy winter snowfall rather than overgrazing.

Any one of the Chamberlain Lakes has good campsites but some are overused. Since the lakes are only about 3.5 miles from Castle Lake, you may elect to follow the Chamberlain Creek trail to its junction with Germania Creek (stay left) instead of camping at Chamberlain Lakes. The geology of this area is interesting, with rocky bluffs breaking the monotony of range and forest. Fall colors are astounding.

The trail stays on the left bank of Germania Creek to the East Fork of the Salmon River. This is about eight miles from the Chamberlain Lakes trail junction and 10 miles from Castle Lake. Once you reach the road, it's a 2.5-mile walk north (to the left) on the road to your vehicle.—*Anna Elizabeth Hammet* □

Note: If you do take the Chamberlain Creek trail, be advised that it is steep [a 2,000-foot drop], and little-used. There are points where it disappears and good map- reading and navigation skills are required. In its upper reaches are the spectacular Chamberlain Creek Falls (visable from the trail), and at the bottom are the Germania Creek Falls. To see these, you'll have to go about one-quarter of a mile out of your way west up the Germania Creek trail. They are not visible from the trail, but you can hear them.]—Jackie Johnson Maughan

Pioneer Mountains

Overview

Please refer to the overview for the White Cloud, Boulder, and Pioneer mountains for general information about the Pioneers.

HIKE 53   *HYNDMAN CREEK*

General description: A day hike in the splendid Pioneer Mountains, the first portion of which is suitable for families
General location: Ten miles east of Hailey.
Maps: Gray's Peak, Hyndman Peak (7.5') USGS quads.
Special attractions: Meadow and aspen groves, wildflowers, fine examples of beaver ponds. An impressive view of Cobb Peak.
Difficulty: Easy to the crossing of Hyndman Creek. Moderate beyond the crossing
Season: Late June to early October.
Information: Ketchum Ranger District, Sawtooth National Forest, Box 2356, Sun Valley Road, Ketchum, Idaho 83340; (208) 622-5371.

The hike: This is a beautiful and an easy hike along a closed road in the upper part of Hyndman Creek, a large drainage which gives access to the heart of the Pioneer Mountains. The hike is through meadows, aspen groves, and patches of coniferous forest. It is ideal for a family outing and picnic. There are many views of 11,650-foot Cobb Peak which dominates the canyon. Many springs

HIKE 53 *HYNDMAN CREEK*

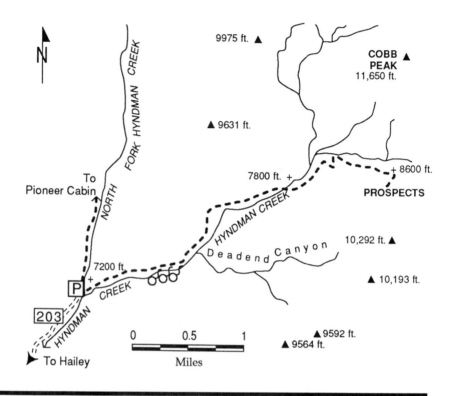

run into Hyndman Creek, and in 1990, at least, these were extensively dammed by beaver. Many spring-fed beaver ponds are perched directly above the creek, an interesting as well as a beautiful phenomenon.

To reach Hyndman Creek trailhead (which is also the trailhead for the North Fork Hyndman Creek), turn off Highway 75 onto the East Fork (of the Big Wood River) road about 5.5 miles north of Hailey. Drive about six miles up the East Fork on a paved road past many new houses to the community of Triumph. Here the pavement ends. 1.5 more miles brings you to the Hyndman Creek Road (FS #203). Turn left onto this improved dirt road and drive up broad Hyndman Creek 3.5 miles past the Johnstone Creek trailhead (access to Pioneer Cabin), then continue about a mile farther to the trailhead. The last mile is mostly on a narrow dugway. If you meet another vehicle, one vehicle may have to back up a substantial distance.

The trailhead is spacious but in the sun. A sign indicates that Pioneer Cabin is four miles up the North Fork. This trail gets the most traffic. The Hyndman Creek trail starts at the locked gate near the trailhead. You immediately cross the North Fork here. This could be a major wade, but fortunately there is a crude footbridge.

The old road, which sees quite a bit of mountain bike use but few motorized vehicles, crosses a meadow and climbs gently into an aspen grove. From this meadow a hiker gets fine views of the rugged peaks at the head of the North Fork. The road, which is slowly returning to nature, takes you gently up the canyon for about three miles to where it crosses Hyndman Creek. The way is filled with meadows, patches of forest, and good views of huge Cobb Peak which rises 4650 feet above the trailhead.

We found a sheep camp near the crossing in early September 1989. Here a crude trail leaves the road to the left and climbs up into the unnamed side canyon. This cross-country route takes you into a splendid basin at the base of 12,009-foot Hyndman Peak, 11,775-foot Old Hyndman Peak, and 11,650-foot Cobb Peak. The route is fairly difficult.

We followed the faint old road to the right and crossed Hyndman Creek instead to continue up the main canyon. The crossing was a long step across several large stones in September, but it could be difficult in early summer's higher water because the creek bottom has still not stabilized from the flood-producing thunderstorm of 1984.

Across Hyndman Creek, you climb up a forested slope on the now fainter roadbed. We found this forest route a very noisy place with the calls of numerous Steller's jays and hawks. Occasional breaks in the forest give stunning views of Duncan Ridge up the left fork. Cobb Peak rises 3,200 feet immediately across the creek on its north side. The road gradually fades out as you near the alpine zone at 8,700 feet below Big Basin. The Gray's Peak USGS quadrangle shows a cabin here, but all we found were a couple of collapsed storage sheds. An old prospect road is still visible on the slope to the south. This is a good place to camp. There are many level campsites and plenty of water. It would make a good base camp for climbing Cobb Peak and exploring the alpine lakes further up-canyon in Big Basin.—*Ralph and Jackie Maughan* □

HIKE 54 *BOULDER CREEK*

General description: This steep, 7.5 mile hike up Boulder Creek to a high ridge in the Pioneer Mountains and back offers a unique wilderness opportunity as short as a simple day hike or else a several day backpack.
General location: About 20 linear miles northeast of Ketchum.
Maps: Standhope Peak, Phi Kappa Mtn. (7.5') USGS quads.
Special attractions: Good fishing at the alpine Boulder Lake, challenging terrain good enough for mountain goat.
Difficulty: Moderate, a steady 1100 foot elevation gain.
Season: Mid-July through September.
Information: Lost River Ranger District, Challis National Forest, Box 507 Mackay, Idaho 83251; (208) 588-2224.

The hike: During the summer of 1984, a severe thunderstorm caused damage to streambeds and trails in this area o f the Pioneers. This included washing out the bridge below the campground across Wildhorse Creek, eroding and closing for a time the road to Wildhorse Mine (stranding several cars), minor rerouting of Wildhorse Creek, and damage to the Boulder Creek trail . A good example can be seen at the far end of the campground. Erosion from Wildhorse

HIKE 54 *BOULDER CREEK*

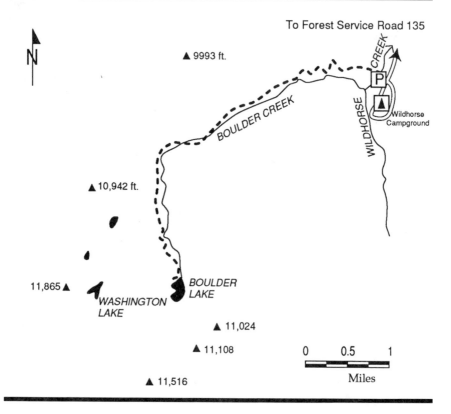

To Forest Service Road 135

N

▲ 9993 ft.

BOULDER CREEK

WILDHORSE CREEK

P

Wildhorse Campground

▲ 10,942 ft.

11,865 ▲

WASHINGTON LAKE

BOULDER LAKE

▲ 11,024

▲ 11,108

▲ 11,516

| 0 | 0.5 | 1 |

Miles

Creek has eaten to the edge of the road to the Wildhorse Mine. The bridge over Wildhorse Creek was rebuilt and opened in 1985.

See the Fall Creek to Suprise Valley trail description for instructions to Wildhorse Creek. Instead of turning left onto the Fall Creek road, follow the main road to the right, paralleling Wildhorse Creek, two miles to Wildhorse Campground.

Parking is available in the Boulder Creek trail access area of the Wildhorse Campground. Although the trail starts at the "No Motorized Vehicles" sign, the hiker will need to ford this creek. Once across, look for the Forest Service sign.

The trail is to the north of the rocky outlet of Boulder Creek. It pulls quickly away, 50 to 100 yards, from the creek. Watch for a large pine tree with blazes. After you enter the trees, the trail is obvious.

Before proceeding on the hike, enjoy the view up Wildhorse Creek of Old Hyndman Peak. With its sharp, steep sides and snowfields, it offers great photographic opportunities at sunrise or sunset. It can be seen only from the Wildhorse Creek area. Hyndman peak is further back and not visible from the campground area.

The first half mile is steep. Switchbacks offer frequent views of the Pioneer

Boulder Lake in the Pioneer Mountains. Keith J. Kempski photo.

Mountains towering over Wildhorse Creek. Once it levels off, the trail passes through alternating pine, aspen, and sagebrush areas. At the head of the canyon is an unnamed 11,865-foot peak which can be seen throughout the hike. Many mistake this peak for the Devils Bedstead. The Devils Bedstead is not in view. It is the rugged peak that encloses Kane Lake in the next drainage to the west. Access to the Devils Bedstead is from the Kane Creek or Summit Creek trails.

The trail passes through two deeply eroded, dry streambeds created by the afore-mentioned thunderstorm. Just before the first crossing of Boulder Creek, you must scamper across one of the streambeds. Looking down, you can see how the force of this stream joining Boulder Creek is causing erosion on the opposite bank. It will be years before the area stabilizes. This is one example of why an area like the Pioneers should be kept in a wilderness condition.

After crossing Boulder Creek, the trail climbs up on the left bank while the creek tumbles through a small canyon on the right. There are occasional overlooks. The trail ascends steadily through pine forest with the creek alongside below.

When a forested ridge appears immediately ahead and to the left, the trail begins a steep climb through deeply rutted switchbacks. Be careful ascending or descending these switchbacks! This section is in desperate need of Forest Service rerouting. While you're climbing, the ridge ahead gives an indication of the elevation which must be gained. After climbing the switchbacks, the trail levels off and crosses Boulder Creek a second time. It climbs the bank and traverses a sagebrush hill about 20 feet above the stream. In a quarter-mile it reaches the lower end of a high alpine meadow area. This meadow is approximately one-half mile long with Boulder Creek meandering through the area, fed by numerous small streams.

The trail skirts the meadow and offers a 180 degree panorama of the rugged canyon walls. Mountain goat can often be seen grazing high on the slopes to the north. Several campsites can be found near the trail. However, camping is marginal because the ground is very wet and irregular. The best camping is found in the conifers across Boulder Creek when you first reach this area.

At meadow's end, the trail starts a gradual ascent, passing around boulders, and eventually meets Boulder Creek on the left. At times the trail is difficult to make out watch for rock cairns. In the last quarter-mile the trail pitches up through rock ledges, still keeping the stream on the left. The last 100 yards are steep and difficult through rocks and talus. Cairns mark the trail which hugs the rock wall on the right. The trail levels off the last 20 yards. Boulder Lake is scenic, rocky, and has marginal camping. Although the area is littered with fire rings, better camping is found in the meadows below. Fishing is good.

It is possible to bushwhack to the upper, trailless lakes from the meadow. There is a faint trail to the lowest lake (9,850 feet). It appears to start at the lower end of the meadow and traverse the meadow about one mile. Finding it from the Boulder C reek Trail is difficult. From the first lake, drop down 100 feet and gradually climb across a rock and talus area to the second lake. From here, the trip to Washington Lake is easy. Fishing is fair. At Washington Lake the hiker can cross a couloir and drop down into Boulder Lake. The trip can be dangerous as it often involves crossing a snowfield and a steep, difficult descent of a streambed. Allow ample time to make the crossing.—*Keith J. Kempski* □

HIKE 55   *IRON BOG LAKE*

General description: A day hike or short backpack to a scenic lake, with a larger lake basin (Fishpole Lake) nearby.
General location: In the southern part of the Pioneer Mountains, about 37 road miles northwest of the town of Arco.
Map: Muldoon Canyon (15') USGS quad.
Special attractions: A short hike to classic Rocky Mountain sub-alpine scenery. There are many wildflowers in these meadowy lake basins.
Difficulty: Moderately easy (due to the short distance).
Season: Late June to October.
Information: Lost River Ranger District, Challis National Forest, Box 507 Mackay, Idaho 83251 (208) 588-2224

The hike: The southern portion of the Pioneer Mountains consists of rugged, glaciated peaks with numerous cirques; many with lakes. Despite their height and cool weather, these mountains have very sparse forests. Although this sometimes makes it hard to get out of the high elevation sun, it does provide for almost constant, scenic views into the distance.

Iron Bog and nearby Fishpole lakes have a reputation as being among Idaho's prettiest. The hiking distance to them is not great. These two aspects, together, make the area sometimes a bit crowded. Fortunately, off-road vehicles have been excluded from area for about a decade now, and some of the localized areas of overuse have healed.

To reach the area, turn off of U.S. Highway 93, 10.5 miles north of Arco onto the Antelope Creek road. This road is paved for the first four miles. Then it's

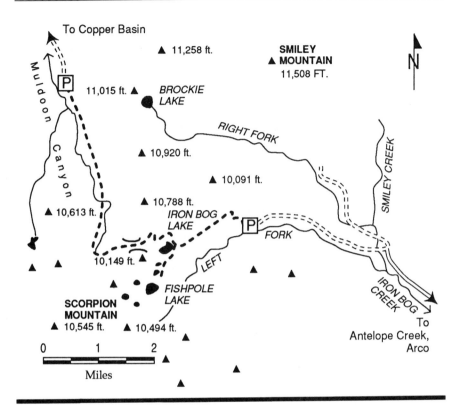

23.5 miles of gravel and dirt to the trailhead, which is in the Left Fork of Iron Bog Creek. From the highway, it's 23.5 miles to the Iron Bog Campground (water). The trailhead is four miles further on a dirt road.

There is a steep grade that may stop non four-wheel drive vehicles about a half mile from the trailhead. Because of this, Challis National Forest is thinking of locating the trailhead about a mile downstream and constructing a new section of trail along the bottom of this delightful little canyon. For the present, however, you may have to walk part of the road to the trailhead.

The trailhead is spacious. Beyond the trailhead a faint jeep track continues a short distance up the stream valley, but the trail to the lake leaves directly (and obviously) to the right (north) and climbs up the mountainside. The trail is signed as closed to all motorized vehicles.

The well-defined trail climbs steeply as it angles up the north canyon slope of the Left Fork of Iron Bog Creek. There are several springs of drinking water in the early season along the trail. A vigorous hiker (dayhiking) can reach the lake in only 45 minutes. Backpackers with a full load will probably require two to 2 1/2 hours.

Due to overuse, it's best to avoid the campsites right on the lake. There are less sensitive spots just before and beyond the lake. There is a tiny lake above

Iron Bog (off the trail), and two small lakes on the way over to the Fish pole cirque (the second being very scenic).

There are fish in Iron Bog and Fishpole lakes. Mule deer and coyote are present as are elk. Pronghorn antelope are surprisingly commonplace, in spite of the high elevation.

To get to Fishpole Lake, walk to the outlet of Iron Bog Lake, descend about 80 feet downhill along the outlet stream, and you should find the trail. It's about a mile and a 450-foot climb to Fishpole Lake. There are four lakes in the Fishpole cirque.

The country around the lakes is meadow and open forest of whitebark pine and Douglas fir. Wildflowers are abundant before September. Large rugged peaks rise behind the lakes.

There is a trail from Iron Bog Lake that climbs about 400 feet over a pass into the head of Muldoon Canyon a long, moist-bottomed, but almost non-forested canyon, ringed by scenic peaks. Muldoon Canyon is an alternative route to Iron Bog Lake. You approach it from Copper Basin. However, it involves using four-wheel drive or walking several miles on a jeep road that is mostly in the sun. Even if you don't come up Muldoon Canyon, the short hike to its open and ruggedly scenic head from Iron Bog Lake is very worthwhile for the view and the wildlife possibilities.—*Ralph Maughan* □

HIKE 56   *EAST FORK—LITTLE WOOD RIVER*

General description: A remote three- or four-day loop trip.
General location: In the proposed Pioneer Mountains Wilderness northeast of Hailey, 22 miles by road.
Maps: Grays Peak (7.5') USGS quad. Muldoon Canyon (15') quad is needed for the Pot Creek spur hike.
Special attractions: Magnificent high mountain views, wildflowers, meadows, cirque lakes, few people.
Difficulty: Moderately difficult due to the relief, some faint, or damaged, trail, and two fords of the Little Wood River.
Season: Late June through September.
Information: Ketchum Ranger District, Sawtooth National Forest, Box 2356, Ketchum, Idaho 83340; (208) 622-5371.

The hike: Most of this grand loop is little-used by hikers; it is seen mostly by hunters in mid-October and a few sheep herders in mid-summer. The hiker is rewarded by grand vistas of the high mountain divide between the headwaters of the Wood River and the Big Lost River. The area has quite a diverse aura, ranging from heavily wooded country and river gorges to alpine meadow and rock.

The loop hike is included in the proposed Pioneer Mountains Wilderness. To date, however, no action has been taken on this wilderness proposal. The Forest Service has closed the area to off-road vehicles. Grazing is allowed up the Little Wood River to the mouth of Box Canyon. My observation in

Head of the East Fork of Little Wood River from the PK Pass trail. Robert N. (Rob) Jones photo.

1982 was that herders have recently done a decent job of moving sheep through the area to prevent overgrazing.

Campsites along the hike are not evenly distributed, being most common at the confluence of watercourses. Fishing is good in the Little Wood River for both rainbow and cutthroat trout, with the best angling being downstream from Iron Mine Creek.

To arrive at the trailhead, take Idaho Highway 75 up the Wood River Valley. The turnoff from the highway is six miles north of Hailey, five miles south of Ketchum. Turn onto the East Fork of the Wood River road and head eastward up the canyon past a burgeoning crop of summer homes.

The road is paved for five miles but then becomes gravel in the vicinity of Triumph. After 5.5 more miles, the road reverts to a rough dirt road and ends a half-mile past the old Mascot lead and silver mine in the headwaters of the East Fork of the Wood River.

The Mascot Mine is private property, and although the trail to PK Pass leaves on the mining property, it's best to drive to the end of the road, which is on National Forest land. Park here by the Johnstone Pass trail registration box and walk the half-mile back to the PK Pass trailhead.

Early in July, the section of dirt road from Federal Gulch Campground to the trailhead may be impassable for passenger cars because of several wet spots. This need not spoil your trip nor require that you walk the four-mile-long section of road to the trailhead. Instead of hiking over PK Pass, simply take the old trail that leaves at the campground and heads east up Federal Gulch over the divide and down Grays Creek, eventually joining the loop at the mouth of Iron Mine Creek. This trail is somewhat faint, but the hike is every bit as scenic as the PK Pass-Little Wood River loop. Of course, you still will have to walk the four miles back to the campground on the road at the end of the hike if you want to make a loop hike.

While the PK Pass-Little Wood River loop could be hiked either direction, I prefer to save the best views for the last, so I recommend hiking over PK Pass first. From the trailhead, look across the stream (East Fork) for a sign marking the trail over PK Pass. Cross the stream (not difficult) and immediately start up toward the pass. It's a climb of 1,300 feet. You pass through avalanche debris, which obliterated the bottom of the trail in 1982. After ascending 1.5 miles through a mixture of mature fir forest and a tangle of low aspen, kept pruned by the frequent avalanches, you'll arrive at PK Pass (elevation 9,325). You can see far down the East Fork as you catch your breath before entering the trees near the summit.

Over the pass, drop into the Iron Mine Creek drainage, where the trail travels along the north side of the creek the entire way (contrary to what's indicated on the topographic map). As you descend, the creek grows rapidly as springs erupt near the trail.

A descent of almost 3,000 feet in 4.5 miles brings you to the Little Wood River. The upper 2.5 miles of the descent is steep, much of it on a ridge covered by low sage. Parts of the trail are rocky due to erosion that has exposed the underlying cobbles. However, after 2.5 miles, an unnamed stream enters from the right and the grade of the trail lessens. Here you enter a Douglas fir forest and come to a hunting camp, evidenced by local "improvements" such as tables. As you walk, look out for stinging nettles along this part of the trail.

The last two miles to the confluence with the Little Wood River drop only 800 feet, as compared to the 2,100-foot descent in the upper 2.5 miles. Deer are commonly seen along this section of Iron Mine Creek.

When you reach the Little Wood River, you'll find a fairly good camping spot and the remains of a cabin, plus good fishing. The Grays Creek trail leads south from here, although it doesn't follow the river which is constricted into a gorge just downstream. The Little Wood River flows through a number of short gorges as it tumbles down from the Pioneer Mountains, prohibiting a continuous trail along it.

From Iron Mine Creek, hike north up the Little Wood River. The trail here has the least relief of any section of the loop. You'll cross seven side drainages and gain 800 feet in the six miles between Iron Mine Creek and the mouth of Box Canyon. The Little Wood River Canyon is narrow, and plates of shale occasionally squeeze the river into a torrent which you can view first-hand from the trail.

The trail follows the west side of the river for 4.5 miles. Here the canyon is narrow, but you get the feeling that there is much more beyond the tops of the steep, rounded hillsides and talus slopes visible from the trail.

Crossing the side streams is easy, but the first crossing of the Little Wood is not. This ford comes about 4.5 miles up from Iron Mine Creek. The crossing in line with the trail has swift water and narrow banks, although it is not a problem in late summer. Earlier in the season, you'd be better off fording about 150 yards upstream, where the stream is wider with a more uniform riverbed.

After this crossing, the trail enters an older forest with a floor strewn with glacial boulders and some old avalanche debris. Here the canyon widens and you get the first glimpses of the peaks at the head of the Little Wood River.

After 1.5 miles of easy terrain, you come to Pot Meadow, a grassy park

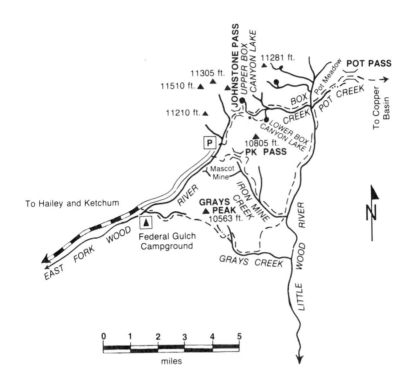

bisected by Pot Creek entering from the east. (Pot Meadow is **not** shown on the Grays Peak USGS map).

You can find some campsites with grand vistas here. The upper part of the meadow has better access to water than the willowy lower part. Deer and elk are commonly seen at the meadow's perimeter.

After crossing Pot Creek, the trail forks. To the right, the trail ascends Pot Creek. The left fork is the continuation of the loop; it crosses the river again to ascend Box Canyon.

The Pot Creek Trail is an ideal side-hike for a lay-over day at Pot Meadow. This trail climbs 2,000 feet to a pass that offers outstanding views down the Little Wood River, up Box Canyon to the west, and across Copper Basin to the White Knob Mountains to the northeast.

The Pot Creek trail (also called the Copper Creek trail) begins by angling over some low hills that appear to be glacial moraines, complete with glacial boulders and, in early to mid-July, a yellow blanket of arrowleaf balsamroot. Amid steadily improving views of the mountains at the head of Box Canyon and the divide, aspens and fir begin to dominate the vegetation. You'll pass several good campsites after climbing 700 feet in about a mile. The last part of the hike is steep, but it's worth it for the scenery. The pass is 3.5 miles from Pot Meadow.

Back at Pot Meadow to continue the loop, the trail skirts the top of the meadow and crosses the river. This wade is not as difficult as the first ford of the Little Wood downstream. Stable logs can usually be found about a hundred yards upstream.

Box Canyon is very scenic, although it's a 2,800-foot haul to its top at Johnstone Pass. The canyon is relatively narrow at first, but broadens within a mile as glacial bowls become visible in its side canyons. Box Canyon Creek thunders through the lower canyon, leaping in numerous cascades. Elephanthead, monkeyflower, and the ever-present arrowleaf often line the trail. After going about one-quarter of the way (it's 4.5 miles from Pot Meadow to the pass), you'll notice that the canyon acquires an alpine atmosphere, with bare, craggy slopes and a boulder-studded valley floor. A large slate mountain (10,391 feet) dominates the south side of the canyon as you climb to the level of Lower Box Canyon Lake. The lake nestles against the inside curve of the mountain. You can most easily reach it by continuing up the trail to where it crosses Box Canyon Creek and then doubling back along the south side of the valley. At the junction of the trail to the lower lake, you'll find the remains of two cabins.

The main trail continues upward below the broken ridgeline on the southwest side of the creek, never straying far from the creek's waters until you are directly below Johnstone Pass, watermelon snow (its red color is produced by an algae) intermittently covers sections of this high trail here until after mid-July.

A half-mile above the cabins, the main trail turns sharply uphill, zigzagging to the pass at a notch which is a hair shy of 10,000 feet. Opposite the pass a faint trail crosses the springs at the head of Box Canyon Creek and leads .3 mile over the low rise dotted with weathered fir to Upper Box Canyon Lake.

At 9,670 feet, the lake, full of cutthroat trout, is usually clear of ice by early July. Several nice campsites, complete with 360-degree mountain panoramas, are available. However, the lake could become congested if very many hikers chose to camp. At the lake, several stumps and other remains mark the site of another old cabin. At this high lake, be certain to use a stove instead of building a fire.

From Johnstone Pass you drop 2,000 feet over a couple dozen switchbacks into the beautiful upper portion of the East Fork of the Wood River. This side of the pass is free of snow long before the Box Canyon side.

Rugged peaks with rumbling cascades ring the head of the East Fork. These are all 11,000 feet or higher. Be sure to stop, look back, and admire these peaks as you trudge downhill. The trail switchbacks in rapid descent through quartz monzonite, similar to granulated granite then it parallels the stream. You'll have to make one easy crossing of the East Fork as you return to your vehicle at the trailhead a little way above the Mascot Mine.—*Robert N. (Rob) Jones*—□

Note: We revisited the headwaters of the East Fork of the Big Wood River in September 1989 and found that the trail over Johnstone Pass was washed out during the great storm of 1984 (see the Fall Creek hike for more information on this storm). As of this writing, the Forest Service has not rebuilt the trail.

The East Fork side of Johnstone Pass has been turned into a huge, steep, sandy gully. It is very difficult to ascend (particularly with a backpack), but relatively easy to descend if one sticks to the middle and "glissades" down.

The Box Canyon side of the pass has been damaged too, making a treacherous descent, but not as difficult as the other side isto ascend. Climbing up the Box Canyon side would not be particularly difficult. Thus, we would advocate to those making this loop to follow Rob Jones' original instructions and begin from PK pass. Be advised, however, that Johnstone Pass may present a difficulty.

Signs of the storm are evident throughout the East Fork. One sees many large erosion gullies scarring various peaks in the area.

The road to the trailhead is rough and steep beyond the primitive Federal Gulch campground. One needs a high clearance vehicle, but not a four-wheel-drive. At the trailhead, a new Forest Service sign grossly underestimates the mileage to Johnstone Pas s and Upper Box Canyon Lake: in truth it is two to 2.5 miles to Johnstone Pass.

Johnstone Pass itself is very scenic, very narrow, and, when we were there, very windy. Gusts we estimated at 70 miles per hour roared through this cleft in the rocks on an otherwise clear, unremarkable day. The head of the East Fork canyon is a magnificent place. Rugged peaks of a glistening whitish-gray mixed with reddish brown rise to over 11,000 feet, and several fairly large waterfalls thunder from clefts in the rocks.—Ralph and Jackie Maughan □

HIKE 57 *FALL CREEK TO SURPRISE VALLEY*

General description: Fall Creek is a moderately easy day hike. Surprise Valley is a beautiful glacier-formed hanging valley above Fall Creek, best done as an overnighter.

General location: 20 Linear miles northeast of Ketchum in the heart of the Pioneer Mountains.

Maps: Standhope Peak (7.5') USGS quad.

Special attractions: Glaciated mountain scenery, access to alpine lakes, impressive erosion scars from a great flood in 1984.

Difficulty: Moderately easy until the climb to Surprise Valley begins. Moderately difficult to Surprise Valley.

Season: July to mid-September.

Information: Contact the Lost River Ranger District, Challis National Forest, Box 507, Mackay, Idaho 83251; (208) 588-2224.

The hike: The Fall Creek trail gives access to both the Right and Left forks of Fall Creek and to Surprise Valley.

Although the mouth of Fall Creek is not impressive, the modest entrance is deceptive. After a mile the trail enters big mountain country. Here glacier-sculpted peaks, horns, and aretes rise around the hiker. Some peaks are almost 12,000 feet high.

The three forks of Fall Creek are textbook examples of hanging valleys.

Access to Fall Creek from Ketchum is by driving past Sun Valley up and over Trail Creek Summit, then down Summit Creek for 22 miles. Turn right here onto the Copper Basin Road. If coming from Mackay or Challis, turn

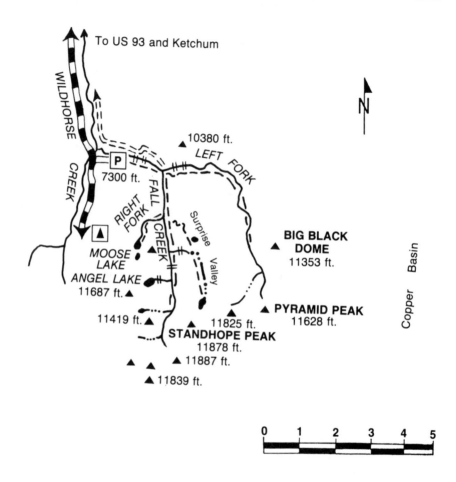

To US 93 and Ketchum

WILDHORSE CREEK

LEFT FORK

10380 ft.

P

7300 ft.

RIGHT FORK

FALL CREEK

Surprise Valley

N

BIG BLACK DOME
11353 ft.

Copper Basin

MOOSE LAKE

ANGEL LAKE
11687 ft.

11419 ft.

11825 ft.

STANDHOPE PEAK
11878 ft.

PYRAMID PEAK
11628 ft.

11887 ft.

11839 ft.

0 1 2 3 4 5

off U.S. 93 at the base of Mt. Borah onto the paved county highway. Take the county road due west across the valley, reaching the Big Lost River as the road enters low, bare, red-rocked mountains. Turn left onto the Copper Basin road 18.5 miles from U.S. 93.

Follow the Copper Basin Road for 2.5 miles, then turn right and go up Wildhorse Creek. Lower Wildhorse Creek is typical Challis volcanic terrain: steep, low, reddish mountains fronted by sage brush bottoms. But up-canyon, toward the head of Wildhorse Creek, stand pointed peaks that stun most tourists. These giants are not the destination, however. Instead, 3.5 miles up Wildhorse Creek turn off the Wildhorse Creek road onto the rough Fall Creek

Road. Drive carefully for about a quarter mile and park near the obvious pack bridge across Fall Creek.

The rough road continues up the hill, passing by the trailhead. the road's continuation provides access to a short, scenic dead-end trail to the lower falls of Fall Creek (.3 mile).

Cross the pack bridge. About 100 yards on the other side meet an abandoned jeep road that is reverting to a pack trail. Follow it through the sagebrush and up the canyon. It climbs moderately and soon enters patches of aspen and conifer.

A pack trail used to go up the right side of Fall Creek from the lower falls. Don't bother. This route was totally obliterated in the great flood of 1984.

As you follow the old road it rises above the stream to gain views of the erosion from the flood. A black cloud settled over the heads of Fall Creek and Wildhorse Creek on August 9, 1984. In just a few hours, it dropped ten inches of rain. The volume of Fall Creek grew to rival the Snake River in flood, uprooting trees, washing away meadows, cutting out streamside cliffs, and accomplishing several hundred years of erosion in a few hours. The evidence of the storm is everywhere in Fall creek and its tributaries.

The old road ends at the Left Fork of Fall Creek. The Left Fork tumbles down from its hanging valley and is not easy to cross before July, although occasionally someone installs a crude bridge. Later, until most of the higher-elevation snow has melted, the flow is subject to daily snow melt volume fluctuation.

The best camping spots in Fall Creek lie just ahead in the forest near the mountainside.

At the confluence of the Left Fork, the main canyon bends at a ninety-degree angle to the south, revealing a grand view. On the right a pointed peak guards the hanging Right Fork Vally, in which lies Moose Lake. A small, rugged horn on the left marks the unseen way to Surprise Valley, your goal. Beyond the horn, witness Standhope Peak, just short of 12,000 feet in elevation.

After the Left Fork crossing, the trail (now an intimate path) winds against the edge of the forest and close to the streamside willows. It is boggy here in the early summer. Next you climb gently across an avalanche chute and soon come to a deep, narrow wash formed by the flood. Scramble down into it and up again. The trial leads into the forest. Soon comes the trail junction for the Right Fork (to the right). Just beyond this point the trail crosses a broad wash created by the flood. The flood-ravaged route (here in the deep forest) is marked with cairns. A quarter mile past the wash, the trail to Surprise Valley exits to the left. The junction is obscure, but the trail is very well cairned. Shortly beyond the junction the main trail up Fall Creek abruptly ends due to damage from the flood. Further travel is very difficult.

The Surprise Valley trail switchbacks irregularly up a very steep, forested, boulder-strewn slope. After climbing about 700 feet, it levels out at a scenic small meadow with a fine view of the white igneous rock beyond—the east wall of Surprise Valley. A spring-fed brook bubbles out of the meadow.

From the meadow on, the trail's track is often faint, but the route is very well marked with blazes and/or cairns. You continue to climb, but not so steeply, into a rocky whitebark pine forest. Eventually the trail tops out and descends to the first lake—a large pond set in the open about two trail miles from and 1,000 feet above Fall Creek. Places to camp are scattered around the lake. The Lakes's outlet is very impressive. Instead of flowing down the valley, it tumbles out of the side of Surprise Valley from a notch and falls directly into Fall Creek. Investigate the falls with care. The lip of the falls is often damp and slippery. It's a long drop into Fall Creek.

The track is faint, but continues beyond the first lake. Keep about 50 yards to the right of the inlet stream to climb the 200 feet to the upper part of the valley—wet meadow bottom with whitebark pine forest on the east side. Look for mountain goats.

Cross to the left side of the creek and hike through the open whitebark forest to avoid the streamside wetness. At the end of the meadow, climb 400 feet up the slope to the deep upper lake. Mighty Standhope Peaks rises directly from its south shore.—*Ralph Maughan* □

Note: The Forest Service recently bridged the flood-created ravines from the great 1984 thunderstorm. They also reconstructed the trail up the main fork of Fall Creek, and partially rebuilt the trail to Surprise Valley. —Ralph Maughan

HIKE 58 *LEFT FORK, FALL CREEK*

General description: A long day hike or overnighter up the least known fork of Fall Creek.

General location: 20 miles northeast of Ketchum in the proposed Pioneer Mountain Wilderness.

Maps: Copper Basin (15') and Standhope Peak (7.5') USGS quads.

Special attractions: An isolated, rarely visited mountain valley with many meadows, volcanic crags, and glacier-carve d peaks.

Difficulty: Moderate due to the faint trail. Relatively easy cross-country after the trail finally disappears.

Season: July through September.

Information: Lost River Ranger District, Challis National Forest, Box 507 Mackay, Idaho 83251; (208) 588-2224.

The hike: Of the three splendid forks of Fall Creek located in the jagged Pioneer Mountains, the Left Fork is the least often seen. This is probably because, from the start of the trail, the country ahead is not nearly as scenic as the view up Fall Creek Valley or the view of the spire-guarded Right Fork. In reality, the Left Fork tributary to Fall Creek is almost a geological duplicate of Fall Creek with an unimpressive entrance that eventually turns to the south to head into beautifully ice-sculpted igneous rock.

The faint, but very easy-to-follow, trail leaves Fall Creek where the old jeep road ends (see the Fall Creek hike description for instructions to this spot). From the jeep road, cross the Left Fork on a log bridge and follow the Left Fork trail up the sidehill at a 90-degree angle from the main trail. You'll climb steeply, switchbacking several times into the hanging valley of the Left Fork. Here in the open, you have a good view across the main canyon toward the Right Fork's hanging valley. The trail does not follow the creek for this first section. The creek is busy cascading in a minor gorge off to your left and below you.

After climbing 500 feet in just .6 mile, the grade lessens, and a welcome spring runs across the trail out of the willows. The trail then fords the Left Fork to

Surprise Valley, Pioneer Mountains. Keith J. Kempski photo.

climb to the left (north) bank. Now you are in the stream valley, and the creek courses lazily below the trail through a maze of short willows.

The trail wanders through open hillside and patches of silvery quaking aspen that adorn the slope made of reddish brown volcanic rock. Flowers wink at you here early in the summer.

Across the stream valley, the opposite slope is covered with a dense forest of conifers. Bare crags of volcanic rock made of the widespread Challis Volcanic Formation poke into the sky above the trail.

At 1.5 miles from the trail's beginning, you begin to climb up the mountainside and away from the stream valley. The topographic maps show the trail continuing right over the mountain and down the other side to Copper Basin. While some semblance of a trail may do this, you should take the first fork to the right that you come to. This fork leads out over a broad sage and grass-covered platform and up the Left Fork Valley. Here, the valley begins its bend toward the south. At first you see, on your left, the brown, featureless scree slopes that form the backside of the Big Black Dome (11,353 feet)—a chunk of sedimentary rock lodged between the volcanics to the north and the hard crystalline, intruded rock to the south. Just below these amazingly smooth scree deposits grow flowers, short willows, and photogenic patches of spruce, fir, and whitebark pine.

As you complete the turn to the south, you'll see the rugged, gray, mostly unnamed peaks at the head of the canyon.

Once you turn the corner of the canyon, the trail is ephemeral, showing up alternately on both sides of the valley. Numerous small springs feed the dense low willows next to the creek. Low flow makes these springs poor sources of water. However, as you continue and enter the land underlain by the hard quartz monzonite of the Pioneer Window, the streamside becomes less mushy and the springs, though fewer, have a better flow.

In the upper canyon, there are many places to camp by the patches of trees with views of the peaks. The odd thing about this pretty place is the lack of continuous forest anywhere in the canyon bottom. Despite a plentitude of moisture and perfect altitude, the trees only grow in isolated clumps. — *Ralph Maughan.* □

HIKE 59 *RIGHT FORK, FALL CREEK*

General description: An overnight hike to a scenic subalpine lake.
General location: 20 miles northeast of Ketchum in the proposed Pioneer Mountains Wilderness.
Maps: Standhope Peak (7.5') USGS quad.
Special attractions: Two lakes in a high glacial bowl, wildflowers, good fishing, the best cross-country route to Angel Lake.
Difficulty: Moderately difficult due to the climb.
Season: July through September.
Information: Lost River Ranger District, Challis National Forest, Box 507, Mackay, Idaho 83251; (208) 588-2224.

The hike: The Right Fork of Fall Creek is yet another hanging valley which drops along with the Left Fork and Surprise valleys, into Fall Creek. The Right Fork is the only one of these three valleys that has a lake with fish Moose Lake. Therefore, it is by far the busiest of the three.

The hike is short from where the trail leaves Fall Creek Valley to Moose Lake, but the elevation gain is considerable 1,535 feet. The trail is well constructed, however, and easy to follow.

Begin about 1.2 miles above the Left Fork of Fall Creek (for instructions to this point, consult the Fall Creek hike description). Cross Fall Creek (there might be a sign here, depending on the previous winter and Forest Service funding) on some logs and begin to hike up into the Right Fork Valley, making several long switchbacks that are not shown on the topographic quadrangle.

A spire guards the entrance to the canyon on the left, and a less rugged big mountain stands to its right. Once you arrive at the cirque, you'll find the spire is really the end of a mile-long spiny ridge.

As you climb through forest and rock, you'll get occasional glimpses of the view back down across Fall Creek to the cream-colored, ribbed wall of the canyon's east side.

As you enter the hanging valley, the grade diminishes but the walk is still anything but level. The two sides of the valley contrast sharply; the left side is of the rugged igneous rock of the Pioneer Window, while the right is softer sedimentary rock called the Copper Basin Formation.

Just before you reach the lake, you'll wander through meadows near the lake's outlet. You can camp here, where rock outcroppings break up the meadow. You'll also find camping spots at the lake on its west side and near the top. Above the lake, a smaller, shallow lake nestles in the rocks.

All of this is set in a large high basin, dominated by nameless peak 11,667 at its head. The only route out of the cirque besides the way you came, is a rough cross-country hike to Angel Lake, a large scenic gem that barely hangs

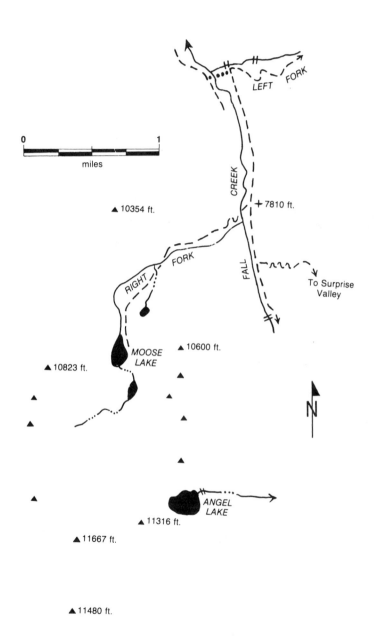

The Right Fork cirque Pioneer Mountains. Ralph Maughan photo.

onto the side of Fall Creek canyon. You can spend a day exploring the cirque or drop over to Angel Lake. Otherwise, side-hikes are limited here. Moose Lake is full of brook trout. Since they tend to overpopulate, you can keep all that you catch.—*Ralph Maughan* □

HIKE 60   *SUMMIT CREEK*

General description: A moderately easy day hike, which is notable for mid-summer wildflowers.
General location: On top of Trail Creek Summit; twelve road miles from Ketchum.
Maps: Phi Kappa Mountain, Rock Roll Canyon (7.5') USGS quads.
Special attractions: Wildflowers, access to the Devils Bedstead.
Difficulty: Moderately easy.
Season: July through September
Information: Lost River Ranger District, Challis National Forest, Box 507, Mackay, Idaho 83251; (208) 588-2224.

The hike: Except for the first quarter-mile and the last three-quarters mile, this trail climbs up a gentle mountain valley. The trail is easy to find and in good condition. Water is easy to locate in the creek and in springs. There are numerous places to camp. The only discordant note is the occasional presence of dirt bikes.

Drive east from Ketchum and Sun Valley for 12 miles to the top of Trail Creek Summit. The trailhead is right on the south sid e of the summit. At the

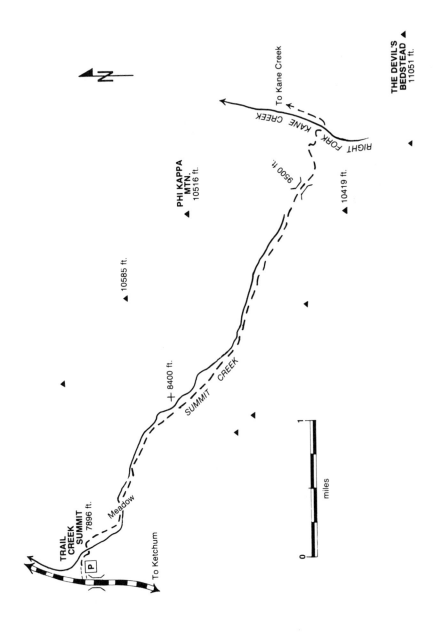

trailhead, you will see an obvious snow measuring device. Park in its vicinity and hike leftward to Summit Creek.

The trail crosses the creek and them climbs steeply for a short distance up a meadowy hillside. There are good views of the Boulder Mountains to the north from this sloping meadow.

The trail soon levels out to head through woods, but before long you come to a lovely, large meadow. In times past, people often lost the trail here as it crossed the meadow, but in 1989 the trail's track was easily visible. After crossing the meadow from left to right, you cross Summit Creek again. From here the trail climbs easily up the canyon, keeping to the canyon's right side. The trail alternates between sub-alpine meadow and forest. Wildflowers blaze from about mid-July to early August.

After about 2.5 miles the trail begins to climb more steeply and you emerge from the forest into a meadow. Bear left at the meadow's far end. Here you drop down a bit to cross a tributary of Summit Creek that comes from the right. After crossing the tributary, keep going straight to climb a minor ridge between the creek you crossed and Summit Creek. After another mile you reach the pass at about 9,500 feet. The Devils Bedstead rises in front of you, and you can see part way down the Right Fork of Kane Creek.

A hike down the Right Fork to Kane Creek is a possible extension of the route. The Right Fork has a fair trail, but you need a good four-wheel drive vehicle to reach the Kane Creek trailhead where you would exit.—*Ralph Maughan* ☐

Sawtooth Mountains

Overview

Perhaps the most famous mountain range in Idaho, the Sawtooth Mountains rise abruptly on the west side of the beautiful and spacious Sawtooth Valley. Near the southern end of the valley, the Sawtooths become the Smoky Mountains, which then extend southward all the way to the Snake River Plain.

The core of the Sawtooth Range is composed of beautiful pink granite, which originated as a molten intrusion into the vast gray igneous formation called the Idaho Batholith which covers most of central Idaho. The hard pink granite, sculpted into walls, peaks, and spires by ice age glaciers, is a mecca for climbers.

The 216,000-acre Sawtooth Wilderness preserves the core of the Sawtooth Mountains and is Idaho's best-known designated wilderness area. Use of the east side of this fairyland of rock is heavy. The western side is relatively uncrowded, and the vast unprotected roadless country that adjoins it is virtually unused.

The entire wilderness is well served with good trails. Access to the east side of the wilderness is easy and features good roads, but the west side involves longer drives, mostly on dirt or gravel roads.

Anglers will find over 300 stunning alpine and subalpine lakes, 60 of which support fisheries. The most common game fish is the brook trout. Unfortunately, many of these brook trout populations are of only small fish due to overpopulation and the inherent low productivity of these high, rock-bound lakes. Wildlife is varied, with most of the Rocky Mountain game species being represented e xcept moose and grizzly bears. Despite all the variety, however, the density of wildlife is low.

A sad note was sounded in 1989, when sockeye salmon failed to return to Redfish Lake. Environmental damage finally interrupted the journey from the Pacific Ocean for good. The species is now probably extinct in Idaho.

Adjacent to the Sawtooth Wilderness west and south is 320,000 acres of unprotected, *de facto* wilderness. Outdoor lovers want to add it to the Sawtooth Wilderness, increasing the size of the protected country to 536,000 acres. This would be one of America's biggest wildernesses. A considerable portion of this country to the west (including part of the existing Sawtooth Wilderness) burned in the Rabbit Creek forest fire of 1994. If logging can be kept out, the *de facto* wilderness area should regenerate quickly, with little lasting harm to backcountry adventure.

The Sawtooth Wilderness is part of the larger Sawtooth National Recreation Area, which gives protection to the pastoral beauty of the Sawtooth Valley and Stanley Basin. It also gives limited protection to the wild character of the White Cloud and Boulder mountain ranges that lie on its east and southeast sides.

HIKE 61   *ALPINE CREEK*

General description: A lovely day hike with opportunities to stay longer and explore lakes not accessible by a regular trail.

General location: In the extreme southern end of the Sawtooth Wilderness. Access is from the Sawtooth Valley.

Map: Snowyside Peak (7.5') USGS quad.

Special attractions: Relatively uncrowded for a trail in the Stanley side of the Sawtooth Wilderness. Numerous beautiful rockbound lakes above the end of the trail.

Difficulty: Moderate before reaching the cross-country part of the hike.

Season: Mid-July to mid-September.

Information: Sawtooth National Recreation Area, Sawtooth National Forest, Star Route, Ketchum, Idaho 83340; (208) 726 -8291.

The hike: Here is a delightful, short trail into the Sawtooths that is not mobbed by people. The scenery is exquisite although there are no lakes by the trailside. The trail is 2.5 miles long and not very steep, climbing only 500 feet, but it takes you a good distance into the jagged Sawtooth Mountains.

From Ketchum, Idaho, take Idaho Highway 75 about 40 miles north to the Alturas Lake road. The paved road takes you to large Alturas Lake after passing through 2.5 miles of meadow and forest. The pavement ends as you reach the north side of this moraine lake. You arrive at Alpine Creek after 1.2 miles on the gravel road. Park here on the east side of the creek. Put on your pack and head up the trail, which follows the creek's east side. Don't cross the creek.

This is a good trail as it heads away from Alpine Creek and into the pine and fir forest. The going is very easy for .3 mile until you begin a 160-foot climb to a shelf. From the shelf you climb with ease around a granite knob, and here you are reward ed with a fine view of Alpine Creek's glaciated canyon,

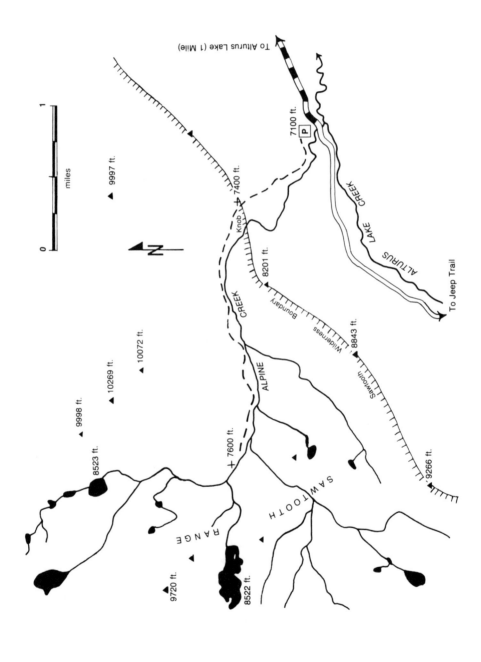

with the rugged gray peaks of the Sawtooth crest rising at the head of this wilderness valley. It's only a mile and a 300-foot climb to this viewpoint.

From the viewpoint near the knob, drop into some forest, from which you'll quickly emerge again onto an open slope (kept open by avalanches) of grass, wildflowers, and sagebrush. The trail wanders again into the forest and emerges in a large avalanche run near Alpine Creek. You'll find good campsites on the valley floor just beyond this display of the force of sliding snow.

The trail's condition deteriorates as you climb gradually through more timber and openings. If you lose the track, just keep to the slope where the going is relatively easy instead of getting down onto the often-wet valley floor.

Finally, 2.5 miles from your vehicle, the trail ends at the creekside in a deep and boggy forest. Just beyond here the valley ends. Three hanging tributaries lie above the main valley, each tributary sheltering numerous trailless lakes. This portion of the Wilderness is being managed to keep it in a trailless condition.

Most people who continue on, head for the largest lake (8,522 feet). There is a angler's route that you can follow for the .6 mile (with a 900-foot climb) to this half-mile-long lake. Hunt for this faint trail on the south side of the creek.

There are about 45 lakes or ponds in the headwaters of Alpine Creek. The larger lakes contain brook trout, but as with so many of the lakes in the Sawtooths, the trout mostly are small due to overpopulation and infertile waters.—*Ralph Maughan* □

HIKE 62 *TOXAWAY-PETTIT LOOP*

General description: A comfortable three-day loop in the spectacular Sawtooth Wilderness.
General location: On the east side of the Sawtooth Mountains facing Stanley Basin.
Maps: Snowyside Peak (7.5') USGS quad.
Special attractions: Alpine and sub-alpine lakes, waterfalls, jagged peaks, fishing, designated wilderness (no machines).
Difficulty: Moderately difficult due to the elevation gain.
Season: Mid-July through September.
Information: Sawtooth National Recreation Area, Sawtooth National Forest, Box 2356, Ketchum, Idaho 83340; (208) 726 -8291

The hike: This is a classic backpacking trip in the Sawtooth Mountains. You'll make an 18-mile loop beginning and ending at a large moraine lake on the valley floor (Pettit Lake). In between, you'll pass a variety of Sawtooth Mountain grandeur, toothed peaks, glacial boulders, mountain lakes, both large and small, many avalanche runs, talus slides, and hard granite cliffs, mountain meadows, waterfalls, cascading streams, and dense stands of lodgepole pine.

You begin at the transfer camp on the north side of Pettit Lake—a well-developed site with restrooms, garbage cans, and designated parking places for perhaps a hundred vehicles (these are not isolated trails).

To get to the Tin Cup transfer camp, turn off of Idaho Highway 75 about 45 miles north of Ketchum onto the signed road to Pettit Lake. Follow this road about 1.5 miles to where a road forks across the lake's outlet. Take the right fork. At the next fork, turn left and go about a half-mile to the obvious parking area at the trailhead.

A brief walk down the trail brings you to the junction with the trail that goes up Pettit Lake Creek and the trail leading up and over into Yellow Belly Creek. It's probably best to take the right fork and climb over into Yellow Belly Creek, making Pettit Lake Creek the last leg of the hike, because a 550-foot-high moraine stands between the two drainages. The prospect of climbing over it is more inviting on your first day when you're fresh than on your last.

Soaking up the view on the Toxaway-Pettit Loop. Ralph Maughan photo.

At the junction, begin the switchbacking ascent of the moraine amid grass, sage, and flowers. The dark blue waters of Pettit Lake sparkle behind you. After about .3 mile you'll reach the edge of the forest. Giant, weathered outlying fir quickly gives way to dense lodgepole thickets as you continue to climb with the trail. You'll have to find some other inspiration besides an anticipation of the view to egg you on—there is no view at the top. From the top, switchback down into the canyon of Yellow Belly Creek, still hiking through lodgepole forest. You arrive at the bottom of the canyon 1.7 miles from your vehicle and join the trail that comes up Yellow Belly Creek. Just a few yards down this trail is McDonald Lake, a somewhat marshy lake with a burn on its south side from the 1981 fire. Larger Yellow Belly Lake, just one-half mile farther down-canyon, has a burn from a 1982 fire.

Head up the canyon, walking almost on the level through more lodgepole forest. After about a mile you climb a short hill and then cross Yellow Belly Creek. There are places to camp in the trees just after the crossing, although they are not highly desirable (no view, mosquitos through July).

Just .2 mile past the stream crossing you begin the 600-foot climb to Farley Lake. In 1982, we did this stretch in the early morning, watching the sun rise over the White Cloud Mountains to the east as we climbed, scaring several deer and elk from early morning cover.

After about .75 mile the trail goes past a small, thundering waterfall on Yellow Belly Creek. Then, in another half-mile you'll cross through a grassy, scrub timber basin through which the creek cascades. Soon you're at Farley Lake (about 1.75 miles from the start of the climb). This pretty lake is full of brook trout, a very common fish in Sawtooth lakes. People have scratched out a few campsites in the decomposed granite between the lakeside boulders, but you'll find much better sites farther up the canyon.

For the next 1.5 miles the trail climbs moderately, but erratically, through small meadows and scrub timber and past large granite boulders and rock.

At 6.5 miles from the trailhead, you come to a junction. The trail to the right leads to Edith Lake, then over a 9,200 foot pass and down to lovely Imogene Lake, which rests in the Hellroaring Creek drainage. Stay on the trail to the left. Soon you'll pass an elongated pond at elevation 8,165 feet. Continue on past this and a smaller pond, then past small Bowknot Lake. One mile and about 150 feet above the junction with the Edith Lake trail, you finally reach big, beautiful Toxaway Lake. Gorgeous peaks rise above the lake as you look toward the head of the canyon. The lake itself is a mile long, making it one of the biggest in the Sawtooth Mountains. You'll find welcome campsites on the north and west sides of the lakes between the trail and the lakeshore. These campsites get a lot of use, however. Please keep them clean and don't build a campfire. Use a stove.

You'll generally find good fishing in Toxaway for brook trout up to a foot—pretty large for Sawtooth brookies.

On the north side of the lake you'll encounter a trail that climbs over Sand Mountain Pass providing access to Vernon, Edna, and Virginia Lakes (all on the other side of the Sawtooth crest) at the headwaters of the South Fork of the Payette River. The trail over Sand Mountain is also an alternative route to Edith Lake and then down into the Hellroaring drainage to Imogene Lake.

To reach Twin and Alice lakes in the Pettit Lake Creek drainage, continue around Toxaway Lake. The trail has been completely rebuilt since the

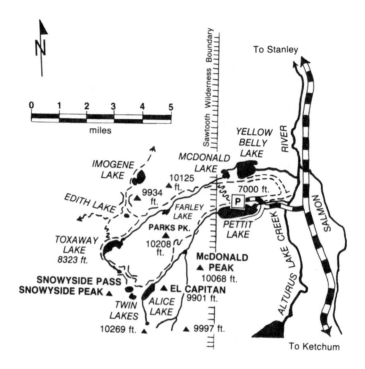

Snowyside USGS quadrangle was published in 1964, so the map is incorrect. You can't get lost, however.

It's a thousand-foot climb and about 1.5 miles from Toxaway to Snowyside Pass (elevation 9,390 feet). The trail rounds big Toxaway Lake and climbs up into a steep canyon that harbors three small lakes. The scenery is sublime as you switchback to the pass. Note that snow often remains here on the northeast-facing slope of 10,651-foot Snowyside Peak until lake July.

From the notch at the pass, start down into the Pettit Lake Creek drainage by following the trail that is lodged into the wide part of a steep wall. Right below you, 500 feet down, is the upper of the Twin Lakes. The trail loops around the north side of the cirque and descends to the Twin Lakes, two sapphire pools situated just below timberline in a wonderful pink cirque basin. Rugged peaks rise all around these fish-filled lakes that are separated only by a narrow rock band. There are good campsites here, too, although the altitude breeds wind.

From Twin Lakes, head east over a saddle and switchback down to Alice

Lake, another large lake, fully the size of the Twin Lakes together. Alice is a scintillating blue, bejeweled with small rock islands and surrounded by sub-alpine fir struggling through the granite. El Capitan thrusts up on the lake's east side, looking somewhat similar to its namesake in Yosemite National Park. The serrated crest of the Sawtooth Range forms the skyline to the south and southwest. Many good campsites are available near Alice Lake, but please don't build new fire rings. Again, it's best to use your stove. You won't be the last party to visit this lake. Think of how it could look in 30 years, given the same amount of use it gets each year, unless visitors treat it gently.

Past Alice Lake, heading down Pettit Lake Creek, walk on the level past two small lakes, then begin a moderate descent through open forest to a creek ford half a mile below the last of the two small lakes. Descend now at a steeper angle for .3 mile to a bridged crossing of Pettit Lake Creek. Continue to descend, switchbacking at times, as the right (northwest) wall of the canyon becomes very rugged and convoluted.

After two miles you'll pass under the rugged cliffs and reach the floor of the lower canyon. Here the atmosphere is moister a nd the trail can be muddy after a summer thundershower. You cross the creek twice, but you can probably get across on logjams or foot logs without having to wade. There are camping spots on the lush flat at the head of Pettit Lake.

Once you reach the shore of Pettit Lake, follow the trail for one more mile on its north side, passing in and out of timber. Here you can take a classic photo of the lake waters and 10,068-foot McDonald Peak rising to the southwest.—*Ralph Maughan* □

HIKE 63   *IRON CREEK TO SAWTOOTH LAKE*

General description: A full day hike to perhaps the most renowned backcountry lake in Idaho.
General location: At the north end of the Sawtooth Wilderness on the crest of the mountain range.
Map: Stanley Lake (7.5') USGS quad.
Special attractions: Alpine lakes, rugged peaks, and photogenic Mt. Regan and Sawtooth Lake.
Difficulty: Moderately difficult (steep) and fairly strenuous if done in one day.
Season: Mid-July to October.
Information: Sawtooth National Recreation Area, Box 2356, Ketchum, Idaho 83340; (208) 726-7672.

The hike: Entire generations of photographers, not to mention amateur camera enthusiasts, have packed their 35-mm, their 2 1/4 inch cameras, and their bulky view cameras with tripods the four miles and 1700 feet to Sawtooth Lake, the largest alpine lake in the Sawtooth Mountains. Photographs of Sawtooth Lake reflecting 10,190 foot Mt. Regan (usually taken from amon g the whitebark pine on its northern end) have graced hundreds of calendars from that of the Sierra Club to the local feed and seed store.

You can make the hike up and back in a day. You can also camp overnight or make this part of a much longer backpacking trip. It's best to camp near

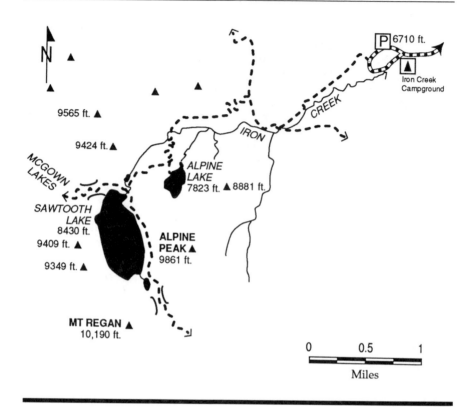

Alpine Lake (below Sawtooth). Here there are numerous camping spots scattered between the rock outcroppings and tres. Camping marginal at Sawtooth Lake due to its location near timberline at 8,400 feet in a large basin on the crest of the Sawtooth Range. Wind and storm are fierce with nothing to break their power as they roar across this expanse of cold water. Use of campfires is prohibited at both lakes.

Drive to Stanley and then continue northwestward on Idaho Highway 21, 2.6 miles to the Iron Creek Road turnoff. Drive 3.2 miles on this gravel, but often badly "washboarded" road, to the Iron Creek Transfer Camp. Here there is plenty of room to park (often in the shade), but expect to see many other vehicles. This is a popular hike. The trailhead also gives access to the Alpine Way Trail.

Start by following the well-built trail through a lodgepole pine covered flat to the wilderness boundary. The boundary is about one mile. A short distance past the wilderness boundary you meet the Alpine Way Trail. Follow this trail to the right. Soon you cross a willowy meadow providing good views of the Sawtooth Mountains. In about a half mile the trail to Sawtooth Lake leaves the Alpine Way Trail at a right angle to left. It heads away from the creek, makes a few switchbacks under large Douglas fir trees, and then climbs steadily until reaching a lovely sub-alpine avalanche meadow with a ford (until August) of Iron Creek. Just beyond the crossing, you begin to climb once more. The trail climbs steeply up a forested mountainside.

A side trail leading to Alpine Lake is reached at a ridgetop after a climb of about 300 feet in .5 mile. This trail to Alpine Lake is a bit hard to see, but the lake can be reached by walking cross-country should you miss it.

Alpine Lake is not an alpine lake. Sub-alpine fir surround it on three sides, framing the view of massive Alpine Peak on its south. As mentioned before, one is much more secure from the elements here than at Sawtooth Lake. On my visit in late July, it rained gently at Alpine Lake but blew fiercely and snowed several inches at Sawtooth Lake.

Continue now upward, switchbacking on top of the rising ridge which parallels Alpine Lake over 100 feet below you. It's a fine view.

The grade flattens as you approach Sawtooth Lake, and you pass by a pond, a possible camping area.

The first view of Sawtooth Lake is the classic one. The trail forks here near the point overlooking the lake. The left fork heads over the crest of range southward, and the right fork climbs to McGown Pass and the high altitude McGown Lakes. These too are a better location for a camp than Sawtooth Lake.—*Ralph Maughan* □

White Knob Mountains

Overview

Despite their height and beauty, the White Knob Mountains remain undiscovered except to the folks living in the Big Lost River Valley. Consequently, the Forest Service tends to forget about managing them for such forest uses as recreation. You can expect indefinite trailheads, poor roads, obscure roads, no other hikers, and possible difficulty recruiting trail companions. But don't let any of those deter you from exploring this magnificent country.

Those not conversant with the White Knobs will likely confuse them with the famous White Cloud Mountains. Their obscurity is underscored by difficult road access and trails no one has bothered to record or mark for posterity, such as the one described as follows. But this is not entirely what makes these peaks 11,000-foot wallflowers. It's mostly their neighbors. To the east are Idaho's highest, the 12,000-foot-plus Lost River Mountains. To the White Knobs' west are the jagged pioneers, which almost reach 12,000 feet and contain many sparkling jewels of alpine water in their heights. These ranges tend to upstage the White Knobs.

The White Knobs boast a number of canyons, but only two major ones— Corral Creek, the subject of the following hike, and Cabin Creek. With 20 or so other Corral and Cabin creeks in Idaho, it's no wonder the area has geographical identity problems.

HIKE 64   *CORRAL CREEK*

General description: A two-day hike into the crystalline core of the White Knob Mountains.

General location: Just east of Copper Basin and just west of Mackay; 100 miles northwest of Pocatello, 150 miles west of Idaho Falls, and 100 miles northeast of Twin Falls.

Maps: Copper Basin and Mackay (15') USGS quads.

Special attractions: Solitude in the most obscure of Idaho's higher (11,000-foot) mountain ranges.

Difficulty: Moderate because of faint trail.

Season: Mid-July to mid-October.

Information: Lost River Ranger District, Challis National Forest, Box 507, Mackay, Idaho 83251; (208) 588-2224.

The hike: Getting to Corral Creek depends on where you're coming from, as it were. From Mackay and the Big Lost River Valley, your objective is to find the Burma Road. This dirt road goes over a lower crest of the White Knobs and then downhill to Corral Creek and Copper Basin.

From Mackay, drive north on U.S. 93 for 9.3 miles, passing Mackay Reservoir which sits at the base of the White Knob Mountain Range. At 9.3 miles, turn left off the highway onto a paved road. Now go for 2.6 miles to a three-way junction. Take the left-most (also paved) of the three forks. Another junction comes after 1.2 miles (turn left here). From this point there are several more road junctions, but now you can see where the Burma Road leads up the mountain side in the near distance. Keep heading for this location. It's 7.8 miles to Corral Creek Summit, elevation 8,728 feet a 2,200-foot ascent. The Burma Road is better than it looks on the old 15' Mackay topo map. Once over the summit, it's 4.7 miles down to the Corral Creek crossing, where you turn left onto a two-wheel track that heads for the trail. If you overlooked Corral Creek, as most travelers do, you'll know you overshot it when you reach Copper Basin one of Idaho's most famous mountain valleys which is 3.8 more mile s downhill.

From Sun Valley or Ketchum, take the well-known Trail Creek Road over Trail Creek Summit, down Summit Creek for 10.3 miles an d turn onto the well-signed Copper Basin Road. Follow this road 15 miles along the East Fork of the Big Lost River to Copper Basin. Continue past the Copper Basin Loop turnoff for four more miles to the Burma Road which crosses the East Fork, then Cabin Creek, and then heads up Corral Creek. At 3.8 miles, turn right onto the two-wheel track mentioned previously.

Now you have rough drive of one to 1.6 miles; the distance you'll be able to go depends on your vehicle. When the going gets too rough, pull off onto the meadow, don your pack, and start walking.

To the southwest, the Pioneer Mountains rake the sky above Copper Basin. From your meadowland vantage point of about 8,200 feet, the White Knobs subtly rise to the east.

Corral Creek itself begins amid grass and wildflowers just below a small lake that's situated in a grassy basin at the foot o f 11,179-foot Lime Mountain. Gathering water from many springs and seeps, it flows slowly down the

HIKE 64 *CORRAL CREEK*

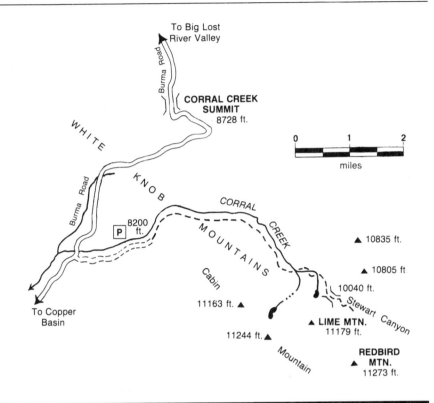

canyon, its course impeded by hundreds of beaver-built ponds.

Because the hike starts at a relatively high elevation and the broad entrance to the Corral Creek Canyon is flanked by low-relief ridges that obscure the view up-canyon, you won't be able to see the big peaks at the core of the White Knob Mountains until you've walked three or four miles.

You walk about a half-mile before the jeep trail finally plays out. This is all meadow country, where Corral Creek splashes off to your left, hidden in the willows. As you enter the canyon, the riparian zone remains broad. The bottoms are filled with grass, willows, and intricate beaver ponds. The trail is faint; however, it always keeps just to right of the damp zone but down off the mountainside. You'll lose it, then find it again. Except for a detour around one hillside spring and one rockslide, the going is relatively easy even when you're not on the pathway.

Gradually the ring of peaks enclosing upper Corral Creek comes into view. They are made of hard intrusive rocks—granite and its close mineral relatives. These peaks contrast with the lesser ridges of the White Knob Mountains, which are made of some limestone, but mostly of the assorted red, pink, brown, and white volcanic siltstones, conglomerates, tuff, and basalt called the Challis Volcanics. To your right rises reddish, double-peaked Cabin Mountain. At the head of Corral Creek you see 11,179-foot Lime Mountain and 11,273-foot Redbird Mountain, the latter actually standing at the head of Stewart Canyon. The peaks ahead to your left are unnamed and slightly less than 11,000 feet.

You'll find camping spots abundant and springs plentiful, but be careful about the water since Corral Creek is intermittently grazed by cattle. You'll want to plan this trip when the cattle are elsewhere. Call the Lost River Ranger District office in Mackay to find out when the drainage is clear of them. Because of all the ponded water, mosquitoes and flies are often numerous.

The trail eventually crosses the headwaters of Corral Creek and climbs over into Stewart Canyon on a high pass (10,040 feet). You'll pass by the lake at the base of Lime Mountain. It's shallow, silty, and barren. On a sunny day, the grassy basin near the lake appears to be a good campsite, but potential wind and storm here, near timberline, make it prudent to camp lower.

There's another lake in the canyon, high on Cabin Mountain. This lake, too, is barren and exposed. A tongue of snow from the mountain still extended into the lake when I visited it in late July. This lake affords a scenic view of the high peaks of the Lost Rivers to the northeast, framed by the rough branches of whitebark pine that partially encircle the lake. You can scramble up Cabin Mountain from the lake, and on its lonely summit ridge you have the best view in Idaho of the Gem State's two highest mountain ranges—the Pioneers and the Lost Rivers.—*Ralph Maughan* □

Smoky Mountains

Overview

Southward in the Sawtooths, the mountains gradually blend into another mountain range, a complicated and rugged mass known as the Smoky Mountains. Here in one chunk lie 337,000 acres of roadless, *de facto* wilderness with rugged mountains, lengthy canyons, sub-alpine lakes, which, with the exception of a few lake basins close to Idaho Highway 75, are visited by only a handful of people.

Mainstream Idaho conservationists of the Idaho Wildlands Defense Coalition are pushing for the establishment of a 130,000 acre Smoky Mountains Wilderness. On the other hand, Earth First! is pushing for a 416,000 acre wilderness which would involve the closure and naturalization of some existing roads. Finally, Idaho's senior senator, James McClure, (who retires in 1990) has introduced legislation in congress for a Smoky Mountains Special Management Area of 115,000 acres instead of wilderness. This would prohibit mining, timbering, and road building, but would also designate certain trails for exclusive use by off-road vehicles, effectively making it illegal to enter large portions of the area unless you were on a motorcycle or a all-terrain vehicle!

The eastern, more frequented part of the Smokies is a beautiful and complicated mixture of volcanic rock, quartzite, sandstone, limestone, and conglomerate. Westward, the most isolated part of the Smokies is built of the generally gray, intrusive quartz monzonite, grandiorite, and quartz diorite of the vast Idaho Batholith which covers much of Central Idaho.

Wildlife in the Smokies is that typical of the wilderness reaches of Central

The Smoky Mountains at the southern end of the Sawtooth Valley. Ralph Maughan photo.

Idaho, meaning most of the big game animals found in the Northern Rocky Mountains except for the grizzly bear . Recently there have been a number of sightings of the rare wolverine.

The Smoky Mountains are under the jurisdiction of the U.S. Forest Service the Sawtooth and Boise National Forests, plus a small portion of the Sawtooth National Recreation Area. For the most current road and trail information contact their offices.

HIKE 65 *PRAIRIE LAKES*

General description: An all-day hike or overnighter to a pretty lake basin with opportunities for a more extended hike.
General location: About 10 miles northwest of Ketchum, just west of the Sawtooth National Recreation Area.
Maps: Baker Peak and Galena (7.5') USGS quads.
Special attractions: Beautiful mountain scenery.
Difficulty: Moderate, with some fairly difficult extensions possible.
Season: Late June through September.
Information: Ketchum Ranger District, Sawtooth National Forest, Box 2356, Ketchum, Idaho 83340; (208) 622-5371.

The hike: Drive 18.9 miles from downtown Ketchum northward on Idaho Highway 75 into the Sawtooth National Recreation Area. Turn left onto the obvious Prairie Creek road. Drive 2.6 miles up this well-used, often dusty road to a nice trailh ead with room for eight to 10 vehicles. Although the road is well-used, be careful; imbedded rocks lurk in its tracks. Ignore the side-road; it's the trailhead to Mill Lake, 2.2 miles away.

Prairie Creek Canyon. Ralph Maughan photo.

HIKE 65 *PRAIRIE LAKES*

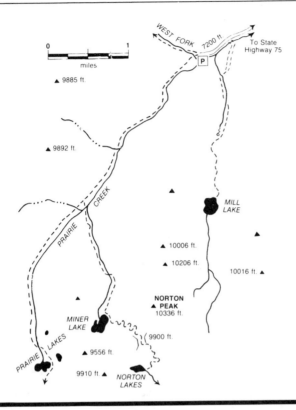

The trailhead is obvious, with a parking place and plenty of signs. It's 4.75 miles from here to the lakes. Unfortunately the way is open to trail machines. Those who demand more immediate solitude might consider taking the trail to the right leading up the West Fork of Prairie Creek.

Assuming you take the left trail, you cross the West Fork and enter the forest, then you climb gently for about a mile to a meadow. Craggy mountains rise to the right and a steep forested ridge to the left. From here you'll ramble through forest and meadow to the junction with the Miner Lake trail at about 2.3 miles from where you began. It's about 1.25 miles and a steep thousand feet to big, shallow Miner Lake—guarded by crags in a tight cirque basin.

Keep to the right at the junction. Very soon you'll come to a small opening where you can see Norton Peak (10,336 feet) rising to the south. (The Smoky Mountains are as high as the Sawtooths.)

Climb at a moderate, but slightly increasing, incline through woods and openings for another mile. The trail gets steep as you approach a convoluted cliff ahead to the right. Pass the cliff and aim for the large grassy meadow. Here you jump over the small headwaters of the creek, climb a hill, and find the lowest lake. The best camping is at the inlet; however, solitude can be found at one of the other three lakes or in the upper basin.

A rough trail leads out of the basin, and, in a mile, it gains the crest. From here you can descend into Norton Creek on the east side of the crest. You can also go a little further, recrossing the crest, and drop into the remote Big Smoky Creek country to the west of the crest. If you drop into Norton Creek, you can descend to its right fork, climb up to Norton Lake, cross difficult a high divide and drop down to Miner Lake, rejoin the Prairie Creek trail, and from there, retrace your steps back to your car. It's a fine three- to four-day loop.—*Ralph Maughan* □

HIKE 66 *WEST FORK PRAIRIE CREEK*

General description: A day hike or overnighter with the opportunity for easy to moderately difficult cross-country travel. This is an alternative to the busy Prairie Lakes trail. It begins from the same trailhead.
General location: 20 miles by road northwest of Ketchum at the Prairie Lakes trailhead.
Maps: Galena (7.5') USGS quadrangle.
Special attractions: Solitude, a large interesting rock slide with a creek that appears and disappears several times. Rapidly changing topography and flora within a short distance.
Difficulty: Moderate. The cross-country section begins easily but eventually becomes moderately difficult.
Season: Mid-June through mid-October.
Information: Ketchum Ranger District, Sawtooth National Forest, Sun Valley Road, Sun Valley, Idaho 83340. (208) 622-5371.

The hike: The scenic Prairie Lakes trail described previously is a busy, widely worn path with many hikers, horses, and some motorbikes. The West Prairie trail leaves from the same trailhead but gets less than a tenth as much use. It can serve as a quiet alternative.

To reach the trailhead, follow the directions for the Prairie Lakes hike. At the trailhead, a sign points to the right indicating the trail's beginning, although no track may be visible on the ground. Walk about 100 yards over an open flat to the obvious West Fork canyon and you will come to a sign indicating the trail is closed to motor vehicles. Here the track leading into a Douglas fir forest is obvious.

You quickly come to West Prairie Creek, a splashing full-sized brook that emerges out of a huge cone of scree just upstream. The scree is the beginning of a large landslide that sprawls down from the craggy peaks on the canyon's right (east) side.

The trail crosses the creek just below the spring (be careful here as the creek bottom is uneven and the stones slippery). Cross it here, nevertheless, and avoid the treacherous scree slope just above the spring.

On the other side of the creek, which is lined with bluebells and monkeyflower in mid-summer, the trail leads up the canyon under forest, but with the scree slide and barren peaks of over 9,000 feet visible to the right. The rock slide is gray with a lot of rose-shaded pieces therein.

Within a quarter-mile the forest thins, then disappears alongside the trail due to the relentless action of many winter snowslides. You emerge into an open

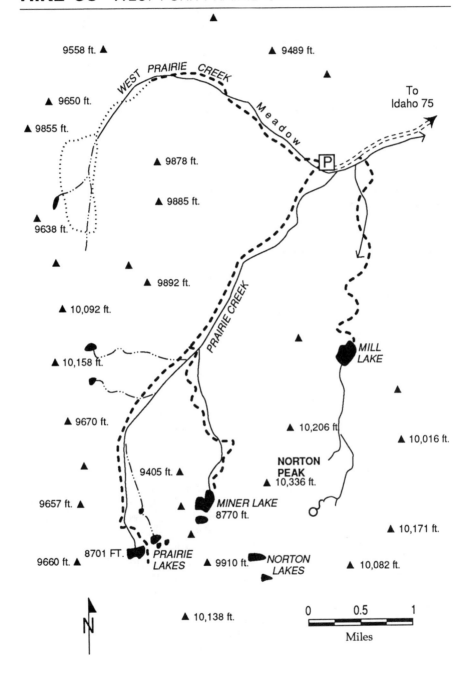

canyon filled with flowers, rock slides, conifer seedlings, and the very few huge Douglas fir that have managed to avoid the avalanches.

The trail climbs steadily up the rock slide along an easy (unless the sun is hot) route. You soon find that the creek has reappeared, flowing slightly below the trail over the rocks, promoting the growth of willows and numerous wildflowers. Soon, however, it disappears again. You gain the top of the slide. .75 mile from its beginning and after an ascent of 420 feet in elevation.

At the top of the slide, you emerge into totally different surroundings, a flat-bottomed, verdant canyon. The trail angles to the extreme left of the grass and willow-filled meadow ahead. The track is faint now becouse the grass grows fast enough to erase the depressions left by boots and horse hooves. If you walk out into the meadow, you will find the creek meandering slowly along.— *Ralph Maughan.* □

HIKE 67 *BAKER LAKE*

General description: A short day hike to a pretty and fishable lake of the Smoky Mountains.
General location: 20 miles northwest of Ketchum.
Map: Baker Peak (7.5') USGS quad.
Special attractions: Wildflower splendor from July into August. A good family hike.
Season: Early July to mid-October.
Difficulty: Moderately easy (steep, but short, 1 1/4 miles to the lake).
Information: Ketchum Ranger District, Sawtooth National Forest, Sun Valley Road, Sun Valley, Idaho 83340. (208) 622-5371.

The hike: Baker Lake sits just beneath the crest of the Smoky Mountains. A small, but rugged, mountain forms part of the Smoky crest just behind the lake.

It's a fairly easy hike to the lake. The trail is obvious all the way as it climbs, quite steeply, through flower-filled meadows to the lake in just 1.25 miles. Total elevation gain is 850 feet. There are plenty of campsites at the lake, although part of the area around the lake is a bit beaten-out (this is a popular trail).

To get to the trailhead, follow Idaho Highway 75 northward from Ketchum for about 15.5 miles. Turn left onto the gravel Baker Creek Road. This road is usually in good condition. It's a pleasant drive of about 9.5 miles to its end where the trailhead is located. There are numerous places to park, but there can also be a lot of traffic. I arrived early on a Wednesday morning in July. There were no vehicles, but upon my return at noon, there were three automobiles, one truck, and a large school bus. The trail itself is closed to motor vehicles.

A few yards past the trailhead, an unnamed tributary of Baker Creek flows over the trail. This requires a wade in June. Beyond this point the trail is easy and obvious, although a few hikers may be confused by trails that leave to the right. These are shortcuts. Please don't take them because they are causing some erosion.

You walk through meadow with some sagebrush and pass under a few large Douglas fir. Then you begin to ascend steeply. The trail quickly climbs to, and

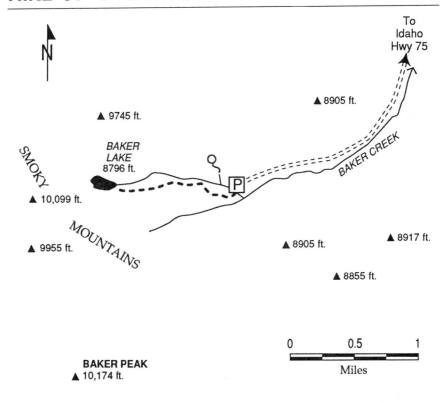

generally stays near, the ridge between Baker Creek and its tributary canyon holding Baker Lake. On my hike, this portion of the trailside was colored with the bright blue of small penstemon all the way to the lake.

Fishing at Baker Lake is catch-and-release using artifical lures only. I didn't fish, but the lake appeared full of seven to 12 inch trout.

The sign at the trailhead indicates that Big Peak Creek is three miles on the trail, but I saw no evidence of a trail to the West Fork of Big Peak Creek. There is a route and a pass into this drainage lying at the head of Baker Creek, but it appears to be a cross-country hike. —*Ralph Maughan* □

Trinity Mountain Area

Overview

Massive Trinity Mountain is an uplift in the Salmon River Range. Please refer to the overview for the Salmon River Mountains for general information about this area.

HIKE 68   *TRINITY MOUNTAIN*

General description: A day hike or easy weekend backpacking trip into a lush and beautiful lake-filled basin.

General location: About 50 linear miles northeast of Mountain Home, Idaho, on an island-like high ridge between the South and Middle Forks of the Boise River.

Maps: Little Trinity Lake and Trinity Mountain (7.5') USGS quads.

Special attractions: Lush and beautiful, but easily accessible, subalpine lakes. Good fishing. Outstanding elk habitat.

Difficulty: Easy, especially if taken as more than a day hike.

Season: July 7 through September.

Information: Mountain Home Ranger District, Boise National Forest, 2180 American Legion Blvd., Mountain Home, Idaho 83647; (208) 587-7961.

The hike: The large basin just east of massive Trinity Mountain is a perfect location to enjoy a weekend of easy hiking and rainbow trout fishing. A road bisects the Trinity Mountain area, providing high elevation access to a lake area that would otherwise be a long hike.

From Mountain Home, Idaho, take U.S. Highway 20 to the northeast to Cat Creek Summit. Then, two miles past the summit, turn off to the left and take a dirt road for 17 miles to Pine, Idaho, and the large Anderson Ranch Reservoir. At Pine, past the reservoir, travel up the South Fork of the Boise River for 8.5 miles and turn onto the Trinity Creek road just before the resort town of Featherville. From here it's 16 miles to the Trinity Mountain area. Generally this road is open, but at times it is closed for Forest Service timber sales. An alternate route is to continue north through Featherville to Rocky Bar, a historic mining area where a road leads up the ridge for 18 miles, proceeding south to the Trinity Mountain area. These roads are narrow but generally passable to sedans. You can camp on the mountain at maintained campgrounds at Big and Little Trinity lakes and also at Big Roaring River Lake.

Follow the turnoff to Big Trinity Lake (the largest lake on the mountain), and go around the west end of the lake to the trailhead. You begin hiking at an inlet creek with a small footbridge. The trail is open for foot traffic only, closed to horses and trail machines.

The trail winds southeasterly through open meadows to cross a creek after a short distance. In the summer, wildflowers fill these meadows. Head toward a saddle, climbing moderately at first. Near the top, switchbacks begin and take you quickly to the top of the saddle at 8,400 feet—600 feet above the trailhead.

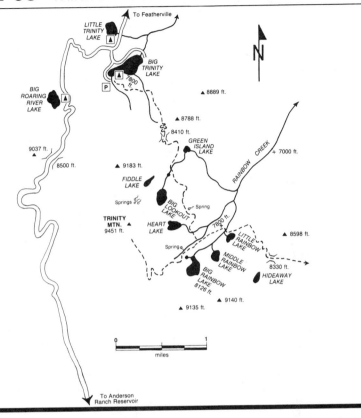

From the saddle, Green Island Lake is clearly visible below. The north face of Trinity Mountain, 9,454 feet, rises to your southwest with a lookout tower perched precariously on its summit.

The basin below holds eight lakes: Green Island, Fiddle Lake, Big Lookout, Heart Lake, and the three Rainbow Lakes, plus Hideaway Lake. Well-maintained trails lead to all of them except Hideaway. The Rainbow Lakes, three miles from the trailhead, are the most popular.

You'll find good camping and fishing at all of the lakes except Green Island, which is surrounded by a swamp and plagued by numerous mosquitoes through most of the season.—*Philip Blomquist* □

The Great Divide

Overview

The Idaho/Montana border is borne on the back of the Continental Divide for several hundred miles. Idaho and Montana are the only two states whose boundary is marked by such a big mountain range. From Yellowstone Park northwestward the divide runs, turning northward into Montana only as it approaches the Bitterroot Mountains.

Despite its prominence on the maps, this area has been hiked or backpacked little compared to other parts of Idaho. Trails are quite scarce, but much of the country is open, making trails unnecessary.

In 1989, however, the Continental Divide National Scenic Trail was dedicated from Canada to the west boundary of Yellowstone National Park. Eventually it will run all the way from Canada to Mexico. The trail still does not physically exist in a number of places on the Idaho/Montana border. The future of the Great Divide is, however, going to be one including more hiking than in the past.

The Idaho border portion of the trail is 253 miles long, entering the state from the north at Chief Joseph Pass and leaving Idaho to the southeast in Yellowstone National Park.

Long neglected by Forest Service management, the Great Divide has seen little recreation, but only scattered development as well. Six important roadless areas along the Great Divide are being proposed for wilderness designation by Idaho and Montana conservationists. These six units of the Great Divide Wilderness are, from northwest to southeast: Anderson Mountain, West Big Hole, Italian Peaks, Garfield Mountain, Centennial Mountains, and Lionhead.

The Great Divide is also divided into three mountain ranges, each separated by a low pass. From Lost Trail Pass north of Salmon southeastward to Monida Pass, where Interstate 15 crosses, they are called the Beaverhead Mountains. Monida Pass eastward to Red Rock Pass are the Centennials, and Red Rock Pass to Reas Pass, next to Yellowstone, are the Henrys Lake Mountains.

This chain of mountain ranges is environmentally important because it provides a corridor for wildlife migration from Yellowstone Park to Central and Northern Idaho and to Western Montana. It is politically significant because it separates Idaho and Montana both economically and culturally. The states are quite dissimilar despite their proximity.

Wildlife is abundant in the remote areas of the Great Divide: deer, elk, moose, pronghorn antelope, coyote, eagle, and black bear are common. Grizzly inhabit the Henry's Lake Mountains, and on occasion may wander all the way from Yellowstone to Central Idaho. From time-to-time wolves have also been sighted.

The major threats to the area are below-cost logging (particularly in the northern Beaverhead Mountains and on the Idaho side of the Centennials), scattered mining, overgrazing in some lower areas, and, increasingly, off-road vehicles scarring the open grassy slopes so common in these mountains.

The public lands on the Idaho/Montana portion of the Continental Divide are under the jurisdiction of the following agencies: Targhee National Forest, Beaverhead National Forest, Salmon National Forest, Idaho Falls District Bureau of Land Management (BLM), Dillon District BLM, and Salmon District BLM.

11,000 foot Cottonwood Peak on the Continental Divide. Idaho/Montana border, Beaverhead Mountains. Ralph Maughan photo.

HIKE 69 *ALDOUS AND HANCOCK LAKES*

General description: A great one-day hike.
General location: 84 road miles northeast of Idaho Falls; 44 road miles to the north-northeast of Dubois, in the mountains behind the town of Kilgore.
Maps: Lower Red Rock Lake (15') Antelope Valley and Kilgore (7.5') USGS quads.
Special attractions: Wildflowers and two easy-to-reach subalpine lakes.
Difficulty: Easy; a fairly level, short, well-kept trail.
Season: Late May to mid-October.
Information: Dubois Ranger District, Targhee National Forest, Dubois, Idaho 83423; (208) 374-5422.

The hike: The most trying feature of this hike is finding the trailhead. This is why we suggest taking the Kilgore and Antelope Valley USGS quads. Even though none of the hike is on these two maps; the access roads are.

Leaving Idaho Falls, drive northward on Interstate 15 for 48 miles to Dubois. Leave the interstate at Dubois, go through this small town and head eastward on Country Road A2. After about 27 miles, a spur from the county road leads a mile north to the small town of Kilgore. As you pass through Kilgore, you come to a T-junction. Go to the left for about .3 mile, then turn off to the

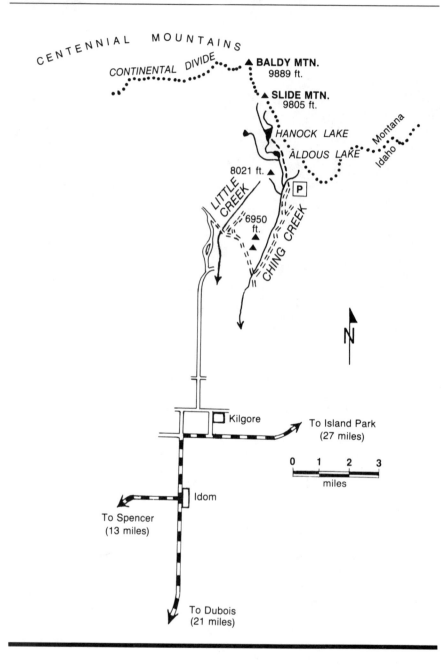

right to head northward straight across Camas Meadows.

After about six miles, you'll begin to enter a canyon and come to a fork in the road. The right fork is marked with a Forest Service sign to Little Creek. Take this fork to the right.

This road follows along the base of the Centennial Mountains for several miles. After a mile, you'll come to the road up Little Creek (to the left). Ignore it and continue straight ahead. 2.5 miles past Little Creek, the road makes a brief jog to the south and comes to a junction. Keep left here. Another quarter-mile brings another junction. Keep left again. Now you swing northward into Ching Creek. Stay to your left at all the forks you encounter until you reach the trailhead.

(As a side note, you can also reach Kilgore by following Country Road A2 from U.S. 20 in Island Park.)

The trailhead isn't developed, but there is room to park about six vehicles. Although it isn't an especially pleasant site, you can camp by your car, and there is plenty of water from nearby Ching Creek. It's wise to boil the water before use.

The old trail to the lakes is closed to off-road vehicles as a result of overuse and past abuse, especially around lower Aldous Lake. Some signs of use are still evident around Aldous Lake, but nature is slowly reclaiming the lakeside. The trail you'll take to the lakes is not the original. It's a new one built to allow the old off-road vehicle road to heal.

The 1.5 mile rerouted trail to Aldous Lake is a biological pleasure as it gently climbs through lodgepole, subalpine fir, and Englemann spruce, which are spotted with green and yellow lichen. Interspersed between groves are patches of small meadows. The trail crosses numerous feeder streams and occasionally approaches the large, roaring Ching Creek which empties from Aldous Lake. The elevation gain to Aldous Lake is only 360 feet, and there isn't much bumping over hill and down dale to get to it.

A variety of mushrooms peek out of the ground. Some parts of the trail are aromatic with pine needles that cover the path and deaden the noise of footsteps. Birds that like high elevations flit about. Elk sign is numerous.

The trail meets the lake near a small dam at the outlet. Aldous is surrounded by stately, healthy trees. Fishing is popular at Aldous, but record-setting fish are not caught here. Numerous ideal camping spots can be found 500 feet from the lake's edge.

Between Aldous and Hancock lakes, the trail is covered with pine needles and steeped in their sweet, pungent scent. With just the right vantage point, you can see the St. Anthony Sand Dunes 50 miles to the south. The trail climbs more steeply than the Aldous trail. It gains 560 feet in elevation and is about 1.5 miles long.

Hancock Lake at 7,900 feet is much rockier and steeper than Aldous. It is surrounded by spectacular landslides with photogenic rocks and boulders right up to the lake's edge. Most of the surrounding trees are dead lodgepole. Due to the rocks and steep shoreline, campsites are more difficult to find. A lot of driftwood lies about from old trees that were caught and died in the high water. Above the lake you can see the Continental Divide ridge of the Centennial Mountains.

The abundance and variety of wildflowers on this hike are overwhelming. Sixteen varieties have been seen in the space of a half-mile: shooting star, fireweed, lodgepole lupine, sego lily, sticky geranium, heartleaf arnica, great Engelmann (white) aster, field chickweed, dwarf monkeyflower, giant-hyssop mint, Indian paintbrush, larkspur, wild parsley, yarrow, cow-parsnip, and pearly everlasting!—*Ann and George Matejko* □

HIKE 70   *SAWTELL PEAK—ROCK CREEK*

General description: A short high-altitude hike which drops into a large basin. Can be an overnight or one-day venture.

General location: About 85 road miles north of Idaho Falls and 35 road miles south of West Yellowstone, Montana.

Maps: Sawtell Peak (7.5') USGS quad.

Special attractions: Spectacular views into Idaho, Wyoming, and Montana with such highlights as the Yellowstone Caldera, Henry's Lake, Island Park Reservoir, Red Rock Lakes, and the Teton and Centennial Mountains. The first two miles of the trail make a good family hike.

Difficulty: Moderate due to rock slides, snow-covered portions of trail, and some consequent precipitous passages.

Season: Mid-June (mid-July in years of heavy snows and late melt) through September.

Information: Island Park Ranger District, Targhee National Forest, Box 220, Island Park, Idaho 83429; (208) 558-7301.

The hike: This is a six mile hike following an old road, closed in 1964, that once led to a watershed restoration project. The route is on, or near, the Continental Divide much of the way, and the first two miles are easy enough to provide a family hiking experience at a high altitude on the Continental Divide. The divide is not accessible at this elevation in many places on the Idaho/Montana border, even by road. This is an opportunity made possible by easy road access to the trail.

This trail is not heavily used except by hunters in the fall. Hikers are advised not to enter the area during hunting season because of its popularity. Another caution is the possibility of thunderstorms. Lightning is a danger on such occasions the first two miles.

After driving north 85 miles from Idaho Falls on U.S. Highway 20, or 35 miles south from West Yellowstone, Montana, on U.S. 20, you take the dirt road leaving to the west directly opposite the Island Park Village condominiums. This road ends about 13 miles later at the top of Sawtell Peak. It gains 3,440 feet in elevation, with the last thousand feet climbing one mile of switchbacks to the mountaintop. Here sits a radar station and your first fantastic view. It's often very windy. If you look down upon the area off to the west, you can see your destination, Rock Creek Basin, and to the southwest, the vicinity of the old road to the basin.

Assuming you have driven to the top of Sawtell Peak to check out the view, drive 1.7 miles back down the mountain to a horses hoe bend in the road which has parking space. Once on foot, double back .2 mile to an old road on the left (west) marked with a sign that indicates motor vehicles are prohibited. This old road is the beginning of the trail. There is no parking at the trailhead

The Continental Divide and Rock Creek Basin in the Centennials. George Matejko photo.

and you must look carefully to find it. It becomes more apparent as you walk along. If you can't find it, you can walk cross-country, angling towards it by leaving from the horseshoe bend in the road.

The trail starts at an elevation of 9,120 feet. Rock Creek Basin is about 8,500 feet in elevation. Although the overall elevation gain or loss is never great, portions of the trail are steep. The first part of the old road is fairly level, with a moderate climb through dead, artistically sculpted white bark pine. You'll also see lodgepole pine and pointed subalpine fir in the area. Winters are harsh, and a constant wind generally blows year round. Vegetation is stunted, but wildflowers are prevalent most of the summer, including August. Some flowers commonly seen are dogtooth violet, phlox, and buttercup.

As the road dips downward, you cross a rock avalanche field of old lava. After about two miles, you leave the Idaho side of the Continental Divide to peer southwest into a toe of Montana. The road now begins to curve and switchback and drops quickly into Rock Creek Basin. In the 1960s, when extensive sheep grazing caused soil erosion problems, sheep were banned from the vicinity. A careful observer can still spot old, barely legible signs forbidding grazing. In parts of the basin, you can see the artificial terraces which resulted from an experimental attempt to restore vegetation and halt erosion. If you came back in another few centuries, you would still see these terraces.

Rock Creek Basin has a perennial stream, appropriately named Rock Creek, that eventually feeds into Henrys Lake. Its roar can be heard miles away. The basin is a rockhound's delight, as it abounds with a variety of rock colors and types. You can find low-lying fir and pleasant camping spots anywhere in the basin.

If you are hiking after the mid-summer months, take water. Early visitors, however, will have plenty of snow and snowmelt for drinking purposes along

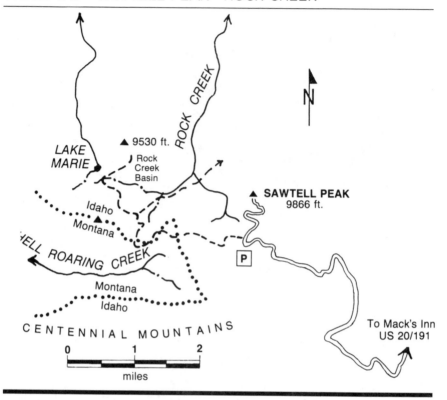

the trail. Due to the high elevation and scarcity of wood, campstoves should be used rather than open fires. Be prepared for cold temperatures and snow no matter what time of year.

Wildlife is abundant. Bear, elk, moose, and deer scat and tracks are common on or off the trail. Looking into the basin, you can often spot big game. Noise carries a long distance in the area, so chances of seeing game are low if you are noisy. Clark's nutcracker, gray jays, and a variety of hawks frequent the territory.

Grizzly bear have been seen in Rock Creek Basin, although this is not a common occurrence.—*Ann Matejko, George Matejko, Ralph Maughan* □

Note: Over 96 thousand acres of the Centennial Mountains in Idaho and Montana are being studied by the U.S. Bureau of Land Management (BLM) as a possible addition to the National Wilderness Preservation System. Despite the high wilderness qualities and absence of any minerals except low grade coal and phosphate, securing wilderness protection of any of these wildlife-rich mountains will be difficult. The major opposition comes from livestock interests and some of the off-road-vehicle enthusiasts. If you want to see this area protected, let your congressional delegates know. In June 1990 the Forest Service officially recommended that none of the Idaho side be protected as wilderness.—Ralph Maughan

HIKE 71 *TARGHEE CREEK*

General description: A long day hike that can be made into an excursion of several days.

General location: 40 miles north of Ashton, Idaho, and 10 miles west of West Yellowstone, Montana, inside of the proposed Lionhead Wilderness.

Maps: Targhee Pass and Targhee Peak (7.5') USGS quads.

Special attractions: Six alpine lakes set amid rolling mountain upland meadows. A climb of Targhee Peak. Wildlife; including grizzly bears, moose, and bighorn sheep. Solitude.

Difficulty: Moderate.

Season: July through September.

Information: Island Park Ranger District, Targhee National Forest, Box 220, Island Park, Idaho 83429; (208) 558-7301.

The hike: It's 4.5 miles to the first lake and an 1,800 foot climb a lengthy nine-mile round trip in a day, but very well worth it. Every step is a beauty, so you don't need to go clear to the lake to enjoy it. If you want to take more time, you can spend a day or two exploring the uplands at the head of Targhee Creek atop the Continental Divide on the Idaho state line.

To get to the trailhead from Idaho, drive to St. Anthony and continue on past Ashton on U.S. Highway 20. Drive up into Island Park and the Targhee National Forest. From Island Park, go across scenic, open Henrys Lake Flat, still on U.S. 20. On the north side of the Flat, ignore Idaho Highway 87, which leaves to the left toward Henrys Lake. Head up into the Henrys Lake Mountains toward the state line at Targhee Pass; but 2.2 miles past the junction with Highway 87, take the dirt road signed "Targhee Creek Trail," which turns off of U.S. 20 to climb up the cutbank on the left side of the highway.

After you go about a mile on this road, you'll come to a junction. Take the poorer road to the right. This road is improperly labeled "jeep" on the Targhee Pass quadrangle. Carefully bounce along for 1.4 miles to the end of this dirt road. Although it is considerably better than just a jeep trail, it can become a quagmire after a heavy rain. There are a number of grassy places to camp on the left near the end of the road just above meandering Targhee Creek.

A jeep road formerly extended all the way to the East Fork of Targhee Creek; but a number of years ago the Forest Service blocked and ditched the road to prevent vehicle access. This has proved a very successful action to improve water quality, protect the abundant wildlife, and greatly increase the solitude of this splendid stream valley. The Forest Service deserves praise for its work here.

At the end of the road, the Targhee Creek trail is obvious. Walk over a hump of dirt dozed up to close the jeep road and continue upward, passing quickly behind a small hill. What's left of the jeep road levels out under a canopy of forest. As you admire nature's reclamation, which is turning the gouge of a road into a path, you soon pass by a transparent forest pond which is fed by underground springs. The spring's outlet waters trickle down to Targhee Creek, slowed by the efforts of many beavers. Targhee Creek itself is filled by willows here and is dammed extensively by beavers as it courses down the stream valley. Above all this greenery, limestone cliffs line the south wall on the canyon.

Toward Black Mountain from the Continental Divide above Targhee Basin. Ralph Maughan photo.

Moose often plod through this broad riparian zone. Elk are common in early summer and late fall. Deer are present all summer.

The trail continues, mostly through dense forest, to a ford of Targhee Creek at the one-half-mile point. This ford is of little consequence in late summer, but before July 15 it is often very difficult. In early season, you can avoid the wade by keeping to the right for a hefty, but scenic, one-mile cross-country trek to where the trail recrosses the creek just past the confluence with small, flower-banked East Targhee Creek. It's a pretty walk, much of it across meadows where springs seep from the limestone to water the bright flowers; but deadfall in the timbered first portion makes part of the cross-country route moderately difficult. If you give up, look for the log that crosses the creek at about one-third of the way.

Past the first ford, the trail breaks into the open. Here there are a lot of camping spots amid meadows of flowers and short willows. Unfortunately, most are near the trail. The distinctive flat-lying rock strata of 10,180-foot Bald Mountain are easily seen on the north side of the meadows.

After about one-third mile, the decaying jeep trail climbs out of the meadow. It gains about 75 feet then drops steeply for a second ford of Targhee Creek. The jeep track and the main trail separate on the other side of the creek. The jeep track switchbacks to its end somewhere up the East Fork. The fainter main trail, which you follow, stays near the creek. As you follow it upstream, it soon leads through an interesting rock passage.

Next, the trail wanders through deep forest containing small, shaded meadows for about a mile as you head up-canyon toward the confluence of main Targhee Creek and the West Fork of Targhee Creek. This section of trail is usually quite muddy. You'll have the feeling of the forest primeval here as you slog along the trail breathing the rank odor of elk and other wild animals.

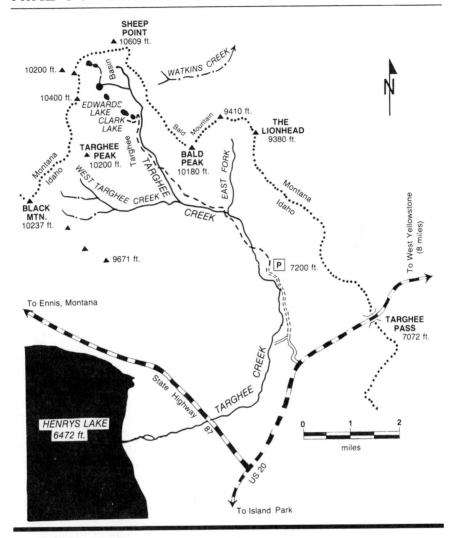

Just before you reach the West Targhee-Targhee Creek confluence, the trail switchbacks up the canyon wall briefly to climb above a mudslide that dates from June 1983.

The mountain ahead with the jumbled orange flanks is Targhee Peak. It rises to over 10,200 feet, guarding the forks of Targhee Creek. We tried to climb it, but were driven down, only 200 feet from the summit, by a lightning storm. According to the U.S. Geological Survey, it is very unstable. An earthquake similar to the Hebgen Lake quake of 1957 could bring down millions of tons of rock, filling Targhee Creek with rubble, just as happened to the Madison River Canyon 10 miles to the north during the 1957 quake. The massive Central Idaho earthquake of 1983 and the numerous small earthquakes that shake eastern Idaho and western Montana are constant reminders of what could happen.

Once past the mudslide, the trail continues to climb gradually upward, entering the canyon to your right. This canyon is called, rather arbitrarily, Targhee Creek. West Targhee Creek, the canyon on the left, is just as big, if not bigger. You'll ascend across a meadow which offers views up trailless West Targhee Creek and southward toward a trident of limestone cliffs. This is a good place for a lunch stop. If you walk across the sloping meadow to where Targhee Creek thunders downhill on the way to its wedding with the West Fork, you'll find a waterfall. Here Targhee Creek leaps over a ledge surrounded by columns of brownish-black schist studded with gleaming mica.

After lunch, you'll follow the narrow path upward in earnest through forest and streamside meadows. The right side of the canyon is a nearly continuous cliff. Forest dominates the west side of the steep canyon.

About midway up Targhee Creek, you cross the creek to the left (west) bank. As you continue upward, you cross a number of small trickles that emerge from the flanks of Targhee Peak. A few have washed out the trail for a brief distance.

Finally, you come to a relatively flat meadow above which the canyon forms an obvious constriction. In the meadow, look for cairns that lead you up out of the canyon to the first lake. This deep blue lake sits at the top of a couple of switchbacks on the edge of Targhee Basin, which harbors five other lakes. From the lake you look across the upper end of Targhee Creek Canyon to the north side of Bald Mountain; a ridge of cliffs, salmon-colored loose rock, and a smattering of conifers. There are some camping spots at this scenic lake, but you can find better ones at or near the other lakes.

Although the trail ends at the first lake, it is easy to find the others. They lie scattered about Targhee Basin, each being about one-eighth mile from the next. The second is Clark Lake. It has a few good campsites with views to the south of the summit of Targhee Peak and of cliffs to the immediate west of an unnamed mountain. After mid-summer, the waters of this lake filter down through the limestone and the site is less desirable.

Of the four lakes above Clark Lake, Edwards Lake (number three) is a bit marginal for camping. All six lakes tend to lose much of their water as the season progresses. Lakes five and six are very close together and are shown incorrectly on the Targhee Peak quadrangle as one lake.

At the north end of the basin is peak 10,609, Sheep Point, the highest of the Henrys Lake Mountains. To the west and northwest rise several 10,000-foot-plus peaks. Targhee Basin is the most northeasterly point of Idaho.

To the east, you can easily cross the headwaters of Targhee Creek, and with little effort you can get over the Continental Divide into another rolling basin that is situated above Watkins Creek. From here you can see across the Madison Valley to the broad, flat, timbered Yellowstone Park country below. Here too, from the correct angle, you see salmon-pink Bald Mountain rise to form two duplicate cones.

If you climb any of the mountain slopes above Targhee Basin, look for bighorn sheep. Use prudence as you walk in the Targhee Creek area, as these mountains retain a few monarchs of the wilderness, the grizzly bear. The Forest Service has designated the area as Situation 1 grizzly bear habitat, the only such area described in this book. Situation 1, to quote from the *Guidelines for*

Management of Grizzly Bears in the Greater Yellowstone Area means the following: "The area contains grizzly population centers (areas key to the survival of grizzlies where seasonal or year-long grizzly activity, under natural, free-ranging conditions, is common) and habitat components exist for the survival and recovery of the species or a segment of its population." You should, therefore, exercise every means of caution, especially in handling food. We had a total of six people on this excursion a good idea in grizzly country.—*Ralph and Jackie Maughan* □

Note: Continuing their good management of the area since the first edition of this book, the Targhee National Forest has closed 1.4 miles more of road up Targhee Creek. To reach the new trailhead, simply follow the good dirt road for about a mile to the obvious well-signed parking lot and horse loading ramp. If for some reason you reach the bridge over Targhee Creek, you have gone about .3 mile too far.

Efforts to designate the area as wilderness have not gone well. Snowmobile interests have decided they want Targhee Basin as a play area and are opposing wilderness designation or, as in the case of Idaho Senator McClure's "wilderness bill," are trying to carve out a curiously-shaped non-wilderness enclave in the center of a Lionhead Wilderness.

Sleeping in my truck near the trailhead in late June 1989, I saw a black bear, a moose, deer, and listened to elk squeal almost all night. This area consistently has as much wildlife as any other place I've visited in Idaho, except perhaps Winegar Hole, just south of Yellowstone National Park near the Wyoming border.—Ralph Maughan

HIKE 72 *SALAMANDER LAKE LOOPS*

General description: Several possible loops near the Continental Divide in a "low" spot of the Centennial Mountains. The hike is a long one-day, or easier, several-day excursion.

General location: North-north east of Idaho Falls in the mountains behind the near ghost town of Kilgore, on the Idaho/Montana border.

Maps: Winslow Creek (7.5') USGS quad.

Special attractions: Beautiful meadows on the Continental Divide. Good wildlife habitat. The opportunity for various hikes from a base camp.

Difficulty: Moderate if done over several days. The difficulty is mostly due to trails whose tread disappears when crossing meadows.

Season: Mid-June to mid-October.

Information: Dubois Ranger District, Targhee National Forest, Box 46, Dubois, Idaho 83423; (208) 374-5422.

The hike: There are several broad low spots in the Centennial Mountains. In these, the distance to the Continental Divide is not so strenuous. This hike describes one such spot with the good fortune to have retained an extensive trail system. These trails may be used to make a number of differing loop hikes (a rare situation in the Centennials where in the past trail systems have often been neglected or destroyed by logging). So far the area described here has remained intact due to lack of high value timber combined with topography

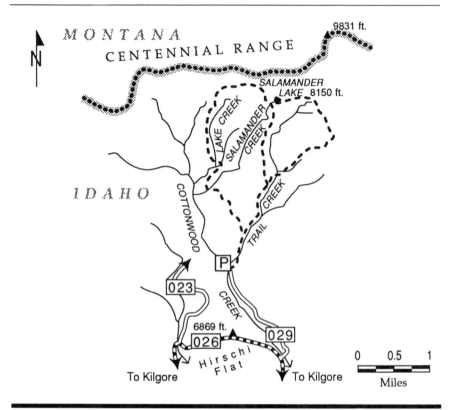

frequently created by creeping soil and small landslides.

To reach the trailhead, follow the instructions for the Aldous and Hancock Lake hikes, but instead of turning onto the Little Creek road (Forest Service #027) after crossing Camas Meadows, continue straight ahead on FS #026. After about .75 mile on #026, take the Cottonwood Creek (#029) road to the right. This road is dirt, unlike the good graveled #026. It's a decent dirt road when dry, but, unfortunately, it becomes poor after a soaking rain. It is not quite two miles on #029 to the trailhead where there is space to park about six vehicles. The parking place is about 100 yards beyond the actual beginning of the trail which is obvious and leads up Trail Creek.

All of these trails are closed to motor vehicles, and a sign so indicates at the beginning. The Trail Creek Trail climbs moderately through small meadows and mixed conifer forest and follows a short distance from the creek for about .5 mile to a new metal sign that reads "Lake Cr." to the left. This is the trail (Lake Cr.) upon which you will return to complete the loop described.

Another .75 mile of moderate uphill brings you to another trail junction and another metal sign indicating Salamander Lake on the trail to the left. This, indeed, is the faster route to the lake. Instead, for a more extensive look at the scenery, I continued up Trail Creek. About .25 mile past the latter trail junction the trail descends slightly to cross Trail Creek (just a hop on rocks in mid-July). It then climbs briefly, levels out and drops down to cross a major tributary of Trail Creek.

From this point on the trail's route is fairly steep uphill. As you climb, you begin to enter larger and larger meadows and gain a view, of the mountainside ahead. Vegetation in the meadows is typical of the 7500-9000 elevation all along the Continental Divide in this locale: beautiful, tall and generally fleshy, forbs such as monkshood, western coneflower, sticky geranium, wild carrot, lupine, bluebells, cow parsnip, and tall cinquefoil, but little grass. The mid-summer growth rate of the forbs is such that they hide the tread of any trail through a meadow not traveled more frequently than every week or so.

Indeed, soon the previously obvious track begins to fade as you ascend through larger meadows. You must be sure to follow the blazes on the trees in order to locate the trail after crossing a meadow. On this part of the loop the blazes are usually obvious (shaped like an upside down exclamation point and often painted red).

You arrive at the highest elevation of the trip when you cross a meadow on a shelf (about 8,500 feet) between two tributary drainages of Trail Creek. Saunter along the shelf through meadowland with clumps of subalpine fir and whitebark pine. This continues until the trail descends sharply to a pond (dry by late summer).

Next, the trail drops about 200 feet rather steeply to Salamander Lake. In this section, just after the trail begins its steepest descent, you may lose the track, as you go down a forb meadow, and be confused by an obvious trail on the meadow's left side. This is an elk trail to a spring. Be sure to continue straight down the meadow. You'll soon pick up the trail's tread and see blazes on the trees.

A small lake, Salamander is shallow and has no fish, but springs keep it full of water. It is a pretty location. The best campsite is on the northwest side of the lake under a thick cluster of spruce and subalpine fir. I found it a good base camp and camped two days.

The trail keeps to the left (southeast) side of the lake, although the tread disappears along the meadowy lakeshore. One or two-hundred yards below the lake outlet is an important trail junction. Here a metal sign indicates "trailhead" straight ahead and "Lake Cr." to the right. To reach the divide and the large loop hike described here, take the right fork of the trail. The beginning of the Lake Creek trail is faint (forbs again), but you will come quickly to a new bridge over Salamander Creek. From the bridge follow the blazes across the forbs, and next across a wet meadow. The trail becomes obvious as it enters the forest and climbs 100 feet to a ridgeline. Here you quickly enter a large meadow, and you can see into Montana. You are not quite yet on the Continental Divide.

The trail immediately disappears in the tall forbs of the meadow, but a plastic "board" with a white arrow is stuck in the ground pointing the way (straight ahead). There are about a half dozen such "boards" every couple hundred yards to lead you across the meadow and down into the head of Lake Creek. You never actually quite climb to the Continental Divide. Between the first and second "board" is a metal sign that points to the divide and also the direction you came indicating "Salamander Lake".

To reach the divide, leave your route at an angle of between 45 to 90 degrees.

Simply keep walking (it's easy) until you are on the divide. You'll find an old barbwire fence (it's down) and a faint trail (possibly a vehicle way that long ago grassed-in). Watch where you came from since the divide is fairly gentle and has a large number of big, similar meadows.

You can follow the divide in either direction about as far as you like. I used it to climb the prominent mountain to the east (with pinkish cliffs and green slopes). This is a climb of about 1,600 feet in a mile (from about 8,200 to 9,800 feet elevation). Simply keep on or near the Continental Divide. The steepness increases with altitude. The last 600-800 feet of elevation gain will occasionally prompt you to scramble.

As I neared the mountaintop, a bald eagle soared, dived at a rodent, and left a pinyon feather as a reminder of this splendid place on the Idaho-Montana border.

On top you find an alpine upland about a square mile in extent. This rolling plateau is covered with scattered whitebark pine, subalpine fir krumholtz, and alpine tundra. Be sure to carry some food and water to the top (unlike myself).

Back on the trail, follow the arrow-imprinted "boards". After about .3 mile, the route swings down into the headwaters of a creek and a streamside meadow. The last "board" did not indicate this change in direction, but the track quickly became obvious. From this point on, follow the blazed trees whenever the tread becomes faint.

Soon the trail leaves streamside and climbs a short distance to a ridge. Just amble down this pleasant ridge between Lake Creek (to your left) and Cotton-wood (to your right). Both canyons are largely not in your sight. After about a mile, you drop down and, in quick succession, cross Lake Creek and one of its tributaries. Both crossings are on bridges. You climb briefly to another ridge. After about .3 mile you descend from this ridge to cross Salamander Creek. You must be very careful here as the trail disappears and the blazes are scattered and old. When you reach the creek bottom, you should find a three-way trail junction with a metal sign indicating "Divide" (pointing to direction from which you've come) and "Lake Trail" pointing down Sala-mander Creek. The sign doesn't point to the plainly obvious track that crosses Salamander Creek on a bridge and goes up the hill on the other side. Cross and go up the hill. You are now 1.25 miles from your vehicle. The trail is sometimes faint as it climbs over a broad ridge and descends to Trail Creek, completing your loop.

The entire loop is good wildlife habitat. Hopefully, it will not be logged. My second morning at Salamander, the sound of two large moose swimming in the small lake greeted me awake.—*Ralph Maughan* □

HIKE 73 *RED CONGLOMERATE PEAKS LOOP*

General description: A one- to several-day loop which climbs to, follows, and descends from the Continental Divide in an isolated, scenic portion of the Beaverhead Mountains.

General location: Sixty miles north-northwest of Idaho Falls on the Continental Divide. The hike is partially in Montana.

Maps: Edie Creek, Fritz Peak, Lima Peaks (Montana) (7.5') USGS quads.
Special attractions: The scenic and rugged Red Conglomerate Peaks on the Continental Divide. Rangeland in excellent condition. Big game and few people.
Difficulty: Difficult in one day due to length, climb, and descent, as well as cross-country segments. Moderately difficult otherwise.
Season: Late June to October.
Information: Dubois Ranger District, Targhee National Forest, Dubois, Idaho 83423; (208) 374-5422.

The hike: East of the Italian Peaks (see Webber Creek to Divide Creek hike) rises yet another cluster of little-known, but high and rugged peaks on the Continental Divide. Shown on most maps as the Red Conglomerate Peaks, the new 7.5' Edie Creek topographic quadrangle calls only the single tallest of these by that name, although from a distance they appear to be similar and comprise a distinct group of peaks; the name would seem to be most appropriately applied to all of them.

This hike describes a loop beginning in Irving Creek at the base of Red Conglomerate Peak (10,250 feet). You climb to the Continental Divide and eventually descend back to the starting point. Both the climb and descent are cross-country. There is a trail in both Irving Creek and near the divide. It's difficult to accurately determine the mileage. I estimate seven to 10 miles total. There are quite a few camping spots near the divide just inside Montana.

To reach the trailhead, leave U.S. Interstate 15 at Dubois by turning onto Idaho Highway 22. Travel west for six miles to a paved county road which leaves to the north from Idaho Highway 22. You travel through farmland on this road and into the scenic basalt canyon of Medicine Lodge Creek. The road is paved for about 15 miles then becomes good gravel. Continue up the gravel road, passing the signed Edie Creek and Webber Creek roads.

The Irving Creek Road leaves to the right 3.2 miles up the Medicine Lodge Road from its junction with the Edie Creek Road. After about three miles up Irving Creek, the road divides into Forest Service Road #187 to the left and #193 to the right. Take #187. This road quickly deteriorates and comes to a mucky crossing of a small creek after about .75 mile. A standard two-wheel drive truck can make it to this point easily. If you have a sedan, watch your oil pan. Park in the meadow and don't try the crossing even in a four-wheel drive vehicle. You'll get stuck (unless it's late summer), and you'll make a mess too.

Walk up Irving Creek from here on a grassed-over vehicle way. The Red Conglomerates rise with rugged splendor to your right. Camping spots abound. You are on Bureau of Land Management (BLM) ground but soon come to the Targhee National Forest boundary, marked by a fence with a gate. Be sure to close this gate and the several others you pass getting to the trailhead.

Just beyond the National Forest boundary, you can begin the loop. There are a number of variations you can take, but it is easiest if you go counterclockwise (this means up Bear Canyon to the Continental Divide). The reason is that Bear Canyon is more difficult to descend than to ascend. I fell twice there while discovering this hike as I descended Bear Canyon (there are many, loose, round rocks on the canyon floor that move more readily when you step downhill).

The shortest loop is to ascend Bear Canyon and descend Red Canyon. Both

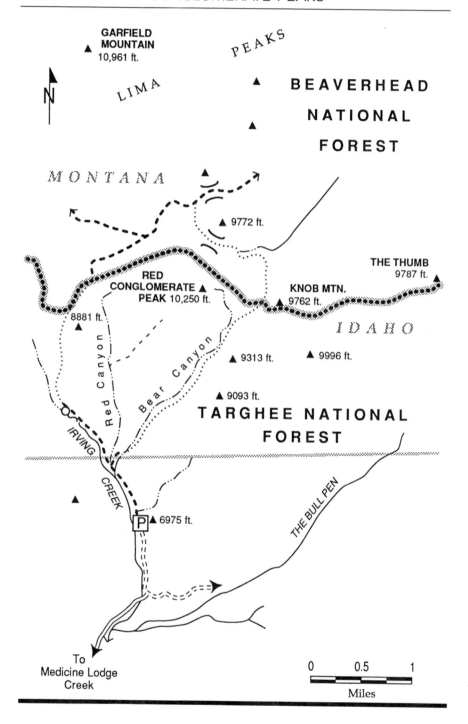

canyon mouths lie at the base of Red Conglomerate Peak just past the forest boundary.

Begin the cross-country ascent by heading up into Bear Canyon. The way is forested, but the canyon bottom is filled with gravel (from decomposed conglomerate rock). The lower part of the canyon is usually dry, but the middle reach has water, at least in spots, most of the summer. The middle reach is scenic with small waterfalls, curious specimens of water-carved conglomerate and other rock types, and huge conglomerate boulders which will require a few short scrambles to get around. The cliffs of Red Conglomerate Peak rise above you in a dramatic fashion.

The canyon gradually narrows and the grade steepens. Water usually will not be found flowing in the upper reach. About 600 feet below the top of the ridge, the canyon forks. Take the right fork. The hike is steep the rest of the way to the pass (9,275 feet), and it may be easier to walk up the grassy mountain slope near the canyon bottom rather than in it.

At the pass is a fine view, especially northward into Montana. The high, bare mountains you see are the Lima Peaks. You're standing well inside of the Garfield Mountain Roadless Area which Montana and Idaho environmentalists propose as a unit in the Great Divide Wilderness. Garfield Mountain (not in sight at the pass) is the highest of the Lima Peaks. Just to your right is Knob Mountain (9,762 feet). It has an impressive north face which you will view shortly as you descend into Montana and the high basin just below you.

You descend into timber, dropping about 300 feet into what was a bright green meadow in mid-July. I found several elk wallows at the meadow's edge.

From the meadow make your way up to the obvious high pass (about 9650 feet) between Divide Point (10,106 feet) and peak 9,772 to its northeast in Montana. As you make this 600-foot climb, there are fine views of Knob Mountain and The Thumb (farther to the east on the Continental Divide). The cliffs of Divide Point rise above you to your left.

Once you're on the pass, just drop down into the drainage below (Little Sheep Creek). The huge bare mountain is Garfield Mountain, which is just short of being 11,000 feet high. You soon come to a fence. Negotiate it and continue downward and you will soon come to a fairly good trail. This is the Continental Divide trail and is marked by new posts and by blazes on the trees.

The trail traverses along the backside of Red Conglomerate Peak through meadows and patches of timber in the draws. There are a number of small springs and creeks near the trail. Hereabout are quite a few camping spots.

Using your Edie Creek USGS quad, notice when you approach the head of Red Canyon over the divide, back in Idaho. Leave the trail, recross the fence and walk to the divide. You will find the top of Red Canyon is a lovely basin, much gentler than Bear Canyon. You can descend this canyon to complete the loop. It appears easier than Bear Canyon, although I expect it is rocky near the bottom. My route instead was to continue along the Continental Divide (but not on the trail for it descends much farther down into Little Sheep Creek northward into Montana). Walking on the divide here is easy, and you have good views of the meadowy mountains that ring the headwaters of Irving Creek. Descend at any time. There is no special route or difficulty except general steepness. The slopes downward into Irving Creek are covered mostly with grass and low-growing sagebrush with patches of timber in the draws. The small pinkish cliffs can be avoided or scrambled over. Note that these cross-country descent routes tend to be the steepest near the bottom.

Once you're down into the canyon, keep to the left side until you come to a spring. The spring emerges just below a grove of tall (and old)jaspen. This is the beginning of Irving Creek. Here you pick up a trail, and it is a pleasnt and easy walk of about a mile back to the forest boundary fence.

Hopefully you will see considerable big game on this loop. The remoteness and fine wildlife habitat of the Red Comglomerates supported a large poaching ring throughout much of the 1980s. The ring was busted in a federa sting operation in the late 1980s. Severe sentences were handed out, and now we hope the number of big game will rise dramatically.—*Ralph Maughan* ☐

HIKE 74 *FREEMAN CREEK*

General description: A short, but relatively steep, five-mile, one-way hike which takes you to the Continental Divide to look down into Montana.
General location: About 12 road miles northeast of Salmon.
Maps: Badger Springs Gulch, Idaho; and Homer Youngs Peak, Montana-Idaho (7.5') USGS quads.
Special attractions: Ruins of Ore Cash mine and long vistas of surrounding mountains, lakes, and snowfields, from the mountain crest.
Difficulty: Moderate; elevation gain of 2,500 feet in last three miles.
Season: Early July to mid-October.
Information: Salmon District, U.S. Bureau of Land Management, Box 430, Salmon, Idaho 83467; (208) 756-2201; or North Fork Rnager District, Salmon National Forest, Box 180, North Fork, Idaho 83466; (208) 865-2383.

The hike: Although the terrain is easy and the trail obvious, this hike's elevation gain to reach the Continental Divide is one to take the wind out of you. This is a spectacular drainage offering several options for additional hiking, climbing, fishing, and exploring a historic gold and silver mine.

This particular piece of mountain property is managed by the U.S. Bureau of Land Management (BLM) in the lower reaches and by the Forest Service in the higher elevations. The jurisdictional dividing line is near the Ore Cash Mine. There is a jeep trail to the mine, but it isn't heavily used. The Forest Service is thinking about closing the trail to off-road vehicles because of its hazards. As a note of caution, you may want to delay this hike until mid-summer because of rockslides, avalanches, and slippery trail conditions. Check with the BLM or Forest Service if you're not familiar with area trail and road conditions.

Drive north from Salmon on U.S. Highway 93 to the hamlet of Carmen. Here, take a right onto a paved, marked road which leads up Carmen Creek for six or seven miles to where Freeman Creek meets Carmen Creek. At this point, the road turns to gravel. Turn right onto the marked Freeman Creek road and travel 2.5 miles to the marked junction of Freeman Creek and Kirtly Creek roads. (This is one-half mile past the last log house.) At the junction, follow the left fork of the road as it leads up into the drainage toward Freeman peak. You can continue for one, perhaps two, miles past this junction, depending on moisture conditions. This is one of those situation in which

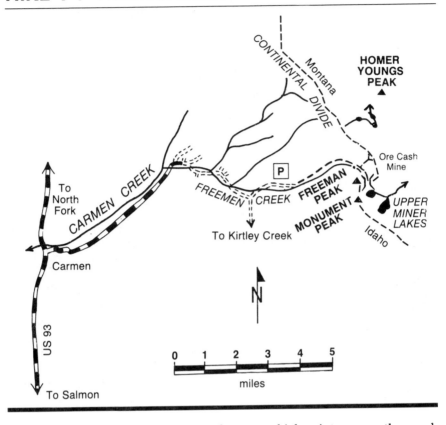

you drive until caution gets the best of you, at which point you can then park in any one of several open, flat spaces.

The road leads into a series of crushed-rock switchbacks and is very easy to follow. Along the way up the canyon you will see the evidence of numerous annual side streams that illustrate the temporary nature of abundant water. Legally, the trail accommodates vehicles all the way to the mine, although one would be ill-advised to drive there. About 4.5 miles in from the fork of Freeman and Carmen creeks, there is a fork in the road leading off to the left, which goes to the mine. The mine was operating in the early 1900s. There is a standing mine shaft in which it is probably inadvisable to do much spelunking. The Salmon National Forest in Salmon has printed information about the mine—you may want to get a copy.

About one-quarter mile further up the trail you come to an old log cabin. From here it is about one mile to the 9,194-foot saddle. From this point on you'll feel the hike, because you gain a thousand feet in under one mile.

The creek canyon is dominated by 10,273-foot Freeman Peak. The trail heads up the canyon to the peak's base and then skirts around behind it to reach the pass. Once you're on the saddle, Freeman Peak is to your southwest. Directly below to the southeast are Upper Miner Lakes, in the West Big Hole

Majestic Freeman Peak in the Beaverhead Range. Ralph Maughan photo.

Proposed Wilderness, at elevations of 8,749 feet and 8,029 feet. The pass puts you on the Continental Divide. You're looking at such beauties as the Three Sisters Peaks, and Montana's Pioneer Mountains. The divide here is walled in by cliffs. Look sharp, as you may be able to see those lovers of precarious positions—mountain goats and bighorn sheep.—*Jennifer Vervoort* □

HIKE 75   *WEBBER CREEK TO DIVIDE CREEK*

General description: A long two-day or easier three or four-day backpack through a wide variety of scenery near, or on, the Continental Divide. A shuttle vehicle is needed.

General location: 65 miles due northwest of Idaho Falls in the Italian Peaks (the highest portion of the Beaverhead Range).

Maps: Heart Mountain, Deadman Lake, Scott Peak (7.5') USGS quads.

Special attractions: Ungrazed canyon bottom (Webber Creek), lakes, stunning peaks which are largely hidden from outside the area, and excellent wildlife observation opportunities.

Difficulty: Moderate when three days are allowed for the hike.

Season: July to mid-October. The lower canyons are accessible in mid-June.

Information: Dubois Ranger District, Targhee National Forest, Box 46, Dubois, Idaho 83423; (208) 374-5422.

The hike: The Italian Peaks, culminating in 11,200 foot-plus Scott and Webber peaks, are the highest part of the Beaverhead Range which forms the Idaho/Montana border for about 250 miles.

In the Italian Peaks, mountain goats and bighorn sheep ply the cliffs. Elk graze the highland meadows and deer the forest. An occasional moose wanders by. Raptors search the land from the sky. Every so often there are reports of grizzly bear and wolves. This is wild territory.

To reach this country, follow the instructions for the Red Conglomerate Peaks Loop, but continue on the Medicine Lodge Creek road past the Edie Creek and Irving Creek side roads. Continue to the crossing of Warm Creek. At this junction take Forest Service Road #280 which quickly climbs to a large and rolling sage and grassland bench. Here there are fine unobstructed views of the Italian Peaks to the left and the Red Conglomerates to the right. The road is improved dirt, which becomes fainter as you progress toward the Continental Divide at Bannack Pass (also called Medicine Lodge Pass). Before you reach the divide, turn left off of the road onto FS road #300 (it should be signed as the "Divide Creek Trail"). Watch for oil-pan-kissing rocks if you have a sedan as you drive the short distance to some shacks called "Cow Camp." Park near here if you don't have a high clearance vehicle. If you do have one, ford the creek and climb to the meadowy bench beyond. You can go about another half mile. Please park if the meadow is wet and your vehicle begins to leave ruts. Leave one vehicle here and shuttle back down Medicine Lodge Creek to the Webber Creek road (FS #196).

The Webber Creek Road leaves the main road about .2 mile downstream from the Edie Creek side road. It's five miles up FS #196 to the Webber Creek trailhead. The road varies from good gravel at the beginning to solid two track at the trailhead. There is a small, unimproved campground at the trailhead with space to park, although it's a squeeze for horse trailers. The trail is obvious and leaves directly at the upstream end of the campground. The Forest Service estimates it's 15 miles from Webber Creek trailhead to Cow Camp and your vehicle.

You start into a narrow, densely-forested canyon with a damp riparian zone. There are a few sagebrush-dominated meadows, however. After 3.5 miles, the canyon begins to open. Willows line the stream bottom and the gray, rugged Italian Peaks appear at the head of the canyon. The massive ice-carved mountain to the left is Webber Peak, nearly 11,300 feet. In the center, partially hidden by a lower pinnacled mountain, is Scott Peak, with a similar elevation. Here you are at the confluence of the South and North Forks of Webber Creek. A short distance to the left, up the South Fork, is a good camping area.

Continue, and head up the North Fork. The peaks draw near, and, after about a mile, you begin the climb into the North Fork's glacial valley.

You gain a trail junction after climbing 900 feet in 1.5 miles. The right hand trail is the one to Divide Creek. Its immediate destination is a 9,400 foot divide between North Webber Creek and the North Fork of Fritz Creek. First, however, you'll want to explore the left fork of the trail.

Up the left trail fork, imposing mountains rise on both sides of the canyon in stepped cliffs and awesome flutted pinnacles. The right wall is the Continental Divide. You gain 400 feet of altitude as you march up the valley of grass, fir, sagebrush, and pine. You arrive quickly at the first of three lakes and beautiful ponds that reflect the convoluted mountains rising with alacrity for over 2,000 feet from their southern shores.

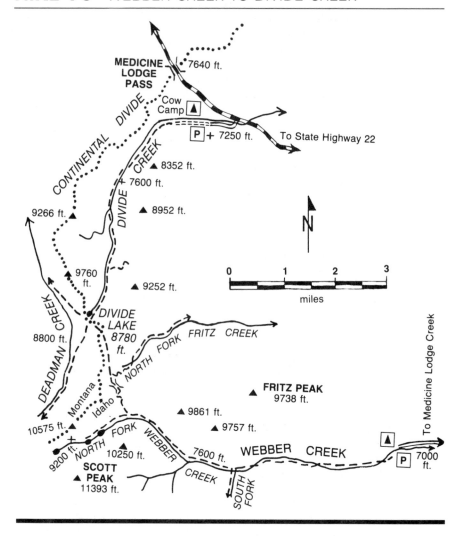

MEDICINE
LODGE
PASS

• 7640 ft.

CONTINENTAL DIVIDE

Cow
Camp ▲

P + 7250 ft.

To State Highway 22

DIVIDE CREEK

▲ 8352 ft.

+ 7600 ft.

9266 ft. ▲

▲ 8952 ft.

N

9760
ft. ▲

▲ 9252 ft.

0   1   2   3

miles

DEADMAN CREEK

DIVIDE
LAKE
8780
ft.

NORTH FORK FRITZ CREEK

8800 ft.

To Medicine Lodge Creek

Montana

Idaho

▲ FRITZ PEAK
9738 ft.

10575 ft. ▲

▲ 9861 ft.

▲ 9757 ft.

▲

9200 ft. NORTH FORK

▲ 10250 ft.

WEBBER CREEK

7600 ft.

WEBBER CREEK

P 7000
ft.

SCOTT
▲ PEAK
11393 ft.

CREEK

SOUTH FORK

These are not lakes for anglers since the rock is pourous. They lose much of their water by autumn. They are a place to camp and admire this hidden valley sandwiched between Idaho and Montana.

Back on the trail for the continuation of the hike, climb 575 feet to the grassy 9,400 foot divide between Webber Creek and North Fritz Creek. On my second trip to the area, we spotted a large elk herd on this pass. You'll want to spend a few moments here, elk or not, to admire the view.

Pressing on to the north, you'll drop into timber and cross the very head of the canyon of North Fritz Creek. A connecting trail descends from this point. It's a fairly good trail except for the steep top of the canyon and a few avalanche debris areas.

The traverse of Fritz Creek completed, you "roll" on down the Continental

Divide Lake viewed from the Continental Divide in the Italian Peaks. Ralph Maughan photo.

Divide. The trail leads slightly into Montana, then Idaho, and so on. The large canyon appearing to your left is Deadman Creek in Montana. This is a beautiful side trip. The Deadman Creek Trail leads to a 9700 foot high pass (between Deadman and Nicholia Creek)—a fine place to observe mountain goats and the sheer north face of the Continental Divide at Italian Peak (for more information see the Hikers Guide to Montana).

As you walk along the Continental Divide, descending slowly, the character of the land changes rather quickly from rocky peaks and cliffs to open, meadowy mountains and mid-elevation meadows filled with tall, fleshy plants (forbs) such as are visible in Deadman Creek below. As is commonplace, the visible track of the trail fades as you go from rocky forest to meadowy upland. To reach Divide Lake, stay on the divide. Avoid the inclination to drop into Deadman Creek or to climb the hills to your right. Aim for the slot at the base of the mountain that rises on the east (right) side of Deadman Creek. The slot holds Divide Lake.

The lake is barely inside Idaho, being separated from Montana by a hundred-foot-high cliff which constitutes the Continental Divide. Divide Lake is a fertile body of water with a rugged cliff on one side, but otherwise surrounded by low grassy mountains and a ring of conifer, giving an appearance reminiscent of a large meadow pond.

There would be quite a few places to camp near the outlet except the site tends to be a bit wet. There are drier places on a bench 50 yards downstream from the outlet.

The last leg of the hike is all downhill. Follow tiny Divide Creek from where it spills from the lake. It gurgles down the narrow, grassy canyon. The canyon deepens rapidly for a mile but then broadens out. Here a trail more obvious than the correct route leads upward to the right. Ignore it and continue through an elk wallow, trying to keep the mud out of your boots. Continue down the canyon. You'll soon find the creekside trail again.

The rest of the way is easy down this 900 foot deep canyon. There are only pockets of timber, but it is painted with wildflowers from July into August. The canyon makes a 90 degree bend (to the east) and ends about a mile above Cow Camp.

Webber canyon is closed to livestock grazing (a rare treat in this country). Livestock are put in Divide and Fritz creeks in the second half of July. If you find cattle in Webber Creek, be sure to report this trespass to the District Forest Ranger in Dubois.—*Ralph Maughan* □

Note: The Forest Service has long supported designating the Italian Peaks as part of the National Wilderness Preservation System. Unfortunately, they have not closed the area to motor vehicles. Dirt bike and all terrain vehicle (ATV) pressure groups seem to be making it a special project to fight wilderness designation here and instead develop a network of trails by means of trail "service" projects. Their presence is considerably more common now than when the first edition of the **Hikers Guide** *was written.—Ralph Maughan* □

Craters of the Moon National Monument and Wilderness

Overview

Craters of the Moon National Monument protects the most geologically unusual regions of one of the most extensive basaltic lava flows on the face of the earth.

In contrast to lava spewed from the summit of a volcano, the molten rock which formed the Snake River Plain erupted from a rift dozens of miles long in the earth's crust. Lava from the Great Rift, as it is known, formed a series of caves (actually lava tunnels), tree molds, spatter cones, and huge craters—a landscape so unearthly that the NASA astronauts trained for the moon landings here.

The landscape is also remarkable for the tenacious life forms that attempt to eke out an existence in the almost barren lava fields. Scattered here and there are pockets of soil which support some grasses, a sagebrush or two, and an occasional limber pine. These little oases are called *kipukas,* a Hawaiian term for an island of vegetation in a sea of lava.

This is a stern, harsh land, very demanding of the plants and animals that live on it and the hikers who visit. Dense fogs can roll in from the Snake River to the south, making travel difficult. It becomes even more difficult when the compass fails to work properly due to the high iron content of the basaltic rocks.

Although the land is harsh, it holds its own special fascination for the discriminating hiker.

Interest in protecting the extensive lava flows adjacent to Craters of the Moon National Park as well as all of the Great Rift is growing. In 1990 Idaho Representative Richard Stallings introduced legislation to establish a Craters of the Moon National Park which would be almost ten times larger than the present national monument.

HIKE 76 *ECHO CRATER*

General description: An eight-mile round trip into the unique desert and lava landscape of craters of the Craters of the Moon National Monument and Wilderness.

General location: About 75 air miles west of Idaho Falls.

Maps: Inferno Cone, The Watchman, and Fissure Butte (7.5') USGS quads.

Special attractions: A moonscape of beautiful, tormented, colorful lava introduces the Great Rift—a huge volcanic fissure in the earth's surface.

Difficulty: Moderatly easy becoming progressively more difficult.

Season: April to October.

Information: Craters of the Moon National Monument, Box 29, Arco, Idaho 83213; (208) 527-3257.

The hike: This is an easy hike, provided you carry adequate water, are in good physical condition, and don't wander too far off the beaten path. Early and late season hiking are preferable to avoid scorching heat coupled with lack of water and shade. You will need to check in at the Craters of the Moon National Monument headquarters for a backcountry travel permit. Off-season hours for the monument are 8 a.m. to 4:30 p.m.; after mid-June, hours are from 8 a.m. to 8 p.m. The monument is a major (for Idaho) developed tourist center. However, the backcountry, while fairly small (68 square miles), seems much larger due to its stark topography.

Drive to Craters of the Moon National Monument, 18 miles southwest of Arco, Idaho, on U.S. Highway 26/93. There is no fee for a backcountry permit, but there is a per-vehicle entry charge and another charge to stay overnight at the developed monument campground. After obtaining a backcountry permit and stocking up on water, drive around the paved loop road to the Tree Molds area and park at the end of the road in the parking lot. The trail begins as an asphalt path leading from the parking lot to the Tree Molds area.

After leaving the parking lot, the trail quickly reverts to dirt and cinders. In approximately one-eighth mile, the trail to the wilderness area leaves the main Tree Mold Trail (to your left, or southeast) and down a short steep bank. Two large square posts mark the junction. Take the wilderness area trail over an iridescent blue pahoehoe lava flow and around the northeast side of Big Cinder Butte (6,516 feet), following cairns. In about one mile, the trail joins the abandoned Monument Road. Turn to your right, and travel toward the notch between Big Cinder and Half Cone Buttes (southeast) entering the Craters Wilderness Area in one-eighth mile. Big Cinder is the largest butte in the monument. The hiking is easy on this abandoned road for somewhat over a mile as you cross Trench Mortar Flat. Keep an eye out for the lava trees about 50 yards off the trail to your right, approximately an eighth mile after topping the low rise between Big Cinder and Half Cone. Here, the rapidly cooling lava at the forefront of a flow encased the bases of standing trees, preserves the trees' outlines in rock for posterity.

While crossing Trench Mortar Flat, stay to your right at a junction with another old road which heads toward Crescent Butte. Mule deer can often be observed on the flanks of Coyote Butte which the road rounds on its left as it begins to fade to a trail. As the road reverts to a trail, it continues to the south, around the west side of Echo Crater (recognizable by the reddish-colored cinders on the upper rim), then swings back toward the southeast, where it fades away completely between the Watchman and the Sentinel. Shortly after beginning the gradual descent from the gap between Coyote Butte and the low cones on the flank of Crescent Butte, you must decide whether to go cross-country to Echo Crater or the Watchman (an easy, obvious cross-country route), or follow the old road around to the Sentinel.

Echo Crater provides the best camp, while the Watchman is somewhat more removed from traveled routes. To reach Echo Crater, break off from the old road soon after leaving Coyote Butte and head across the cinders towards the low lip of the crater on the northeast side. There are no developed trails, but travel through the sage is relatively easy in this section as you parallel the Great Rift. Bobcats are occasionally seen in the vicinity, and mule deer are common in the Craters backcountry. Enter Echo Crater from the low spot in the rim. Two different camping environments are available in the crater, one amid limber pine in the lower portion, and another surrounded by juniper/sagebrush in the higher section. More than two parties create a crowded situation. A short jaunt up the southeast ridge of the cone takes you to the red cinder "peak" at 5,850 feet, a 20-minute walk. Fair views of some of the cones and the cairns making the site of Bearsden Waterhole in the Great Rift can be seen from the rim.

Bearsden Waterhole is about .75 mile east of Echo Crater in the most discernable part of the rift. The waterhole is in a small, 20-feet deep depression, and you must climb down from the northwest edge (an easy route) to reach the small cave. There's usually water here into the summer, but check with the Park Service since the water supply fluctuates greatly from year to year. Snow and ice with a few inches of water are generally present into June following a normal snow year. Please take only the minimum you need, as local animals and birds rely on this supply. In addition, there's enough animal-human activity to warrant treating or boiling the water. Little Prairie Waterhole, an eighth-mile further southeast in the rift from Bearsden, and assorted crevices in the rift, generally hold snow and sometimes water in the spring.

Continuing a mile southeast of Echo Crater, along the Great Rift, will take you to the Watchman, a relatively old cone with a more recent, darker flow on the northwest face. Limited camping is available, with the best under a limber pine on the north edge of the cone. There's enough room for a small party.

Hiking becomes more difficult beyond the Watchman, primarily because of thick brush (wear pants). Split, Fissure, and Sheep Trail Buttes are progressively scattered in line with the rift. An intermittent and unreliable waterhole is located in the northwest depression of Sheep Trail Butte. To the southeast of Sheep Trail Butte lies the Vermilion Chasm, nearly at the edge of the designated wilderness. Venturing from the rift area leads you onto the Little Prairie Aa Flow to the north, or the Sawtooth Aa Flow to the south. This is rough, boot-eating terrain. Just say the Hawaiian names describing the lava: *pahoehoe* (pronounced "pah-hoh'-eh'hoh'eh'—a ropy, wrinkled lava) and *aa* (pronounced "ah'-ah'—rough, jagged lava), and you get an onomatopoeic

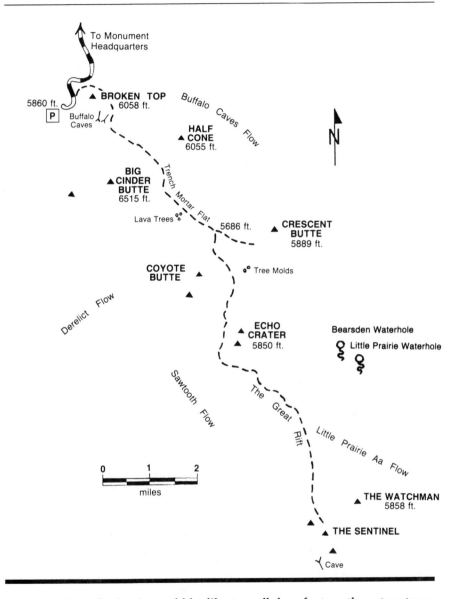

representation of what it would be like to walk barefoot on these two types of flows. There's a catch, of course, because fractured pahoehoe can be as brutal to traverse as aa. Despite what your boots may think of this hike, you will never forget its stark, unearthly beauty.—*Robert N. (Rob) Jones*

Big Hole Mountains

Overview

Hugging the border of Idaho and Wyoming is a lengthy mountain range bearing three names. To the north, as it emerges out of the volcanic rock of the Snake River Plain, this range is called the Big Hole Mountains. In its middle, between Idaho Highway 31 and U.S. Highway 26, it is referred to as the Snake River Mountains (refer to the overview for the Snake Rivers for more information about this part of the range). South of U.S. 26, its highest portion, entirely in Wyoming, bears the title, "Salt River Range." Despite these aliases, it is all one beautiful chain of mountains.

The Big Hole portion is a generally forested, semi-circular area of steep, but relatively low, intensively dissected mountains. To the south, the Snake Rivers are less forested, mostly because of the action of countless avalanches, and are 1,000 to 1,500 feet higher.

These mountains are built of numerous sedimentary rocks, pushed into complicated jumbles of rock by thrust faulting. The material of these mountains (and of all mountains near the Wyoming border) was once many miles to the west. It was pushed eastward by the forces of continental drift.

This geology allows for hypothetical pockets of oil and natural gas. The oil industry has been exploring the Overthrust Belt of Eastern Idaho for almost a generation. They have been unsuccessful, but have nevertheless waged a strong campaign against wilderness designation.

The Big Hole and the Snake River Ranges abut a vast area of wild country to the north and northeast in Wyoming—the Greater Yellowstone country. You can hike from U.S. 26 at the south end of the Snake Rivers northward to the Tetons and Yellowstone National Park and only cross one paved highway and one dirt road. The rest is wild. Moreover, the Big Holes, Snakes, and Salt Rivers provide an important corridor for big game to migrate from the Yellowstone country down to southwestern Wyoming, eastern Idaho, and northern Utah.

The entire area is geologically active and tremblers frequently shake the area of the state border. Another large quake is possible.

The Big Hole Mountains, due to their relatively low elevation, provide early summer hiking. The 220,000 acre roadless area to the south, in the Snake Rivers, is large enough to allow you a week-long backpacking vacation.

Idaho and Wyoming environmentalists have been trying for years to preserve these roadless areas as designated wilderness. They have been successful in keeping them roadless, but, unless wilderness designation arrives soon, these pristine areas may fall to the oil companies and the increasingly well funded dirt bike and all-terrain vehicle lobbies.

HIKE 77 *BLACK CANYON TO BIG BURNS*

General description: A two-day hike through wild mountains surprisingly close to the city of Idaho Falls.

General location: Northeast of Idaho Falls in the Big Hole Mountains, 33.5 miles by road to Black Canyon.

Maps: Garn's Mountain and Wheaton Mountain (7.5') USGS quads.

Special attractions: Early season hiking near Idaho Falls. Steep, scenic low mountains cloaked with a beautiful mixed forest that opens in spots to give views of the surrounding wild country.

Difficulty: Moderate except for a difficult wade of Big Burns Creek in early summer.

Season: Mid-June to mid-October.

Information: Palisades Ranger District, Targhee National Forest, 3659 E. Ririe Highway, Idaho Falls, ID 83401; (208) 523-1412.

The hike: Although barely reaching 9,000 feet, the Big Hole Mountains just east of Idaho Falls and west of the Tetons are an easily accessible, often overlooked, large block of wild country. Over 80,000 acres (125 square miles) of these mountains and canyons are *de facto* wilderness.

Despite close proximity to the intensively farmed and populated Upper Snake River Valley, grizzly bears are still observed from time to time in these mountains, although there are probably no permanent silvertip inhabitants.

You can hike here in mid or even early June, and there are lots of trails, although most are lightly maintained at best.

While the hike from Black Canyon to Big Burns Creek is not quite a loop, it does not require a lengthy shuttle with a second vehicle. You can walk the road that fills the two-mile gap in the loop in less than an hour.

Big Burns Creek is a good-sized stream in a large canyon. Black Canyon is smaller. Both are scenic and contain fairly good hiking trails. They are connected by the very lush and narrow Little Burns Canyon, which also has an acceptable trail.

From Idaho Falls, drive east on U.S. 26 for 13.7 miles. Here, turn off the highway to the left onto the paved Heise Road. Follow this road, which crosses the South Fork of the Snake River, for 4.1 miles and you come to the resort of Heise Hot Springs. One mile past the hot springs, the road forks. The paved road to the left goes to Kelly Canyon ski area. Take the gravel road to the right which follows the South Fork of the Snake River for 14.2 miles from Heise in a very scenic drive to the mouth of Big Burns Canyon. In some places the road is a good 40-mile-per-hour gravel highway, while in others you slow to 10 miles per hour to bump over ungraded basalt outcroppings or large-diameter gravel. It's 1.5 more miles on the road to the mouth of the Black Canyon.

The South Fork of the Snake River, particularly in the vicinity of Big Burns Creek and upstream, provides extraordinary wildlife habitat. Moose, elk, deer, bears, bighorn sheep, and all types of waterfowl frequent the area—it's also a nesting area for the endangered American bald eagle and for the golden eagle. The Idaho Fish and Game Department has identified the South Fork as the number one threatened wildlife habitat in the state of Idaho.

Thousands of anglers and hunters boat the South Fork each year. Here, between Big Burns and Black Canyon, dozens of fertile and slightly warm springs emerge just below the dirt road, bursting into riparian ponds brimming with wildlife.

For years, various dams that would destroy this river have been promoted. Originally, a high dam at the mouth of Big Burns Creek was planned. It would have backed water all the way to Palisades Reservoir, displacing hundreds of people along with wildlife. In recent years, plans have been scaled down, calling for only a 20- or 30-foot high dam at Burns Creek. This has the "advantage" of only ruining the river. Why a dam is needed is subject to a various number of conflicting justifications. Let your representatives know how you feel about this issue.

Drive up into Black Canyon, the mouth of which is guarded by a vine-covered tower of volcanic conglomerate rock. The road continues for about a mile. Park on one of the meadows before a road sign announces "Black Canyon Trail."

Walk past the sign along a four-wheel drive trail. The jeep trail becomes a pack trail after about a mile at the second crossing of Black Creek.

The pack trail winds through deciduous and evergreen forests, crossing the creek eight or nine more times. These are jumps or small log crossings except in the early summer, when you may have to wade. The woods that cling to the fertile sedimentary rock of these mountains glow in various shades of healthy green.

After the last creek crossing (2.2 miles from the starting point), the trail turns and climbs quickly into a small, steep side-canyon. Fill your water bottles in the spring at the bottom of the side canyon. This is the last water until you reach Little Burns Creek.

Now you march a rousing 1,200-foot climb to the Black Canyon-Little Burns divide (7,600 feet). The trail is faint but stays to the bottom of the side canyon where the shade of the Douglas fir keeps it from becoming a bramble way. Just before the divide, you'll emerge from the forest into a clearing. Here, if you walk out to the point overlooking Black Canyon, you get quite a view down-canyon over green forest to the Snake River, at the base of the mountains, and to the farmlands beyond. Up-canyon you look right at the face of Black Mountain, its gray, flat-bedded sedimentary slopes scoured by thousands of winters of avalanches.

At the divide, a signed trail continues to climb up the ridge. It leads on to the West Fork of Pine Creek. Your trail leads to the left *down* the ridge. Then, after about 50 yards, it drops steeply into Little Burns Creek for a switch-backing thousand-foot descent. Here you pass many forest windows looking across Little Burns to the divide between it and Big Burns Canyon.

After a mile of descent, as the headwater rivulets of Little Burns Creek flow together, you'll reach a trail junction. Here the Little Burns Creek trail splits as it comes uphill towards you. To the right, a well-signed trail fork climbs out of Little Burns and offers access to many trails after crossing the shoulder of Piney Peak. Go to the left here and continue down Little Burns Canyon.

Just below this trail junction are some clearings. This is a good, and as of 1982, pristine, area to find camping spots. Further down the canyon, narrow walls prevent camping.

Little Burns is a narrow, very scenic, well-vegetated canyon. It is closed to

HIKE 77 *BLACK CANYON TO BIG BURNS*

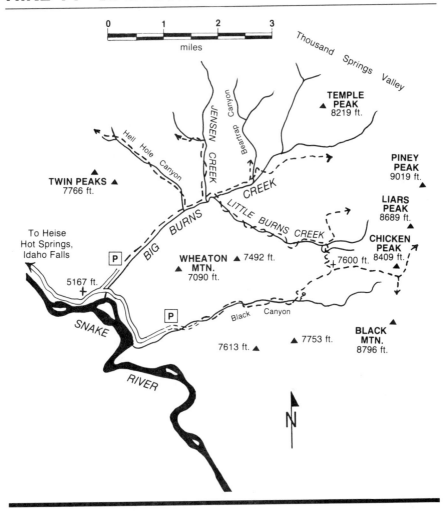

grazing. There are many unimpeded views of the canyon slopes which are covered with fir, aspen and brush, and balding spots near the rims.

The trail is not wide, but it is easy to follow. Well-bounded by brush (much of it wildrose), it fords Little Burns Creek five times in the upper reaches and four in the lower part of the canyon. For .75 mile in the middle, there are no crossings. At the bottom of the canyon, you are greeted with a ford of Big Burns Creek. This is cold and swift through June, but only moderately dangerous even early in the season. There are three nice big springs in Little Burns; one is of exceptional beauty.

After wading Big Burns Creek, you step out into a much larger canyon with forested slopes hiding most of the rough limestone cliffs. The canyon bottom is quite meadowy in its middle reaches, and there are many places to camp. The trail is easy to find and easy to walk on. Flowers bloom through June.

Topographic maps show a trail to the head of Big Burns and up a tributary, Beartrap Canyon, leading to Thousand Springs Valley. Actually these trails largely disappear, leading the unwary into a tough, but scenic, bushwhack.

Both Big Burns and Little Burns creeks are closed to fishing. In them spawn the rare Snake River fine-spotted cutthroat trout.

From the confluence of Little Burns Creek, the trail goes down Big Burns for three miles to the road. You pass side trails that lead up Jensen Creek and Hell Hole Canyons. Despite what the map shows, you never have to ford Big Burns Creek again. The lower miles of the canyon are an impressive walk below large cliffs.

During the weekdays, you will see few people in these canyons. On weekends, expect to see day hikers and a few trail machines in the lower stretches. Motorized vehicles can't negotiate the recesses of upper Big Burns or of Little Burns, however.

During the Forest Service's Roadless Area Review Inventory II (RARE II) study, the public supported wilderness classification for these mountains at a ratio of three to two. However, the oil and gas companies' vote counted most. Since RARE II, it has all been leased for oil and gas exploration.—*Ralph Maughan* □

Snake River Mountains

Overview

Straddling the Idaho-Wyoming stateline, just south of Grand Teton National Park, lies a series of steep, rugged peaks, the Snake River Range. Although not quite as high as the granitic Tetons, a few limestone peaks of the Snake River Range reach altitudes in excess of 10,000 feet.

The Snakes, more commonly referred to as the Palisades Backcountry, comprise a wild land resource of nearly a quarter-million acres. This acreage is divided almost evenly between Idaho and Wyoming. The area's extreme steepness and heavy winter snowfall make it prime avalanche country, which results in a diverse mosaic of vegetation types along the mountainsides, ranging from open alpine meadows and avalanche paths to dense forest. Snow may linger in the deep canyons well into July, when melting snows in the high country reappear as gushing springs along the porous limestone hillsides.

Grizzly bears are still sighted from time to time in the Palisades Backcountry, which is considered part of the eight-million-acre Greater Yellowstone Ecosystem. This ecosystem is a virtually intact chunk of big game habitat centered around Yellowstone National Park itself.

Although the U.S. Forest Service has attempted to open the Palisades to oil and gas development in recent years, conservationists hope that Congress will recognize the importance of the 200,000 acres of wild country to the environmental health of the Yellowstone Ecosystem and protect the Palisades as a wilderness area.

For more information about this area, please refer to the overview for the Big Hole Mountains.

The Snake River Range from Palisades Reservoir. Ralph Maughan photo.

HIKE 78 *BIG ELK CREEK*

General description: A big, easily accessible canyon, with many inviting side-trails offering an intimate exploration of the Snake River Range.

General location: 47 miles southeast of Idaho Falls; 65 miles northeast of Pocatello.

Maps: Mt. Baird, Palisades Peak and Teton Pass (7.5') USGS quads.

Special attractions: A scenic gorge in mid-canyon and an extraordinary number of avalanche runs throughout the hike.

Difficulty: Easy, except for early summer stream crossings in the hike's upper portion.

Season: Late June through September.

Information: Palisades Ranger District, Targhee National Forest, 3659 E. Ririe Highway, Idaho Falls, ID 83401; (208) 523-1412.

The hike: Less used than Palisades Creek, Big Elk Creek has an easy trail leading up a broad, open, scenic canyon. Your hike in this canyon can be as short as a couple of hours, or you can turn it into a four- or five-day exploration of the Snake River Range. Happily, this trail, like the Palisades Creek trail, was closed to trailbikes beginning in 1983.

To get to the trailhead, drive on U.S. Highway 26 from Alpine, Wyoming,

HIKE 78 *BIG ELK CREEK*

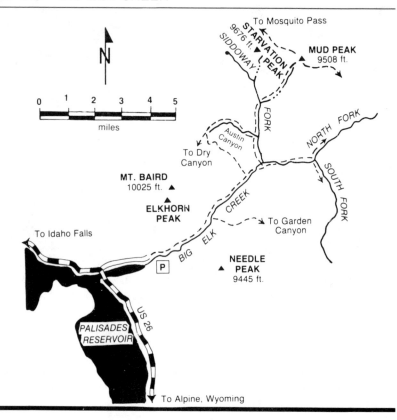

or southeast from Idaho Falls, passing through Swan Valley and along part of Palisades Reservoir. At the Big Elk Creek arm of the reservoir, a signed dirt road to Big Elk Creek leaves the highway. Drive 2.5 miles on this dirt road to the trailhead, which is the end of the road.

Walk from the car up a short side hill and into the forest, almost immediately crossing a perennial spring (an important source of water if your bottle isn't full.)

Like Palisades Creek, Big Elk is a substantial stream, running swift and cold into mid-summer. The trail does not cross the creek until you are almost to the Siddoway Fork of Elk Creek. There are a lot of good campsites along the creek; most are within sight of the trail, however.

For three miles the canyon stays wide, offering frequent views of the steep, partially forested slopes of the Snake River Range as you pass in and out of the patchy forest. The canyon narrows as you pass Hells Hole Canyon and follow the trail right alongside the stream. Limestone walls rise steeply for 600 feet above you. Just past this gorge, in early to mid-summer, a falls leaps over an alcove to the left of the trail and onto a bed of grass and tall wildflowers.

As you approach the Cabin Creek tributary, the forest thickens. The swamps under the trees look like moose habitat, which indeed it is. The Forest Service keeps this area ungrazed by domestic livestock.

A very scenic, but faint, trail in the Cabin Creek drainage leads up over the ridge and onto the grassy top of Austin Canyon. This, however, involves a difficult 2,100-foot climb. It's easier to do this side hike in the other direction, from Austin Canyon to Cabin Creek.

The main trail crosses Big Elk Creek just below its confluence with the Siddoway Fork (five miles from the trailhead). You can't ford the stream until early July, although a tough quarter-mile bushwhack and scramble can get you into the Siddoway Fork as much as three weeks before you can wade across the Big Elk.

The Siddoway Fork is a substantial tributary canyon, narrower than Big Elk Creek. The side-trail winds up this canyon through many delightful little meadows and patches of forest. Eventually, the Siddoway Fork trail gives you access to the pretty Austin Canyon Trail or to the main crest of the mountain range running north and south between Swan Valley and Jackson Hole.

The main trail crosses Big Elk Creek several more times in the remaining 1.5 miles from the first ford to the junction of the North Fork and South Fork of Big Elk. This section is best hiked in late July or August to avoid high water.

The forks of Big Elk Creek have beautiful, subalpine elk summer pasture, except when livestock are present. Some years the area gets a rest; others the livestock are not put in until August 1. Check with the Forest Service if you want to avoid sheep or cattle.

Perhaps the most interesting thing about this canyon is the astounding number of avalanche paths that run down the mountains. There are hundreds of them—so many that Big Elk Creek Canyon has only patchy forest. The open places where snow thunders down in the winter become flowered meadows in mid-summer with the larger chutes having melt streams until then.

The natural phenomenon of abundant avalanche slides is common in this part of the Middle Rockies. You'll see even more dramatic examples in the Snake River Range if you hike up Garden Canyon or the Dry Fork of Wolf Creek.—*Ralph Maughan* □

HIKE 79 *LITTLE ELK CREEK*

General description: A short, but very steep day hike that climbs through a lush canopy of vegetation to emerge in alpine meadows and end on a pass offering endless views of Idaho and Wyoming.

General location: 47 miles southeast of Idaho Falls.

Maps: Mt. Baird, Palisades Dam, and Palisades Peak (7.5') USGS quads.

Special attractions: A "Sound of Music" panorama in the upper third of the trail, with a chance of seeing cliff-dwelling mountain goats.

Difficulty: Difficult due to steepness.

Season: Late June through September.

Information: Palisades Ranger District, Targhee National Forest, 3659 E. Ririe Highway, Idaho Falls, ID 84301; (208) 523-1412.

The hike: Little Elk Creek is not a trail for the weak, lazy, or inexperienced. It's a long, steep three miles. Going down is hard on the knees and feet as

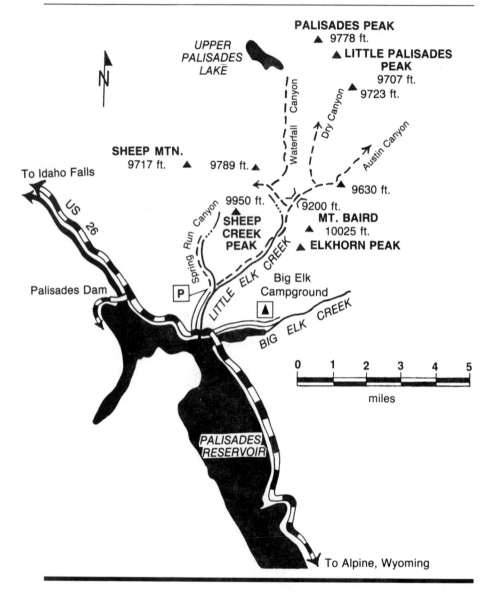

you do a lot of braking; going up should prepare you for the Olympics. From the trail's beginning at 5,960 feet to your destination, a nameless mountain at 9,630 feet, it's a 3,670-foot climb.

To get to Little Elk Creek, drive from Idaho Falls to the Palisades Reservoir on U.S. Highway 26. Once you pass the dam at the reservoir's north end, it's another 2.5 miles to the Little Elk Creek turnoff on your left (east). The dirt road leads in for about one mile to where the creek in Spring Run Canyon forks with Little Elk Creek.

The Little Elk Creek trail. Ralph Maughan photo.

Just before the fork with spring-fed Spring Run Creek, park at the trailhead. Here, trails take off to both the right and the left. Take the trail to the right and wander up Little Elk Creek under a canopy of aspen, fir, and cottonwood. Underneath, grass and tall flowers such as sticky geranium, cinquefoil, arrowleaf balsamroot (in the early summer) and western coneflower (in the late summer) line the edges of the intimate, easily followed path. At one-half mile and at one mile respectively, two small streams flow in from the left. Until you reach the second stream, the trail is deceptively gentle.

The lower two thirds of the hike is forested, but as soon as you pass the side stream one mile from the trailhead, the route becomes increasingly steep.

For the first 2.5 miles or so, the trail follows Little Elk Creek and the route is obvious. You'll pass three small tributaries on your right and two on the left. The last two you pass form the headwaters of Little Elk Creek.

After you pass the headwaters and a set of switchbacks, you'll see two side-trails in the next one-half mile leading off to the left. Stay right. The upper third of the main trail fans out into a fine panorama of bare cliffs, green hills, and flowers. The patient hiker will probably observe mountain goats on the cliffs during morning and evening hours. The problem with the last stretch to the top of the mountain is exposure to the elements—the heat of the sun or rain or lightning. Once on top you can enjoy the view of the reservoir behind, unnamed 9,000-foot-plus peaks all about, Palisades Peak (9,778 feet) and Little Palisades Peak (9,707 feet) ahead, and the Tetons in the distance beyond them.

After reaching the pass at 9,200 feet, the trail quickly crosses the headwaters of Waterfalls Canyon (for more information, see the Waterfalls Canyon Hike). Then it goes right over peak 9,630 and down the other side, where a trail to the left forks to Dry Canyon and eventually Upper Palisades Lake. Here at the top of Dry Canyon, the right trail fork drops into Austin Canyon. This will take you to the Siddoway Fork of Elk Creek. All of these trails intersect with many others to keep you busy for several days without really going very far.

Whether you are traveling up or down Little Elk Creek Canyon, take some drink mix for snowcones. You can usually count on a snowbank for cool refreshment at the divide through July.—*Ann and George Matejko* □

HIKE 80 *PALISADES CREEK*

General description: An easy, but often busy, trail into the rugged Snake River Mountains.

General location: Near the Wyoming border about 45 miles east of Idaho Falls and 65 miles northeast of Pocatello.

Maps: Palisades Peak and Thompson Peak (7.5') USGS quads.

Special attractions: A beautiful, cliff-lined canyon with a lake, lush vegetation, a beautiful stream, and lots of wildlife due to livestock closure.

Difficulty: Easy from the trailhead to the Waterfalls Canyon trail. Difficult above due to stream crossings.

Season: Mid-June to November for the lower portion; mid-July to October for the upper section.

Information: Palisades Ranger District, Targhee National Forest, 3659 E. Ririe Highway, Idaho Falls, ID 83401; (208) 523-1412.

The hike: This is probably the most popular hiking trail into the Snake River Mountains. This canyon and its tributaries are managed as the "Palisades Backcountry" by the Targhee National Forest. The management direction is to keep this environment suitable for near-primitive recreation.

The trail up the canyon is quite easy to hike on and to follow, although it can get muddy after major rainstorms and in the early season. Palisades Creek is popular for good reason—splendid scenery; lots of moose, deer, and some mountain goats in the canyon; and good fishing. Also, no grazing of domestic livestock has spoiled the canyon's lushness.

As a result, plenty of people come up Palisades Creek, often so many it's hard to find a good camping spot. In the lower canyon, the feeling of the wild retreats until after Labor Day. Palisades Creek has the greatest number of visitors during the period from Wednesday through Sunday. Monday and Tuesday see significantly fewer people. despite all the use the canyon gets, however, it has been kept remarkably clean under the administration of the Targhee National Forest.

To reach the trailhead, drive about 52 miles from Idaho Falls eastward on U.S. Highway 26. Continue through the small towns of Swan Valley and Irwin, and turn to the left off the highway onto a gravel road at the unincorporated community of Palisades. The road sign says "Palisades Creek."

After about two miles, the gravel road ends at the Palisades campground, set right in the mouth of the V-shaped opening to mountain beauty beyond. Parking for hikers is to the left just before the campground entrance and the bridge over Palisades Creek. The horse transfer area is on the other side of the bridge and to the right.

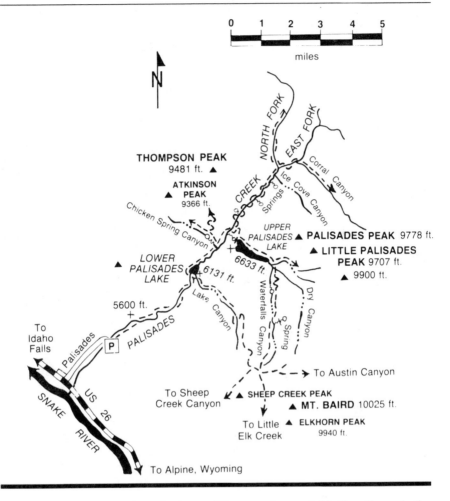

You can find the trail easily by walking up the road leading through the campground. Walk past a Forest Service information sign and into the narrow mouth of the canyon. Palisades Creek splashes beside the trail (earlier in the season, it *thunders* beside the trail). The creek never gets very low because much of its flow comes from year-round springs emerging far up the canyon and up its tributaries. Fortunately, the creek is bridged as far as Lower Palisades Lake. It isn't bridged above the Waterfalls Canyon Trail, however; you'll have to ford it time after time.

Despite the rugged, steep mountains rising above the canyon, its bottom is forested, shaded by both evergreens and deciduous trees. From its beginning at the campground, Palisades Canyon is 2,000 feet deep. Further upstream, it's over 3,000 feet deep. After about a mile, near the first bridge, the canyon opens up into a large amphitheater. Here, temporarily out of the forest that fills the canyon, you can see the great cliffs lining the canyon's side slopes.

Palisades Creek brawls down the mountainside. Ralph Maughan photo.

Look for mountain goats whenever you have a good view of the cliffs.

The trail proceeds three more miles (sometimes following the stream, other times climbing to about 75 feet above it) up the generally narrow canyon to a landslide that impounds Lower Palisades Lake. A short, switchbacking climb up the slide brings you to the lake. Here you'll find good, but used-looking, campsites. The next reasonable campsites are 1.5 more miles.

Moose haunt the area from the lower lake on. The lake has pretty good fishing for cutthroat trout. The stream below has only fair fishing due to high water until later in the summer, although in late June, anglers sometimes take large spawning trout out of the torrent. Better fishing lies ahead upstream and also at Upper Palisades Lake.

To continue, cross the bridge at the lake's outlet and walk up the north side of the canyon past the lake and the low willow marsh at its head. Continue past pretty Chicken Springs Canyon, where you'll see a Forest Service cabin. About a quarter-mile past the cabin there are a number of campsites. The area right around Chicken Springs is closed to camping to encourage regrowth of the area. It was formerly denuded by excessive camping.

Chicken Springs Canyon itself is a pleasant walk. The springs rise about .75 mile up the canyon. Just before you reach the springs, the steep Thompson Peak trail goes up the hillside (marked by a sign but with no obvious track at firest). The Atkinson Peak Trail proceeds up Chicken Springs Canyon, past the springs (there's no water above them), into a timbered, wider part of this side canyon; and then it climbs steeply to meet the Thompson Peak Trail. Chicken Springs got its name from the abundance of blue and ruffed grouse nearby. Moose are also common in the canyon.

Back on the Palisades Trail, it is about a half-mile from Chicken Springs to where you ford Palisades Creek for the first time. Just past the ford is a junction with the popular Waterfalls Canyon Trail. There used to be a foot bridge here, but it washed out in 1982. The ford is moderately swift, about 60 feet wide and about 2.5 feet deep in mid-summer. When run-off is at its maximum (usually between mid-June and the first of July), however, the ford may be very difficult. (See note at end.)

Probably 99 out of every 100 people go up the Waterfalls Canyon Trail rather than continuing up Palisades Creek. As a result, you can find real wilderness solitude by being the one that stays in the main canyon.

Past the ford, Palisades Creek diminishes in size but is still substantial. It's hard to cross it until mid-July. This is important to note, because you quickly come to the first of 22 fords! The canyon narrows in this section and becomes very beautiful, with many springs and intermittent streams flowing out of the wide canyons: Big Dry, Little Dry, Dead Man, Lost Spring, Ice Cove. Ice Cove Canyon is misnamed "Ice Cave Canyon" on most maps. You'll see the ruins of a cabin at the mouth of Dead Man Canyon. The trail here is partly overgrown and often wet, as it diverts water from the creek. The hiking isn't easy, especially with the trail constantly going back and forth across Palisades Creek, but it's well worth your effort. There are a number of places to camp. The best, however, is at the grassy, partially wet flat at the junction of the North and East forks of Palisades Creek—the end of this trail description.

If you want to explore further from the East Fork-North Fork junction, primitive trails go up each fork. And these, in turn, have numerous side branches providing you with opportunities for fine wilderness hikes.

The best season for the lower portion of the canyon (to the first lake) is mid-June to late July. Above the lower lake, mid-July to mid-August may be best because the creek is low enough to wade and the upper canyon is still very green. Fall is also a lovely time to visit the canyon. Cooler weather makes hiking more comfortable, eliminates the bugs, and offers relative quiet and solitude. September transforms the canyon in to a tapestry of color.—*Ralph Maughan* □

Note: A new bridge has been built over Palisades Creek where the trail crosses to go to Upper Palisades Lake, making access to Upper Palisades Lake and Waterfalls Canyon easier and feasible earlier in the season. This trail has a high priority for rebuilding during the 1990s.—Ralph Maughan

HIKE 81   *RAINEY CREEK LOOP*

General description: An two-day loop of about twelve miles in the northern end of the Palisades Backcountry.
General location: About 45 miles east of Idaho Falls near Swan Valley and Pine Creek Pass in the Snake River Range.
Maps: Fourth of July Peak, Thompson Peak (7.5') USGS quads.
Special attractions: A nice loop offering the option of climbing several mountains and connecting with many side trails.
Difficulty: Moderate.
Season: July to late October.
Information: Palisades Ranger District; Targhee National Forest, Box 3659, Idaho Falls, Idaho 83401. (208) 523-1412.

The hike: Rainey Creek is the large broad-mouthed canyon a few miles north of Palisades Creek and due east of the town of Swan Valley. There is a road up Rainey Creek which ends a little over a mile below its two forks. Formerly this road extended all the way to the forks (as shown on the Thompson Peak USGS quadrangle), but it has been closed, converted to a trail, and a trailhead built near the mouth of Road Creek, a side-canyon.

A second trailhead is located at the top of this loop. Its access is a road leaving Idaho Highway 31 at Pine Creek Pass. The road leads down into the North Fork of Rainey Creek's headwaters, where it ends.

The trails are in generally good condition and easy to follow, but use of the lower trailhead involves two fords of Rainey Creek proper (a major undertaking before snowmelt ends in late June or early July). The trail crosses the forks with abandon, but one can hop across on the rocks by mid-August. Earlier, you may want to hike in tennis shoes. Dirt bikes are allowed on all these trails, and their use is heavy on the old road bed in Rainey Creek's main canyon and on the trail that connects the upper North with the upper South Fork. Motorized use is light in the two forks, however, because of rocky portions of the trail, tall forbs trailside (including stinging nettle) in mid-summer, and the necessity of riding through the rocky-bottomed creeks many times.

To reach the upper trailhead, take the well-signed, improved dirt road at Pine Creek Summit off of Idaho 31. Drive to its end in the bottom of the North Fork of Rainey Creek. The North Fork trailhead is very large with horse loading ramps, a latrine, and trail information signs.

For the trailhead in lower Rainey Creek, drive about a mile south of the town of Swan Valley on U.S. Highway 26. Turn left (to the east) at the LDS Church onto a signed, paved county road. From here it's about seven miles to the trailhead.

HIKE 81 *RAINEY CREEK LOOP*

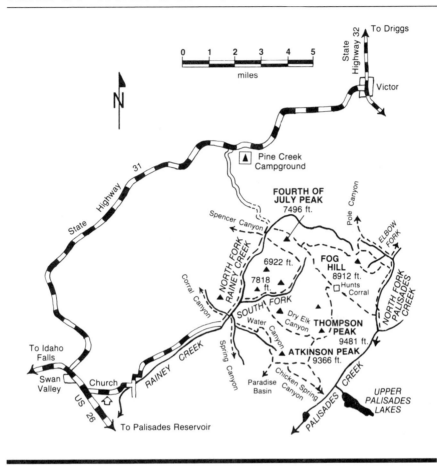

The road soon becomes gravel and leads into the obvious mouth of Rainey Creek Canyon. Drive to the end of the road. The trailhead is spacious with horse loading facilities. Unfortunately there is little shade.

The description here follows from the lower trailhead.

Follow the abandoned road bed as it runs against the north slope of Rainey Creek canyon. The mountain rises to your left, and springs gush out below the trail to form extensive beaver ponds amidst the willows of this broad, fertile bottom. After about a half-mile, you must ford Rainey Creek. Beyond this ford the old road narrows, forming more of a trail which leads through thick willows. In July 1987 I surprised a bear and her cub as I was jogging through, but by mid-summer you're much more likely to pass a herd of cows. A quarter mile further you pass Corral Canyon on your far left and soon come to the second ford. Just after wading here, you come to a gated, barb-wire fence. Please reclose the gate. From here the trail is level, and very easy all the way to the forks.

Just beyond Corral Canyon, you'll notice some burned timber high on the south slope of the canyon. This is the result of Spring Canyon Fire One and

Two in 1987 and 1988. The same general area burned two years in a row! This burn is barely visible from the loop trail, but the total area covered just above the creek is extensive.

There are numerous camping spots under the cottonwood trees at the forks. Hop across the North Fork and start up the South Fork Trail. It soon begins to climb moderately and the canyon abruptly narrows. Soon you emerge from forest cover into an open, scenic reach with cliffs, numerous rockslides, and many creek crossings. You soon come to Dry Elk Canyon. A trail heads up this heavily-burned canyon and to the South Rainey/Palisades Creek divide.

Once past Dry Elk, the canyon becomes less rocky, but the bottom remains largely free of trees. It slowly widens and eventually broadens into a relatively gentle headwaters area of mixed conifer, aspen, and small meadows.

As you reach this area, you come to a trail fork near the creek in an eroded area due to dirt bikes and use of the crossing as a sheep driveway. A sign here indicates it's 2.5 miles to the North Fork of Rainey Creek (to the left) and three miles to Hunt's Corral on the right. The trail to Hunt's Corral suffers from excessive use by dirt bikes and the mentioned sheep driveway. Although it's not readily apparent, another trail continues up the South Fork here. It's unsigned and not on the Forest Service or the USGS quadrangle. It climbs up a minor ridge to Fourth of July Peak. This is an alternative route to the North Fork trailhead.

The bench just above the creek to your right is an area with plenty of good camping sites. These are generally lacking further back down the South Fork.

Take the trail fork to the left and climb moderately 400 feet to a pass. The trail is easy to follow as it goes through aspen, conifer, and small meadows. At the summit there is an impressive view of a peak back down in the South Fork.

From the summit the trail drops downward in heavy timber as it descends 400 feet to a beaver pond area. Here the country opens up and you climb again—this time about 150 feet to the top of a secondary ridge. This portion of the trail has the best views of the entire trip. You see the rugged peaks of the divide between the two forks of Rainey from meadows and through open stands of quaking aspen. Once on the secondary ridge, the trail follows its top all the way down to the trailhead in the North Fork of Rainey Creek. As you approach the trailhead, the trail becomes very wide, the result of dirt bikes and many hikers on brief walks.

Walk to the downstream end of the trailhead to pick up the North Rainey Creek trail. It is almost level starting out through open willowy country. The trail begins to descend and the canyon bottom becomes lush with tall forbs and willow fields. In 1989 beaver had been busy building new ponds here.

Eventually you enter a scenic rockslide area similar to the one on the South Fork. The trail descends more steeply here, and at the bottom of the slide area, you find yourself in the deepest part of the canyon. This doesn't last, however, because you arrive at the place where the forks form Rainey Creek in about .75 mile.

Rainey Creek is a good place watch for moose. Elk and deer are common too. As mentioned, black bear are seen on occasion.

Idaho environmentalists propose the drainage as part of the Palisades Wilderness, and the Targhee National Forest is currently managing it as part of the Palisades Backcountry. Unlike Big Elk Creek and Palisades Creek, however, pressure from the timber and oil industry are a major obstacle to its permanent protection as wilderness.—*Ralph Maughan* □

HIKE 82 *INDIAN CREEK LOOP*

General description: A near loop hike with lots of opportunity for side trips and more extended excursions.

General location: Just inside the Wyoming line in the southern end of the Snake River Range 69 linear miles southeast of Idaho Falls.

Maps: Alpine, Ferry Peak, Mt. Baird, and Observation Peak (7.5') USGS quads.

Special attractions: Beautiful subalpine scenery, numerous wildflowers, wildlife.

Difficulty: Moderate.

Season: Mid-June to mid-October. (Be aware that Wyoming hunting season opens in early September.)

Information: Palisades Ranger District, Targhee National Forest, 3659 E. Ririe Highway, Idaho Falls, ID 83401; 208/523-1412.

The hike: Indian Creek is the southernmost of the Snake River Range's major canyons. Its two forks provide beautiful hiking areas. The South Fork completes the roster of Snake River Range canyons that drain into Idaho.

The South Fork trail takes you from aspen and fir forest to a beautiful subalpine cirque basin that holds two ponds, rolling wildflower meadows, wildlife, and lots of room for cross-country exploration and access to other trails. The North Fork trail follows a narrower canyon with spectacular rock walls and a beautiful waterfall into the basin at its head.

To approach Indian Creek, drive 73 miles southeast of Idaho Falls on U.S. Highway 26, passing through the town of Swan Valley and traveling alongside the Palisades Reservoir. (If you are approaching from the other direction, Indian Creek is seven miles north of Alpine, Wyoming.) As you near Indian Creek, swing down the canyon from a hill above the reservoir to a green, wide-mouthed canyon. Right in the middle of the canyon mouth, turn to the left off the highway. Follow a gravel road up the canyon through pastureland and meadows punctuated with clumps of aspen. After about two miles you'll come to a fork in the road. The left fork heads up the North Fork Indian Creek; the right fork leads to your destination. The road up the South Fork is good, but the North Fork road is poor.

The road up the South Fork ends 2.1 miles past the road junction. There is a bridge across the creek (and a horse corral) just before the stateline. The road drops to creek side and ends in a quarter-mile.

It's best to park in the stateline lot because the creek is eroding the section of the road beyond and there is nowhere to turn around at road's end.

The trail leads into the forest and comes to a creek crossing—the only crossing for quite a way up the canyon. It's an easy crossing in the summer, but in June the water level rises daily with snowmelt. (Bring wading shoes and be careful then.)

Above the crossing, the trail keeps to the north side of the creek, undulating but climbing gently and steadily through pine, cottonwood, aspen, and fir forest.

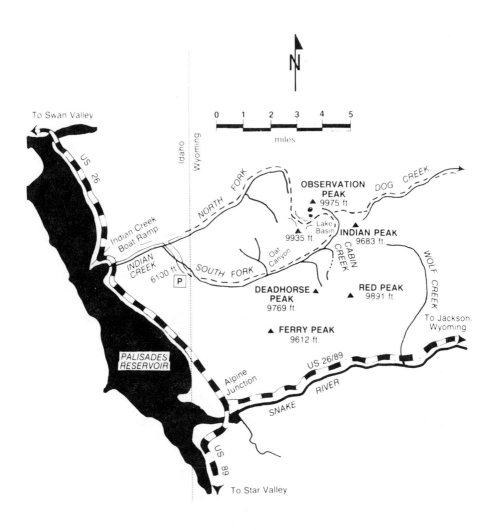

The trail crosses occasional rockslides and avalanche chutes. After about two miles, you'll reach the tributary of Oat Canyon where you'll find a perennial stream. The cliffs and talus slides of 9,612-foot Ferry Peak rise above the greenery to the south, providing your first good view of the mountains. From here the visuals improve quickly and steadily. Above Oat Canyon you are greeted with a long meadow established and maintained by the power of avalanches. Here you'll find a pleasant combination—hospitable camping with a good view. In early summer water thunders down from the avalanche-chisled side canyons.

Above the meadow the trail climbs steeply, about 600 feet in one mile, to another meadow, which is one-half mile long. The meadow lies between the tributary canyons of Deadhorse and Cabin Creeks, both of which contain faint trails inviting exploration.

At this meadow the South Fork assumes a subalpine aspect, an increasing openness framed by pointed stands of dark green alpine fir and Englemann spruce. After an easy crossing at the head of the meadow, you begin to climb again. After a 200-foot, quarter mile climb, you come to a hunting camp at the edge of a spruce and fir grove. Here one year on June 18 we encountered a tent-burying snow storm. Such storms are common in the Snake River Mountains in early June: snow flurries, hail, and maybe even an inch of two of snowfall as late as July 4.

From this grove at 8,000 feet, the trail continues its steep climb. After 1.25 miles you gain a thousand feet to intersect the trail from Dog Creek. Go to the left at this junction, following the now open, rolling countryside. A half mile brings you to Lake Basin, located slightly north of the trail. The trail to the North Fork of Indian Creek turns abruptly left in the meadow at the Forest Service marker and climbs the ridge into the next basin. The trail to Lake Basin continues north to encounter two ponds (perhaps the upper pond could be called a small lake). Both are set in cirques below 9,975-foot Observation Peak and its unnamed 9,800-foot associates.

The lower pond is fed by springs just to its north and northwest, A pretty brook runs out of the pond for a few yards and drops down a cave. Both ponds offer beautiful views and good camping. However, the springs of the upper pond may dry up by late August. Some years in late summer sheep are put out to graze in Lake Basin. Then the ambiance is quite different. By then, you may also encounter a stray band of trail machinists. By and large, however, the canyon is beautiful, wild, and remote. The wildflowers are splendid until mid to late July.

An extra day of hiking can be added by camping in Lake Basin and climbing Observation Peak. A "herd path" trail begins approximately 20 yards north of the upper pond outlet. The path is a long, straight traverse which skirts the top of the treeline and intersects a ridge trail at a flat spot east and below the summit of Observation Peak. There is a spectacular 360 degree panorama here—the Grand Tetons and Jackson to the north, the snow-capped Wind Rivers to the east, the Palisades Reservoir and Caribou Mountains southward, and the wilderness peaks of the Snake River Mountains to the northwest.

From Lake Basin you can complete the loop hike by following the trail over two ridges as it takes a roundabout route down into the North Fork Indian Creek. The trail crosses a short ridge out of Lake Basin through a series of switchbacks. At the top it begins a gradual descent into the next basin. Good views of the South Fork drainage and Snake River Mountains are provided. You cross an avalanche chute and meadow to a lake with several good campsites. Around the lake, the trail is indistinct, but it can be clearly seen climbing the second ridge to a 9,500 foot couloir. The trail up this ridge is deeply eroded and needs rebuilding.

At the pass are good views of Observation Peak and the surrounding Snake River Mountains as well as the North Fork drainage. From here it is approximately nine miles to the trailhead.

The trail drops into and crosses another basin to intersect with the Big Basin Trail. Be careful—at the junction the Big Basin trail turns left, indicated by a marker on a tree. The main trail continues straight ahead.

After a steep, downhill section, you encounter a horse camping area at 8,600 feet. Scattered sites are suitable for camping if the smell of horses is not objectionable. Water is readily available from small streams forming the upper waters of the North Fork.

Crossing a level plateau, you encounter a junction with the South Fork Elk Creek trail. Past this junction the trail begins a very steep descent of 1,000 feet down a series of switchbacks to the headwaters of the North Fork at 7,600 feet. The North Fork originates with two streams cascading down a headwall into a large, beautiful basin. This is an excellent rest area but finding good camping is difficult because of heavily vegetated, rocky and unlevel terrain.

The North Fork is a slightly narrower canyon that has considerably different features than the South Fork. The trail begins a gradual descent through lush meadows of forbs which sometimes obscure the trail and makes walking difficult. Streams from numerous side canyons feed the North Fork and hiking is muddy at times.

Just before reaching Garden Canyon, the trail climbs to a narrow ledge 50 feet above the stream. Looking down instills uncertainty and most hikers tend "to lean into the mountain" while covering this section of the trail. At the junction with the Garden Creek Trail, the North Fork trail is about 100 feet above the stream and you will be greeted with spectacular views of rock formations towering above the stream bed. You may have to ford Garden Creek.

A trail marker indicates it is four miles to Lake Basin. At Garden Canyon it is another 4.5 miles to the North Fork trailhead.

Garden Canyon is a lovely, lush side canyon, kept partially free of trees by avalanches. A number of small waterfalls and cascades stream from its sides. There is a camping spot in its mouth.

The last section of trail, through undulating terrain, is easy. You cross the North Fork approximately one-half mile before the trailhead and recross it again immediately before reaching the your destination. The crossings can cause some difficultly until July, but if the going is too difficult, you can avoid them by keeping to the north side and bushwhacking the half mile to the trailhead.—*Ralph and Jackie Maughan and Keith Kempski* □

HIKE 83 *WATERFALLS CANYON TRAIL*

General description: A moist and scenic tributary canyon to Palisades Creek that contains a large lake.

General location: 49 miles southeast of Idaho Falls; about 66 miles northeast of Pocatello.

Maps: Palisades Peak and Thompson Peak (7.5') USGS quads.

Special attractions: Beautiful springs, a large, fertile lake dammed by a landslide; and a beautiful waterfall in the top of the canyon.

Difficulty: Easy to the end of the lake. Moderate above the lake due to steepness and a somewhat faint trail.

Season: Late June to early October.

Information: Palisades Ranger District, Targhee National Forest, 3659 E. Ririe Highway, Idaho Falls, ID 83401; (208) 523-1412.

The hike: For directions to the trailhead, see the Palisades Creek hike description. Follow that hike description to Lower Palisades Lake. Pass Lower Palisades Lake and continue on the trail until you come to a bridge over Palisades Creek.   The faint trail on the other side of the creek at the crossing goes on up Palisades Creek. You should take the obvious trail that leads into the timber and uphill. We saw a big bull moose in the pond at the base of the hill.

A giant landslide fell off the mountain ages ago, filling the mouth of Waterfalls Canyon. The trail switchbacks easily up this slide to the impounded lake, a 375-foot climb. Halfway to the lake, the lake's waters emerge from the slide as a beautiful, large spring that cascades down into the forest toward Palisades Creek. This spring is a major reason why Palisades Creek runs high year-round.

As you approach the lake, notice the bulges of earth in the tops of the avalanche runs in the mountains surrounding the lake. The earth remains unstable in this area.

The lake itself is deep and cool, with numerous coves. Abundant cutthroat trout live in the fertile waters that filter down from the limestone and phosphate rock of the mountains. As you walk along the east shore of the lake, the trail stays about 75 feet above the lake. The mountain slope plunges steeply into the lake's water.

To find a campsite at the lake, either follow the spur trail that leads along the landslide dam where you first see the lake, or walk to the lake's inlet. At the inlet area, two stream flow into the lake. Camp on the hill between the two streams.

Here at the inlet at the south end of the lake, the trail passes an old sod-roofed cabin, built in 1915, that was used for about a decade by a trapper.

One-quarter mile above the lake's inlet, you come to the well-marked Vacation Canyon junction. Keep to the right, cross the creek, and continue up Waterfalls Canyon.

The upper part of Waterfalls Canyon was left hanging above the lake by a glacier. You'll climb a steep 500 feet into the upper canyon. At the top of our climb in early July, we found the trail disappeared into a deep snow-melt pond. Only a month later, the pond had vanished to be replaced by a flowery meadow.

The trail climbs gradually now, wandering through patches of forest and meadow. In early summer, water still runs in the creek; at times, the creekbed and the trail are one and the same. As you near the end of the canyon, a spectacular cascade plunges 920 feet down the east wall of the canyon. Its waters flow into a pond. Early in the season, a second waterfall adorns the opposite canyon wall.

Beyond the falls, the trail leaves the broad canyon bottom and climbs about 1,200 feet to a large open basin just below timberline. You are near the highest peaks of this mountain range here. They surround the basin with their rugged cliffsides.

At 5.5 miles from the trail's beginning, you'll reach the junction with the Little Elk-Sheep Creek Trail. The Little Elk Fork of the trail continues southward, passing over into Little Elk Creek on a 9,200-foot-high divide. (For more information, see the Little Elk Creek hike.) At this divide, another trail leaves to the east, snaking along the top of Waterfalls Canyon. It passes right over an unnamed 9,630-foot peak and forks into either Dry Canyon or Austin Canyon. The Dry Canyon route will take you back to Upper Palisades Lake, completing a scenic loop.

The Sheep Creek fork heads westward. You can climb to a high divide at 9,600 feet and pass just south of an unnamed peak that is just over 9,900 feet high. Here you gain a sublime view of the Tetons and all of the other nearby mountains. You can elect to go south, descending into Sheep Creek, or take the trail that goes to the northwest, dropping into Lake Canyon. The latter choice provides a grand loop that takes you down to Lower Palisades Lake.

Lake Canyon's trail is faint and a bit overgrown as it descends from the basin just below the high divide. It runs through wet meadow and forest that is kept fairly open by winter's avalanches. In the mid-reaches of Lake Canyon rise sheer cliffs. It's common to see mountain goats on these.

No permanent stream runs through Lake Canyon, but there are snowmelt streams in the cliff-walled basin near the high divide. They run until mid-July in average snow years.

The best season for this hike is probably late July, when the flowers are in full bloom. You'll find camp spots abundant in upper Waterfalls Canyon and upper Lake Canyon. Trail traffic is light once you are past Upper Palisades Lake.—*Ralph Maughan* □

Note: Lightning strikes on Labor Day 1994 caused a large forest fire adjacent to Upper Palisades Lake. The Palisades Lake fire burned 2,000 acres on the northeast and east sides of the lake.

Caribou Mountains

Overview

The Caribou Mountains are a relatively unknown range in the Overthrust Belt of Eastern Idaho. They parallel the Big Hole, Snake River, and Salt River mountains which lie across the valley to their east.

Topography is rather unique—numerous ridges interspersed with small, high elevation stream valleys.

There are three fairly large roadless areas in these mountains. On the west side of Palisades Reservoir and Swan Valley, the Bear Creek roadless area is over 100,000 acres (about 160 square miles).

To the south between the McCoy Creek road on its north (FS #087) and the Tincup Highway (Idaho Highway 34), lies the Caribou Roadless Area. Just south of the Tincup Highway is the Stump Creek Roadless Area. Both Caribou and Stump creeks are over 80,000 acres in size.

All three are notable for abundant elk herds. Deer and moose are common as well. These mountains are also especially notable for having unstable slopes. Landslides and earthflows are commonplace, a major reason why you may still enjoy their wild character. Roads are largely not feasible.

Trails are abundant, but often not well maintained. Most of the Caribou, but not the Bear Creek or Stump Creek, Roadless Area is closed to dirt bikes and ATVs in the summertime.

Within the Caribou Roadless Area, a large forest fire, The Trail Creek Fire, burned in the summer of 1988, particularly near the head of Jackknife Creek. A fire was overdue in this country, and, after this renewal, the landscape is rapidly regenerating. It appears the only long-lasting damage will be the bulldozer lines used to fight the fire.

HIKE 84 *BEAR CREEK*

General description: A five-mile day hike along a popular fishing stream.
General location: 52 road miles southeast of Idaho Falls of the west side of Palisades Reservoir.
Maps: Palisades Dam, Red Ridge, and Commissary Ridge (7.5') USGS quads.
Special attractions: Easy access to an area which is in one of the major outdoor recreational centers in southeastern Idaho.
Difficulty: Moderately easy.
Season: Early June to late October.
Information: Palisades Ranger District, Targhee National Forest; 3659 E. Ririe Highway, Idaho Falls, ID 83401; (208) 523-1412.

The hike: Evidently most of the hikers who visit Bear Creek are there to enjoy its excellent fishery. Many elk hunters walk the canyon and ply the ridges in season. The mountains surrounding the Palisades Reservoir and the reservoir itself, of course, are extremely popular recreation sites.

The drive from Idaho Falls to the Palisades Reservoir over U.S. Highway 26 is most scenic once past 20 some miles of farmland, beyond which you meet and follow the Snake River. Turn off Highway 26 at the north end of the reservoir at the marked Palisades Dam road, which leads over the dam itself. Once over the dam, the road is gravel for the next 7.2 miles to the trailhead. There are an abundance of other roads of varying quality that leave the access road, including the Elk Creek-McCoy Creek road, but the route to Bear Creek is adequately marked, as is the trailhead.

The trout in Bear Creek are Snake River cutthroat, which are fast becoming rare throughout the upper Snake River drainage. This is due to overharvesting

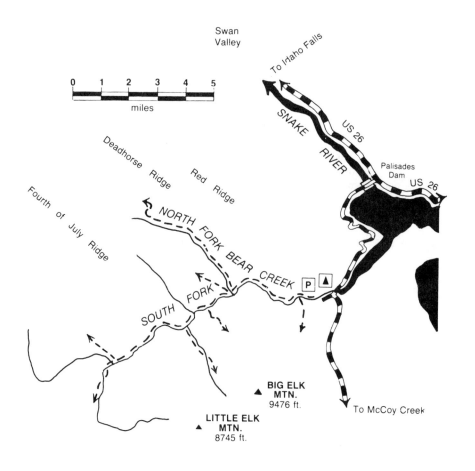

and hybridization with the introduced Henrys Lake cutthroat.

The mountains drained by the creek are medium sized by southeast Idaho standards. The highest peak drained by Bear Creek is 9,476-foot Big Elk Mountain. The trail up this stream valley is gentle, rising only a thousand feet from the trailhead to the end of South Fork, Bear Creek's longest tributary.

After about a half-mile walk through rather dense riparian underbrush, the trail leads you into an open valley of mostly grasses and sagebrush. Occasionally the trail forks, usually with one path leading to the creek and the others heading up the various side-canyons.

Hikers are cautioned that the temptation to disregard Forest Service trail markers is great, as most of the trail signs seem to point uphill. However, the low route is no easier than the high one, and disregarding the signs will ultimately mean more work—such as fording the creek or walking back to

Down Jensen Creek toward Black Mountain, Caribou Mountains. Ralph Maughan photo.

the trail. In the spring of the year, or even in early summer, the three- to five-meter-wide creek may be a formidable obstacle.

In late summer or early fall, if the hiker doesn't mind wading knee-deep, the way can be shortened considerably by fording, thus avoiding the steep bypasses that often widely skirt the valley floor. There are at least six such crossings in the five or so miles from the trailhead to the North Fork of the Bear Creek junction. One can save probably .75 mile and perhaps as much as an hour's walking time by fording the creek.

While the south wall of the valley is forested mostly by subalpine fir and Douglas fir, the north side generally remains open. The open side, where the trail is, is thinly wooded with a few aspen, Utah juniper, and even an occasional cottonwood at the lower elevations.

The valley floor's vegetation cover varies from dense eutrophic beaver ponds to open sagebrush flats. Most of the floor is open enough to easily walk across, except where beaver ponds inundate and thick covers of willow and alder have developed.

Upstream of the junction with the North Fork, the valley which is often called the South Fork from this point, narrows somewhat to become more of a canyon. Here the streambed dominates the terrain and alternates from gravelly bars to grassy flats of eutrophied beaver ponds. Most of the camping and fishing takes place above the North Fork junction.

There are several side trails branching off from Bear Creek. The more important of these are Muddy Creek, South Fork of Falls Creek Road Trail, and the North Fork of Bear Creek. The North Fork trail is a good one, worth a walk up it at least part of the way. All of these trail junctions are marked by Forest Service signs indicating the mileage.—*George Wentzel* □

HIKE 85 TINCUP CREEK

General description: A three mile, day hike to the summit of Tincup Mountain, or a two- to three-day trip to the headwaters of Tincup and Jacknife Creeks.
General location: 11 miles east of Wayan, Idaho.
Maps: Tincup Mountain, Caribou Mountain, Lanes Creek (7.5') USGS quads.
Special attractions: Count on solitude in this sanctuary for elk, deer, and moose.
Difficulty: Easy to Tincup Mountain, moderate to the headwaters of Tincup and Jackknife Creeks.
Season: Early June through October.
Information: Soda Springs Ranger District, Caribou National Forest, 421 W. 2nd So., Cedar View Plaza, Soda Springs, Idaho 83276; (208) 547-4356.

The hike: The Caribou Mountains are characterized by colorful gray and red clay soils which make for a "painted forest", but these same soils slump-out and erode naturally at a high rate. Road building is devastating, causing "blowouts" both above and below a roadcut.

These beautiful, fragile mountains contain the second highest concentration of elk in the state of Idaho for size of land mass. Large populations of moose and mule deer also inhabit the area. The entire range is in need of wilderness designation to protect its fragile watershed and outstanding wildlife habitat and populations (see the Caribou Mountains overview)

This country, little known except for a few hunters and Forest Service personnel, is accessed via Idaho Highway 34 in Tincup Creek Canyon. From Soda Springs, Idaho, drive north on Idaho Highway 34 to Wayan. Tourist information about the marshy Grays Lake National Wildlife Refuge and the Caribou Mountains can be obtained at Wayan. From Wayan continue east on Highway 34 for about 11 miles; this will put you in Tincup Creek Canyon.

There are three good access trails on the north side of Highway 34 which lead up to the Tincup Mountain trail. Watch for Rich Creek, Bear Creek, and Corral Creek signs on the north side of the highway.

The Rich Creek Trail drops down into Tincup Creek and is the trail to take if you want to spend a day fishing on a beautiful mountain stream. If you prefer a ridgeline hike, you'll want to take the Bear or Corral Creek trails which lead to the summit of Tincup Mountain.

The Tincup Mountain Trail proceeds north onto the Jacknife-Tincup drainage divide ridge. This ridge route provides a good overview of the Tincup-Jacknife country and the Caribou Mountains off to the north. A pleasant day hike to the summit of Tincup Mountain (8,184 feet) will provide a good overview of the southern end of the Caribou Mountains, including Stump Creek, to the south. This is prime elk, moose, and deer habitat, so keep your eyes open for these magnificent animals.

If you want to make your hike into a backpack, continue north on the Tincup Mountain Trail.

Beyond the north slopes of Tincup Mountain you will walk along a narrow, precipitous ridgeline. Here the West Fork of Jacknife Creek breaks off abruptly into a deep, rugged canyon below. Further north lies the Jacknife-Tincup divide ridge. It has a bright green color and stands out from the

HIKE 85 *TINCUP CREEK*

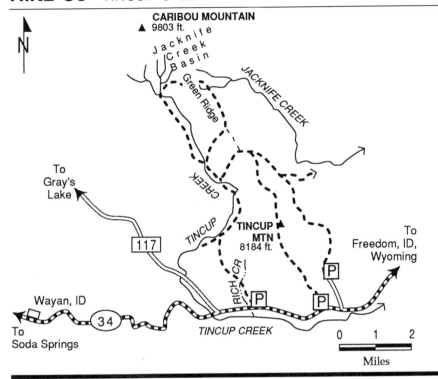

surrounding slopes. I have long called it "Green Ridge". As you walk along Green Ridge you will have the south slopes of Caribou Mountain as your guiding landmark. Eventually, you'll arrive at the beautiful subalpine meadows encompassing the headwaters of Jacknife and Tincup Creeks, just below the highline ridge on the south slope of Caribou Mountain. Choose a stand of subalpine fir or quaking aspen to camp under, out of the meadows.

On the way out you can either backtrack the way you came, or loop back out along the Tincup Creek trail, which parallels this willow-lined creek until it breaks away and then turns back to the Rich Creek trail, and down to Highway 34. Note that continuation down Tincup Creek beyond where the Rich Creek trail leaves can be tough going.—*Mike Panting* □

HIKE 86 *PINE CREEK—PALISADES RESERVOIR LOOP*

General description: An overnighter in one of Idaho's best and least known wildlife areas.
General location: 52 miles southeast of Idaho Falls on the west side of the Palisades Reservoir.
Maps: Palisades Dam (7.5') USGS quad.

Special attractions: Easy access to a backcountry area with outstanding bird and wildlife viewing opportunities.

Difficulty: Moderately difficult due to the faint trail from Van Creek to the Bear Creek inlet, a total climb of 1,800 feet and descents of 2,400 feet.

Season: June (when Bear Creek can be forded) to late October.

Information: Palisades Ranger District; Targhee National Forest, 3659 E. Ririe Highway, Idaho Falls, Idaho 83401. (208) 523-1412.

The hike: This is a hike in splendid big game country. Part of the hike is along the shore of man-made, but beautiful, Palisades Reservoir. The Caribou Mountains just west of the reservoir, including this hike are part of the Poker Peak roadless area, which is being recommended for wilderness even by Idaho's anti-wilderness politicians.

The hike provides a good opportunity to see elk and moose as well as birdwatching. The presence of so much game also makes for many game trails that are sometimes confusing to the hiker.

The northwest unit of the Caribou National Forest is administered by the Targhee National Forest. Except for the area described in this hike, it is open (although contested) to trail bikes and other motorized travel. An occasional trail biker will use the Pine Creek trail to complete a loop with the Poker Peak trail. However, due to lack of trail maintenance, equestrians use only the Pine Creek and Poker Peak trails.

For directions to the trailhead, see the Bear Creek hike, but as you near the Bear Creek trailhead, take the road that turns left (south) across Bear Creek and becomes the Elk Creek Road. The Pine Creek trailhead is approximately one half mile down the Elk Creek Road on the left. Parking is at the trailhead or the horse trailer parking area back at the bridge.

Before starting the loop from Pine Creek, it's best to check the water level of Bear Creek; the complete loop includes fording this stream at the end of the hike near where it runs into Palisades Reservoir. Here Bear Creek is traveled by great blue herons, flocks of ducks, and other birds which find homes in this marsh and riparian area.

The trail starts with a gentle climb along Pine Creek for a mile. Once across, the ascent becomes steeper with frequent switchbacks. Water is not available again until going down the Landslide Creek Trail. The climb presents excellent views of the Caribou Range to the west.

After climbing to meet the ridge on the right, 1400 feet above the trailhead, you cross a wide open sagebrush pass for approximately a quarter mile. About two miles from the trailhead, the Poker Peak and Landslide Creek trails intersect the Pine Creek Trail at the end of the pass. Palisades Reservoir is another 2.5 miles down the Landslide Creek Trail.

The Landslide Creek Trail is a moderate descent of 1900 feet through dense wooded areas and meadows. In 1989, the trail had not been cleared of downfall, slowing descent and requiring alertness to trail markings. Take care to locate blaze markings on trees while crossing meadows which make sections of the trail difficult to find.

The descent offers frequent views of the reservoir and Blowout Canyon of the Snake River Mountains to the east.

About one mile beyond the Poker Peak/Pine Creek trail junction is a small stream crossing. This is the first easily accessible water since the Pine Creek

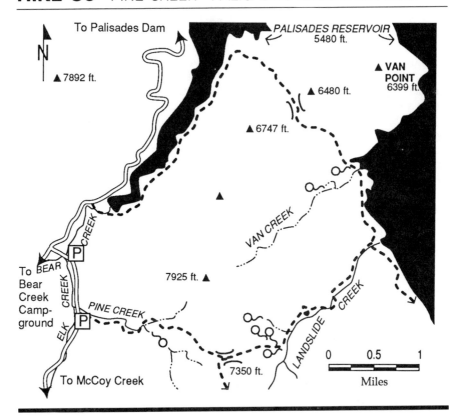

crossing. (Before it intersects with this stream, the trail runs parallel to another stream for a half mile. This stream is below and in heavy brush.) Another half-mile down, the trail skirts a mountain pond. On the topo map it appears to be a likely camping spot. However, it's a mud hole. Take care to go around the pond to the outlet to pick up the trail. Otherwise, you'll wander in a maze of game paths.

Before reaching the Palisades Reservoir, the trail levels off through a thick meadow area and skirts a series of old beaver dams across Landslide Creek.

Nice camping, complete with a fire pit and outhouse, is available at the Palisades Reservoir. While the shoreline area is not exactly a wilderness retreat, there is a minimum of human intrusion and an abundance of wildlife—bald eagles, great blue herons, pelicans, moose, elk. The rushing waters of Landslide Creek block out the noise from across the reservoir and only an occasional motorboat disturbs the tranquility.

At the reservoir, a shoreline trail intersects the Landslide Creek Trail. Follow the shoreline trail north toward Van Point. The trail is flat and far enough from the reservoir that it's not visible. As you approach Van Creek, the trail disappears into a maze of paths—some made by animals, others by boaters.

(From Van Creek to the Bear Creek inlet, the trail is poorly marked. As on the Landslide Creek Trail, take care to read the topo map, locate tree blazes, and keep a sharp eye for the meandering trail in meadow areas.)

Crossing the Van Creek inlet, the shoreline trail climbs a ridge to the northeast of the creek. From here, it begins a 400 foot ascent through a long meadow to a saddle, with Van Creek to the left as you climb.

After crossing the saddle, the trail descends toward the Palisades Dam. After a half-mile, it veers to the left (west) to cross a wooded ridge and descends about 100 feet above the water on a steep slope. (The Bear Creek inlet is a favorite spot for boaters. It is not unusual to pass anchored boaters drinking beer and lounging in the sun while you hike toward the trailhead.)

The trail is not well-marked where it veers west. Game trails continue straight and parallel a stream to the shore of the Palisades Reservoir. The shore offers good camping when water levels are low. It's possible to return to the shoreline trail by following the shore and bushwhacking up the steep slope as the shore becomes an impassable cliff.

After three miles, the trail passes the Bear Creek Campground across the bay. Stay high on the hill and continue for another half mile. The trail then drops down to the water and you will have to ford Bear Creek. From this point, the Pine Creek trailhead is one mile south on the dirt road.—*Keith J. Kempski* □

Bannock Range

Overview

This long, but discontinuous, mountain chain begins at Pocatello and runs southward to Utah, ending on the west side of Cache Valley. The Bannock is mostly a low ridge, but it boasts a number of exceptions—at Scout Mountain, at Elkhorn Peak, and at Oxford Peak. Small roadless areas partially surround these uplifts, and from the summits you gain fine views of the country where the Middle Rockies merge into the Great Basin country of Nevada and northwestern Utah.

Geologically speaking, the Bannock Range is among the most complex of the many minor ranges of the Idaho/Wyoming border.

The West Fork of Mink Creek Roadless Area is perhaps the best of the wild pockets in this range. It is easily accessible from Pocatello, and it occupies, oddly enough, one of the lower secitons of the Bannock. These mountains are public land, generally administered by the Caribou National Forest.

HIKE 87 OXFORD PEAK

General description: A two-day tripwhich puts you in line for several small peaks, a cross-country scramble up Oxford Peak, and a visit to an old mine site.
General location: About 42 miles southeast of Pocatello near Malad Summit.
Maps: Downey West, Malad Summit, and Oxford (7.5′) USGS quads.

Special attractions: An area lightly used by humans that is close to major population concentrations.
Difficulty: Moderate.
Season: June to October.
Information: Malad Ranger District, Caribou National Forest, Box 142, Malad, Idaho 83252; (208) 766-4743.

The hike: This portion of the small, long, narrow, Bannock Range is not heavily used for recreation. However, cattle are grazed in the area, and you may wish to check with the Forest Service about such grazing before setting a date for your hike. The area is open to off-road vehicles, but they don't use it extensively.

This description will not tell you how to reach the summit of Oxford Peak which dominates the vicinity; instead, this hike will take you some 5.25 miles to Gooseberry Creek and an old mine site.

Travel south of Pocatello on Interstate 15. It is about 31 miles to the exit to U.S. Highway 91 and the town of Downey. Do not take the left turn off Highway 91 into the Downey business district. As you leave the Downey townsite, take a right onto paved U.S. 191. This road goes back toward the interstate and Malad Summit. (If you were to follow it to its end, which you won't, you would skirt to the west of the very mountains you wish to visit). After about two miles there is a bend to the right, a gravel pit on the right, and you cross Marsh Creek. Just after you cross Marsh Creek, take a left onto the Aspen Creek Road. It leads due south. Stay on the main road, ignoring side roads to the left and right. After about two miles you'll come to a fork. Take the right fork. This is the Cherry Creek Road; the other is the Aspen Creek Road. From here it's about 5.75 miles to the Cherry Creek Campground. Again, do not take any side roads, but follow the main road, which remains in good condition throughout.

About two miles before you reach the campground, you will enter the Caribou National Forest. Since it is public land, there is not problem with access to the campground or trailhead. The road ends in a fork. The right fork crosses the creek to end at the campground. The left fork turns into a jeep track leading up the left fork of Cherry Creek. Take the left fork, continuing for about another one-quarter mile. To your right (south) leaves the Middle Fork of Cherry Creek and trails that lead to it and to Mine Creek. Don't take these trails; instead, take the one straight ahead going east up the Left Fork of Cherry Creek.

Be careful to treat drinking water along this route, as there are beaver ponds all along the way. The ponds are exceptionally scenic, however, along with the aspens and evergreens, especially in the later afternoon sun. There are only a few campsites between the trailhead and the saddle, which is about three miles from the trailhead.

The time of season you take this hike will determine when you'll run out of water since there are only a couple of annual sidestreams coming in from the southslopes of the canyon. Have some drinking water in your pack when you reach the saddle, especially if you plan to stay around for the view, or to sleep on top of one of the hills.

It is a steady 1,200-foot climb to the saddle at 7,200 feet. At the saddle you

HIKE 87 OXFORD PEAK

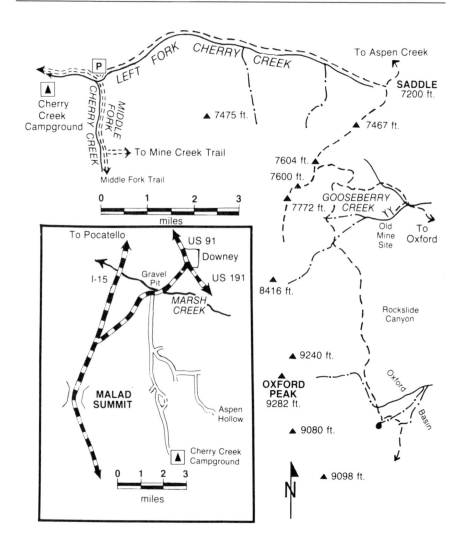

look over into Cache Valley to the east. The trail to the left (north) takes you back down towards Downey. If you follow the right fork (south) you'll bump over four small unnamed peaks, (7467, 7,604, 7,600, and 7,772 feet). To the west, Elkhorn Peak provides a beautiful relief for the sun setting behind it.

Continuing your journey from the first knoll, it is about half a mile to the second knoll (7,604 feet). There is a side-trail at the top which takes off to the right (southwest). If you keep on the main trail, just as you begin to descend the knoll, you'll come to another side-trail on the left (east) that leads to

Gooseberry Creek and beyond to Oxford Basin.

To get to Gooseberry Creek, drop down about a thousand feet on a winding trail about a mile long. In the first quarter-mile you'll come to a fork. Take the left fork to drop into Gooseberry Creek. Another quarter-mile and you'll come to a crossing of a fork of Gooseberry Creek. Although shown as a perennial on the USGS map, this fork was dry in September. Meander down following the creek bed until it joins with another fork of Gooseberry Creek. Here the trail splits, with one branch leading to the right for maybe .2 mile to the mine site. It you follow this trail a little over a half-mile, you'll come to a dirt road that goes three miles to town of Oxford.

There are a few old buildings at the mine site. I was happy to find a creek running through here in September. (Bring extra fuel to boil water because of the cattle in the area).

To get to Oxford Basin, you start from the second knoll, taking the same fork as you would to get to Gooseberry Creek. However, at the next fork, go right instead of left. You'll gain about 200 feet in elevation as you double back up the mountain a bit to cross, in about a quarter-mile. Gooseberry Creek, which begins as a spring up in the hills on your right. You will have noticed a low ridge in the distance to your left on which Oxford, at 9,282 feet, is the highest point. Oxford Basin is to the east of that ridge. This basin contains a small lake at 7,043 feet. The lake drains to the east. Beyond the lake the map shows the trail continuing for at least another eight miles in various directions, none of which come out at the Cherry Creek Trailhead.—*Karen Swafford.* ☐

HIKE 88 *WEST FORK OF MINK CREEK*

General description: A pretty six-mile round trip hike, very suitable for families; or an eight-mile point-to-point hike ending at the Gibson Jack Creek trailhead.

General location: A few miles south of Pocatello in the northern end of the Bannock Range.

Maps: Clifton Creek, Pocatello South (7.5') USGS quads.

Special attractions: Wildflowers from mid-May to mid-June; rare ungrazed range and forest land which is closed to all motorized vehicles.

Difficulty: Easy to the beaver ponds. Moderately easy to Gibson Jack Creek.

Season: Mid-April to mid-November.

Information: Pocatello Ranger District, Caribou National Forest, Federal Bldg.; Pocatello, Idaho; (208) 236-7500.

The hike: The West Fork of Mink Creek area presents a long and successful history of environmental restoration. The Bannock Mountains were overgrazed long ago, but grazing in the West Fork of Mink and nearby Gibson Jack Creek ceased in the early 1900s when these canyons were closed to the grazing of domestic livestock in order to protect Pocatello's municipal water supply.

For over a half century after the livestock closure, however, drainage from a muddy wagon, and later, a jeep track was allowed to fester into the city

HIKE 88   *WEST FORK, MINK CREEK*

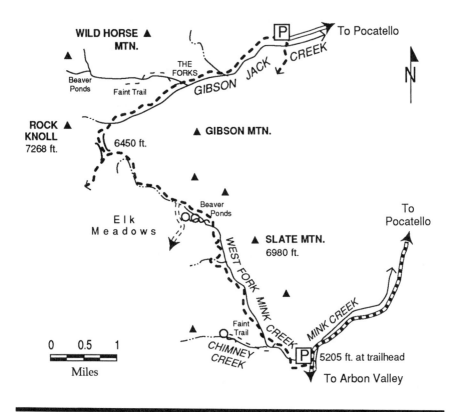

water. In the early 1970s this pollution of the city's water was finally stopped when the Caribou National Forest closed the area to four-wheel drive vehicles. Still, the use of trail motorcycles and all-terrain vehicles was permitted to continue until the late 1970s when strong pressure from environmentalists overcame Forest Service resistance. The West Mink Trail was closed to all forms of motorized recreation.

The trail is very popular today as the only trail of length in the area for nonmotorized uses. It is also shady right from the trailhead, well-maintained, and close to Pocatello.

Drive southward from the center of downtown Pocatello on South Arthur street until it becomes the Bannock Highway. Follow this road for about eight miles to the national forest boundary. You will pass subdivisions, orchards and a couple of country clubs, but the buildings cease at the forest boundary to be replaced by low, brushy mountains with patches of aspen and fir with thick vegetation in the bottom of Mink Creek canyon—typical of the highlands of southeast Idaho.

The paved road winds up Mink Creek. Ignore the paved road to the left (to the East Fork of Mink Creek, Justice Park, and Scout Mountain) that leaves about a mile past the forest boundary. Continue until you are 3.2 miles past the forest boundary. Turn right just past a small greenstone cliff on the right side of the road and the Pocatello City water intake structure in the stream on the left. Park here at the spacious West Fork trailhead or follow the dirt jog .10 mile to another parking place next to gate which marks the trail's start.

This good trail, no longer recognizable as an old jeep trail, leads directly up the canyon, mostly in the shade, climbing moderately past willow, quaking aspen, river birch, chokecherry trees, and beaver ponds. A few large old growth Douglas fir tower over the low-growing deciduous forest.

After rising 200 feet in about a half-mile and crossing the creek once over a culvert, the trail passes a clearing on the left. A side trail descends to the clearing. This is a common destination for those on a stroll. The side trail crosses the clearing and the creek and climbs up a thickly vegetated side canyon (Chimney Creek). In the 1960s, this was a road, but now it is an overgrown faint trail. You can follow it for a half-mile alongside a spring-fed brook that bubbles between numerous beaver ponds. The trail ends at a cool spring covered by a small structure built to protect the water's purity.

The main trail continues up the West Fork Canyon. An open slope of sagebrush (and in late May many wildflowers) rises steeply to the right and a more gentle, forested slope is on the left.

You cross the creek on a deteriorating bridge and the trailside is enveloped in forest. In about a half mile you enter a Research Natural Area. This protected area extends from the West Fork of Mink Creek over the top of Slate Mountain and down into Gibson Jack Creek. Ungrazed land such as this is such a rarity in southeast Idaho as to be of scientific importance, hence the designated natural area. The tall flower stalks you find here in August cannot be found in nearby drainages. Dust and noxious weeds are commonplace instead.

Finally after about three miles and an elevation gain of 900 feet, the grade lessens and you arrive at the beaver ponds. These are at the headwaters of the West Fork. Their number, structure, and size varies from year-to-year, although in 1989 I saw more than at any time since I've been visiting the area (first in 1972). In the last several years, visitors have occasionally seen moose at the beaver ponds. Moose are colonizing the highlands of southeast Idaho and northern Utah. The ungrazed ponds area is excellent habitat.

Continuing to the top of the ponds you find a number of small structures originally built to protect Pocatello's water at its spring source (the water was piped directed from the springs, but now is collected and treated at the bottom of the West Fork canyon).

Soon you come to a fence, gate and a primitive road. Beyond lies cow and off-road vehicle country. You'll be impressed by the difference. You can follow the road up the hill to the left to Elk Meadows—a place of tall, virgin Douglas-fir; aspen; and small meadows—unfortunately also of too many cows after about June 20. There has been some discussion of changing grazing schedules to keep cows out until late July. So perhaps by 1992 or so, Elk Meadows will be pleasant well into the Summer.

The undulating topography and forest at Elk Meadows screen views of surrounding mountains and valleys, and every year a few people get lost briefly in this small area. Carry a map and a compass hgere is you do any cross country hiking.

If you continue straight up the "road" (which is actually a broad trail) instead of climbing to Elk Meadows, you climb gently up the now broad, shallow, streamless, but pleasant canyon, for about a mile until you come to a signed trail junction indicating Gibson Jack Creek to the right. You quickly cross over a wooden cattle guard and fence and begin the drop into Givson Jack Creek Canyon.

Once again you are in an area closed to grazing. The trail descends through lush meadow with aspen and some large Douglas-fir. Here the flowering forbs often stand six-feet tall in mid-summer. You cross a creek several times, but it is usually dry by late summer.

Soon the trail begins to contour down an open dry hillside. Below the trail in the canyon bottom, however, you view a pretty and moist area along the creek. There are many beaver ponds, and the opposite side of the canyon has a heavy stand of Douglas-fir.

Before long you come to a bridge over the creek. This marks the "forks." A sign "no motorized vehicles" indicates a vhicle closure up the fork to your left. This is a shady canyon with a faint, unmaintained trail.

Continue down Gibson Jack Creek. The excellent trail eventually moves away from the riparian zone into rangeland with views of the Portnef and Pocatello Mountains in the distance to the east. This rangeland is beautiful in late May and June, but hot and dry later. You soon come to the trailhead where there is room for four or five vehicles.

To reach the Gibson Jack Creek trailhead follow the directions for the West Mink onto the Bannock Highway, but turn onto the Gibson Jack road 4.7 miles south of the center of Pocatello, and directly opposite the Juniper Hills Country Club. It is 2.2 miles from the highway to the trailhead.

To protect the purity of Pocatello's water, overnight camping and dogs are not allowed in the muicpat watershed area of the West Fork and Gibson Jack Creeks.

On weekends and in the late summer afternoons, you'll find the West Mink Creek trail busy with hikers, horses, or those pedaling mountain bikes. It's popularity is such that the USDA Forest Service is experimenting with alternate day use by mountain bikes one day and hikers/equestrians the other day. Be sure to check on the day before your drive to the trailhead. In the winter, the West Fork is a popular cross country ski trail of intermediate difficulty.

Motorcycles were finally removed from the Gibson Jack Trail in 1993. An alternative route was developed for their use. This Gibson Jack Trail is very popular in May and June before the temperatures turn hot. Hikers admire the late spring wildflowers made possible by the exclusion of livestock grazing.—*Ralph Maughan* □

Albion Mountains

Overview

South of the Snake River plain begins the Great Basin, most of which is in Nevada and Western Utah. The Great Basin consists of many long, but narrow, north/south trending ranges separated by broad, usually arid, valleys. The streams a rising in the mountains usually have no drainage to the ocean (although this is not the case in Idaho).

The Albion Range is just southeast of the farming town of Burley. It's the highest mountain range south of the Snake River, culminating at 10,339 foot Cache Peak. The other Great Basin mountains of southern Idaho are the Jim Sage, Cottrell, Black Pine, Sublett, Deep Creek, Bannock and Portneuf (although perhaps the latter two could also be considered part of the Middle Rockies). Hiking trails are few in these areas but the open aspect of many slopes makes cross country hiking feasible.

The heights of the Albion Mountains possess a small roadless area, and which Idaho conservationists are promoting for a Cache Peak Wilderness, and several beautiful sub-alpine lakes.

At the southern end of the range, the soft Cassia granite has been exposed to the elements and eroded into numerous oddly-shaped monoliths domes, pinnacles, huge boulders. This area, called the Silent City of Rocks, was recently turned into a national reserve by Congress. This gives the area protection from vandalism and is promoting the development of hiking trails, sanitation facilities, camping and picnicking facilities.

The Silent City of Rocks is a splendid area for rock climbing or an easy family outing in late spring or fall. □

HIKE 89　　INDEPENDENCE LAKES

General description: A three-mile hike to four lakes nestled high in the Albion Mountains.
General location: 35 road miles southeast of Burley.
Maps: Cache Peak (7.5') USGS quad.
Special attractions: A fantastic view of Mount Harrison, the Jim Sage Mountains, and the rugged ranges of south Idaho all set in an oasis surrounded by the semiarid Snake River Plain.
Difficulty: Moderate to easy.
Season: Mid-July to mid-October.
Information: Burley Ranger District, Sawtooth National Forest, Rt. 3 Box 3650, Burley, Idaho 83318; (208) 678-0430.

The hike: Independence Lakes are nestled in a basin near the top of 10,339-foot Cache Peak and Mount Independence at 9,950 feet. From these lakes, Mount Harrison is visible to the north, the Jim Sage Mountains to the southeast, and (if you climb Cache Peak), City of the Rocks, a favorite rock-climbing area, is visible to the south.

HIKE 89 *INDEPENDENCE LAKES*

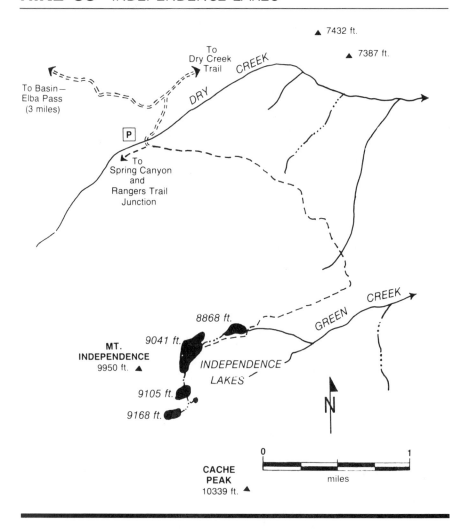

▲ 7432 ft.

▲ 7387 ft.

To
Dry Creek
Trail

CREEK

DRY

To Basin—
Elba Pass
(3 miles)

P

To
Spring Canyon
and
Rangers Trail
Junction

GREEN CREEK

8868 ft.

9041 ft.

MT.
INDEPENDENCE
9950 ft. ▲

INDEPENDENCE
LAKES

9105 ft.

9168 ft.

N

0 — 1
miles

CACHE
PEAK
10339 ft. ▲

Drive about 20 miles south of Burley on Idaho Highway 27. Turn left (east) shortly after you enter Oakley onto the paved road which leads to Elba. Continue to climb for about 12 miles to the Basin-Elba Pass. Here, turn right (south) onto a road which gets continually rougher as it follows the ridge past the Pot Holes. From the pass it is about five miles to the trailhead. About a mile from the pass you'll come to a signed road to Stinson Creek. Instead of following it, keep to the right. When you reach the Pot Holes turnoff, keep to the left. From there it is about another two miles to the trailhead. The last mile of this road is very rocky and warrants caution if you're in a passenger vehicle. Once, to my amazement, I saw a schoolbus at this trailhead.

There is plenty of parking at the unmarked trailhead on Dry Creek. From

Dry Creek, the trail follows an old road through forest for about two miles. This part of the trail climbs gently from 7,800 to 8,000 feet. As the trail circumvents to the east of Mt. Independence, there are good views of Elba Basin and the Raft River Valley to the east. The Jim Sage Mountains are also clearly visible, along with most of the other ranges in southeastern Idaho.

During the last mile, the trail turns sharply to the west and climbs straight up for over 800 feet to the first lake. The second lake is the largest, sitting approximately 200 feet higher than the first.

Camping is poor, due mainly to the many rocks. However, the scenery and fishing are first class. Rainbow trout may be caught in the first lake and cutthroat in the largest lake. In 1973, Arctic grayling fingerlings were planted, but they don't seem to have survived. There are no fish in the upper two lakes.—*Philip Blomquist* □

Note: Grayling were replanted in the second lake in 1987 and again in 1988. During my visit in 1987 the second lake was excellent for 18 inch cutthroat trout. —Philip Blomquist

HIKE 90 *SILENT CITY OF ROCKS NATIONAL RESERVE*

General description: An area of fantastic granite monoliths primarily suitable for day hiking.
General location: About 25 linear miles southeast of Burley, Idaho. About 40 road miles south from the Interstate 86/ 84 exchange.
Maps: Almo, Cache Peak (7.5') USGS quads.
Special attractions: Pillars, knobs, cliffs, pinnacles, and hoodoos of soft granite; easily accessible in a new National Reserve. Extreme southern Idaho has the only pinyon pine in the state.
Difficulty: Easy to moderate trails. Easy to difficult cross country.
Season: Late March through October.
Information: Burley District, Bureau of Land Management, Rt. 3, Box 3650, Burley, Idaho. 83318. (208) 678-5514. National Park Service, Visitors Center, Almo, Idaho 83312.

The hike: After many years of effort by local residents to protect this small, but unique area of oddly eroded granite, Congress established the Silent City of Rocks National Reserve in 1988.

The national reserve status (which is weaker than a national park, monument, or wilderness area) should put an end to spray painting of rocks and off-road vehicle abuse. It will also provide for maintenance and construction of trails, interpretation, picnicking, and a campground. The grazing of domestic livestock may also be reduced eventually.

The rocks (many of which have names such as Bath Rock, the Arrow, Turtle Rock) are a popular destination for rock climbers. I still remember the cold, gray, March day in 1973 at the City of Rocks that I first roped up under the guidance of the Idaho State University Outdoor Program.

The most common access to the area is on Interstate 84, then to the small town of Malta. From Malta take Idaho Highway 77 toward the mountains, and then turn left at Conner Junction (to the south on a paved county road) to the tiny, beautiful hamlet of Almo. Here the pavement ends. Follow the

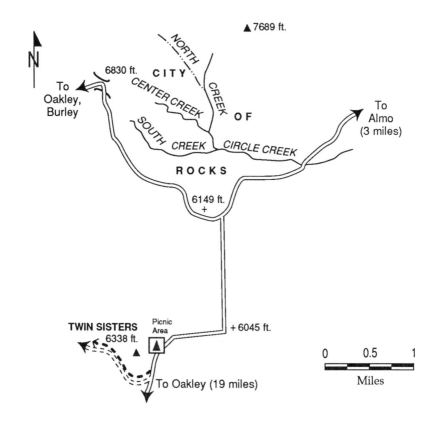

▲ 7689 ft.

N

6830 ft. C I T Y

NORTH CREEK

To
Oakley,
Burley

CENTER CREEK

SOUTH CREEK

CIRCLE CREEK

O F

To
Almo
(3 miles)

R O C K S

6149 ft.
+

TWIN SISTERS Picnic Area
6338 ft. + 6045 ft.

To Oakley (19 miles)

0   0.5   1

Miles

gravel road for a mile south of Almo and turn right and follow this gravel road about four miles past the ruins of a stone house and a few outlying rocks to another junction. Left, to the south, the road leads to the Twin Sisters (giant, isolated rocks and a BLM picnic area). Keep right. Soon you pass a number of short side roads leading to informal parking, picnicking, and camping areas among the rocks. Here too a number of unmaintained trails leave to descend among the rocks into South Creek, a common destination for an easy, family dayhike. Access is also available south from Burley to Oakley on Idaho Highway 27 then south up the paved, then gravel Forest Service road to the Rocks. This road takes you over a pass and snow blocks the road until about late May.

You can hike up South Creek, or, if you are at its mouth (where the country opens up), you can continue northward on a discontinuous, but easy, trail to Center Creek. Beyond Center Creek, a series of spotty trails leads to North Creek. You can walk up either Center or North Creek, following halting trails or cross country routes. Undoubtedly, as the national reserve gets functioning, the path of the trails will be firmly determined and signed. Certain trailheads will be improved and others closed and abandoned. In the meantime keep a close eye on the specific rocks (for use as guideposts) if you continue beyond South Creek. Otherwise, it may be hard to find your way back easily, although getting seriously lost here would be very difficult.

The best season here is late spring and the month of September. Summertime can be quite hot. Spring brings rangeland wildflowers and, generally, pleasant temperatures. The mild month of September (although nights can be quite cold) features the gold coats of quaking aspen. Access opens when the snow melts (March or April).—*Ralph Maughan* □

Bear River Range

Overview

The Bear River Range is a northward extension of Utah's Wasatch Mountains. Most of the Bear River Range is in Utah, but it ends abruptly about 20 miles north of the border at Soda Point near Soda Springs, Idaho. The most impressive view of these rugged, but only moderately glaciated mountains is on their west side where, for over 40 miles, they form the backdrop of Cache Valley, Utah-Idaho.

In the mid-80s Utahans successfully rallied to protect a medium-sized roadless area from Logan Canyon northward to the Idaho line as the Mt. Naomi Wilderness. This roadless area extends northward a way into Idaho, ending just south of Cub River Canyon.

Idaho environmentalists are proposing that 24,000 acres of this area in Idaho be added to the Mt. Naomi Wilderness. All but the most anti-environmental politicians in Idaho have been supporting this basic proposal. I grew up at the base of the Bear River Mountains, and the righteousness of keeping development off these slopes was one of the first thoughts I remember about environmental protection.

The Mt. Naomi area in Idaho is scenic but has few trails. The canyon bottoms are full of dense, low-growing maple and oak and therefore difficult to passage. There is an old jeep road in Sugar Creek. A number of other trails exist on maps but are absent, or nearly so, on the ground.

Most of the more gentle, east side of the Bear River Range was developed long ago with a network of dirt roads. Timbering has been extensive, and now its lower slopes are being subdivided for second homes. However, in the headwaters of St. Charles Creek, a valuable roadless area remains. The Forest Service burdened it with the unlovely name of the Worm Creek roadless area back in 1978 during its second Roadless Area Review and Evaluation (RARE II). The Caribou National Forest also recommended it for wilderness designation. Since then, however, pressure from off-road vehicle and oil and gas interests have caused them to drop this proposal. Idaho and Utah environmentalists, however, are proposing a 35,000 acre "Cache Crest" Wilderness, the new name accurately reflecting this crest and eastern slope scenic area.—*Ralph Maughan* □

HIKE 91 *ST. CHARLES CANYON-HIGHLINE TRAIL*

General description: A day or weekend hike along a spectacular ridge in the proposed Cache Crest Wilderness.

General location: On the east side of the Bear River range in extreme southeast Idaho, just north of the Utah border. 73 miles southeast of Pocatello and 57 miles by road from Logan, Utah.

Maps: Egan Basin, Paris Peak (7.5') USGS quads.

Special attractions: A walk along a high,, meadowy ridgeline, with precipitous views down Cub Creek Canyon to the west and of Bear Lake in the east.

Difficulty: Moderate.

Season: Late June through September.

Information: Montpelier Ranger District, Caribou National Forest, 431 Clay, Montpelier, Idaho 83254; (208) 847-0375.

The hike: St. Charles Canyon is not used heavily by hikers, although the lower, roaded part of the canyon is popular in summer months because of nearby Bear Lake and Minnetonka Cave. The Caribou National Forest also maintains three campgrounds in the canyon, but not many venture beyond the end of the road.

From Logan, Utah, drive 40 miles through Logan Canyon to Bear Lake. Continue on U.S. Highway 89 for 14 miles to just north of St. Charles, Idaho. Turn left onto the paved road up St. Charles Canyon.

From Pocatello, Idaho Falls, or Preston, take Idaho Highway 36 just north of Preston and travel over the crest of the Bear River Mountains to Ovid, Idaho. Drive southward on U.S. 89 from Ovid through Paris and Bloomington to the St. Charles Canyon road. This is about 12 miles south of Ovid. Still another route is U.S. 30 through Soda Springs and Montpelier, then six miles on U.S. 89 to Ovid.

Drive eight miles up St. Charles Canyon on the paved road. A few hundred yards past Cloverleaf Campground, turn off onto a dirt road to the right. Continue now on this dirt road for about 200 yards and park. The trailhead begins here. Follow the trail (an old road) for several hundred more yards through aspen trees to a bridged crossing of St. Charles Creek. Fishing is good both here and downstream.

About a mile above the bridge the trail forks. To the left is the Snowslide Canyon trail, and to the right, the North Fork of St. Charles Creek. Take either fork, as both lead to the Highline Trail. Together they make a loop back to where you are standing. Both trails lead steeply uphill through aspen and then fir to the Highline trail, which is right on top of the ridgeline at about 9,000 feet, running north and south. The North Fork Trail stays quite close

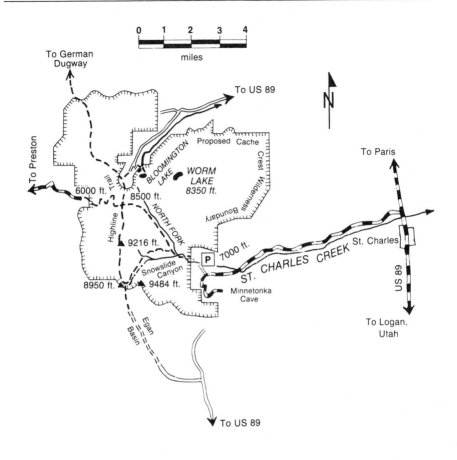

to the creek, but the Snowslide Trail keeps above and north of Snowslide Creek most of the way. It finally drops to the floor of Snowslide Canyon after passing above a spring-fed pond, where it is common to observe wildlife.

Upper Snowslide Canyon is a nice place to camp in early summer, but later the creek dries up there. In Snowslide Canyon, the trail may become faint near the top as you walk through small meadows, with many dense patches of false hellebore. If you lose the trail, bear slightly more west than south and you will reach the Highline Trail as you gain the ridgetop.

The last 1.25 miles of the North Fork trail leave the creek and climb a thousand feet, mostly through meadow, to the Highline trail.

Approximately two miles of the Highline trail separate Snowslide from the North Fork canyon. The hike here is a sublime, undulating ramble on the mountain crest as the trail wends its way through grass and flowers and past occasional struggling conifers. To the east, 12 miles away, you see the blue waters of Bear Lake. To the west, the mountainside plunges in a no-nonsense fashion almost 3,000 feet to the floor of Cub River Canyon. To the southwest, you can see across green Franklin Basin to the highest peaks of the Bear River Range in the Mt. Naomi Wilderness area (mostly in Utah). At the south end of the Highline trail, you look southward to green, peaceful Egan Basin, surrounded by dark green mountains of low relief, all densely forested.

If you are interested in more than a loop hike, you can continue on northward for some distance past the junction with the North Fork of St. Charles Creek trail with the Highline trail. It's six miles over more open ridgetop and quite a bit of karst topography to the end of the Highline trail at the German Dugway near the head of Paris Canyon. Much of the proposed Cache Crest Wilderness is karst, with its limestone caves, sinkholes, ponds, depressions, and disappearing lakes. Unfortunately the Highline Trail receives increasing attention from the ORV crowd.

The proposed wilderness area is good habitat for deer, elk, blue grouse, and an occasional moose. In mid-summer, the grazing of sheep and cattle can be heavy, and camping becomes a bit limited due to a lack of level spots next to a season-long water supply.—*Philip Blomquist and Ralph Maughan* □

Hells Canyon

Overview

Many claim that Hells Canyon is the deepest gorge on Earth. Some uphold that it is "merely" the deepest gorge in North America. However, relief and exposure are only one aspect of the precarious balance of Hells Canyon and the surrounding glacier-carved canyon country which reaches west to Oregon and Washington's Blue Mountains and east to Idaho's Little Salmon River Valley: in terms of geology, botany, scenery, and historical significance, the Hells Canyon Country is a story unto itself.

In the era before full occupation by settlers (a mere 110 years ago), the Hells Canyon environs were home to various bands of the Nez Perce Tribes who were led in their latter years by the renowned Chief Joseph. The land in this region was so bountiful that the Nez Perce word for "land" (also decipherable as "wilderness") had an interchangeable meaning with "food".

The canyon bottom is a furnace of inversion-induced heat in summer: lower in elevation, warmer, and climatically isolated from the cold, snow-mantled upland regions.

One hundred miles of the Snake River is still free-flowing, 67 of which is designated under the National Wild and Scenic Rivers Act. This section of river and its immediate tributaries represent the largest watercourse still in a predominantly wilderness condition in the lower 48 states. Including the adjoining Wallowa Mountains in Oregon, well over a million acres of roadless land remains, about half of which is designated wilderness.

Most of these protective classifications are a result of the 1975 Hells Canyon National Recreation Area (NRA) which established a 652,000 acre NRA in recognition of the need to protect the unique and irreplaceable values of Hells Canyon.

In modern times the native peoples are not to be found in Hells Canyon. (They were driven out in 1877 by the U.S. Calvary in one of the saddest chapters in Native American history.) Yet, their artifacts and homesites remain. The Hells Canyon country is identified as one of the most significant archaeological sites in the American West. Part of the area is designated as a National Archaeological Sensitivity Area.

Wildlife is diverse and abundant, mainly due to the diversity of vegetation and climate in a relatively concentrated area and also because of the predominantly wild character of the landscape. In addition to supporting one of the two largest elk herds in North America, this is the habitat of a healthy predator population: a wide variety of hawks and other birds of prey including osprey, and bald and golden eagles which winter in the depths of the canyon. Peregrine falcons have recently been introduced on the canyon's rim. Relatively large numbers of predatory mammals exist, including black bear, cougar, lynx, marten, and fisher. There have even been recent sightings of grizzly bears in the Lord Flat area on the Oregon side. (These were thought to have been extinct in Oregon for over 50 years.). Unfortunately, fish and wildlife agencies have dismissed urgings for investigation and confirmation of sightings.

Salmon and steelhead, although greatly diminished from historic levels, retain significant populations despite interference from numerous downstream impoundments. Good potential for increased anadromous fish runs exists, provided the habitat is maintained. In addition, the prehistoric sturgeon also inhabit the Snake River here. A variety of other rare or infrequent species, such as the great grey owl, bighorn sheep, and Franklin's grouse, find a haven in Hells Canyon.

Despite the bounty, grace, and unique features of Hells Canyon, the rush to consume and develop it has been almost overwhelming. The latter-day struggles that have taken place over the fate of these lands have been nearly as hard fought and bitter as the wars between the Nez Perce and the U.S. Calvary. The initial controversies began in the late 1950s and raged over the "use" and "ownership" of the Hells Canyon Country. Conservationists, recreationists, and Native Americans engaged the hydro and resort developers and timber companies in administrative and legal skirmishes that lasted nearly 20 years.

The timber companies coveted the old growth ponderosa pine, while the hydro-developers had varying visions of huge dams, one of which (High Mountain Sheep) would have reached over 700 feet up the canyon wall and flooded 75 miles of the Snake. The site of this dam is still in evidence via a painted inscription imposed high on the rocks. This, along with other sites, remains as a reminder to those who were involved in the initial controversies of the narrowly avoided doom which culminated with the passage of the Hells Canyon National Recreation Area (Public Law 94-199) on New Year's Eve, 1975.

This law protected 67 miles of the Snake River and 26 miles of the Rapid River from dams as well as designating 194,000 acres of wilderness. It also set restrictions on developmental activities among its goals to protect and maintain the myriad of natural phenomena within the 652,000 acre NRA.

While the victory of 1975 was tremendous, the controversy is far from over. The U.S. Forest Service, entrusted with management of the Hells Canyon NRA, has instead instigated an enthusiastic program of timber extraction which emphasizes the removal of old growth pine and fir in the undesignated wild regions of the NRA.

A power conglomerate has recently proposed two dams on the lower section of the Snake River, immediately below the Wild and Scenic River boundary. The proposed damsites would flood the remaining 33 miles of the free flowing portion of the Snake River, which has been studied and recommended for wild and scenic status.

The Forest Service has also proposed constructing a large developed recreational vehicle park at Pittsburg Landing, an area of highest archaeological sensitivity. It is the former location of Indian villages and contains petroglyphs, pictographs, lithic scatters, and other invaluable remnants of the past.

Forest Service timbering activities in the Hells Canyon NRA have completely overshadowed the pursuit of legislatively mandated goals for protection of fish, wildlife, wilderness, scenic, and unique ecological values. Logging and road-building projects in the NRA are concentrated in the most critical strongholds of ecological integrity.

Only 30 percent of the NRA is forested, and what little forest exists is of utmost importance of wildlife. Since the establishment of the NRA, over 100 million board feet of timber has been contracted for removal, with no respite in sight as more large timber sales are planned in roadless areas. The places so vital to the birthing of new generations of wildlife are dwindling.

Unfortunately, the prospect looms of having to "reprotect" what was presumed protected when the NRA was passed. Current management practices in the NRA have inspired calls for both litigation and additional legislation. Investigation of options for litigation has begun, and discussion of legislative proposals is proceeding. In 1986 a bill was introduced in Congress to strengthen protection of the area with additional wilderness designations and other measures, but it was defeated.

Chief among alternative proposals is the suggested application of National Park and Preserve status, an option that could more fully protect the area and allow traditional activities such as hunting to continue.

The Hells Canyon Preservation Council, formed in 1960 to preserve the qualities which define the deepest gorge on earth and its surrounding terrain, has recently reformed to continue the effort to keep Hells Canyon intact. For additional information regarding Hells Canyon, or to become part of this non-profit organization, please contact the HCPC at Box 903, Joseph, Oregon 97846.

This write-up is abridged and excepted with permission from Ric Bailey's, "Hells Canyon Gapes in Splendor," *Columbiana*, vol. 2, no. 1, 1989, pp. 11-13, 69.)

HIKE 92 *SEVEN DEVIL'S LOOP*

General description: A 27 mile loop circumnavigating the rugged and well-named Seven Devils Mountain Range.

General location: Seventeen miles west of Riggins in the Hells Canyon Wilderness.

Maps: He Devil, Oregon-Idaho (15') USGS quad.

Special attractions: A little-used wilderness in big, big country which offers magnificent views into Hells Canyon, some 30 lakes (many with fish), and much wildlife (golden eagle, mountain goat, cougar, and black bear).

Difficulty: Strenuous.

Season: Mid-July to mid-September

Information: Hells Canyon National Recreation Area, Box 832, Riggins, Idaho 83549. (208) 628-3916.

The hike: This is an excellent loop hike because each day offers fine views and each night a place to camp by either lake or stream. The terrain is rugged with a good deal of elevation loss and gain.

The Seven Devils can create their own weather as storms sweep off Lord Flat on the Oregon side of Hells Canyon and recirculate over these pinnacled mountains. The west side is where one encounters the fiercest weather. We spent one night at Echo Lake holed up in the tent while the wind whipped rain and dime-sized hail stones down on us. The west side of the range is also where we saw mountain goat and golden eagle. The east side, which includes the Rapid River, is heavily forested and here we saw much sign of and, indeed, a black bear.

Hells Canyon is visible from lookout points on the west side of the range. It is approximately 8,000 feet deep measuring from the top of the Seven Devils to canyon bottom. A 67.5 mile free-flowing stretch of the Snake River here, and 26.8 miles of the Rapid River, were designated as a Wild and Scenic Rivers under the Hells Canyon National Recreation Area Act. (See Hells Canyon Overview). This act, along with protecting Hells Canyon from dams and other "improvements", also established the 194,132 acre Hells Canyon Wilderness. Although inclusion of the Seven Devils proper in the wilderness was never contested, the Rapid River was due to its valuable timber (see Rapid River hike). The Seven Devils area, and the beautiful Lord Flat visible during much of this hike, is still under threat from logging and road building. Presently, the Hells Canyon Preservation Council is working for National Park, National Preserve, and National River status for portions of this magnificent country (See Hells Canyon overview for more information).

From U.S. Highway 95, take the signed road just south of Riggins which leads west to the Seven Devils Trailhead. This gravel road climbs 5,400 feet in 17 miles. Be sure to bring water as there is none at the trailhead. The road is passable for sedans, although the last four miles require shifting down to first gear. Trailers are not recommended. Windy Saddle Campground is the point at which the trailhead is located, but if you spend the night, the Seven Devils Campground (one half mile further) is nicer and less exposed. (Take your own water.)

To get a full view of this country, you might want to take the Heaven's Gate Road to the lookout tower. The road is nicely graded for the first 11 miles, then a new logging road is being built at the sharp curve at milepost #11. From there up, the road is rocky, worn from gully washes (no waterbars), and is almost four-wheel drive. New logging is in evidence. From the end of the road, it is a quarter mile walk to the top.

The 1957 He Devil USGS map makes this loop look easier than it is because

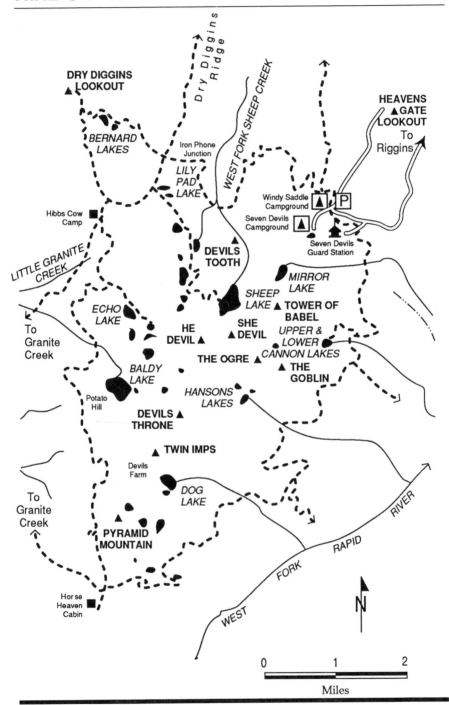

the scale is 15' and covers four times the area of the 7 1/2' maps. It is important to secure a copy of the photo-copied Forest Service map (available at the trailhead register). The USGS map does not show many of the lake trails or give the names of many mountains. We recommend doing the route counterclockwise, saving the easiest part (from Lower Cannon Lake to the trailhead) for last and taking the toughest portion (Windy Saddle to Bernard Lakes) first.

The trail starts by dropping 480 feet through forest to the East Fork of Sheep Creek. It then climbs 1,000 feet to cross the northern spur of the Seven Devils range. Here you can look back and see the Heavens Gate Lookout at 8,407 feet and the dirt road leading to it. As the trail skirts west and then south, it drops 1,300 feet to the West Fork of Sheep Creek. In this section the Devils Tooth monolith dominates the weird and wild looking terrain. The trail heads west, contouring the head of the West Fork for approximately one mile, then climbs yet again for 400 feet to the Dry Diggins Ridge Trail. So far you have covered about five linear miles, but climbed some 1,400 feet

This point is named the Iron Phone Junction and portions of the old downed telephone line still lie abandoned near the trail. At this major junction, we encountered some fishermen who were camped at Basin Lake. Although we did not fish ourselves, we were told that the Seven Devils country is good for cutthroat, rainbow, brook, and Dolly Varden. Rather than turning south (which would make for a shorter loop), we continued northwest to Bernard Lakes and the Dry Diggins Lookout. We chose to add this extra three-plus miles in order to climb to the lookout and thereby get a good view of the Snake River and Hells Canyon 6000 feet below. From the lookout you'll see evidence of the 1988 forest fires.

It is a little over a mile and 300 feet elevation gain to the second of the Bernard Lakes. We camped on the southeast side. Scouting the entire lake, we looked for signs of previous visitors, and found nothing, absolutely nothing, not even a campfire ring.

The next day we left our packs at the bottom of the trail to the lookout, and climbed the approximate 240 feet to the top. It was here we had our first sighting of mountain goat. Our second sighting occurred when we stopped for lunch on point 8,099 (Three Creek Peak), about .75 of a mile south on the portion of the Bernard Lakes Trail which leads back to the main trail. This animal was very large and very white as we watched it through binoculars.

The final three-quarters of this trail swings south southeast to descend 240 feet back to the main trail. This junction is not signed. After the junction, you will continue south through open then sparsely wooded country to the signed Potato Hill and Little Granite Creek Trails above Hibbs Cow Camp. Stay to the left and this will put you on the Potato Hill Trail. Don't be confused by the fact that there are two junctions very close together. They are both signed and lead to the same aforementioned places.

From the Dry Diggins Lookout junction to Echo Lake, it is about three miles. (There is a trail to Echo Lake, although the USGS quad doesn't show it.) The 1988 forest fires burned much of the Little Granite Creek drainage, though not up to the lake itself. This forested lake is about 200 feet above and one rocky mile from the main trail. The rugged cirque basin that cradles it is headed by the He Devil, at 9,393 feet the highest in the range.

Back on the main trail, it is about 1.5 miles to the cut-off trail to Baldy Lake.

The trail drops 160 feet west through forest then contours generally south to cross the southern most fork of Little Granite Creek. It is a steep (500 feet), one mile climb to Baldy Lake, one of the most heavily used sites (comparatively speaking—we saw two people). Baldy Lake itself is splendid. Here you are able to see the He Devil, Mt. Belial, the Devils Throne, and the Twin Imps. This country might remind you of the "Midnight on Bald Mountain" segment of Disney's classic *Fantasia*.

From this point to Cannon Lakes, we saw no one. It is about 4.5 miles and 1280 feet of elevation gain to the southern end of the range and the Horse Heaven Junction just below the Horse Heaven Lookout. In spite of the effort, this is probably the most outstanding section of the loop. You are heading due south above timberline for almost the entire trek. While a poet might not find the right words to describe this country, a pair of golden eagles did, circling and calling to each other in their odd, high voices.

Once past Horse Heaven, you begin a slow, easy downhill walk. The trail here, as is true of most of the Seven Devils, is good as you head east. Once you turn north, you're on what's called the Boise Trail. The aspect of the land changes dramatically as you descend into old growth forest. In mid-August we saw much evidence of bear—huge piles of scat full of berries, and rotten overturned logs. At one point a large and delicate spider web was built from tree to tree across the trail. While there are many lakes on this side of the range, we found trails to none. It is another 7.5 miles to Hanson Creek where we camped (although there is plenty of opportunity to stop sooner). There is one trail (about 1.5 miles before Hanson Creek) which leads down to the Rapid River. Stay to the left.

Hanson Creek itself is not remarkable. The land is slumping and full of dead-fall and most difficult to get to. However, the water is clear and we drank without treating it. We camped on a little open rise to the north of the creek. That morning as I made my way to the creek, I heard something moving in the trees. I banged the aluminum pans I was carrying to warn whatever it was that I was there. Later that morning, as we bathed in the sun in absolute privacy, a little bear (possibly a yearling) sauntered out of the trees, looking very surprised to see us. I fired my pistol in the air, wishing in retrospect I'd fired my camera, and it took off.

It is another easy three or so miles of contour through forest cover and occasional deep woods to Cannon Lakes. It is about a 240 foot climb of less than one mile to Lower Cannon Lakes. Here we saw what seemed like a lot of people and the campsites were obviously used quite often. However, at Lower Cannon Lake we were able to find a nice, private campsite by crossing a rather difficult boulder field on the south side of the lake. The site is located at the inlet to the lake. We saw woodpeckers and pikas.

The peaks surrounding the Cannon Lakes are the Goblin, the She Devil (the biggest—located at the head of the canyon), and the Tower of Babel. The other third of the lower lake is an open slope of deadwood, due to a forest fire back in 1962. There are small, hungry cutthroat in the lake.

The hike from Cannon Lakes to the trailhead is four miles, in good condition, and rises about 240 feet. The junction is marked and occurs on a rise just after you cross Cannon Creek.—*Jackie Johnson Maughan and Margaret Hansen* ☐

HIKE 93   *RAPID RIVER*

General description: A three-season, little-used hike along a river spectacular enough to have been named a federal Wild and Scenic River.
General location: 35 road miles northwest of McCall, Idaho.
Maps: Heaven's Gate and Pollock Mountain (7.5')USGS quads.
Special attractions: Early spring and late fall hiking. In the spring this area features big game and cascades of wildflowers on steep slopes. It has a unique grove of Pacific yew and is closed to recreational vehicles.
Difficulty: Easy.
Season: Mid-March to December.
Information: Slate Creek Ranger District, Nezperce National Forest, HC 01 Box 70, Whitebird, Idaho 83554; (208) 839-2211.

The hike: Take Idaho Highway 55 northwest from McCall to New Meadows. At New Meadows, head north approximately 3 0 miles on U.S. Highway 95. You will come to the marked all-weather gravel road to the Rapid River Fish Hatchery and picnic area. Turn left onto this road. Drive the three miles west to the hatchery. The trailhead is located just barely past the administrative buildings before the road turns left to the hatchery picnic area. You'll need to park well off the road so others can get by.

This is a three-season, undiscovered paradise. You can walk approximately 11 miles (with little elevation gain or loss) along the main fork of the Rapid River without getting your feet wet, because a bridge has been thoughtfully placed everywhere the trail crosses the river. Within the first half mile, the trail enters a narrow canyon, and the walls seem to close in. It you hike this area in the spring, look to the high cliffs for white-throated swifts. These swallow-sized birds with white gorgets (throats) are such adept aviators that their habitat is listed as "open sky." Swifts are known to mate in flight. If you look intently, you can see their acrobatics high in the blue, cloud-brushed skies.

In about 1.5 miles, the trail crosses the Rapid River. Another 1.5 miles after the crossing, you'll enter a unique area, for here there grows a tree called the Pacific yew. The yew is a special evergreen because its trunk is red and smooth and divides into thick auxiliary branches more like a proper maple or sycamore than an evergreen. This yew provides great shade with its thick, dark green foliage. The Pacific yew is decidedly out of its normal seaboard range here in Idaho; this grove marks the furthest place east it has managed to call home.

One mile further upstream, the trail again crosses the river. Just one-half mile past here, the trail forks to the West Fork of Rapid River. This is a possible campsite. The West Fork is also part of the Wild and Scenic River System. This trail leads you in about three miles to McRae Ranch. Go another five miles or so and you come to the toes of the Seven Devils Peaks and the Idaho side of the Hells Canyon Wilderness.

By continuing up the main fork of Rapid River, you'll find two more trails that exit to the west in the next four miles (Dutchoven Creek and Wyant Creek). After these trails (which may or may not be maintained), the main trail crosses the Rapid River near Castle Creek and then, doubles back to the west side of Copper Creek. There are bridges at these crossings.

As you walk along the Rapid River, keep your eyes open for herds of

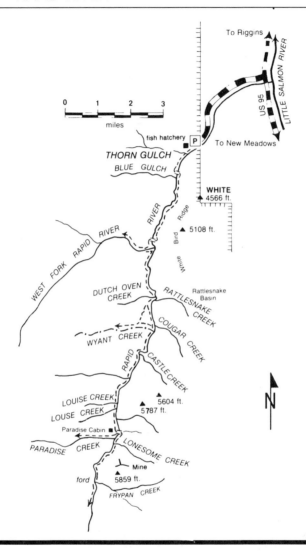

To Riggins

LITTLE SALMON RIVER

US 95

To New Meadows

fish hatchery P

THORN GULCH

BLUE GULCH

WHITE
▲ 4566 ft.

RIVER

Bird Ridge

▲ 5108 ft.

White

WEST FORK RAPID RIVER

RIVER

DUTCH OVEN CREEK

RATTLESNAKE CREEK

Rattlesnake Basin

COUGAR CREEK

WYANT CREEK

RAPID

CASTLE CREEK

LOUISE CREEK

LOUSE CREEK

▲ 5604 ft.
▲ 5787 ft.

Paradise Cabin ■

PARADISE CREEK

LONESOME CREEK

ford

Mine

▲ 5859 ft.

FRYPAN CREEK

0 1 2 3
miles

N

wintering deer and elk in early spring. During the spring, these herds have often been seen above the main trail on the high grassy slopes. In the winter and spring, when confined to the canyon, the animals are highly susceptible to disturbance. Make a special effort not to bother them.

The trail stays on the west side of Rapid River for two more miles to where it parallels Paradise Cabin. Here, it crosses the river again. You've got about 1.5 miles of trail left before you hit Frypan Creek, which flows down into the canyon from the east. At this point it is necessary either to ford Rapid River or to do a 1.5 mile cross-country hike on high ground. The ford can be difficult in high water season.

Upstream of the West Fork confluence, there are places to camp all along the river. Side streams are frequent throughout the hike and become more numerous the farther upstream you go.

There are many loop routes you can do once you get about two miles and beyond past the ford. One such loop goes to the source of the Rapid River and back along the North Star Trail. Another climbs toward the Seven Devils following the Black Lake Fork of Rapid River.

The Rapid River Wild and Scenic River Corridor, including the West and Main Forks, is about 26.8 miles long and one-half mile wide. It was designated as Wild and Scenic as part of the congressional legislation which created the Hells Canyon National Recreation Area in 1975. However, the land surrounding the corridor was not officially protected. That surrounding the first six miles of Main Fork and all of the West Fork is closed year-long to recreational motorized vehicles by the Nezperce National Forest. As you go farther upstream and the river enters the Payette National Forest, no such protection from ORVs exists. Even the Nezperce closure is temporary and subject to change in individual forest planning. It does not preclude road building for timber harvests. Timber roads are encroaching from all sides and will eventually sign the area's death certificate if efforts aren't made to protect the entire canyon. Your voice is needed in that effort.

The canyon is still wild enough to have been at least eyed by the Forest Service for inclusion as wilderness in the Hells Canyon National Recreation Area. The Rapid River flows into the Little Salmon River to its east to mix waters with the main Salmon and eventually the Snake River. The fish hatchery near its mouth is a good indication that dams do ruin fish runs. Construction of Idaho Power's Brownlee, Oxbow, and Hells Canyon dams on the Snake River in the 1950s and 1960s exterminated the salmon runs in the upper Snake. To make amends and undo the destruction, Idaho Power was required to work with the Idaho Department of Fish and Game to build the hatchery to restock the world famous Chinook salmon run. The Rapid River's Wild and Scenic status was granted partially to protect this hatchery.

Although some tourist manuals claim that the hatchery is a success, the Chinook salmon is in fact, although not yet by law, an endangered species in Idaho. This is a bitter contrast to the early 1960s, when there were so many salmon in tributaries as far south as the Weiser River that you could practically walk across the water on their backs.— *Jerry Dixon* □

Note: The trail now climbs about 200 feet up the right side of the canyon from the fish hatchery road instead of leading directly up the canyon along the streamside. After about .75 mile, the trail drops down to the stream. This canyon is very scenic from the start. Even a short hike is worthwhile.

I've rarely seen water as clear and transparent as Rapid River. Nevertheless, logging activities continue to threaten its headwaters.

Those planning a trip here for the first time should note that the canyon is usually too hot for pleasant hiking in the summer. Rattlesnakes and poison ivy are common, but the high quality trail makes their avoidance easy when forewarned as here.— Ralph Maughan

Boulder Mountains

Overview

Most people think the Boulder Mountains lie just north of Ketchum and due south of the White Clouds. However, a vast, mostly unknown portion of the Boulders actually lie east of the White Clouds. East Pass Creek is located in this part of the Boulders. Please refer to the overview for the White Cloud, Boulder, and Pioneer mountains for more general information about this area.

HIKE 94   *EAST PASS CREEK*

General description: A two-day, nine-mile backpack into a remote part of the Boulder Mountains with opportunities for side trips and a long, mostly cross-country loop connecting East Pass Creek with Herd Creek.
General location: 100 miles north of Twin Falls, 125 miles northwest of Pocatello, and 105 miles northeast of Boise in the eastern part of the White Cloud-Boulder Mountains Proposed Wilderness.
Maps: Meridian Peak and Bowery Peak (7.5') USGS quads.
Special attractions: A rugged canyon with a beautiful waterfall. Solitude.
Difficulty: Moderate due to a 1,300-foot climb at the start and an infrequently maintained trail.
Season: July through September.
Information: Lost River Ranger District, Challis National Forest, Box 507, Mackay, Idaho 83251; (208) 588-2224.

The hike: To get to the trailhead, drive either to Ketchum and over the gravel Trail Creek road, or to Mackay and then northward on U.S. Highway 93, turning off onto the paved county highway at the base of Borah Peak.

If approaching from Ketchum, drive eight miles past Trail Creek Summit down Summit Creek. From the eastern approach, drive 20 .7 miles west from the turnoff from U.S. 93, passing the Copper Basin turnoff. From either direction, you then turn off the main road onto the road up the North Fork of the Big Lost River. Head up this broad stream valley on the graveled 15-mile-per-hour road. It's 11.4 miles to the undeveloped meadow trailhead at Hunter Creek.

The North Fork of the Big Lost is a gentle and scenic stream valley, filled with meadows and willows. Lightly timbered mountains, built of the colorful Challis Volcanics, rise to the right. High mountains, with more timber and more typical of the higher parts of the Boulder chain, rise across the stream valley on your left as you drive up the North Fork. Moose were recently introduced into the North Fork.

As you near the end of the North Fork road, be sure to keep to the right of the stream. The road to the trailhead leaves to t he right just before the main road makes its only crossing of the North Fork.

It's a rough mile on this road to where the trail begins. Drive carefully. Park at the meadows at the mouth of Hunter Creek, which is the obvious canyon

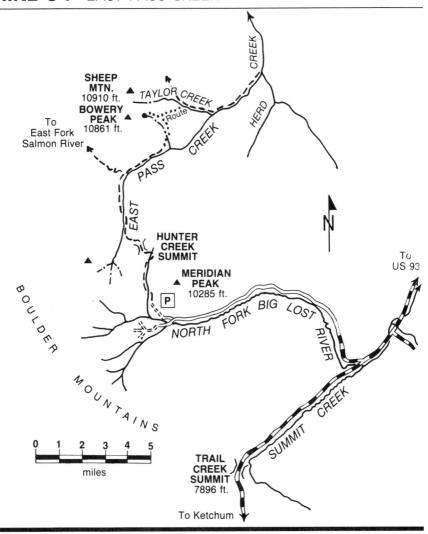

running upward to the north of the head of North Fork Valley. As you begin, the magnificent peaks at the head of the North Fork command your attention. They rise to almost 11,800 feet at Ryan Peak.

Start up the canyon. You'll soon find the trail on the right side of Hunter Creek. The trail is easy to follow as it climbs 1,300 feet in three miles to Hunter Creek Summit at 9,400 feet. You cross Hunter Creek a couple of times (no problem) as you climb the pleasant, mostly forested canyon to the pass.

At the pass, don't be misled and follow the trail that goes along the ridge crest. Instead, go straight down into East Pass Creek, dropping steeply for 700 feet in less than a mile on a trail that has several eroding routes. You end the descent at a grassy meadow. This is a good place to camp, where the headwaters of East Past Creek splash by and unnamed peaks, most well over 10,000 feet, rise around you.

At the meadow's lower end, a mountain with rugged pinnacles and cliffs comes into view down-canyon. For the next three miles, its intriguing form looms closer and closer. The canyon deepens as you walk down East Pass Creek. Two miles below the meadow, East Pass Creek leaps off a ledge, forming a major waterfall.

Below the waterfall, the canyon gets deeper still and begins to dry out. Sagebrush begins to appear in the meadows. Clumps of aspen appear among the conifers. The trail passes right under the pinnacled mountain, and the canyon bends toward the east. After about two more miles, however, the trail peters out as it approaches a gorge. This is the end of the trail. If you decide to camp in this vicinity, there are plenty of sites back near the base of the pinnacled mountain. You can continue by making a 2,200-foot cross-country climb out of the canyon to the unnamed lake that rests in the cirque below the east face of 10,861-foot Bowery Peak. It's a difficult climb to this barren, pristine lake. From the lake you can climb to the ridgeline that includes Bowery Peak and Sheep Mountain and various unnamed summits of this high northerly extension of the Boulder Mountains. From the ridge you gain a rare viewpoint of the White Cloud Peaks that lie to the west across the East Fork of the Salmon River. The high southern portion of the Boulder Mountains sweeps around to the southwest. To the east is a tall, treeless ridge that encloses Herd Creek and, rising beyond, the peaks of the Lost River Mountains.

You can get into the Herd Creek country by descending from the lake into Taylor Creek and following a trail down Taylor Creek to East Pass Creek below the gorge that blocked your passage. When you come to the confluence with Herd Creek, head up it into open Challis volcanic country. Follow the ridgeline here for several miles in a loop back to the North Fork of the Big Lost River. This cross-country loop is about 20 miles long.—*Ralph Maughan* □

Note: It's 1.3 miles on Forest Service road #477 to a small, grassy trailhead that has been constructed since the first edition. Here there are a few small conifer providing partial shade, and there is room for a half dozen cars or trucks and a few horse trailers. In 1989 a sign indicated that the Hunter Creek Trail was closed to motor vehicles. The trail climbs steeply (but just briefly) up the hill to the right of the trailhead.—Ralph Maughan

East Pass Creek in the Boulder Mountains. Ralph Maughan photo.

HIKE 95   *NORTH FORK TRAIL*

General description: A one- or two-day hike into the heart of the big, rugged Boulder Mountains.

General location: 13 miles north of Ketchum in the Sawtooth National Recreation Area at the headwaters of the North Fork of the Big Wood River.

Maps: Amber Lakes, Galena Peak and Ryan Peak (7.5') USGS quads.

Special attractions: A hike from forest to rock. Numerous wildflowers, springs, cascades, and avalanche runs which op en the forest for views of the rugged scenery.

Difficulty: Easy to the bend in the canyon (two miles). Moderate above the bend due to an increasingly faint trail. Difficult from the head of the canyon to Ibex Pass due to elevation gain and some route-finding.

Season: Late June through September.

Information: Sawtooth National Recreation Area, Star Route, Ketchum, Idaho 83340; (208) 726-7672.

The hike: This hike is typical of the Boulder Mountains: It's a beautiful walk sliced between tall, rugged mountains, but there's no lake as a destination. The lack of lakes keeps trail traffic quite low even though this hike is in the popular Sawtooth National Recreation Area (SNRA), only a five-mile drive from SNRA's headquarters building. Even so, the North Fork trail is relatively busy compared to nearby trails up the East Fork of the North Fork, Eagle Creek, and Murdock Creek.

From downtown Ketchum, drive north on Idaho Highway 75 into the SNRA. Just past the entrance sign where the highway crosses the Big Wood River, take the road to the right that leads to, and past, the SNRA headquarters building. At headquarters you can get plenty of information about hiking and other features of the SNRA. The building is set right in the mouth of the North Fork Canyon, 8.2 miles from downtown Ketchum.

Continue on the dirt road for 5.1 miles up the North Fork Canyon, passing Murdock Creek and the East Fork (of the North Fork) tributary canyons. The dirt road slowly deteriorates from good to just fair. The trailhead, with parking room for seven or eight vehicles, is located exactly at the end of the road. There is a trail register at the beginning of the trail and a sign announcing "no motor vehicles allowed."

The trail is obvious as you pass the trail register and climb steeply, although briefly, into the forest on the right (east) side of the North Fork. The trees are large and the forest deep, so it is surprising when after one-third mile, you suddenly pop out into the sun to cross the first of many avalanche chutes one of the features that make this trail so scenic. Here you drop down and cross the river to avoid a large cutbank just out of sight upstream. The ford is not difficult after early summer , but nearly impossible before. The trail stays in the open and on the west side of the North Fork for about one-third mile before it crosses back. These two fords are the only ones necessary on this hike.

The trail passes in and out of forest but remains generally in the open. The clearings are due to the megatons of snow that thunder down the walls of the canyon in the winter. Between the trailhead and the up-canyon junction

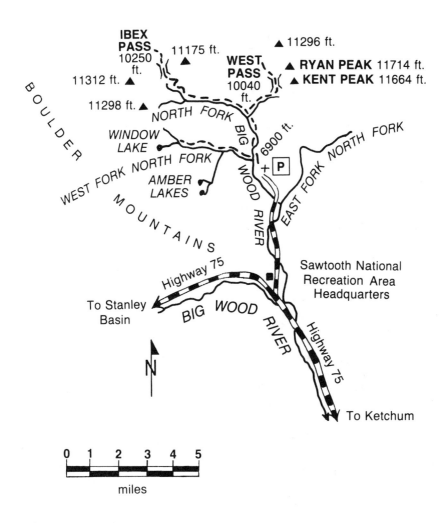

with the trail to West Pass (about two miles), you cross eight major avalanche chutes.

The hiking continues at an easy pace until you see a steep side-canyon ahead to the right, where a waterfall leaps. The West Pass Trail climbs up this canyon, ascending 2,900 feet in just two miles to West Pass, then descending into West Pass Creek. To find the start of this trail, keep on the main trail after sighting the falls and side-canyon until you cross a meadow. The West Pass Trail leaves on the far side of this meadow. It's a very faint track until you reach the trees on the meadow's northeast side, then it becomes obvious.

After this trail junction, the main trail bends gradually to match the canyon's north-to-west right angle turn. Soon it begins to climb moderately as the canyon's grade increases. At the same time, the trail becomes less distinct. You may even lose it briefly as you walk through the lush, tall wildflowers. Fear not—it is always easy to relocate the trail.

One and a quarter miles past the bend, the canyon's grade decreases, and you can find places to camp for about a half mile. Most of these spots are not large, however, and many are near springs—either an advantage or a problem depending on whether you prefer carrying water or slapping mosquitos. The awesome views of the Boulder Mountains from any of these campsites should take your mind off the mosquitos. The mountains in this canyon look like a blend of the Snake River Range of eastern Idaho and the volcanic Absarokas of the eastern border of Yellowstone National Park. You will perhaps perceive other likenesses; whatever they may be, you are sure to sit and stare.

Back on the trail, you soon come to the end of the canyon. Unnamed peaks here rise over 11,000 feet. Cross-country scrambles beckon the vigorous to the south, west, and north. The trail, however, leads to the crest to the north-west, Ibex Pass, at 10,250 feet.

The trail becomes fainter as you begin the ascent to Ibex Pass, but there are numerous cairns to guide you when the track disappears. A sharp watch for these piles of rock will lead you to the pass.

In 1982, a Ketchum resident complained about how the cairns, a recent addition, had ruined the solitude of the upper North Fork country by giving access to the pass. He used this example to question the whole concept of the SNRA. As you hike this faint path, however, ask yourself whether the slight increase in trail traffic since the SNRA's creation in 1972 is worse than coming over the top one day to see Tyrannosaurus Mining, Ltd., laying out mine, mill, road, tailings pond, and trailer camp. This was essentially the alternative when Idahoans decided to ban mining, except existing valid claims, from these mountains. In fact, the path to Ibex Pass has existed for years. Anyone with maps and some experience could, and did, get to the pass without need of cairns as guide.

The path becomes more alpine. You cross several headwater rivulets and rise ever upward. Toward the top, as you pass timberline, you find a distinct path up through the talus. Ibex Pass itself is abrupt; the trail goes right down the other side to Ibex Creek. It's a little difficult to find the pass on the topographic quadrangle maps, because the pass lies exactly where the Ryan Peak and the Galena Peak quads intersect.

Here, at 10,250 feet, you gaze northward across the East Fork of the Salmon River to where 11,820-foot Castle Peak rises above the rest of the White Clouds. Castle Peak may be the most famous mountain in Idaho; still, not many people ever see the giant peak from the south.

At the pass, bare rock mountains rise to both your right and left. Hopefully, in a few years here, you will be standing in a congressionally designated White Clouds-Boulder Mountains Wilderness. The proposal for a 450,000-acre continuous White Clouds-Boulder Mountains Wilderness is being advocated by all major Idaho conservation organizations. The White Clouds-Boulder Mountains area contains one of the nation's largest roadless mountain areas.—
Ralph Maughan ☐

The windswept crest of the Boulder Mountains from Ibex Pass. Ralph Maughan photo.

HIKE 96 WEST FORK, NORTH FORK BIG WOOD RIVER

General description: A day hike into a rugged portion of the Boulder Mountains in the proposed Boulder-White Cloud Mountains Wilderness.

General location: Thirteen miles north of Ketchum in the Sawtooth National Recreation Area.

Map: Amber Lakes (7.5') USGS quad.

Special attractions: Rugged mountain scenery, wildflowers.

Difficulty: Moderately easy.

Season: July through September.

Information: Sawtooth National Recreation Area, Star Route, Ketchum, Idaho 83340; (208) 726-7672.

The hike: The trail up the West Fork of the North Fork of the Big Wood River is a shorter, slightly steeper version of the North Fork Trail. You may see deer or elk along its approximate 2.5 mile length. You can camp near the trail's end, but this is usually a day hike. The trail is closed to motorized vehicles.

The trailside is generally forested, but views begin about mid-way; and it becomes open with fine scenery in a large meadow where the trail ends.

The trailhead is the same as for the North Fork Trail (see the North Fork Trail for access directions). At the trailhead, ford the North Fork and pick up the obvious trail on the other side. There is a trail register box here. In late summer, you may be able to find a crossing on a log.

Walk through a dense forest of lodgepole pine and Douglas fir for about a quarter mile into the mouth of the canyon. The canyon narrows as you enter and you begin to climb. After a gain of about 200 feet, the trail levels out near the creek (which is the only reliable source of water on the hike).

About a mile from the trailhead, a faint trail leaves to the left at a spot near the creek. Here you can see across the canyon to a steep side-canyon. This is Amber Gulch. Cross the creek here if you wish to scramble up to Amber Lakes in the top of Amber Gulch. This essentially is a cross country hike involving a gain of 2,000 feet in just two miles. If you do it, keep to the left (east) side of the gulch. The lakes are barren, but beautiful. Camping spots are in the meadows below the lakes.

If your destination is not Amber Lakes, continue on the obvious main trail which climbs briefly at a steep grade uphill to the right to avoid a tangle of avalanche debris. Next you enter an open area, climb into forest again, and repeat the process several times. Finally you arrive at an open willowy flat. As you continue up the canyon, the willows largely disappear to be replaced by a lovely wildflower meadow, which is ringed by peaks at least 11,000 feet high.

The trail ends at the end of the meadow. This is marked by a shallow slot-like gorge from which the West Fork pours.

From here it is possible to continue cross country to the head of the canyon, traverse down into the North Fork, and make it a loop hike back to the trailhead. This is a rugged route involving high elevation.—*Ralph Maughan* □

HIKE 97 *TRAIL CREEK LOOP*

General description: A nine-mile near loop well suited for a day hike. It leads up a canyon and behind two mountains to descend another canyon.
General location: About 16 miles east of Ketchum in the Boulder Mountains.
Maps: Rock Roll Canyon and Meridian Peak (7.5') USGS quads.
Special attractions: Magnificent views on a good trail which covers varied terrain; includes a waterfall and several cool wading pools.
Difficulty: Moderate.
Season: Mid-July through September.
Information: Ketchum Ranger District, Sawtooth National Forest, Box 2356, Sun Valley Road, Sun Valley, Idaho 83340; (208) 622-5371.

The hike: If day hikes were judged on a scale of 10, the Trail Creek Loop is a 10-plus. The walk is a leisurely one which takes the hiker from 7,800 feet at the trailhead, to just over 10,000 feet at the pass, to coast in a gentle descent back to the starting point. This hike illustrates the intrinsic value of loop hikes not a single step is retraced, and the chances of encountering others using the trail are minimal. (See update note at the end).

The initial goal is to get high into the headwater country of Trail Creek to its West Fork. From Ketchum drive northeast and through Sun Valley some 13 miles on former Idaho Highway 75 over Trail Creek Summit. The road is posted as hazardous and mountainous, but it actually isn't that bad. Turn left (north) at the Park Creek Campground onto the Park Creek Road and continue for about three miles. Park where the road forks at the old sheep pens and walk west (left) up the West Fork of Trail Creek. It is better to begin the loop in a westerly direction so the sun will be at your back.

The first mile follows a logging road. As the logging road ends, the ascent begins. For the next mile, keep the creek to your left as the trail, which is excessively axe-blazed, traverses the north side of a wooded slope. It is about a three-mile hike to the windy pass which crosses the ridge. There is a bowl on either side of the pass. In the bowl on the west side are several small unnamed lakes fed by meltwater.

As you cross the ridge, you can drop down into the bowl just off the trail to the north. There is a spring in the center of the bowl and this makes a cool, mossy lunch site perfect for sunbathing. The views from here are unsurpassed in the Boulders. You are surrounded with excellent examples of mountains sculpted by the shifting ice of the Pleistocene epoch. If you decide to climb any of the four peaks over 10,000 feet that surround the bowls, be on the alert for possible storms rolling in from the west. This is no place to be during a summer electrical storm!

From the viewpoint at the bowl, fanning out below, is one of the most beautiful drainages imaginable. If it's early in the year, stay to the left of the main headwater fork of Trail Creek as it forms below the bowl and pick up the descending trail at treeline. If in late summer or early fall, when the country is less snowbound, you can freestyle any route with which you feel comfortable as long as you stay between the two headwaters forks. By listening, you can find the confluence of these forks about a thousand feet below the ridge, where the trail can be located in a meadow adjacent to the creek.

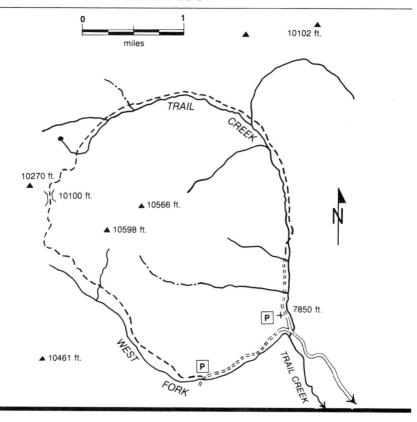

Once you have regained the trail, it's an easy five-mile walk to the trailhead. The trail follows Trail Creek through woods and small clearings. Late afternoon shadows define and highlight the varieties of this remarkable forest. Trail Creek has an enticing waterfall and several cool wading pools. The trail crosses the creek to a logging road, and then it's only a mile or so to your vehicle.

There are at least two springs on either side of the pass, but until then there are none of any dependability on the West Fork. There are several which merge on both sides of Trail Creek as you descend. Look for deer, elk, and possibly a bighorn sheep. The meadows are often lush with wildflowers. Bring your insect repellent, particularly for defense against the deerflies at the higher altitudes.—*Craven Young* □

Note: Although this hike was just as beautiful in 1989 as when Craven Young described it in the first edition, the Forest Service was logging the bottom of the loop, ruining it. Because of this, it is now probably best to drive to the end of the road in either fork and do it as an in-and-out hike instead. A loop would require walking 1.5 to 2 miles on dusty logging and woodcutting roads.—Ralph Maughan

HIKE 98 *HIGH RIDGE TRAIL*

General description: A fairly quiet trail that leads to a very scenic view of the highest peaks of the nearby Pioneer Mountains and of Trail Creek Gorge at their base.
General location: Thirteen miles by road from Ketchum, just beyond Trail Creek Summit, in the most southerly part of the Boulder Mountains.
Maps: Rock Roll Canyon (7.5') USGS Quad. You may also wish to take the Phi Kappa Mtn. (7.5') quadrangle to help interpret the view.
Special attractions: Spectacular views of glaciated peaks and a deep stream gorge.
Difficulty: Moderately difficult.
Season: Early July to "Rock Roll Point." The trail to Basin Gulch is accessible as soon as you can ford Trail Creek (second or third week in June).
Information: Ketchum Ranger District, Sawtooth National Forest, Box 2356, Sun Valley Road, Sun Valley, Idaho 83340; (208) 622-5 371.

The hike: The High Ridge trail begins at Cold Canyon in the upper reaches of Trail Creek; or alternatively in Lake Creek, a tributary of the Big Wood River, with access from Idaho Highway 75. It is an eight-mile, point-to-point hike between the two, but the description presented here is of only the first four miles from Trail Creek to a high overlook ("Rock Roll Point") above Trail Creek Gorge. Rock Roll Point is so designated here because it is located at the upper edge of Rock Roll Canyon, a very steep defile that descends into Trail Creek Gorge a few miles above Sun Valley.

To reach the undeveloped trailhead, drive up the Park Creek road, which is just a half mile past (east of) Trail Creek Summit . As you begin to descend into upper Trail Creek on the Park Creek Road (about a mile from the road's junction with the Trail Creek road), a dirt road appears at your left. Drive down it. The road drops down a short grade to Trail Creek where the stream is meanders through a meadow just before plunging into its famous gorge. Park in the sun by the creek or 50 yards back under the lodgepole pine-shaded bench just above the meadow.

Ford Trail Creek in the meadow (7710 feet); it is an easy wade after the snowmelt. After fording the creek, go up the obvious jeep track on the other side. You walk along an old logging trail on a lodgepole-covered flat near the mouth of Cold Canyon. The old track ends after about a quarter mile, and you climb very steeply on the trail, gaining about 200 feet, into Cold Creek Canyon. The trailside forest changes to spruce and fir because a moister microclimate prevails in the canyon.

The trail continues to climb at brief intervals amidst lengths of relatively level trail until you break out of the forest at about 8,300 feet. Here in the open, the trail immediately becomes fainter. You keep to it by following the rock cairns that have been placed alongside the pathway. You now have a view of the steep cirque headwall at the canyon's top and, downstream, of the portion of the Boulder Mountains which rise just north of Summit Creek (Summit Creek is the geographical divide between the Pioneer and Boulder Mountains).

The trail crosses Cold Creek exactly at contour 8,600 feet on the map. Look carefully for cairns on the other side. They direct you into, and through, small conifers (struggling back after an avalanche) and up the south side of Cold Creek Canyon for a very steep (but short) climb into Basin Gulch. This steep climb is through the timber, reaching the divide of 9120 feet in about a third of a mile.

You drop about 200 feet, descending mostly through limber pine, to the relatively flat floor (flat compared to Cold Canyon) of Basin Gulch. Peak 10,458, the most southerly of the Boulders, rises grandly above the basin. There are places to camp in the basin and some springs as well as the stream. It is a more suitable place for a camp than Cold Canyon. The Sawtooth National Forest is designating Basin Gulch as a research natural area for limber pine, however, and you may want to check to see if camping will be permitted in the future.

Looking down the "gulch", you can see part of Trail Creek Gorge, but a much better view comes as you climb over into Basin Gulch's other fork. To do this, follow cairns that lead you into the timber for another brief, but steep climb, over the divide between the two forks of Basin Gulch (a 300 foot climb this time, and not quite as steep as that out of Cold Canyon).

Just beyond this 9,200 foot high divide between the two forks of Basin Gulch, the trail breaks out into the open, high above the gulch's south fork. Here is an awesome view down into Trail Creek gorge, in which the road clings to the very steep, avalanche-scored slope that rises from the gorge's depths all the way to the peaks of the Pioneer Mountains. Basin Gulch, as seen from the gorge, is one of the scenic highlights of the Trail Creek Road. Each year, tens of thousands of people admire it from below as its stream cascades down the salmon pink mountainside into the abyss. Of course, only an infinitesimal percentage view the scene in the opposite direction.

The trail is narrow across the top of this fork of Basin Gulch, but it seems gripped to the side of peak 10,458; and the going is fairly easy as you traverse to Rock Roll Point, climbing gently most of the way.

The point is obvious. Its elevation is about 9450 feet. The trail reaches it and swings around for about a 110 degree turn across the top of Rock Roll Canyon, which plunges about 2600 feet in .75 mile into Trail Creek. You can continue on the trail along the top of Trail Creek Gorge to the ridgeline and eventually down into Lake Creek if you wish and have a second vehicle to pick you up. Most people stop at the point, however. They admire the tremendous view of the gorge and of the high peaks of the Pioneers that rise immediately to the southwest. Then they head back to their car parked in upper Trail Creek.—*Ralph Maughan* □

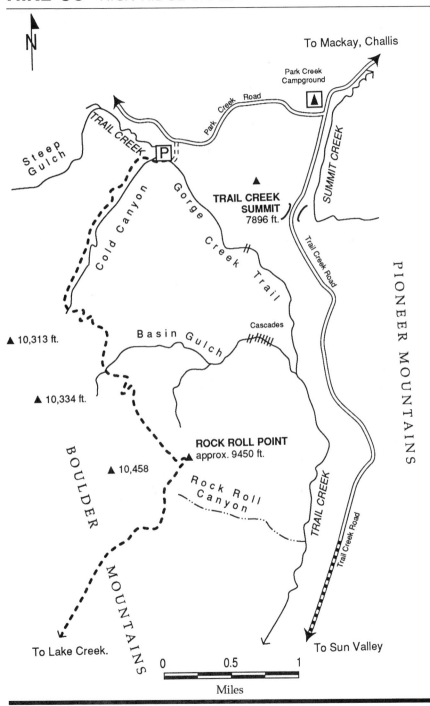

N

To Mackay, Challis

Park Creek Campground

Park Creek Road

TRAIL CREEK

Steep Gulch

P

Cold Canyon

Gorge Creek Trail

SUMMIT CREEK

▲
TRAIL CREEK SUMMIT
7896 ft.

Trail Creek Road

▲ 10,313 ft.

Basin Gulch

Cascades

▲ 10,334 ft.

PIONEER MOUNTAINS

ROCK ROLL POINT
approx. 9450 ft.

▲ 10,458

Rock Roll Canyon

TRAIL CREEK

Trail Creek Road

BOULDER MOUNTAINS

To Lake Creek.

To Sun Valley

0   0.5   1

Miles

Mt. Bennett Hills

Overview

South of the town of Fairfield, which is situated in the broad valley called the Camas Prairie, rise some hills. They are usually little-noticed as the travelers' attention will be on the high Soldier Mountains to the north or the late May wildflower displays on the Camas Prairie itself.

These hills are named the Mt. Bennett on behalf of its highest point (Mt. Bennett at 7,485 feet elev.). From the south, near the Snake River at Kings Hill, Glenn's Ferry, or Bliss, along Interstate 84, these "hills" appear to be a substantial mountain range, offering over 4000 feet of relief, measured from the Snake River.

The area can be thought of as bounded by U.S. Highway 20 from Mountain Home on the west, the Camas Prairie on the north, Idaho Highway 75 and the Snake River Plain on the east, and the Snake River on the south. The Hills are thus about 40 miles in length and 15 in width.

Most of the area is managed by the U.S Bureau of Land Management, but there are private holdings scattered on the north and the south. These lands block direct access to the highest part of the area on the northwest side. BLM management emphasizes grazing, and maintained hiking trails are nonexistent. However, the existence of numerous canyons make for places relatively free of cows. The open nature of the country also makes trails unnecessary in many places.

Sagebrush seems to be the dominant plant, but in the canyon bottoms, especially those with water and little livestock grazing, rangeland plants rarely seen elsewhere are common. The higher hills also have isolated stands of quaking aspen and fir. The relatively low elevation of the Mt. Bennett Hills coupled with their considerable relief makes this a good hiking area from March to early June.

The most impressive aspect of these low mountains is the odd rock formations formed from "welded volcanic ash" or "tuff" in the middle part of the range. The formations are particularly impressive in the Little City of Rocks, Burnt Willow Canyon, and the large Gooding City of Rocks area. The latter two are described as hikes in this book.

This volcanic rock has eroded into complicated and weird pinnacles, knobs, and pillars often called "hoodoos." The generally dark brown rock is commonly "painted" by exceptionally bright yellow and orange lichen growth. The hoodoos extend westward considerably beyond the Gooding City of Rocks into Dry Creek and Catchall Creek.

The more isolated recesses of these hills have deer, elk, bobcat, and even a few bear. Coyote are common throughout the area. The two rock "cities" and the Black Canyon/Burnt Willow Canyon area are being pushed for wilderness classification by Idaho conservationists—their name, collectively, being the Camas Trail Proposed Wilderness.

HIKE 99 GOODING CITY OF ROCKS

General description: Two separate hikes through fantastic rock "hoodoos".
General location: In the Mt. Bennett Hills south of the Camas Prairie and Fairfield.
Maps: Fir Grove Mountain, McKinney Butte. USGS (7.5') quads.
Special attractions: Odd rock formations in intimate canyon settings. Wildflowers. A springtime hike.
Difficulty: Four-mile Canyon is a stroll. Coyote Creek loop is moderately difficult due to a lack of trail and the need for route-finding ability.
Season: May through October. Best from mid-May until mid-June.
Information: Contact Shoshone District, Bureau of Land Management, P. O. Box 2B, Shoshone, Idaho 83352. (208) 886-2206.

The hike: The hoodoos and pinnacles of ancient volcanic ash flows, welded together by time and pressure, are at their most impressive in the Mt. Bennett Hills at the Gooding City of Rocks and the nearby Little City of Rocks.

The most scenic parts of the Gooding City of Rocks are the canyon portions. In the canyons, the attraction of the odd rock formations is supplemented by small creeks (in spring and early summer) and intimate streamside meadows. In addition, many of the canyon bottoms are generally not grazed by domestic livestock, a rarity in the public rangelands of the West where typically all rangeland is under grazing permit and is generally greatly modified from pre-settlement conditions. Thus, there are plants you normally do not see and more wildlife, even including elk and an occasional black bear.

To reach the City of Rocks area, follow the directions for Burnt Willow Creek hike, (Hike 100) but instead follow the good dirt road for several more miles beyond the intersection with the poor dirt road leading to Burnt Willow Canyon. Then turn left at the obvious junction, which usually is signed.

Follow the signs to the City of Rocks and park near the rock with the whited-out sign (still legible) "City of Rocks."

Don't go down this road if it is muddy. You will probably get stuck even in a four-wheel drive. Fortunately, this dirt road is a fairly good when dry, and it dries in about 12 hours after a rainstorm.

Following are descriptions of two separate hikes at the City of Rocks—one short and easy; the other a lengthy loop

Fourmile Creek

This is an easy hike. Most is a stroll. From your parking spot near the whited-out sign, walk through the hoodoos off in an easterly direction. You will soon descend into Fourmile Creek (a shallow canyon). The only thing you have to remember is to carefully note where you descended, for finding your way back could be momentarily confusing because of the maze of similar appearing hoodoos.

The canyon bottom is only from five to about 50 feet wide, but it is meadowy with a rivulet gurgling its way along in May and early June. Walking is easy amidst the dark brown rocks splotched with bright yellow and orange lichens.

After about a mile the canyon opens up, dries, and the rocks become less

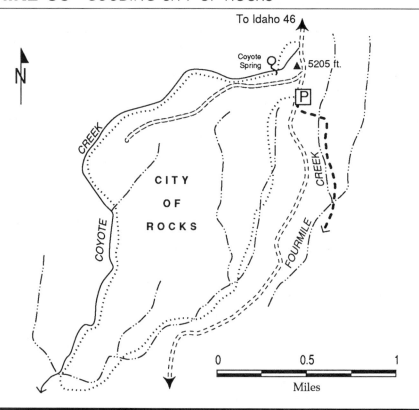

To Idaho 46

Coyote
Spring

▲ 5205 ft.

N

CREEK

CITY

OF

ROCKS

COYOTE

CREEK

FOURMILE

0   0.5   1

Miles

numerous. There are many places to camp as the canyon begins to open up. Return to your vehicle the way you came.

Coyote Creek Loop

This complete hike is a long day hike or a comfortable overnighter. It would probably be considered moderately difficult because of the need for map-reading skills, several narrows, and lack of a trail. It is not strenuous, however. Mostly it involves walking along meadows beside tiny streams.

If you are not planning to do the entire loop (perhaps you will only want to walk to the narrows and return), **make a careful note of where you descended and of the several similar-appearing side-canyons which you soon pass.**

The hike immediately leads down a scenic, shallow canyon much like Four-mile Creek. The rocks become more impressive as you continue. Some look like giant chickens; others like toadstools. There are a number of windows or arches in the rocks too.

You are approaching the narrows of East Coyote Creek when you come to a narrow pour-off with a pool below in May and much of June. This barrier

Pinnacles of welded volcanic ash in Coyote Creek. Ralph Maughan photo.

is easy should you choose to wade. Downstream from the pour-off, the rock formations soon become higher and take on a very bizarre appearance, and soon you are in the narrows! You may want to wade, but the wading is easy, complicated only by the presence of some brush. If the day is cool, the narrows may be uncomfortably cold since they are in the shade and often windy. I saw no poison ivy here (or anywhere in the City of Rocks). You should watch for rattlesnakes, however. They are scattered throughout the Mt. Bennett Hills.

After about a quarter-mile, the narrows end abruptly. The canyon widens and the stream disappears. From here to the junction with coyote Creek the canyon is more open, but still scenic. The stream rises and disappears several more times. You do pass by two large hoodoo-lined side canyons on your right, but you will know they are not Coyote Creek because they are smaller than the canyon you are following. They do make an interesting side hike.

You reach Coyote Creek 1.5 to two miles below the narrows when the East Fork is joined by a side-canyon larger than the one you have been following. In May this canyon has two or three times the flow of its east fork.

Head up Coyote Creek. It is fairly easy walking and filled with impressive rock formations from the beginning. In addition to hoodoos and pinnacles, there are quite a few natural arches (perhaps better described as "windows" in the rocks). I found the canyon very beautiful.

Coyote Creek has two sets of narrows. The first one you will encounter is easy although you may have some shallow wading. The second is the more spectacular, but you must climb about 40 feet up the left side of the canyon and go around part of the upper narrows. This is not at all difficult, but exercise caution.

A large side canyon enters at the upper narrows. Its mouth is blocked from easy entry by a ten-foot high cliff. In spring a waterfall spills over the cliff. Its entrance is guarded by five or six, 50-foot pinnacles that look like the upright femur bones on some giant.

Above the upper narrows the stream disappears briefly and the rocks shrink in size. I spotted a rattlesnake here. They try hard to get out of your way, but you should always walk with care. Use of a walking stick may give you comfort in more ways than one. Rattlesnakes like sunny areas near water where there are places to hide.

Continue following Coyote Creek to its origin at a ugly, grazed out area and water trough called Coyote Springs. All but the last quarter mile is scenic. The only difficulty is choosing the correct fork of the canyon as you head upstream. The rule to follow is this: in every case where the forks are large enough to be confusing, choose the right fork.

From Coyote Springs, follow the dirt road a quarter mile back to your vehicle.—*Ralph Maughan* □

HIKE 100 *BURNT WILLOW CANYON*

General description: A one or two-day late spring hike.
General location: In the Mt. Bennett Hills south of the Camas Prairie near Fairfield.
Maps: McHan Reservoir, Thorn Creek SW (7.5') USGS quads.
Special attractions: A spring hike, wildflowers, volcanic rock formations.
Difficulty: Moderate to moderately difficult due to the lack of a trail.
Season: May through October. Late May and early June are best.
Information: Contact Shoshone District, Bureau of Land Management, P. O. Box 2B, Shoshone, Idaho 83352. (208) 886-2206.

The hike: The southern and eastern portions of the Mt. Bennett Hills are cut with many volcanic-walled canyons. Most have cliffs of basalt and welded volcanic ash tuff. The latter often erodes into strange shapes (hoodoos). Such hoodoos are most prominent in the Gooding City of Rocks (see hike 99), but they are common throughout these "hills."

Burnt Willow Canyon is typical of many of these canyons. It is, however, fairly accessible by road. Although the canyon is hot and generally without water in the summer, for about a month in late spring it is green, has a clear-flowing stream, and is filled with wildflowers, particularly blue camas and arrowleaf balsamroot.

To reach the canyon, turn off of Idaho Highway 20 a few miles east of Fairfield onto Idaho Highway 46 which leads south. Turn right onto the good dirt road about 14 miles south of the 46/20 junction. The dirt road junction is at the base of a distinctive flat-topped butte. Here a Bureau of Land Management (BLM) sign reads "Fir Grove 7, Coyote Springs 8, City of Rocks 9". To reach this road from Goodding, travel north about 17.5 miles on Idaho Highway 46.

After 2.8 miles turn on to a poor dirt road leading south (leftward). Park your vehicle and put on your hiking gear as soon as the road begins to climb out of the shallow canyon (this is the head of Burnt Willow about .75 mile from the turn-off). If the road is muddy, do not start down it. It is terrible when muddy. Fortunately, it dries out fast. Instead, walk the short distance to the head of Burnt Willow Canyon.

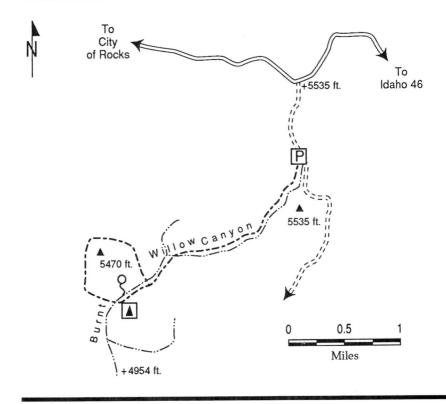

Walk down the shallow canyon, which gradually deepends. It is somewhat difficult going for a short distance as there are many watermelon-sized basalt boulders in the creek bed. Soon, however, the way eases and the canyon walls sport dark brown hoodoos that are brightly "painted" with almost fluorescent colors of yellow and orange. Blue camas line gurgling Burnt Willow Creek, which has carved pretty patterns in the welded volcanic ash in places.

There are a few marginal camping spots, but it is best to wait until you have walked several miles and reached the middle portion of the canyon to camp. Here it suddenly widens, the hoodoos disappear, and the creek banks are lined with willows. There are many places to camp plus a spring in the middle of a meadow. Filter, boil, or treat the spring's water since the area is sometimes grazed by cattle.

Below this wide area the canyon narrows again and eventually sprouts more hoodoos. An alternative I took rather than continue on down the canyon was to climb out here for a look at the country above the canyon rim. I went up the open side canyon on northwest side of the meadow (this is the right side when you are oriented downstream). I soon came to a plateau between Burnt Willow and the head of Black Canyon to the west.

I contoured around Hill 5,407 and descended back down into Burnt Willow

Canyon, passing through a narrow rimrock band of black basalt. From the shoulder of Hill 5,407 there is a good view of Burnt Willow Canyon and the distant snow-capped (in May) Soldier Mountains to the north. Avoid following the jeep road. This takes you too far to the west and down into the headwaters of Black Canyon.—*Ralph Maughan* □

APPENDIX

Finding Maps

Every hike in this book lists the U.S. Geological Survey topographic maps appropriate for the hike. These maps provide the most detailed description of the lay of the land and are really a necessity for all but the most developed trails. The maps can often be found at a university library, as such libraries also serve as federal depositories. They might also be found at local libraries or at the following list of vendors. However, it is probable that the critical map may not be immediately available, in which case you'll need to order it directly, for about $2.25, from the Western Distribution Branch, U.S. Geographical Survey, Box 25286 Federal Center, Denver, Colorado 80225. You can also obtain an Idaho index of all USGS quadrangles from this source. There is a $1 handling fee for orders of less than $10.

Idaho Vendors of USGS Topographic Maps

Boise
Jensen-Graves Co. Sawtooth
    Mountaineering, Inc.
The Bootworks, Inc.

Bonner Ferry
Bonners Ferry Herald

Coeur D'Alene
Gary's Sport Center
The Bookseller
Wilderness Mountaineering

Driggs
Elk Billiards & Sportshop
Mountaineering Outfitters

Idaho Falls
Conant's Landing
Hollady's Incorporated
Mountain Trading Co.
Solitude Sports, Inc.

Ketchum
Backwood's Mountain Sports
Dick Alfs Fly Shop
Galeana Lodge
Sturtevant of Sun Vally
The Elephant's Perch

McCall
May Hardware, Inc.
Medley Sports, Inc.

Moscow
Northwestern Mtn. Sports

Nampa
Big Sky Maps

Palisades
Snowball's 26, Inc.

Pocatello
 Idaho State University Bookstore
Jimmy's All Seasons Angler
Sunset Sports Center
Western Auto Assoc. Store

Priest River
Priest River Times

Rexburg
Mountain Works, Inc.
Porter's Book Store

Saint Anthony
Henry's Fork Anglers, Inc.

Saint Maries
The Paperhouse

Salmon
River City Book & Good Food Supply

Sandpoint
The Outdoor Connection
Vanderfords

Stanley
Redfish Lake Lodge, Inc.
Sawtooth Interpretive Assoc.
Stanley General Store

Sun Valley
The Snug Co.

Twin Falls
Blue Lakes Sporting Goods
Newton's Sports Center

The next most useful maps to the hiker are the "travel plans" to the individual forests. These show, although in greatly reduced detail, all the developed trails and those which are closed to off-road vehicles. You can also obtain the general map to each forest. Copies of the travel plans are free, while the forest maps cost $1. Both can be obtained from the addresses listed with each hike or from respective regional offices. For forests located north of the Salmon River, contact U.S. Forest Service, Northern Region, Federal Building, Box 7669, Missoula, Montana 59807; for those south of the Salmon River, contact U.S. Forest Service, Intermountain Region, 324 25th St., Ogdan, Utah 84401.

U.S. Bureau of Land Management maps are not standardized like those of the Forest Service. You can, however, write for them from the addresses listed with specific hikes or by contacting the BLM, Idaho State Office, 3948 Development Ave., Boise, Idaho 83705.

About the authors:

Ralph Maughan, a professor of political science at Idaho State University, author of a guide to the remote Teton Wilderness, draws on over two decades of wilderness experience and leadership in such groups as the Sierra Club, the Greater Yellowstone Coalition, and the Idaho Environmental Council. He was recently honored by the Idaho Conservation League, on the 25th anniversary of the passage of the Wilderness Act, as a wilderness preservation leader.

Jackie Johnson Maughan, an instructor of English at Idaho State University, has published two outdoor recreation books related to women, poetry and short stories, just completed a novel, and is presently working on a second novel based on the grizzly bear. She has over fifteen years of wilderness and conservation experience.

HIKING NOTES

HIKING NOTES

HIKING NOTES

FISHING

Angler's Guide to Alaska
Angler's Guide to Minnesota
Angler's Guide to Montana
Beartooth Fishing Guide

FLOATING

Floater's Guide to Colorado
Floater's Guide to Missouri
Floater's Guide to Montana

HIKING

Hiker's Guide to Alaska
Hiker's Guide to Alberta
Hiker's Guide to Arizona
Hiker's Guide to California
Hiker's Guide to Colorado
Hiker's Guide to Hot Springs in the
  Pacific Northwest
Hiker's Guide to Idaho
Hiker's Guide to Missouri
Hiker's Guide to Montana
Hiker's Guide to Montana's
  Continental Divide Trail
Hiker's Guide to Nevada
Hiker's Guide to New Mexico
Hiker's Guide to Oregon
Hiker's Guide to Texas
Hiker's Guide to Utah
Hiker's Guide to Virginia
Hiker's Guide to Washington
Hiker's Guide to Wyoming
Hiking Softly, Hiking Safely
Trail Guide to Glacier National Park

MOUNTAIN BIKING

Mountain Biker's Guide to Arizona
Mountain Biker's Guide to Central
  Appalachia

Mountain Biker's Guide to Northern
  New England
Mountain Biker's Guide to Southern
  California

ROCKHOUNDING

Rockhound's Guide to Arizona
Rockhound's Guide to Montana

SCENIC DRIVING

Arizona Scenic Drives
Back Country Byways
California Scenic Drives
Oregon Scenic Drives
Scenic Byways
Scenic Byways II
Trail of the Great Bear
Traveler's Guide to the Oregon Trail

WILDLIFE VIEWING

Arizona Wildlife Viewing Guide
California Wildlife Viewing Guide
Colorado Wildlife Viewing Guide
Idaho Wildlife Viewing Guide
Indiana Wildlife Viewing Guide
Montana Wildlife Viewing Guide
North Carolina Wildlife Viewing Guide
North Dakota Wildlife Viewing Guide
Oregon Wildlife Viewing Guide
Texas Wildlife Viewing Guide
Utah Wildlife Viewing Guide
Washington Wildlife Viewing Guide

PLUS—

Birder's Guide to Montana
Hunter's Guide to Montana
Recreation Guide to California
  National Forests
Recreation Guide to Washington
  National Forests

Falcon Press Publishing Co. • Call toll-free 1-800-582-2665

BRING ALONG A COMPANION

On your next trip to the great outdoors, bring along *Wild Country Companion*. This new FalconGuide includes state-of-the-art methods for safe, no-trace traveling in North America's backcountry. Whether you're on foot, horse or bike, this book offers new ways to sustain our outdoor recreation resources.

Wild Country Companion
By Will Harmon
Illustrated by
Lisa Harvey
160 pp., 6 x 9",
charts, softcover.

For more information on this and other Falcon Press books visit your local bookstore.
*Or call **1-800-582-2665***